People and Computers XX – Engage

Nick Bryan-Kinns, Ann Blandford,
Paul Curzon and Laurence Nigay (Eds)

People and Computers XX – Engage

Proceedings of HCI 2006

 Springer

Nick Bryan-Kinns BSc, MSc, PhD, PGCAP, AKC
Queen Mary, University of London, UK

Ann Blanford BA, MA, PhD, MBCS, CEng, CITP
University College London, UK

Paul Curzon BA, MA, PhD, PGCertHE
Queen Mary, University of London, UK

Laurence Nigay BSc, MSc, PhD, Habilitation, IUF Professorship
Université Joseph Fourier – Grenoble 1, France

Typeset by *Winder.*

British Library Cataloguing in Publication Data
A catalogue record for this book is available from the British Library

ISBN-10: 1-84628-588-7   Printed on acid-free paper
ISBN-13: 978-1-84628-588-2

9 8 7 6 5 4 3 2 1

Springer Science+Business Media, LLC
springer.com

Contents

Connecting with Others   83

Interaction for Me   117

Interactions in the Wild   175

Mind, Body, and Spirit 237

Preface: Engage!

This volume contains the refereed papers to be presented at the 'HCI'06: Engage' conference at Queen Mary, University of London, 11–15 September 2006. 'HCI'06: Engage' is the 20th annual British HCI Group conference.

It was a difficult task to select thirteen long papers from the 53 submitted (an acceptance rate of 1 in 4). Ten of the thirteen papers come from two European countries (UK and France) and the three remaining ones from North America and Japan. All the papers have been reviewed by independent peer reviewers and meta-reviewed by one of the Program Committee members. The three Technical Co-chairs considered all the reviews paper by paper and identified a first set of selected papers. Six papers were taken to the Program Committee for full discussion. The final decisions were taken by the Program Committee members and were always based on specific justified comments rather than scores.

The volume also contains seven refereed short papers. 84 short papers were submitted from which 36 have been accepted for presentation at the conference. The Programme Committee then selected seven short papers amongst the 36 accepted short papers to be included in this volume.

The papers reflect the exciting and evolving nature of human–computer interaction (HCI), a multidisciplinary and crucial research field for computing technologies. We nevertheless note the very low proportion of industry-only authored papers, and we need to consider new ways of engaging industry people in the HCI conference.

An innovation this year has been to introduce themes. We wanted to engage the HCI conference with six core themes:

1. *At the Periphery* – how can ambiance engage? Disappearing technologies – such as ubicomp, mixed media, and ambient intelligence – still engage us even though we cannot directly interact with them.

2. *Enthralling Experiences* – what draws people in? Performance, aesthetics, emotion, and creativity: powerful engagement can be a means or an end.

3. *Connecting with Others* – what happens around and through technology? Interacting with colleagues and friends is helped and hindered by the connecting technology.

4. *Interactions for Me* – what improves my experience? Technology can be dehumanising but it can also improve working and social life enormously.

5. *Interactions in the Wild* – how does technology breach boundaries? The borders between management, chaos and control change as interactions leave the desktop and go mobile.

6. *Mind, Body, and Spirit* – how does diversity impact? People are different so interactions should span age, ability, culture and gender.

Our goal was not to limit the topics of interest for the conference. Indeed the six proposed themes capture some of the established favourite ideas in the HCI field but also suggest new collaborations and approaches for opening the conference to new communities. Moreover the proposed themes are not independent but intertwined: they did not define a preset structure for the technical program that would have influenced the selection of papers. It is consequently natural that the papers could fit into several themes. We organized the papers along the six themes trying to encourage interesting relationships going beyond the contribution of any single paper.

Under the theme 'At the Periphery', one paper concerns cross-modal ambient displays combining a public ambient display with a personal cross-modal display. The second addresses the difficult question of evaluating systems for everyday life such as computational jewellery. The systems studied in the two papers are used in a mobile context that also contribute to the theme 'Interactions in the wild'.

The theme 'Enthralling Experiences' brings together five papers. One paper studies the olfactory interactive design for engaging game play. A further two focus on aesthetic and hedonic qualities as complementary to usability for enthralling experiences. A fourth paper studies the effects of pre-existing mood and music in connection with involvement while the last paper is dedicated to interface affect and familiarity in the context of a learning environment.

'Connecting with Others' encompasses studies on computer-supported collaborative work (CSCW). One paper considers how to enable both collocated and remote participants to engage in collaborative work simultaneously while a second focuses on the design of a mobile collaborative system for crime scene investigation. This last paper also focuses on shared awareness in a mobile context ('Interactions in the Wild').

'Interactions for Me' brings together two papers on new interaction techniques for target acquisition, one for pen-based interaction and one based on perspective view. A third paper under this theme focuses on the effect of motivation on procedural errors. Finally a fourth paper is dedicated to a particular application domain, e-shopping, exploring the usefulness of interactive animations.

'Interactions in the Wild' brings together three papers addressing the design and development of augmented reality and mobile systems. One paper is dedicated to the development of an augmented surgery system by focusing on output multimodal interaction. Three papers focus on the design of mobile systems, including location discovery tasks on mobile devices, a real time bus information system, and awareness/access to mobile services.

Finally a conference on HCI would not be complete without a session dedicated to the diversity of users. The theme 'Mind, Body, and Spirit' includes two different points of view on this. First, one paper highlights the impact of cognitive/visual style of users for evaluating visualization techniques and in particular the PieTree. Second, two papers address the challenge of visually impaired users: one paper is dedicated to accessibility as well as usability of websites while the second focuses on constructing bar graphs using a force feedback device for visually impaired users.

We hope that the themes and the collated papers will engage the reader in an exciting book that provides a valuable stimulating source of information for researchers and practitioners in HCI. The editors are grateful for the help given by the conference committee members and the vast team of reviewers who gave their time and energy to creating an engaging conference and book on HCI!

Nick Bryan-Kinns, Ann Blandford, Paul Curzon & Laurence Nigay

June 2006.

The Committee

Conference Co-chairs	Nick Bryan-Kinns *Queen Mary, University of London, UK*
	Patrick G. T. Healey *Queen Mary, University of London, UK*
Technical Co-chairs	Ann Blandford *University College London, UK*
	Paul Curzon *Queen Mary, University of London, UK*
	Laurence Nigay *Université Joseph Fourier – Grenoble 1, France*
Panels	Olav W. Bertelsen *University of Aarhus, Denmark*
	Adrian Williamson *Graham Technology plc, UK*
UPA UK liaison	Caroline Jarrett *Effortmark Ltd, UK*
Workshops	Stephanie Wilson *City University, UK*
	Helen Sharp *Open University, UK*
Tutorials	William Wong *Middlesex University, UK*
	Paola Amaldi *Middlesex University, UK*
Short papers	Tony Stockman *Queen Mary, University of London, UK*
	Bob Fields *Middlesex University, UK*
Interactive experiences	Willem-Paul Brinkman *Brunel University, UK*
	Peter Wild *University of Bath, UK*
Doctoral consortium	Panos Markopoulos *Technische Universiteit Eindhoven, The Netherlands*
	Angela Sasse *University College London, UK*
Posters	Dimitrios Rigas *University of Bradford, UK*
Lab overviews	Fraser Hamilton *Designed for All, UK*
Website, Submissions,	Marc Fabri *Leeds Metropolitan University, UK*
and Registrations	Dave Clarke *Visualize Design, UK*
Treasurer	Sue White *Queen Mary, University of London, UK*
Student Volunteers	George Papatzanis *Queen Mary, University of London, UK*
Banquet Fairy	Jenn Sheridan *Lancaster University, UK*
Sponsorship	Caroline Jarrett *Effortmark Ltd, UK*
	Helen Petrie *University of York, UK*
Publicity	Paul Cairns *University College London, UK*
Informal Advice	Ann Light *Queen Mary, University of London, UK*
BCS Events Chair	Anxo Cereijo Roibás *University of Brighton, UK*
BCS Group Link	Adrian Williamson *Graham Technology plc, UK*
	Fintan Culwin *South Bank University, UK*
Previous Conference Chair	Tom McEwan *Napier University, UK*

The Reviewers

Dima Aliakseyeu	*Technische Universiteit Eindhoven, The Netherlands*
Françoise Anceaux	*Université de Valenciennes, France*
Chee Siang Ang	*City University, UK*
Anjali Arora	*New York University, USA*
Mattias Arvola	*Linköpings Universitet, Sweden*
Sandrine Balbo	*University of Melbourne, Australia*
Lisa Battle	*Lockheed Martin, USA*
Gordon Baxter	*University of York, UK*
Russell Beale	*University of Birmingham, UK*
Reinhold Behringer	*Leeds Metropolitan University, UK*
Jacob Biehl	*University of Illinois at Urbana-Champaign, USA*
Stuart Booth	*Foolproof, UK*
Jan Brejcha	*Univerzita Karlova v Prague, Charles University Praze, Czech Republic*
Lorna Brown	*University of Glasgow, UK*
Anxo Cereijo Roibás	*University of Brighton, UK*
Jim Chen	*University of Portsmouth, UK*
Luigina Ciolfi	*Ollscoil Luimnigh, Ireland*
Gilbert Cockton	*University of Sunderland, UK*
Karin Coninx	*Universiteit Hasselt, The Netherlands*
Murray Crease	*NRC-IIT, Canada*
Steve Cummaford	*University College London, UK*
Andy Dearden	*Sheffield Hallam University, UK*
Gavin Doherty	*Ollscoil Átha Cliath, Coláiste na Tríonóide, Ireland*
Claire Dormann	*Carleton University, Canada*
Emmanuel Dubois	*IRIT, France*
Lynne Dunckley	*Thames Valley University, UK*
Alistair Edwards	*University of York, UK*
David England	*Liverpool John Moores University, UK*
Nicolas Esposito	*Université de Technologie de Compiègne, France*
Elena Fadeeva	*AUTODESK, Inc., USA*
Rod Farmer	*The University of Melbourne, Australia*
Sue Fenley	*University of Reading, UK*
Sally Fincher	*University of Kent, UK*
Peter Gardner	*University of Leeds, UK*
Satinder Gill	*Middlesex University, UK*

Nina Reeves	*University of Gloucestershire Business School, UK*
Tony Renshaw	*Leeds Metropolitan University, UK*
Jens Riegelsberger	*Framfab UK Ltd, UK*
Dave Roberts	*IBM, UK*
Patrick Roth	*Université de Genève, Switzerland*
Elyse Sanchez	*Pathfinder Associates LLC, USA*
Eunice Ratna Sari	*TRANSLATE-EASY, Indonesia*
Corina Sas	*Lancaster University, UK*
Jennifer G. Sheridan	*Lancaster University, UK*
Frances Slack	*Sheffield Hallam University, UK*
Andy Sloane	*University of Wolverhampton, UK*
Georg Strøm	*Københavens Universitet, Denmark*
Alistair Sutcliffe	*University of Manchester, UK*
Desney Tan	*Microsoft Research, USA*
Josie Taylor	*Open University, UK*
William Thimbleby	*Swansea University, UK*
Phil Turner	*Napier University, UK*
Susan Turner	*Napier University, UK*
Katerina Tzanidou	*The Open University, UK*
Judy van Biljon	*University of South Africa, South Africa*
Robert Ward	*University of Huddersfield, UK*
Michael Wilson	*CCLRC, UK*
Michele Zanda	*IMT, Lucca Institute for Advanced Studies, Italy*
Elena Zudilova-Seinstra	*Universiteit van Amsterdam, The Netherlands*

At the Periphery

Crossmodal Ambient Displays

Patrick Olivier, Han Cao, Stephen W. Gilroy & Daniel G. Jackson

Informatics Research Institute, University of Newcastle upon Tyne, Newcastle upon Tyne NE1 7RU, UK

Tel: *+44 191 246 4939*

Email: *p.l.olivier@ncl.ac.uk*

URL: *http://homepages.cs.ncl.ac.uk/p.l.olivier*

Ambient displays have for some time been proposed as a means of providing situated information to users in public spaces in a manner that minimizes the invasive nature of traditional displays, and reduces the distraction caused to bystanders. We explicitly address these shortcomings and present a novel information display framework called a crossmodal ambient display. CrossFlow is a crossmodal ambient display prototype for indoor navigation, that exploits aspects of crossmodal cognition in providing users with the facility to decode temporally multiplexed information in an animated ambient display. We describe a number of benefits of crossmodal ambient displays relating to both privacy and performance. Initial user studies have demonstrated that, compared to traditional navigation aids such as maps, crossmodal displays have the potential to significantly enhance the navigation performance of users whilst at the same time leading to a reduction on the cognitive load imposed by tasks such as navigation.

Keywords: ambient displays, crossmodal cognition, crossmodal displays.

1 Introduction

Ambient displays have been a topic of investigation in ubiquitous HCI for a number of reasons. In part they have been the result of a growing need and desire to situate computer interfaces in the everyday environments of users. As such they have been a response to observations as to the recent increase in the density of information displays in public spaces such as shopping malls, airports, and any environment in which a number of organizations compete to attract the attention of users to their products and services. Indeed, as the number of information and service providers in a public space increases there is often a disproportionately large rise in the density and heterogeneity of public displays.

Ambient displays are one proposal for an information display framework that can address the visual clutter and resulting detrimental impact that heterogeneous public displays place on the occupants of a space. In essence they are embedded in their environment, often utilizing unused physical and visual aspects of everyday objects in the provision of an information channel that is easily ignored. The recent popularity of ambient displays also reflects a rise in interest in notions of user experience, and in particular, the aesthetics of the user interface and the links between user interface design and traditional art and design. Portrayals of ambient displays such as informative art try to leverage aspects of everyday objects and artistic genres as a means of embedding dynamic information in our everyday environment.

However, ubiquitous computing remains committed to the paradigm of the handheld computing device, and the provision of information in a manner that is personalized to the user and to the user's location. Many issues arise as a result of the constraint of requiring a traditional interface on a handheld device. Some of these are technical, such that providing personalized and spatially contextualized information to users requires reliable and fine-grained tracking of user positions in a space. Positional tracking in indoor environments remains a significant technical challenge and has significant implications in terms of the privacy and security of users.

The provision of information through a handheld display can also undermine the broader goal of situating information services in users' physical environments. As the rise of mobile phone usage readily demonstrates, interaction with a personal computing device often leads to a degree of disconnection from one's environment as cognitive resources are turned inwards towards our personal information and communication space. Our goal is to address the shortcomings of both traditional ambient displays, which to date have not been capable of supporting tasks which require both highly situated and personalized information provision (such as indoor navigation), through their integration with handheld devices. As such we aim to bridge the divide between personal computing in the form of handheld computing and display devices and developments in situated and ambient displays.

We briefly summarize work in the fields of ambient and peripheral displays in Section 2 and introduce our notion of a crossmodal ambient display and its underlying cognitive motivation in Section 3. We describe the prototype crossmodal ambient navigation system in Section 4, and the results of a preliminary user study in Section 5.

2 Ambient Displays

Peripheral displays aim to deliver information to users effectively and efficiently without demanding their full attention. Ambient displays extend this notion beyond the desktop or head-mounted configuration of traditional peripheral displays, by embedding aesthetically pleasing display in a user's everyday environment, either through specialized display technologies (e.g. floor lights), projection, or by dynamically controlling properties of familiar objects such as fountains and mobiles. Furthermore, an ambient display is embedded in an environment in a manner that is not inherently tailored to any particular user. To date, most ambient displays convey general information (e.g. news, stock values, weather, traffic congestion and human activity) for groups of users, though a small number of examples support personalized mappings [Prante et al. 2004; Vogel & Balakrishnan 2004].

Ambient display research has involved the of a number of prototypes that aim to utilize highly aesthetic and peripheral, representations. For example, InfoCanvas [Plaue et al. 2004], Informative Art [Redström et al. 2000] and AROMA [Pedersen & Sokoler 1997], each incorporates abstract design elements, motivated by different styles of visual art, to represent information. With a greater emphasis on the aesthetics of everyday design, the Active Wallpaper, Water Lamp, and Pinwheels [Wisneski et al. 1998] artefacts all attempt to map information changes (e.g. weather, stock values) to system state changes in a 'calm' and 'subtle' manner, with a view to minimizing the attentional demands placed on a user engaged in some other task in an environment.

The majority of peripheral displays are visual in character. Visual peripheral displays developers have a sophisticated understanding of the nature of visual cognition and aim to present information in a timely manner which appropriately matches the time-sharing strategies utilied when users are performing two related tasks simultaneously. However, when the dual or multiple tasks become too demanding, the visual channel is easy overloaded and errors increase. Audio Aura [Mynatt et al. 1998], ambientROOM [Ishii et al. 1998], and AROMA [Pedersen & Sokoler 1997] have explored auditory and/or olfactory, multimodal ambient displays to exploit other perceptual channels. A key aspect of our proposal in the use coordinated modalities to achieve effective personalized use of an ambient display.

3 Cognition and Crossmodal Ambient Displays

3.1 *Crossmodal Cognition*

Psychological research into attention, over many decades, has demonstrated that an information processing bottleneck (i.e. one-at-a-time processing) and an attendant limitation in the information processing capability of humans in multiple task conditions. However, overwhelming evidence demonstrates that some information from unattended sources ultimately reaches higher stages of processing [Luck & Vecera 2002], which presents the possibility for people to receive information in a manner that that does not require their full attention. More recently, empirical research in cognitive neuroscience has given rise to the notion of crossmodal attention, a term used to refer to capacities and effects involved in the process of coordinating (or 'matching') the information received through multiple perceptual modalities [Driver & Spence 1998a]. Recent studies reveal extensive crossmodal links in attention across the various modalities (e.g. audition, vision, touch and proprioception). With respect to ambient display design, it has been demonstrated that some crossmodal integration can arise preattentively [Driver & Spence 1998b].

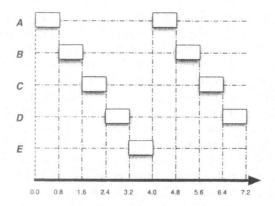

Figure 1: Temporal multiplexing of the crossmodal cues.

While empirical programs of research address the precise mechanisms of crossmodal integration, and in particular crossmodal spatial attention, our goal is to incorporate these insights in the development of new ambient display techniques. As we demonstrate in Sections 4 and 5, the crossmodal ambience framework integrates a public ambient display and a personal crossmodal display cue. This facilitates the anonymous access of publicly displayed information, without resorting to the tracking technologies, and personal visual displays, that are so characteristic of many ubiquitous computing designs.

3.2 Crossmodal Ambient Displays

In a crossmodal ambient display, information (which may contain both public and private components) is displayed throughout the whole physical extent of a shared information space. In contrast to a conventional ambient display, the crossmodal ambient display temporally cycles through information of potential interest to users in a space. Thus, in the case of our indoor navigation application, directions to different locations in the space (including exits) are projected on the floor of an environment one-at-a-time on a fixed time cycle. For example, in time-slot 1, directions to destination A are displayed at all locations in the physical space, in time-slot 2, directions to destination B are displayed, and so on until the directions to destination A are repeated (see Figure 1).

The user identifies (or decodes) which time-slot in the cycle is relevant to their own request for directions through the utilization of a crossmodal cue (e.g. a sound or vibration) issued by the personal mobile computing device. That is, either in response the user's request for directions, or on entry to the physical space, the user's device communicates with the ambient display infrastructure to establish the schedule of time-slots when the different directions will be displayed. In other words, the personal mobile device displays private information cues, that only individual users can perceive, that allow users to decode the ambiently displayed public and/or personal information.

Note that the directions displayed at a location depend on the direction of the destination from that location. Again we can contrast this with traditional handheld notions of navigation, whereby there is a requirement to track the position of a user and present directions salient to the specific location of the user. We can contrast these two configurations in terms of the multiplexing of information displayed. In traditional mobile device applications, incorporating tracking, information is spatially multiplexed. That is, the position of a user is known and information specialized to the location of the user is displayed on the user's device. In the crossmodal scenario information is temporally multiplexed and information relevant to a location is displayed at all locations (in our case through projection on the floor of the environment) at a specific time.

Unlike traditional mobile configurations (e.g. a hand-held visual display with tracking) the information is clearly displayed in a manner that is visually accessible to any occupant of that space. Whilst this might be criticized as potentially undermining a user's privacy, crossmodal ambient displays address the problem of privacy by anonymizing the user. The crossmodal cue (e.g. the vibration or sound) that the user is provided with (to indicate in which time-slot their information is being displayed) is hidden from other occupants of the space. In addition, other, redundant, information may be projected in the unused time-slots with a view to making the personal information (e.g. in this case the directions the user is requesting) less discoverable. Furthermore, since the user only requests the schedule of the time-slots for an environment the ambient display infrastructure has no more detailed information as to which time-slot (i.e. which directions) the user wants access to.

We explored our design idea through a crossmodal ambient display prototype named CrossFlow, for indoor navigation, and evaluated it in a dual task experiment with nine participants. In accordance with our design hypothesis as to the use of a cognitively well founded coordination of modalities, we found that the participants had significantly higher performance when using CrossFlow for indoor navigation as compared to a traditional map. Furthermore, users of CrossFlow also performed better in terms of performance of the primary task of the dual task paradigm, implying that it had significantly lower attentional requirements. These results have implications for the design and evaluation of novel navigation tools, information displays and multimodal user interfaces.

4   Indoor Navigation with CrossFlow

As modern architectural spaces increase in their size and complexity, wayfinding in unfamiliar indoor environments also becomes more challenging. Conventional handheld maps, as well as stationary signs such as poster maps, landmarks and directional signs, need users to know their locations and the locations of destinations in order to formulate their navigation plans. Recent mobile computing proposals and products mostly propose that the user either pays full attention to a personal display (typically a small screen on a handheld device) or that they listen to verbal instructions. In the former case users must continuously refer to both their location and the location of their destination, both on the electronic map and in the physical environment, which may cause interruptions of the navigation task and may even provoke dangerous situations [Kray et al. 2005].

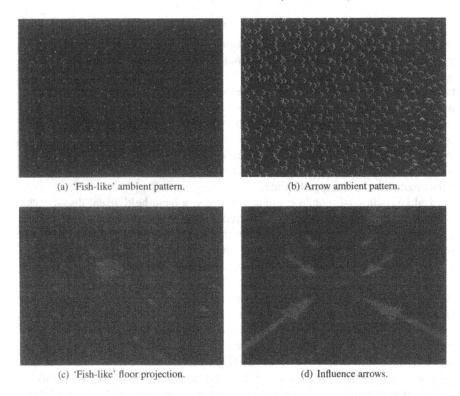

(a) 'Fish-like' ambient pattern.   (b) Arrow ambient pattern.

(c) 'Fish-like' floor projection.   (d) Influence arrows.

Figure 2: Ambient display designs and the influence arrow design tool.

Furthermore, in real world navigation tasks, people often have multiple other tasks to undertake whilst they are finding their way to a particular destination in the environment (e.g. taking care of children, transporting luggage, making a phone call, or simply just thinking about a problem as they move from one location to another). Few navigation systems aim to support multiple task handling during navigation.

CrossFlow is a prototype indoor navigation system, based on our notion of a crossmodal ambient display design, and embodies our framework for integrating public ambient displays and personal cues across modalities. The prototype is designed for use by a user with a mobile phone inside large unfamiliar buildings. The time-multiplexing technique described in Section 4 prompts users as to which directions correspond to their destination of interest. Advantages of such an indoor navigation system include: low cost, no requirement for sensing or tracking of the users, and the maintenance of user privacy.

4.1 Ambient Display Design

CrossFlow uses aesthetically pleasing ambient displays combined with a crossmodal cue on a user's personal mobile device to provide direction information. The ambient display for directions was designed to be as peripheral and calm as possible. Figure 2 includes two examples of the raw display, Figure 2a shows an animated 'fish-like' pattern, the elements of which orientate themselves and flow in the direction of the destination, and Figure 2b an arrow-like pattern that does not translate but animates between different directions. Once projected, the elements of the design (i.e. individual fish or arrows) are approximately the size of a hand, and have a visual intensity that integrates with the floor giving the appearance of a sparkling carpet. Figure 2c shows a close-up of the projection on the floor of the experimental region.

At any point in time, and at every location in the space, directions are displayed for a user to follow in order to reach a particular destination. Thus in Figure 2a the flowlines configure themselves to form paths (around any attendant obstacles) towards the crosshair indicating the location of the destination. The pattern changes every 800ms, during each time-slot all elements in the projected display have the appearance of swimming towards the same destination along the designed paths. Similarly, for the design in Figure 2b the entire arrow set points along the designed paths to the same destination. During the next time-slot, the elements undergo an animated transition in configuring themselves for the next destination.

The configuration of the pattern is achieved using configuration files to set parameters that control the design, size, density, and dynamic properties of the individual elements (rate of movement and visual persistence), and the duration and number of time-slots of the display. Influence arrows are used to interactively configure the direction of motion during each time-slot. Figure 2d shows a set of influence arrows which a designer interactively manipulates to control the direction of flow at locations in the environment. Influence arrows give the designer the flexibility to specify local flow tendencies for the pattern, which are aggregated for the final pattern. Thus a designer will configure the influence arrows to steer the flow around obstacles and away from sites that are not intended to lie on the path to a destination. Influence arrows may be interactively added, scaled, and rotated to attain the desired pattern of flow, and a key press binds the configuration to a time-slot. In Figure 2 we can see that a convergent pattern has been specified where all flow is directly towards the location of a white disc placed on the floor.

4.2 Crossmodal Cues

The second element of a crossmodal ambient display is the design of the crossmodal cue on the personal device. A personal mobile device, in this instance a Microsoft smart phone, issues a crossmodal cue in the form of one or both of:

1. a vibration for the duration of the corresponding time-slot; and

2. an audible high pitch sound coordinated with the onset of the time-slot.

We have yet to study empirically the impact of the different cues on the effectiveness of the display and in our initial evaluation we use both modalities simultaneously.

The crossmodal cue causes the user to pay attention to the directions shown by the public ambient display in the corresponding time-slot and induces a subtle switch of the user's attention. The personal mobile device connects to a central server to synchronize the time-slots at the beginning of navigation and to receive the schedule of time-slots and their mappings to the numerical keys of the navigation interface on the mobile device (which simply asks the user to press the number corresponding to the destination required). When the user selects a new destination the personal mobile device presents a cue in a different time-slot corresponding to the display of directions to the new destination.

5 Preliminary User Study

We ran a preliminary study to explore the effectiveness and efficiency of the crossmodal ambient display system as a personal navigation tool. The goal of the study was to inform our understanding of crossmodal ambient displays, in particular:

- To determine if the use of a crossmodal ambient display system can improve human performance for a navigation task in comparison to the use of a standard map.

- Provide an understanding of the impact of the use of a crossmodal ambient display on the performance of primary task during navigation.

- Explore the notion of ambiance through the measurement of subjective reports of mental workload.

5.1 Study Design

The study used a within subject design. We utilized one independent variable, type of task and navigation tool used, with two levels of treatment:

1. navigation using a map in a dual-task condition (answering arithmetic questions and navigating); and

2. navigation using CrossFlow in a dual-task condition (answering arithmetic questions and navigating).

We also measured user performance on the primary task (answering arithmetic questions) in the absence of navigation. The dependent variables included time of completion, time taken per arithmetic question, accuracy undertaking primary task, navigation errors, and perceived mental workload.

The 9 subjects, both male and female, were aged between 20 and 30 years old and had no discernible visual or physical impairments. The mathematical ability of each participant was elicited through a screening questionnaire prior to the study. An initial evaluation of performance on arithmetic questions yielded a mean time per question of 4.0 seconds and a mean accuracy of 97%.

The primary task involved answering a set of arithmetic questions posed one-by-one by the experimenter whilst the subject undertook the navigation task. Each subject was videoed and their responses for the questions were recorded during the experiment by the experimenter. The secondary navigation task was for the subject to find 5 targets (out of 15 targets displayed) with the aid of either a map or CrossFlow. Around the experimental area there were 15 containers positioned at different locations within the projected image. 5 out of the 15 containers held navigational information for the user.

Figure 3: Map and CrossFlow conditions.

In the case of the map, the subject was given the name of the first target container, and subsequent target containers contained the name of the next destination. In the CrossFlow condition, the containers provided the number to be entered into the phone for the next target. The 10 containers that were not valid destinations contained the statement 'this is an incorrect location'. The use of these 'distracter' targets was with a view to adding a degree of real world complexity and ambiguity for both the map and CrossFlow conditions. As the experiment was conducted in a relatively small space, as compared to an airport, it was necessary to have a significantly denser array of locations for the user to navigate between (see Section 6 for a discussion of this aspect of the experimental design).

5.2 Procedure

In an initial phase, each subject answered 18 arithmetic questions as a briefing task. The briefing task was intended to evaluate the baseline performance of each user with regards to the primary task. Subjects were asked to try to answer all the arithmetic questions correctly, and no time limit was enforced. On completion of the briefing task each subject navigated in the experimental area (10.0×6.5 meters) to find 5 targets out of the 15 targets under both conditions. Figure 3 shows the experimental area with a sample distribution of the targets used in the two conditions. The order of presentation of the conditions for each subject was randomized, as was the set of destinations used for a subject.

Condition 1 was undertaken with the aid of a simple map and subjects gave spoken answers to the arithmetic questions posed by the experimenter. On finding a target, the subject read the name of the next target from the container and continued. The subjects were told that answering the arithmetic questions was the primary task which would not stop until all designated 5 targets were found. No time requirement was placed on the subjects. In the second condition, the primary task was the same, and navigation task was completed with the CrossFlow system. Each subject used a SPV E200 smart phone and the five 800ms time-slots, corresponding to the five destinations, cycled every 4 seconds and utilized both an auditory and vibration cue as described in the previous section. On discovery of each target, the subject selected the number of the next target on the keypad of the phone.

Condition	Map	CrossFlow
Total time (secs)	133	80
Time per question (secs)	8.5	6.1
Questions correct (%)	84	98
Navigation errors	1.2	0.4
NASA-TLX score	79	60

Table 1: Mean performance measures for the map and crossmodal ambient display conditions (9 subjects).

Five measures were collected:

1. the completion time for the navigation task in each condition;

2. the time spent answering each of the arithmetic questions in the briefing phase and in the two conditions;

3. the accuracy of arithmetic question answers;

4. the number of navigation errors; and

5. a subjective measurement of mental workload using the NASA Task Load Index (NASA-TLX) [Hart & Staveland 1988].

5.3 Results

Our hypotheses were supported in terms of primary and secondary task performance, total completion time, and the subjective reports of mental workload. The descriptive statistics reveal that in contrast with a map the use of CrossFlow resulted in better performance in all aspects.   Table 1 presents the mean measures for the two conditions.

5.3.1 Comparison of Primary Task Performance

The performance for the primary task was compared across the briefing task, and the two dual-task conditions: navigating using the map and navigating using the crossmodal ambient display system. Two aspects of the performance on the primary task were considered:

- time taken to answer arithmetic questions; and

- the percentage of correctly answered questions.

With respect the time taken, a one-way repeated measures ANOVA revealed very significant differences between performance without and with the navigation task ($F(2,16) = 42.28$, $p < 0.001$). A post hoc paired samples t-test further show that the average time taken to answer an arithmetic question in the dual-task condition decreased very significantly from using the map to using CrossFlow, $t(8) = 6.60$, $p < 0.001$. The mean time when using CrossFlow was 28% quicker than when using the map.

To compare accuracy, a one-way repeated measures ANOVA revealed that the differences were significant between conditions ($F(2,16) = 4.89$, $p = 0.022$). A post hoc two-tailed paired samples t-test shows that the difference of the accuracy of processing arithmetic questions was only marginally significant between the map and CrossFlow conditions, $t(8) = -2.26$, $p = 0.054$, with the mean accuracy using CrossFlow being 17% higher than for the map.

5.3.2 Comparison of Secondary Task Performance

The performance on the secondary (navigation) task was compared for the map and CrossFlow condition according to two criteria:

- total time spent finding 5 destinations (total time in the dual-task condition); and

- number of navigation errors in discovering the 5 destinations.

Navigation errors were recorded formally when subjects addressed the wrong location, i.e. subjects incorrectly identified a distracter location as the next destination and when users returned to a previous prior destination in order to ascertain the location of the next target. In the map condition subjects averaged 1.2 navigational errors and for CrossFlow the average was 0.4. In is apparent that for such a small scale experiment (both in terms of the spatial scale of the navigation problem and the number of subjects) few conclusions can be drawn from such a low error rate.

As for the total time taken, a paired samples t-test showed that the total time spent on the whole experiment in the dual-task condition decreased significantly from using the map to using CrossFlow, $t(8) = 3.457$, $p = 0.009$.

5.3.3 Comparison of Judgements of Mental Workload

A paired samples t-test was conducted on the subjective judgements of the subjects in each of the two conditions using the NASA-TLX rating of mental workload. The results show a significant reduction in the perceived mental workload when using CrossFlow as compared to the map, $t(8) = 6.24$, $p < 0.001$.

5.4 Discussion

The experiment compared the effectiveness of CrossFlow with a traditional map for navigating an indoor environment. The results indicated that subjects using CrossFlow performed better on both the primary (arithmetic question answering) and secondary (navigation) tasks. This can be explained in terms of the ambient nature of CrossFlow as supported by the NASA-TLX reports, and we observe that the attention bottleneck effect is apparent for subjects in the map condition.

Although the experiment supports the utility of the crossmodal ambient display system, informal observations of subject behaviour should be incorporated in future design iterations of both the system design and the experimental design. For example, subjects tended to pause more with the crossmodal ambient display system in order to gradually hone in on the correct target, as shown by the projected images. One of the subjects paused for a particularly long time as he struggled to find the next target, which was actually right beneath his feet. This situation can in the main be attributed to the artificially small spatial scales over which subjects had to move and as such is a shortcomings of the experimental design. However, a truly flexible ambient display design would take account of the local configuration, including the proximity of destinations to each other, and mediate against the state of confusion that this subject found himself in.

Another artefact of the small experimental area is that the dense array of destinations meant that the directions indicated by the display appeared vaguer than would have been the case in a larger area with larger targets. In a number of cases a subject needed to step out of the experimental area in order to gain some perspective on the display and find the next target. Finally, the aesthetics of the experience was not addressed in the experimental set-up, though informal subject feedback received after the study revealed that subjects felt at ease with the system and most found CrossFlow fun to use and helpful.

6 Conclusion

We have proposed an interaction framework which aims to bridge the gap between ambient displays and personal mobile HCI through exploiting aspects of crossmodal cognition. We utilized this framework in the construction of CrossFlow, a crossmodal ambient display prototype for indoor navigation, and demonstrated a significant increase in the navigation performance of users of CrossFlow over the users of a map. Based on our empirical studies there is significant support for both the utility and desirability of crossmodal ambient displays. Evaluation of the prototype has shown that crossmodal ambient displays can support faster, more accurate and less cognitively demanding navigation than a traditional map.

Serious notice must be taken of the physical configuration of our preliminary evaluation and its ecological validity. In the real world, navigation tasks take place over significantly larger distances, and landmark identification is a significantly smaller component (in terms of time taken) of the navigation task than in our experimental set-up. Furthermore, people do not generally navigate while performing mental arithmetic and the spaces they occupy are usually populated by other people undertaking a range or activities. We intend to address these observations in a multi-user study on a larger spatial scale.

The small distances involved in our preliminary study are potentially detrimental for CrossFlow, as the shorter the distances are between the destinations, the greater the impact of the user having to wait for the time-slot corresponding to the next destination. In the worse case users will have to wait 4 seconds for the full cycle of directions, and this time is comparable to the time required to move between destinations. However, this is clearly going to be less time that users will typically require to identify a destination on a map and to decide upon appropriate landmarks by which to navigate.

One final bone of contention is the very classification of CrossFlow as an ambient display. In traditional terms, few ambient displays support explicit tasks such as navigation, and even fewer provide even the low level of interaction afforded by CrossFlow (selection of a destination). Our position is not only to consider ambiance in relation to the user – indeed no display is ambient when a user attends to it – but instead consider the incidental bystander's view of the display. We feel it is unlikely that such a person would associate the calm and somewhat aesthetic nature of the display with traditional information systems. Indeed though it remains to be demonstrated, we feel that bystanders would struggle even to identify which occupants of the space are using the system and which are not (especially if a user uses the vibration of a phone in their pocket as the crossmodal cue). From the perspective of the bystander CrossFlow is highly ambient.

The use of crossmodal perception to index temporally multiplexed information has significant potential for applications other the navigation. Although the requirement for floor projection (in this configuration) is onerous, this is outweighed by the fact that there is no need for tracking, which is particularly difficult for in-door environments. We also see potential for crossmodal displays (ambient or otherwise) to address the public-private divide through the display of public, but anonymized, information.

References

Driver, J. & Spence, C. [1998a], Attention and the Crossmodal Construction of Space, *Trends in Cognitive Sciences* **2**(7), 254–62.

Driver, J. & Spence, C. [1998b], Crossmodal Attention, *Current Opinions in Neurobiology* **8**(2), 245–53.

Hart, S. & Staveland, L. [1988], Development of NASA-TLX (Task Load Index): Results of Empirical and Theoretical Research, *in* P. Hancock & N. Meshkati (eds.), *Human Mental Workload*, North-Holland, pp.139–83.

Ishii, H., Wisneski, C., Brave, S., Dahley, A., Gorbet, M., Ullmer, B. & Yarin, P. [1998], ambientROOM: Integrating Ambient Media with Architectural Space, *in* C.-M. Karat & A. Lund (eds.), *CHI'98 Conference Summary of the Conference on Human Factors in Computing Systems*, ACM Press, pp.173–4.

Kray, C., Kortuem, G. & Krüger, A. [2005], Adaptive Navigation Support with Public Displays, *in* R. St. Amant, J. Riedl & A. Jameson (eds.), *Proceedings of the 10th ACM International Conference on Intelligent User Interface (IUI 2005)*, ACM Press, pp.326–8.

Luck, S. J. & Vecera, S. P. [2002], Attention, *in* H. Pashler & S. Yantis (eds.), *Stevens' Handbook of Experimental Psychology, Volume 1, Sensation and Perception*, John Wiley & Sons, pp.235–86.

Mynatt, E. D., Back, M., Want, R., Baer, M. & Ellis, J. B. [1998], Designing Audio Aura, *in* C.-M. Karat, A. Lund, J. Coutaz & J. Karat (eds.), *Proceedings of the SIGCHI Conference on Human Factors in Computing Systems (CHI'98)*, ACM Press, pp.566–73.

Pedersen, E. R. & Sokoler, T. [1997], AROMA: Abstract Representation of Presence Supporting Mutual Awareness, *in* S. Pemberton (ed.), *Proceedings of the SIGCHI Conference on Human Factors in Computing Systems (CHI'97)*, ACM Press, pp.51–8.

Plaue, C., Miller, T. & Stasko, J. [2004], Is a Picture Worth a Thousand Words?: An Evaluation of Information Awareness Displays, *in* W. Heidrich & R. Balakrishnan (eds.), *Proceedings of Graphics Interface 2004*, A. K. Peters, pp.117–26. http://www.graphicsinterface.org/proceedings/2004/.

Prante, T., Stenzel, R., Röcker, C., Streitz, N. & Magerkurth, C. [2004], Ambient Agoras: InfoRiver, SIAM, Hello.Wall, *in* E. Dykstra-Erickson & M. Tscheligi (eds.), *CHI'04 Extended Abstracts of the Conference on Human Factors in Computing Systems*, ACM Press, pp.763–4.

Redström, J., Skog, T. & Hallnäs [2000], Informative Art: Using Amplified Artworks as Information Displays, *in* W. E. Mackay (ed.), *Proceedings of DARE 2000 on Designing Augmented Reality Environments*, ACM Press, pp.103–114.

Vogel, D. & Balakrishnan, R. [2004], Interactive Public Ambient Displays: Transitioning from Implicit to Explicit, Public to Personal, Interaction with Multiple Users, *in* S. K. Feiner & J. A. Landay (eds.), *Proceedings of the 17th Annual ACM Symposium on User Interface Software and Technology (UIST'04)*, *CHI Letters* **6**(2), ACM Press, pp.137–46.

Wisneski, C., Ishii, H., Dahley, A., Gorbet, M. G., Brave, S., Ullmer, B. & Yarin, P. [1998], Ambient Displays: Turning Architectural Space into an Interface between People and Digital Information, *in* N. A. Streitz, S. Konomi & H.-J. Burkhardt (eds.), *Cooperative Buildings: Integrating Information, Organizations, and Architecture. First International Workshop, CoBuild'98*, Vol. 1370 of *Lecture Notes in Computer Science*, Springer-Verlag, pp.22–32.

Plotting Affect and Premises for Use in Aesthetic Interaction Design: Towards Evaluation for the Everyday

S. Kettley & M. Smyth

Human Computer Interaction Research Group, Napier University, Edinburgh EH10 5DT, UK
Email: *{s.kettley, m.smyth}@napier.ac.uk*

This short paper presents an experimental approach to the difficulty of evaluating interactive systems as artefacts for everyday life. The problem arises from the event-like nature of the user-centred evaluation session, as distinct from 'being' or the 'ongoing flow' of daily life, and from the dynamic complexity of the lifeworlds of users in human centred design approaches. In analysing the data from a recent project investigating the aesthetic and utilitarian figurations of a wireless system of computational jewellery, it was found that the participants made references to a range of notional lifeworlds, and that the premises for use attached to these varied in type. An overview of the evaluation procedure, including pre and post task sessions with the user group, is given, and the results from the project discussed.

Keywords: user experience, lifeworlds, premises for use, designing for the everyday, meaning making, evaluation, wearable computing, computational jewellery.

1 Introduction

Over the past two years, the first author has been engaged in the concept design and realization of a suite of wirelessly networked jewellery for a friendship group. This was developed as part of her doctoral program looking at user experience with Wearable Computers for 'the everyday', and at Contemporary Craft as a rich metaphorical resource for this and other design disciplines [Kettley & Smyth 2004; Kettley 2005]. The Wearable Computing community has been interested for some time in mainstream markets [DeVaul et al. 2001; Starner 2001; Watier 2003] but

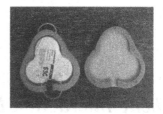

Figure 1: Hand built Speckled jewellery nodes pendant detail and battery in custom case.

has had little opportunity to consider the less tangible aspects of user needs and experiences. At the same time, the notion of the lifeworld has emerged as important in some human centred approaches to Interaction Design [Agre & Horswill 1997; Hallnäs & Redström 2002]. The lifeworld is an emergent framework of meanings and shared language that allows individuals to empathically interact with one another; Agre & Horswill [1997], for example, defined it as a shared understanding of functionality, tools and affordances, while Hallnäs & Redström [2002] emphasize the metaphorical presence of objects as constitutive of this subjective space. This paper describes an approach more in tune with the latter, in its view of objects as un-decidable until brought into play, and thus as capable of supporting more than one *figuration* or meaning. The term *figuration* needs some introduction, and is used here in manner of Actor Network Theory, indicating a giving of 'a figure, a form, a cloth, a flesh to an agency'. Latour gives an example in which an agency is variously figurated as 'imperialism', 'the United States', 'Bush Junior', and 'many officers from the Army and two dozen neo-con leaders' to illustrate how an agency assumes an identity [Latour 2005]. Such figuration requires some commitment on the part of the user, and this method seeks to analyse users' utterances for this commitment with respect to their own and other imaginary lifeworlds. It is suggested that the resulting matrix of premises for action plotted against four notional lifeworld distances gives an indication of the participants' openness to the presented concept designs, and their willingness or ability to find a place for them within their own lifeworld.

2   The Networked Jewellery

The intuition informing the project was that jewellery, as a sub-genre of Contemporary Craft, might offer an interesting approach to some of the issues facing wearables with regards the industry's hopes for a more mainstream market [Kettley & Smyth 2004; Kettley 2005; Wallace 2004; Wallace & Press 2004]. Five neckpieces were built using traditional methods at the jeweller's workbench, incorporating a prototype Speckled Computer[1] in each. These nodes were able to identify each other within a range of about twenty metres, and used a range of coloured LEDs to indicate to the wearer the identity and approximate distance of other individuals in the group. Figure 1 illustrates examples of the hand-built Speckled jewellery nodes.

[1] See http://www.specknet.org/ for details of the Speckled Computer.

Figure 2: Out-of-the-box evaluation.

Figure 3: task-based evaluation Royal Museum of Scotland.

3   Towards an Holistic Evaluation Method

The researchers were interested in how women in a friendship group figurated the objects as either jewellery (aesthetic) or communication devices (utilitarian). However, this very question posed problems for the evaluation, in its embodiment of a false dichotomy. It was quickly apparent that the women themselves did not have such a problem, as they explored blended figurations, seeing the work as 'like nothing else', as 'useful jewellery', and as being able to 'stand on its own as it is'. The problem was that these more interesting understandings of the work were emerging not from the data from the task-based evaluation, but from the less formalized sessions that had been intended to reveal the lifeworld of the friendship group. Seeing the centrepiece of the evaluation as task-based reified the designs as communication devices, when the research was asking questions about metaphorical meaning. The solution was twofold: firstly, to treat all the gathered data as being of equal importance, and secondly, to treat affective reactions and rationalized premises for use as of equal importance, each capable of indicating a level of attraction on a sliding scale of potential acceptance and commitment to the object.

The friendship group were with the project for two years in total, initially taking part in the 'probe' activities mentioned above and, at regular intervals, giving affective feedback on sets of prototype jewellery (this was the third). They were therefore familiar with the broad idea of computational jewellery at the stages being analysed here, eighteen months later. There was a wealth of visual and verbal data available to the researcher from throughout the project, and the initial analysis, using Grounded Theory [Strauss & Corbin 1994] but restricted to the tasks at the Museum (details below), was expanded to include three data sets:

- an *'out-of-the-box' session* in the home of one of the women, in which aesthetic responses were implicitly sought, but which delivered far more (Figure 2); in this session, a video camera on a tripod, a handheld camcorder and a tape recorder were used to capture interactions;

- the *task-based evaluation* in the Royal Museum of Scotland and the newer Museum of Scotland, in which the women were first asked to use the jewellery to locate others across three floors of the building, and in the second to compete in teams, 'collecting' exhibits while concealing their whereabouts from rivals (Figure 3); during these tasks, each participant had her own 'research buddy' who captured talk aloud protocols and movement on video; and

- the individual *debriefing interviews* in which it was imagined the two figurations would merge in narrative reflection; these were administered both by post and over the phone, mixing note taking with participants' own written responses

The resulting experimental analysis technique focused on one particular theme that had emerged from the larger analysis, and categorized premises for use as being of a notional distance from the participant's own lifeworld. It was found in the analysis of the friendship group's interactions with the networked jewellery, that they explored broadly four of these spaces; *immediate scenarios* ('if she went away, you know, if she went out the front door, it would stop'; 'you can talk about me!') enacted as a result of the evaluation session itself, for example within Ch's home (Figure 2); *their own lifeworld(s)* ('you're not really going to be going out with six people are you'... you're probably only be going to be looking for one person...'); *other people's worlds* ('you know who would like it... autistic children'; 'it would be quite useful for a deaf person... where instead of you know, standing at the door and say its so and so... if she's got one hanging inside her door...'); and *fanciful worlds* ('I think you should make one in platinum and gold... diamonds and a tiara... you could make tiaras!'; 'beam me up Scotty!').

4   Notional Lifeworld Distance

Figure 4 shows such utterances coded as premises for action or as exhibiting affect (positive or negative), plotted against these notional lifeworld distances along the x-axis, and against a relative scale of attraction on the y-axis. The key indicates at which point in the evaluation procedure the comments were made. In this case, it can be seen that the instances from the earlier informal session are noticeably spread out, as the women tried to make sense of the jewellery with reference to a wide range of associations and ideas. Relating the jewellery to other people's needs resulted in imaginary but realistic scenarios of use for the deaf, disabled children, and school

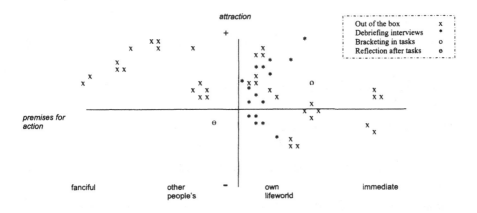

Figure 4: Attraction and premises for action.

children on a trip. The physical characteristics of the setting for the out-of-the-box evaluation also allowed for the investigation of immediate scenarios. Only two instances of these codes were found in the reflective spaces in and around the tasks at the museum (bracketing within tasks and reflection after tasks), but the debriefing interviews generated all those instances concentrated around the area that would suggest positive appropriation of this concept design, underlining the importance of including the metaphorical and the narrative in evaluation. In the own lifeworld area, an interesting outcome was that the aesthetic comments predominantly came from the out-of-the-box evaluation, while those from the interviews generated more scenarios of use, and bound aesthetics to the participants' own strategies for levels of display in their habitual dress.

5 Conclusions

That task based evaluations tell us how useful or robust something is, is not a great surprise, but that informal situations for experience with systems need to be explicitly built in to deliver a more holistic evaluation of a concept, while not shocking news, is still a relatively novel approach. Similarly, that the observer has an affect on the situation being studied is not news, but to be able to account for that impact in more detail is valuable. To refine this technique, Interaction Design will of course require further case studies and investigative research. It was found in this project that plotting responses in such a way visualized the different evaluative situations and their respective outcomes and supported the analysis of the participants' overall response to the concept as positive, in a way that would have been obscured by the task-based evaluation alone.

References

Agre, P. & Horswill, I. [1997], Lifeworld Analysis, *Journal of the Artificial Intelligence Research* **6**, 111–45.

DeVaul, R. W., Schwartz, S. J. & Pentland, A. S. [2001], MIThril: Context-aware Computing for Daily Life, http://www.media.mit.edu/wearables/mithril/MIThril.pdf, last accessed 2006-06-08.

Hallnäs, L. & Redström, J. [2002], From Use to Presence: On the Expressions and Aesthetics of Everyday Computational Things, *ACM Transactions on Computer–Human Interaction* **9**(2), 106–24.

Kettley, S. [2005], Crafts Praxis as Design Resource, *in* P. Rodgers, L. Brodhurst & D. Hepburn (eds.), *Crossing Design Boundaries*, Taylor & Francis, pp.545–9.

Kettley, S. & Smyth, M. [2004], The Materiality of Wearable Computers, *The Design Journal* **7**(2), 32–41.

Latour, B. [2005], *Reassembling the Social: An introduction to Actor Network Theory*, Oxford University Press.

Starner, T. [2001], The Challenges of Wearable Computing: Part 2, *IEEE Micro* **July-August**, 54–67.

Strauss, A. & Corbin, J. [1994], Grounded Theory Methodology: An Overview, *in* N. K. Denzin & Y. S. Lincoln (eds.), *Handbook of Qualitative Research*, Sage Publications, pp.273–85.

Wallace, J. [2004], Sometimes I Forget to Remember, Invited presentation at 'Challenging Craft' international conference. Paper can be obtained via http://www.challengingcraft.org through the Guest Speaker item or directly from http://www2.rgu.ac.uk/challengingcraft/ ChallengingCraft/pdfs/jaynewallace.pdf, last accessed 2006-06-14.

Wallace, J. & Press, M. [2004], All This Useless Beauty, Paper presented at Pixelraiders2 conference. Proceedings issued only on CD-ROM by the organizers. See http://www. pixelraiders.org/.

Watier, K. [2003], Marketing Wearable Computers to Consumers: An Examination of Early Adopter Consumers' Feelings and Attitudes Toward Wearable Computers, Master's thesis, Georgetown University. http://www.watier.org/kathy/papers/Marketing% 20Wearable%20Computers%20to%20Consumers.pdf, last accessed 2006-06-08.

Enthralling Experience

Smell Me: Engaging with an Interactive Olfactory Game

Stephen Boyd Davis, Gordon Davies, Ruba Haddad & Mei-Kei Lai

Lansdown Centre for Electronic Arts, Middlesex University, Cat Hill, Barnet, Hertfordshire EN4 8HT, UK
Email: *{s.boyd-davis,g.davies}@mdx.ac.uk*

The paper describes an artistic project which produced some valuable findings in relation to olfactory interactive design. It records a process of discovery in a largely unfamiliar area of interaction. The paper describes how the many difficulties which people have in discriminating, recalling and identifying smells were used as the substance of engaging gameplay. Both theoretical and practical issues are discussed, including the role of olfaction in creating a sense of complete realism, and its use to create affect and to promote engagement. Issues of specifying and controlling odour are discussed, as are problems arising from the nature of olfactory perception. A digital olfactory game is described and evaluated. The paper may seem to undermine the whole idea of using the olfactory channel, and leaves it an open question how useful olfaction may eventually prove. It is admitted that significant problems await the design of olfactory experiences.

Keywords: olfactory, digital game, engagement.

1 Introduction

We describe an artistic project with some valuable lessons for olfactory interactive design, charting a process of discovery in largely unfamiliar territory. Using rudimentary components we created an interactive digital game which places the player's sense of smell at the centre of the experience. The aim is to answer the question: What should the designer of interactive systems know about olfactory design? Much of our answer to this central question will consist of further questions – questions which the interactive media designer ought to ask at an early stage in any proposed development. We are not claiming to have all the answers, but this paper will still we believe be useful. There are so many questions and problems, that we may seem to undermine the whole idea of using the olfactory channel, and we believe it is indeed an open question how useful olfaction may eventually prove. We can confirm that significant problems await the design of olfactory experiences.

Given the unfamiliarity of olfactory interactive design, we outline here some of the key issues and indicate which were found to be most pertinent in our own work. We prioritized the issue of the user's (player's) engagement with the experience, though we also comment on other aspects of the use of odours in interactive systems.

2 Context

The context of the development is an electronic arts teaching and research centre in the art and design department of a UK university. We approach human computer interaction from a different perspective than would be expected in a computing science department, adopting an informal, playful approach to project development. Some projects arise not from perceived need but from curiosity about the potential of novel technologies. Despite the informality of our approach, we encourage taught students and researchers to investigate users' responses to the projects they make, an approach which is still uncommon in 'creative' departments [Boyd Davis 2005]. In the work outlined here, we made a small formal study of users' reactions. This is supplemented with informal observations, and feedback from players, arising when the work was displayed in a public exhibition. We have defined the project as an 'artistic' endeavour on the grounds that it conforms neither to a process of careful scientific investigation nor to those of classical game design. Instead it is an open, exploratory investigation which nevertheless yields useful insights into users' engagement with odour in a digital context.

3 The Appeal of Olfaction

The psychology, and even the physiology, of olfaction are areas of discovery and debate. Only in 2004, a Nobel Prize was awarded to Axel & Buck for their work (published from 1991 onwards) on odorant receptors and the organization of the olfactory system [Nobel Foundation 2004]. It is difficult to find undisputed information on how odour is processed, and therefore hard to say in what ways users may respond to its use in interactive systems.

3.1 Olfaction for Realism and Completeness

Smell is missing from most interactive digital user experiences. This is the case even where an involving sense of 'total' realism is sought, such as in virtual reality or video games. In the hierarchy of media used for realist purposes, vision is given the greatest attention, followed by sound, supplemented – for the ordinary consumer – by primitive haptics such as the use of 'rumble' vibration in the handset of games consoles. Attempts have been made, sometimes not wholly seriously, to exploit odour as an additional channel in gameplay. For example Sierra Entertainment's 1996 game *Leisure Suit Larry 7: Love for Sail* included a scratch-and-sniff card which the player was instructed to use at certain points in the game. In *Fragra* [Mochizuki et al. 2004] the player wears a head mounted display (HMD) with a wired olfactory device. When the player catches an object with the VR glove, she or he can smell it and is required to match the odour with the relevant image. This is one of very few games which treat olfaction as an aspect of the gameplay itself, rather than as a reinforcement of another sensory experience.

Several HCI researchers have discussed the potential of olfactory display. Barfield & Danas [1995] defined an olfactory display and discussed many of the issues of both principle and practice which needed to be taken into account. More recently, Kaye [2004] has provided a useful overview, including documenting various not wholly successful attempts to commercialize the use of digital control of odours. Several studies concern the use of scents to convey information, such as in notification systems, more than using scents as ambient odour to affect users emotionally. For instance, Kaye [2001, pp.86–91] used two scents, mint and lemon, to represent the stock market going up or down in the *Dollars & Scents* project. However, Bodnar et al. [2004] suggested, on the basis of experiment, that olfactory notification is less effective in delivering information than visual and auditory modes, though they note that this may be caused by the relative unfamiliarity of users in dealing with odours as denotations of information, an issue we encountered in our own work.

It seems certain that if it were easy and convenient to deliver odours as part of a realist interactive experience, as is wanted in many games, it would be done. However, it can be assumed that true realism would often be avoided. Just as the corpses in many video games conveniently fade away rather then visibly decomposing, we can assume that an analogous approach would be taken with the use of smell. If odours were routinely used in video games, it also seems likely that they would generally be used redundantly with other channels: the player would see fire, hear it and smell it. However it could also be used to give substantive information such as alerting the player to a danger they would otherwise not detect.

3.2   Olfaction for Affect and Engagement

Odours are reputed to have a particularly direct effect on emotions and memory, though the subject is fraught with controversy [Laing et al. 1991]. It is sometimes suggested that the connection of the areas of the brain responsible for processing smell to the limbic system provides a direct route to the brain's emotional centre [Carter 1999, p.114]. While it is popularly claimed that odours motivate us and affect our emotions directly [Barille & Laroze 1995], others disagree and tend to explain the power of odours in relation to the context and previous experiences [Engen 1991]. A unique odour can trigger distinct memories from childhood or from emotional moments – positive or negative – later in life. Famously, the majority of Proust's three thousand pages of fictional memories in *A la recherche du temps perdu* arise from the distinctive scent of a small cake dipped in tea [Proust 1913-27]. That odour is an important factor in retrieving memory is not disputed, though the mechanisms are. Issues in identifying odours are complicated by differences, not always easy to establish, between discrimination, recall of scents achieved without being able to identify them, and full naming recognition. All these aspects were explored in our work. Prior familiarity with odours makes them easier to identify. The memory of a certain odour cannot be retrieved by making a conscious effort, whereas visual or auditory memory can be retrieved. While trying to recall a certain odour, people tend to recall the image associated with that smell. For instance; they recall a picture of lemon when attempting to recall a lemony odour [Engen 1991]. Practice improves the ability to discriminate and to recall. Supplementary information can reinforce or undermine olfactory discrimination. If a single odour is presented in three different bottles, it will likely be perceived as three different odours.

4 Practical Issues for an Olfactory System

Issues of perception, recall and recognition are not the only source of problems for the interaction designer. Practical difficulties arise from the lack of an agreed model for the specification of odour, the elusive physical character of odour, and therefore of its control. Implementation issues include controlling the intensity and direction of odour emission, cancellation of odours after emission, offering a variety of odours, combining odours, responsiveness of the emission mechanism, and cost. In our case we chose to build a crude odour emission system based on shop-bought components. Experimentation with one of the proprietary digitally controlled scent emission systems had proved unsatisfactory.

4.1 Specifying and Controlling Odour

An interactive system incorporating odour requires the following components: a source of odours, comprising the odorous substances and some mechanism, either to excite them such as heating, or to transmit the substance such as by a spray, or the odour of the substance such as by a fan; a (human) user; and a control system whose inputs respond to user actions and whose outputs include a mechanism for controlling the emission source or sources. Issues arise both in terms of specifying odours and controlling them.

When dealing with the visual, a range of usable models is available for specifying colour (despite difficulties caused by contextual factors such as lighting and device characteristics) of which the most common for digital media is red, green, blue (RGB). Such is not the case with odour, where even the theoretical existence of primaries is a matter of dispute. Though Amoore [1963, 1970] broke down odour into a number of basic types – camphoraceous, musky, floral, peppermint, ethereal, pungent and putrid – and it certainly now seems that different parts of the sensory mechanism are specialized to respond to particular odour stimuli [Lawless 1997], this is not to say that there is necessarily a set of pure odours at the centre of these categories which when combined will produce most or all odours, in the way that RGB can be combined to create most colours. There are also difficulties in specifying the intensity of a smell since this is perceived very differently for different odours.

A further problem is in the control of odour, arising from its physical character. Since odours for interactive media need to be made available to the user at a particular time and intensity for a particular duration, an appropriate parallel here might be with MIDI-specification of basic note information in relation to time. A musical note may be turned on using a MIDI device, and it may be turned off. However, with odours, there are problems both in starting and stopping. Starting an odour may be difficult to achieve with good timing, because the emission source must be activated and odour carried through the air to the nose of the user; and stopping an odour is extremely difficult. Stopping emission of the odour may not be followed by complete absence of the odour for some time, even where a fan is used to exchange the air in the space.

In the desire to transmit the odour to the user rapidly and with a fine degree of control, one obvious solution is to pipe the smell to the user's nostrils. Apart from the intrusiveness of this solution, there is another, more interesting problem. It has been noticed that increasing the flow rate to the nose artificially makes an odour seem stronger, even though the perceived intensity remains constant when flow rate is varied naturally by sniffing [Teghtsoonian et al. 1978]. To avoid some of these problems, Yanagida et al. [2004] have been developing a series of prototype devices on the theme of an 'air cannon', which locate the user's nose and direct a small vortex ring of scent towards that location.

4.2 Problems with the Human Component

In addition to difficulties with the specification and delivery of odours, several issues arise from the properties of the user. There are differences in sensitivity to odours between individuals [Lundstrom et al. 2003]. These may be genetic, or may be related to the user's gender, age, medical factors including whether or not they smoke, and the degree of practice the user has had. An additional issue is that prolonged or frequently repeated exposure to an odour causes it to be perceived less strongly. This last is one of the most obvious limiting factors on any system design which might be adopted.

The issue of preferences between users is, as one would expect, affected by prior experience including cultural factors. Individual preferences differ widely so that the smell of a bonfire may invoke happy memories of firework displays for one, and sad feelings of the end of the year for another [Carter 1999, p.114]. It has been suggested that much of the supposed emotional power of odour is not inherent in the odours themselves but in the memories they evoke [Engen 1991]. Fortunately our system used only three scents, all of which were from commercial air-fresheners and had presumably been designed to be likely to please. Preference was not a feature of the game we devised.

5 The Physical Design

We explain first the physical structure of our setup, and give the rationale for this design in the light of the issues already discussed. The setup comprises the following elements:

- The odour emission source: three shop-bought aerosol air-freshener sprays were housed in a simple rectangular cabinet faced with a gauze screen. The odours were, nominally, Lavender, Jasmine and Citrus. In this paper the scent-names are capitalized to indicate that we are referring to synthetic odours with these names, not the real substances which these names would normally denote. Odours are gently driven towards the player, from the side (i.e. downwards in Figure 1), with the help of a low-powered fan behind the aerosol devices.

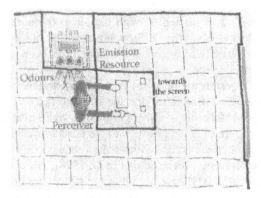

Figure 1: Working sketch of the physical layout of the project.

- The player, seated, faces (towards the right in the figure) a keyboard, of which a few keys are used as a controller for movement within the game, not for alphanumeric input.

- There are stereo speakers and a projection screen. The digital projector is out of the player's view.

- The control system is a computer running a project within Macromedia Director MX 2004, supplemented by the 'xtra' SerialXtra by Physicalbits, which is used to interface the Director project to the emission source. The computer is out of the player's view.

Trial and error was used to determine the best location for the odour emission source. Given that the odours in our case were delivered as aerosol spray, it was important that they should not be fired towards the player's eyes and face.

As supplied, each air freshener is normally activated by its own inbuilt battery-operated timer which completes a circuit at predetermined time intervals. Completion of the circuit causes a certain amount of scented liquid to be released as an aerosol spray. We bypassed the timer so that the air freshener was activated simply by the presence of the current from the battery, and then used three relay channels (one for each of the three air fresheners) from an 8-channel set connected to the serial port of the computer. By using the software component SerialXtra by Physicalbits as an intermediary between Macromedia Director and the serial port, we were able to switch on or off any channel of the relays from within the multimedia authoring and delivery package. In most cases, the triggering of an emission is entirely under the control of the software, so that, for example, as the user travels a road in the game environment, a series of smells is generated in random order. In one sub-game within our project, however, the user can choose to 'place' odours in the game environment and in this case the appropriate smell is emitted when they do so.

Inside each air freshener, as purchased, the timer triggers the rotation of a toothed wheel. This is converted by a cam into a downward motion which pushes

Figure 2: A built-in cam mechanism depresses the button of the aerosol as a toothed wheel rotates.

down the cap of the aerosol (Figure 2). The electrical power which is applied must be strong enough to push down the cap, while the spring in the aerosol button must have sufficient strength to push it back on release. Therefore, the position and the height of the aerosol are crucial. We have tried to use other spray bottles in addition to those supplied for use in the device, without success.

6 Gameplay Design

The use of odours as an element in gameplay is not confined to digital systems. Kumiko are games played during the Japanese Incense Ceremony, which depend on identifying which incense scent is being burnt. A small number of commercial games are made by a French company, for example *Loto des Odeurs* which combines a game of chance with players' skills in identifying smells of fruits, flowers and foods (http://www.sentosphere.fr/). Physically the *Loto* game consists of players' game-cards and thirty small jars of scented substances.

We created a series of small games, under the umbrella title of *Smell Me*, each exploring slightly different aspects of the basic idea. We aimed to exploit some of the many difficulties of recalling and identifying odours already outlined above, making them the substance of the gameplay. It might seem that with only three odours to play with, users would find the games trivially easy, but this proved not to be the case. Players found the games hard, in some cases harder than we intended. The difficulties experienced by players arose mainly from their difficulty in identifying odours, not from other aspects of the game play such as navigation, the game rules, or issues of manual control.

Though players could play the games in any order, the design was contrived to encourage them to play the simplest game first. This was intended to provide a surreptitious form of training, preparing the player for the other games. Nearly all players took the default route through the games. The fictional scenario across the suite of games was a playful 'primitive' society living in a landscape of fruits and flowers.

Figure 3: In Collect Me players travel forward on a straight road. As each scent is emitted, the player must label it by selecting one of three icons.

Figure 4: A scene from the mini-game Mix Me in which players must identify a scent within a mixture.

The first game, *Collect Me*, deals with simply recognizing the odours within a game context (Figure 3). A succession of odour emissions occurs as the player views a fanciful tree. Instruction is given using voice-over. An object appears in the space before them, whose image can be switched using a single keyboard key to any of three icons representing the three respective odours. So, as each scent is emitted, the player must label it by selecting one of the three icons. Scoring uses a simple counter for successful identifications. A count-down timer discourages the user from playing very slowly as a way of making the game easier. In *Kiss Me* the player must identify a certain odour which they have experienced earlier. Within the game scenario, the player is identifying each of six masked women as his wife by correctly identifying her scent. The penalty for error is a virtual slap in the face, for success, a virtual kiss. These outcomes are represented audiovisually. *Drop Me* gives users an opportunity to define their own meanings for the odours. The player is invited to use them as olfactory traces, marking locations in a maze in order to make it easier to discover the way out in the sequel game *Follow Me*. *Mix Me* (Figure 4) was designed to deal with recognizing the components of mixtures of odours.

7 Engaging with Odours

Two forms of evaluation were carried out. The game was tested with sixteen subjects using a small usability and evaluation workshop on university premises, responses being elicited using a post-play questionnaire. In addition, approximately forty

Rating assigned by players	1	2	3	4	5
How difficult was it to play the game? (1 = very easy)	7	4	3	1	1
How difficult was the game to navigate? (1 = very easy)	7	6	1	2	0
How much were you satisfied with your performance? (1 = not at all)	1	3	8	3	1
How much did you enjoy using your sense of smell in the game? (1 = not at all)	0	0	3	9	4

Table 1: Trial results for 16 subjects based on a post-use paper questionnaire. 10 male, 6 female. Age range: 20 to 34.

users played the game when it was displayed as part of an exhibition in London in September 2005. Informal observations were made of users at play, and players were invited to give their views of the experience. Similarly, a dozen players were studied at a subsequent display of the work as part of a conference on games.

The suite of games as a whole was not found to be easy. Even though we had devised the mini-game *Collect Me* to be simple, players found even this introductory game remarkably hard. For players to simply grasp that the game relied on olfactory skills turned out to be difficult, due probably to its unfamiliarity. Interacting using the sense of smell in any context is not common, let alone as part of a digital game. However, after approximately two minutes, most players got used to the game idea.

In the formal evaluation, the subjects were first-year undergraduates (6 males) and the remainder postgraduate students (4 males, 6 females), studying respectively on programmes in games design and interactive media design. Ten out of sixteen users play games at least once a week. All were in their 20s or early 30s. A basic questionnaire concerning the reactions of players (Table 1) was administered immediately after play.

Most players found the game suite easy to play overall. Navigation of the game environment was scored as somewhat easier than the overall game, with 13 finding navigation 'very easy' or 'fairly easy', and none finding it very difficult. Asked whether they were satisfied with their own achievement in the game, an overall majority of the players chose the middling value. In answer to the key question, 'How much did you enjoy using your sense of smell in the game?' all players chose ratings in the upper half of the rankings.

Having watched the players at play, we would have to qualify the impression that the game overall was 'easy'. The results of the informal study of users were in some ways as instructive. We present the findings here in relation to the range of topics which emerged.

Identification of scents:

- Players generally report that they can detect differences between scents, but they have great difficulty saying which is which. However, their performance improves after initial problems.

- The two flower scents were particularly problematic because of their general similarity. It was easy to tell the difference between fruit scents and flower scents, but the scents of Lavender and Jasmine were experienced as too similar. It would be better to use scents which are widely distributed across a gamut. This has implications for scalability: a large number of scents would be increasingly 'close' to one another in the gamut, especially if the odours were limited to those found generally pleasing.

- The great majority of players reported that after the initial 'training' period in which, after becoming accustomed to the game idea, their performance improved, their ability to discriminate subsequently deteriorated. This fits with what is known about repeated or prolonged exposure to odours.

- In *Collect Me*, approximately 65% of players found it difficult to distinguish two flower scents (Lavender and Jasmine), but found it easier to identify the scent of Citrus.

- In *Kiss Me*, approximately 80% of the users could not correctly recall the target smell. Nevertheless this game was well liked, suggesting that – in common with any game – difficulty, provided it is set within the right scenario, can make an engaging basis for an olfactory game.

- In *Mix Me*, 90% of the users could not identify the components of mixed scents. Knowing what we do now about the difficulty of identifying even three individual scents, this is not surprising.

- Some potential players refused to play on the grounds that they believed they did not have a good sense of smell. Smokers lacked confidence initially, but seemed to have no less success than non-smokers. In the formal evaluation, only 1 out of 16 users who identified every scent correctly has been a smoker for over 10 years.

Location of the odour emission system:

- Players were intrigued by the mechanism for odour delivery. Some guessed quite wrongly that the scent was coming from the audio speakers in front of them! Most were surprised when told that the scents were coming from beside them, suggesting that even with a strongly directional delivery system such as aerosol spray, directionality can be obscured by players' concentration on other tasks.

- Curiosity about the source led many players, once they had identified it, to turn directly towards the source, especially during emission. Given that the design was intended to obviate this, this was obviously a failing, and a potential health hazard.

- In early trials, the distance between the player and the source was quite large and the odour not easy to discern. Often two players teamed up, one taking up a position near the source, the other at the keyboard.

General reactions to the concept:

- The great majority of visitors (approximately 85%) found the game suite interesting and considered it innovative. Of these, slightly more than half thought it an idea worth developing further.

- Habitual game players adapted more rapidly to the game than non-players, despite the unfamiliarity of the olfactory element.

- Gender seemed not to be a factor. Age among adults was not a factor, but children generally were uninterested.

- A number (approximately 20%) started to play, found the gameplay too difficult and confusing and quit immediately.

Suggestions from players

1. Some players suggested applications for the game such as in calming the mentally disturbed. However, others noted, as we did, that the game excited players rather than calming them.

2. It was suggested that we link the game to sensors, so that according to the player's heart rate (for example) the odour would change. This might be able to deal with the objections to the previous point, though basing an automated response on interpretation of bio-data is itself not straightforward.

Though, as we have said, some potential players were not interested in the game, a very significant proportion began to play. Of those, the great majority remained playing the game, though not always for very long. While playing, players were thoroughly engaged with the experience. Informal questioning about the mini-games within the suite showed that Kiss Me was found difficult but was liked most. *Mix Me* and the maze games *Drop Me* and *Follow Me* exceeded many players' tolerance for difficulty. *Collect Me* was relatively easy but not liked as well as *Kiss Me*. It seemed that engagement was promoted particularly in *Kiss Me* by the close fit between the player's task and the imaginary scenario proposed in the game. Many players laughed as they understood the nature of the task and then attempted to identify their 'spouse' by scent.

In retrospect, we realized we had made some assumptions which proved incorrect. Male players were expected to like the game less than females, but this was not the case. We expected children to be excited by the concept, but generally they were not. Even those children who started the game soon abandoned it. This may or may not have arisen from the olfactory aspect or from other aspects of the game design: we are not currently able to say.

For most players, as we hoped, the difficulty of discriminating, recalling and identifying scents made an engaging basis for digital gameplay.

8   Discussion

We have noted several difficulties in designing with odour, here drawing attention to just two problems specific to the design process. Storyboarding smells is hard, but repeated run-throughs of the developing project using real odours suffer from the designers' own decreasing sensitivity during repeated or prolonged exposure. At a more fundamental level, it is all too easy when designing with odour to carelessly elide designer intention with user perception. If we say 'At this point there is a smell of lavender', do we mean the moment when the transmission of the odour is designed to begin, or the imprecise time when the user becomes aware of the odour? This is an unfamiliar problem: we are accustomed when designing for vision, and even sound, to ignore time differences between the production of the stimulus and the onset of the sensation.

8.1   Odour for Information

If usability is 'the extent to which a product can be used by specified users to achieve specified goals with effectiveness, efficiency and satisfaction' [ISO 1998] then a number of serious problems arise with the use of odour, both in relation to informational use (effectiveness and efficiency) and affective aspects (satisfaction).

Our work confirmed previously reported problems in using odour as a vehicle for information. *Smell Me* was intended to provide an environment that encouraged users to play with their sense of smell, using the scents as information. However, we observed that some players still relied on the sense of hearing and sight to play the game. They paid conscious attention to the sound of the aerosols, even using them to 'cheat' in identification tasks.

Some user difficulties in discriminating the chosen scents probably arose from the fact that we used inexpensive synthetic odours designed for domestic use rather than created for the task. However our experience suggests that finding a range of odours which are acceptable but which are also all discriminable, under real-world rather than laboratory conditions, will be hard.

Since, as noted, timing is problematic, the informational use of odour in any context where the timing of the sensation alters the meaning will also be a problem. This is likely to be the case where visual or auditory information within a dynamic stream is intended to work with odour as a unified message. These timing problems interact with difficulties in discerning individual odours within mixtures, so that if one odour lingers it will confuse the perception of another which was nominally delivered later.

8.2   Odour for Engagement

If odour is intended, not as primary communication, but to augment a multimedia experience by making it more immersive and thereby, arguably, more engaging, there are lessons to be learned from its use in other media. Odour in film has been notably unsuccessful with both critics and public. Though it is claimed that rose oil and an electric fan were used in a Pennsylvania film theatre in 1916, and later attempts included Aroma-Rama and Smell-o-Vision – and a film, Scent of Mystery in 1960, in which odour carried significant plot information – the recurring popular verdict is that 'some things are best left to the imagination'; that odour is 'one of the worst movie ideas ever' [Smith & Kiger 2006]. Equally ominously for digital media, Wired magazine chose *iSmell* as one of its 'Empty Promises' of 2001 [Manjoo 2001], while in 2004 when *Scent Mail* was first proposed, journalist Barry Fox called it 'one of the daftest ideas I've heard about in 25 years of writing about technology' [BBC World 2004]. It seems therefore that augmentation by odour is likely to suffer considerable popular resistance. We assume that it was the playful context of our own project which made it largely acceptable to users.

Where odour is used to help complete an immersive user experience, an at first sight trivial problem requires the designer's attention. Emission devices tend to divide between those like ours, or the air cannon of Yanagida et al. [2004], which transmit reasonably rapidly on demand but in which the mechanism makes a perceptible noise, and those which are silent because they use heat-vaporization, but where the latency between control signal and user sensation is worse. The noise of an odour mechanism obviously tends to interfere with the transparency of the experience, drawing attention to its technical mediation. Using headphones and a constant soundtrack could mask such extraneous sounds.

The game within *Smell Me* which enjoyed the greatest popularity was *Kiss Me*. The engagement which this game produced seemed to arise partly from the close fit between the fanciful scenario (the search for the wife) and the use of scent. Kissing and scent fit well together, as does, by convention, the identification of scent with woman. Scent was able to lend to the normally mechanical experience of gameplay using keyboards and controllers, monitors and speakers, an appropriate sensual element which fitted well with the 'story'. To borrow a term from film theory, scent was a convincing part of the *diegesis*, that is, it was integral to the fictional world, rather than seeming like an extrinsic addition.

It is generally acknowledged that level of difficulty in a game is best conceived not as a fixed uniform quality, but as a dynamic property which is designed to strike a balance, on a continuing basis, between the extremes of being too easy so that the player becomes bored and being too hard so that the player is frustrated [Csikszentmihalyi 1975, p.49]. We have admitted that some of the tasks we set around odour in our games were too difficult to be engaging, but also noted that it was not the easiest game that was best liked. It might seem that the problem of the player's decreasing sensitivity during exposure could fit with the need for games to progressively increase in difficulty: odour-based tasks would inevitably become more difficult during a play session. However there are two problems: games are often required to increase in difficulty across multiple sessions, whereas desensitization is a temporary artefact of exposure during a single session; also, returning to the point mentioned above, the difficulty experienced may be of the wrong kind. The user's decreasing ability to discriminate odours seems likely to be perceived as *extra-diegetic*, that is, not a meaningful part of the game scenario but an extrinsic frustration akin to being unable to see or hear clearly the outputs of a more conventional game.

Basing their work on Csikszentmihalyi's, Salen & Zimmerman [2003, p.338] proposed eight objectives in game design. It may be useful in conclusion to look at the role of odour in relation to these, in light of our project. Though the objectives relate to game design, they may help identify broader issues of engagement with interactive media.

Tasks should offer a chance of completion, a challenging activity that requires skills. The difficulties of odour identification create an engaging challenge. It is known that skills in odour recall and identification can be improved through practice, making it possible to design games which offer an increasing level of difficulty to match players' increasing skill.

Tasks should merge action and awareness such that the activity becomes spontaneous, almost automatic. Odour clearly has the potential to augment a multimodal experience, which might lead to a more fully engaged concentration. However we have identified many impediments to a seamless game experience including practical issues such as extraneous noise and the cumbersome nature of the delivery mechanisms. At present, the novelty of the experience is also an impediment to its being transparent in the way this objective seems to demand.

The task has clear goals. It is certainly possible to propose clear goal-directed tasks involving odour, as we have shown.

The task provides immediate feedback. Odour tends not to provide clear feedback to the user, for the many reasons outlined above. However, odour in the real world behaves similarly, so it can be argued that in some cases the imprecision of computer-controlled odour could evoke realistically the character of odour in the real world. In any case, Salen & Zimmerman's demand for immediacy is questionable: many games deliberately do not reveal to the player all they need to know immediately.

The task leads to deep but effortless involvement. In principle, odour can prompt retrieval of lost memories, it is highly evocative, but, when mechanically mediated, it may also interrupt user concentration on the current task.

The task facilitates a sense of control over one's actions. By augmenting a multimodal sense of realism, odour may help to make the virtual world seem more completely responsive to the player's actions. Odour offers an additional plaything which the user may be allowed to manipulate. However, there are many difficulties in achieving rapid or fine control over odour.

Concern for the self disappears during the task; sense of self emerges as stronger when the flow task is completed. Odour has, in principle, the capacity to transport the user in imagination, removing them from the real world context in which the interaction takes place. In practice, current technologies are obtrusive and militate against overlooking the mechanical mediation of the experience.

The sense of duration of time is altered. If the (admittedly fictional) experience of Proust's hero is anything to go by, decades may be evoked by a fleeting experience of an odour. However, nothing practical on this aspect was discovered during our brief trials. Players seemed to take the smells as present and immediate, not as alluding to smells from another time in their experience. Evocation through odour is highly personal.

What we have learned in this project has partly confirmed accepted wisdom from other forms of design – such as the need for a maximal fit between the individual components of the user's experience and the overall scenario, which we have related to the concept of *diegesis* – but it also alerted us to issues which are unique to designing with interactive odour: difficulties in conceptualizing, specifying and controlling. For this project, unfamiliarity produced issues of its own. It created difficulties for us as designers during planning, and we believe also had a significant effect on the reactions of users. Even if we had approached our investigation more formally it would have been difficult to guard against, on the one hand, problems arising from users' inexperience in dealing with odour-based digital experiences (which seemed to make their tasks exceptionally hard) and, on the other, novelty appeal, where we almost certainly benefited from the fact that none of our players had ever played an odour-based game before.

In designing with odour in an interactive context, though there are fundamental problems arising from the nature of odour, and many practical difficulties in both design and delivery, the intriguing potential makes us want to pursue the idea. For the future, the conceptual difficulties and practical issues suggest that, should it ever become possible to directly stimulate the brain in order to *simulate* the perception of distinct odours, then this would eventually be a far easier solution than any of those we tried, or than any of the developments based on real odours currently being explored around the world.

References

Amoore, J. E. [1963], Stereochemical Theory of Olfaction, *Nature* **198**(4877), 271–2.

Amoore, J. E. [1970], *Molecular Basis of Odor*, Charles C. Thomas.

Barfield, W. & Danas, E. [1995], Comments on the Use of Olfactory Displays for Virtual Environments, *Presence: Teleoperators and Virtual Environments* **5**(1), 109–21.

Barille, E. & Laroze, C. [1995], *The Book of Perfume*, Flammarion.

BBC World [2004], Click N Sniff, Video article by Tayfun King, June 10th 2004, http://www.bbcworld.com/content/clickonline_archive_23_2004.asp?pageid=666&co_pageid=3, last accessed 2006-05-11.

Bodnar, A., Corbett, R. & Nekrasovski, D. [2004], AROMA: Ambient Awareness through Olfaction in a Messaging Application, *in* R. Sharma, T. Darrell, M. Harper, G. Lazzari & M. Turk (eds.), *Proceedings of the 6th International Conference on Multimodal Interfaces (ICMI'04)*, ACM Press, pp.183–90.

Boyd Davis, S. [2005], It's Art, but is it HCI? – Testing the Boundaries., *in* N. Aykin (ed.), *Proceedings of the 11th International Conference on Human–Computer Interaction (HCI International 2005)*, Lawrence Erlbaum Associates. Published on CD-ROM.

Carter, R. [1999], *Mapping the Mind*, Weidenfeld and Nicholson.

Csikszentmihalyi, M. [1975], *Beyond Boredom and Anxiety: The Experience of Play in Work and Games*, Jossey-Bass.

Engen, T. [1991], *Odour Sensation and Memory*, Praeger.

ISO [1998], ISO 9241-11 International Standard. Ergonomic Requirements for Office Work with Visual Display Terminals (VDTs). Part 11: Guidance for Specifying and Measuring Usability. International Organization for Standardization, Genève, Switzerland.

Kaye, J. [2001], Symbolic Olfactory Display, Master's thesis, Massachusetts Institute of Technology.

Kaye, J. [2004], Making Scents: Aromatic Output for HCI, *Interactions* **11**(1), 48–61.

Laing, D., Doty, R. & Breipohl, W. [1991], *The Human Sense of Smell*, Springer.

Lawless, H. T. [1997], Olfactory Psychophysics, *in* G. K. Beauchamp & L. Bartoshuk (eds.), *Tasting and Smelling*, second edition, Academic Press, pp.125–74.

Lundstrom, J., Hummel, T. & Olsson, M. [2003], Individual Differences in Sensitivity to the Odour of 4,16-Androstadien-3-one, *Chemical Senses* **28**(7), 643–50.

Manjoo, F. [2001], Vaporware 2001: Empty Promises, http://www.wired.com/news/technology/0,1282,49326,00.html. last accessed 2006-05-11. Refers to the Wired article 'You've Got Smell!' by Charles Platt, http://www.wired.com/wired/archive/7.11/digiscent. html, last accessed 2006-05-11.

Mochizuki, A., Amada, T., Sawa, S., Takeda, T., Motoyashiki, S., Kohyama, K., Imura, M. & Chihara, K. [2004], Fragra: A Visual–Olfactory VR Game, SIGGRAPH 2004 Sketch.

Nobel Foundation [2004], Press release: The 2004 Nobel Prize in Physiology or Medicine, http://nobelprize.org/medicine/laureates/2004/press.html, last accessed 2006-05-11.

Proust, M. [1913-27], *A la recherche du temps perdu*, Bibliothèque de la Pléiade. Originally translated into English with the title 'Rememberance of Things Past' by C.K. Scott Moncrieff (completed in separate editions by Sydney Schiff and Frederick A. Blossom). Recent translations into English use the title 'In Search of Lost Time'.

Salen, K. & Zimmerman, E. [2003], *Rules of Play: Game Design Fundamentals*, MIT Press.

Smith, M. J. & Kiger, P. J. [2006], The Lingering Reek of Smell-O-Vision, Article in Los Angeles Times, 2006-02-05.

Teghtsoonian, R., Teghtsoonian, M., Berglund, B. & Berglund, U. [1978], Invariance of Odor Strength with Sniff Vigor: An Olfactory Analogue to Size Constancy, *Journal of Experimental Psychology: Human Perception and Performance* **4**(1), 144–52.

Yanagida, Y., Kawato, S., Noma, H., Tomono, A. & Tetsutani, N. [2004], Projection-based Olfactory Display with Nose Tracking, *in Proceedings of IEEE Virtual Reality Conference 2004 (VR'04)*, IEEE Computer Society Press, pp.43–50.

Measuring the Aesthetics of Reading

Kevin Larson[†], Richard L. Hazlett[‡], Barbara S. Chaparro[§] & Rosalind W. Picard[¶]

[†] *Microsoft Advanced Reading Technologies, One Microsoft Way, Redmond, WA 98052, USA*
Email: *kevlar@microsoft.com*

[‡] *Johns Hopkins University School of Medicine, 2045 York Road, Baltimore, MD 21093, USA*
Email: *rlhazlet@jhmi.edu*

[§] *Software Usability Research Laboratory, Wichita State University, Wichita, KS 67260-0034, USA*
Email: *barbara.chaparro@wichita.edu*

[¶] *MIT Media Laboratory, 20 Ames Street Cambridge, MA 02139, USA*
Email: *picard@media.mit.edu*

Aesthetic considerations are as important as usability for human-computer interactions, but techniques for measuring aesthetics have been elusive. In this paper, we use the domain of reading to develop new measures of aesthetics. These measures could be applied to any domain. Reading is arguably the most ubiquitous task that people perform on computers. To date, reading research has focused on reader performance, which is typically measured by reading speed and comprehension. But many typographic improvements that make a more beautiful document show little to no measurable difference on traditional performance tasks. We conducted six studies that found two measures that successfully detect aesthetic differences: improved performance on creative cognitive tasks after text is optimized, and reduced activation in the corrugator muscle that is associated with frowning.

Keywords: reading, typography, aesthetics, emotion, affective user interface.

1   Introduction

Reading has arguably the longest and richest history of any domain for scientifically considering the impact of technology on the user. From the 1920s to the 1950s, Miles Tinker [1963] and other researchers ran hundreds of user tests that examined the effects of different fonts and text layout variables, such as the amount of vertical space between each line of text (called leading). Their research focused on user performance, and reading speed was the favoured measure. They charted the effect of the manipulated variables on reading speed, looking for the point at which their participants could read the fastest. Their assumption was that faster reading speeds created a more optimal experience. Printers and publishers eagerly consumed this research.

In recent years, some of these variables have been reexamined as the technology and capabilities evolve with the advent of computers and computer screens. Dillon [1992] examined how to design textual information for an electronic environment. Boyarski et al. [1998] examined the effect of fonts that were designed for computer screens. Dyson & Kipping [1998] examined the effect of line length on computer screens. Larson et al. [2000] examined the effect of 3-D rotation on reading. Gugerty et al. [2004] demonstrated a reading performance advantage with the Microsoft ClearType display technology.

Some typographers argue that the focus for decades on traditional measures of user performance does a disservice to the design of text and documents. Bringhurst [2004] argues that the goal of good typography is to invite the reader into the text. The appropriate measure of invitingness is not reading speed or comprehension, but rather something that other measures have not been able to capture: aesthetics.

In this paper, we first describe two studies that inspired us to investigate aesthetics, and then describe a series of four more studies in which we experimented with two novel measures of aesthetics: creative cognitive tasks and facial muscle measurements. Before discussing the studies, we briefly explain some of the factors that are important to typographers for designing beautiful text.

2   The Art of Typography

Typographers are attuned to subtle features when they design and set type. One such feature is symmetry. It is surprisingly difficult to make and render symmetric type. Each stroke across a font needs to be of equal weight – if one vertical stem is heavier than the next, the relative darkness appears as a dark spot on the page. As shown in Figure 1, the white space *within* characters also needs to be balanced – for example, if the space under one arch of an m is narrower than the other arch or narrower than the arch of the n, this letter appears as a dark spot on the page. And the white space between characters needs to be equal to complete the desired symmetry.

To create the desired evenness across a page, typographers use a variety of techniques, including ligatures, kerning, small caps, and old-style numerals. Ligatures are special-combination characters that a type designer creates for a font when two characters clash with each other. The most common use of ligatures is for the letter pairs *fi* and *fl* because the top of the *f* looks uncomfortable with the dot on the *i* and the top of the *l* respectively. Kerning is the technique of adjusting the

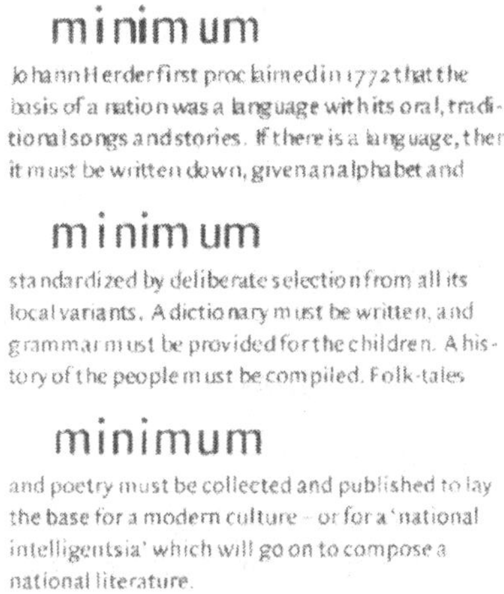

minimum

Johann Herder first proclaimed in 1772 that the
basis of a nation was a language with its oral, traditional songs and stories. If there is a language, then
it must be written down, given an alphabet and

minimum

standardized by deliberate selection from all its
local variants. A dictionary must be written, and
grammar must be provided for the children. A history of the people must be compiled. Folk-tales

minimum

and poetry must be collected and published to lay
the base for a modern culture – or for a 'national
intelligentsia' which will go on to compose a
national literature.

Figure 1: The first paragraph shows uneven stroke weight and uneven spacing both within characters and between characters. The second paragraph shows only poor spacing between characters. The third paragraph shows symmetry both in characters and spacing.

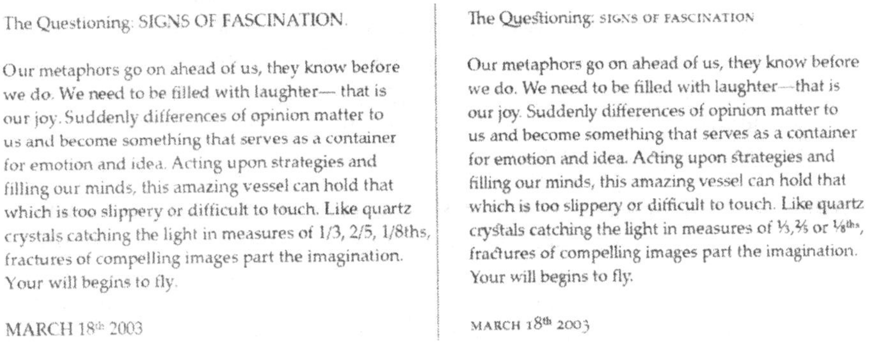

The Questioning: SIGNS OF FASCINATION.

Our metaphors go on ahead of us, they know before
we do. We need to be filled with laughter— that is
our joy. Suddenly differences of opinion matter to
us and become something that serves as a container
for emotion and idea. Acting upon strategies and
filling our minds, this amazing vessel can hold that
which is too slippery or difficult to touch. Like quartz
crystals catching the light in measures of 1/3, 2/5, 1/8ths,
fractures of compelling images part the imagination.
Your will begins to fly.

MARCH 18th 2003

The Questioning: SIGNS OF FASCINATION

Our metaphors go on ahead of us, they know before
we do. We need to be filled with laughter—that is
our joy. Suddenly differences of opinion matter to
us and become something that serves as a container
for emotion and idea. Acting upon strategies and
filling our minds, this amazing vessel can hold that
which is too slippery or difficult to touch. Like quartz
crystals catching the light in measures of ⅓,⅔ or ⅛ths,
fractures of compelling images part the imagination.
Your will begins to fly.

MARCH 18th 2003

Figure 2: The paragraph on the left contains no OpenType features. The paragraph on the right demonstrates OpenType ligatures, kerning, small caps, old-style numerals, and subscript and superscript features.

---

default letter spacing to create more even spacing. Small caps and old-style numerals are necessary to reduce the large block that gets created on pages that use a large number with several digits or capital letters in a row, such as in an acronym, like HCI. Small caps are the shape of capital letters, but are comparable in size to lowercase letters. Like lowercase letters, old-style numerals have ascenders and descenders.

All of these techniques and dozens of others are now available to typographers for on-screen use with a technology called OpenType. Figure 2 shows an example of OpenType-adjusted text.

Most typographers believe that OpenType features benefit users, but there are many areas of controversy in the typography community about what is best for the user. For example, typographers have not determined if a serif font or sans serif is more appropriate for reading a textbook. Reading speed and comprehension are the primary scientific measures for testing typographic differences. In two performance studies, we discovered that reading speed and comprehension failed to detect differences between two kinds of typographic page manipulation, despite there being a large apparent difference in the two document types.

3 OpenType Reading Speed Study

In this study, we have participants read text with and without OpenType features.

Participants: Twenty college students (10 male, 10 female) with normal or corrected vision participated in the study and received compensation of $25. Participants were not told the purpose of the study until after its completion.

Materials: Text passages were chosen from college board practice examinations that included approximately 800 words (mean = 830.17, s.d. = 33.55). The documents with OpenType incorporated ligatures, kerning, small caps, old-style numerals, and subscript and superscript; the documents without OpenType did not. Text documents were randomly presented on Dell Inspiron 5100 laptops with a 15-inch display with 1400×1050 native resolution. Participants saw documents on two pages. They selected an arrow at the bottom of each page to go to the next page or the previous page. No scrolling was required. They read the documents at a distance of approximately 50cm while being automatically timed.

Procedure: In each condition, participants spent approximately 30 minutes reading three documents. We asked them to read each document at their own pace. After reading each document, participants answered eight comprehension questions about the document. They could look up the answers in the documents, but were advised that they had only five minutes to do so. After reading all three documents, the participants were administered the NASA Task Load Index to assess Mental Workload. Participants then took a short break and repeated the procedure with a different set of three documents for the other condition. After both conditions were completed, we showed the participants a sample page with images of the two conditions and asked them to state which layout they liked best. We counterbalanced the order of the two conditions and six passages across participants to ensure that each passage occurred equally in the two conditions.

3.1 Results

Reading performance: We averaged the reading rate in words per minute across documents for each condition. Participants in the OpenType condition read at a rate of 194.73 words per minute (s.d. = 48.17); participants in the no OpenType condition read at a rate of 195.89 words per minute (s.d. = 55.64).

We then computed the comprehension scores as a sum score out of a total eight possible. Participants in the OpenType condition comprehended 4.67 questions on average (s.d. = 1.11); participants in the no OpenType condition comprehended 4.73 questions on average (s.d. = 1.02). A paired-samples t-test revealed no reliable differences across conditions for reading speed, $t(19) = 0.21$, $p = 0.84$, or comprehension, $t(19) = 0.18$, $p = 0.86$.

Mental Workload (NASA Task Load Index): Participants had a reliably higher Task Load Index (TLX) after reading the documents with no OpenType document condition (mean = 48.9) than after reading the OpenType documents (mean = 37.7), $t(19) = 2.79$, $p = 0.01$.

Preference: 55% of the participants preferred the OpenType format; 45% preferred the no OpenType format. A Wilcoxon Z test showed no reliable preference for either layout format, Z (N=20) = 0.447, $p = 0.66$.

Results from this study showed that OpenType formatting affected neither reading performance nor document preference. The participants indicated that they did not notice much difference between the two versions and had a hard time choosing which one they preferred. Some participants noticed the smaller caps and different style numbers in the documents with OpenType, but said they preferred the larger caps and numbers in the documents without OpenType. Despite the failure of traditional performance measures to distinguish the two aesthetic conditions, the NASA-TLX did capture a statistically significant difference.

3.2   Page Setting Reading Speed Study

In this study, we have participants read online text with and without enhanced page setting. Enhanced page setting included the optimal use of headers, indentation, figure placement, and quote blocking.

Participants: Twenty college students (10 male, 10 female) with normal or corrected vision participated in the study and received compensation of $25.

Materials: Figure 3 shows an example of the poor page setting and optimized page setting conditions used in this study. Optimized page setting includes good headers, indentation, figure placement, and quote blocking. Text passages and presentation were the same as the ones that we used in the OpenType reading speed study.

Procedure: The procedures were the same as the ones in the OpenType reading speed study.

3.3   Results

Reading performance: We averaged the reading rate in words per minute for documents for each condition. Participants in the optimized page setting condition read at a rate of 185.60 words per minute (s.d. = 47.22); participants in the poor page setting condition read at a rate of 183.38 words per minute (s.d. = 51.36). Comprehension scores were computed as a sum score out of

The following excerpt is from Eyes on the Prize, the companion guide to the public television series on America's civil rights struggle. During the 1930s National Association for the Advancement of Colored People (NAACP) attorneys Charles H Houston, William Hastie, Thurgood Marshall charted a legal strategy designed to end segregation in education challenging segregation in Houston believed that the battle against segregation had to begin at the highest academic level in order to mitigate fear of race mixing that could create ever greater hostility and reluctance on the part of white judges. After establishing a series of favorable legal precedents in higher education, NAACP attorneys planned to launch an all out attack on the separate-but-equal doctrine in primary and secondary schools. The strategy proved successful. In four major United States Supreme Court decisions precedents were established that would enable the NAACP to construct a solid legal foundation upon which the Brown case could rest. Missouri ex rel. Gaines v. Canada, Registrar of the University of Missouri (1938); Sipuel v. Board of Regents of the University of Oklahoma (1948); McLaurin v. Oklahoma State Regents for Higher Education (1950), and Sweatt v. Painter (1950).

In the Oklahoma case, the Supreme Court held that the plaintiff was entitled to enroll in the university. The Oklahoma Regents responded by separating black and white students in cafeterias and classrooms. The 1950 McLaurin decision ruled that such internal separation was unconstitutional.

In the Sweatt ruling, delivered on the same day, the Supreme Court held that the maintenance of separate law schools for whites and blacks was unconstitutional. A year after Herman Sweatt entered the University of Texas law school, desegregation cases were filed in the states of Kansas, South Carolina, Virginia, and Delaware, and in the District of Columbia asking the courts to apply the qualitative test of the Sweatt case to the elementary and secondary schools and to declare the separate-but-equal doctrine invalid in the area of public education.

The 1954 Brown v. Board of Education decision declared that a classification based solely on race violated the 14th Amendment to the United States Constitution. The decision reversed the 1896 Plessy v. Ferguson ruling that had established the separate-but-equal doctrine. The Brown decision more than any other case launched the equalitarian revolution in American jurisprudence and signaled the emerging primacy of equality as a guide to constitutional decisions; nevertheless, the decision did not end state-sanctioned segregation.

THE FOLLOWING EXCERPT IS FROM EYES ON THE PRIZE. THE COMPANION GUIDE TO THE PUBLIC TELEVISION SERIES ON AMERICA'S CIVIL RIGHTS STRUGGLE

During the 1930s National Association for the Advancement of Colored People (NAACP) attorneys Charles H. Houston, William Hastie, Leon Ransom, and Thurgood Marshall charted a legal strategy designed to end segregation in education. They developed a series of legal cases challenging segregation in graduate and professional schools. Houston believed that the battle against segregation had to begin at the highest academic level in order to mitigate fears of race mixing that could create even greater hostility and reluctance on the part of white judges. After establishing a series of favorable legal precedents in higher education, NAACP attorneys planned to launch an all-out attack on the separate-but-equal doctrine in primary and secondary schools. The strategy proved successful. In four major United States Supreme Court decisions precedents were established that would enable the NAACP to construct a solid legal foundation upon which the Brown case could rest. Missouri ex rel. Gaines v. Canada, Registrar of the University of Missouri (1935); Sipuel v. Board of Regents of the University of Oklahoma (1948); McLaurin v. Oklahoma State Regents for Higher Education (1950), and Sweatt v. Painter (1950).

In the Oklahoma case, the Supreme Court held that the plaintiff was entitled to enroll in the university. The Oklahoma Regents responded by separating black and white students in cafeterias and classrooms. The 1950 McLaurin decision ruled that such internal separation was unconstitutional.

In the Sweatt ruling, delivered on the same day, the Supreme Court held that the maintenance of separate law schools for whites and blacks was unconstitutional. Herman Sweatt entered the University of Texas law school, desegregation cases were filed in the states of Kansas, South Carolina, Virginia, and Delaware, and in the District of Columbia asking the courts to apply the qualitative test of the Sweatt case to the elementary and secondary schools and to declare the separate-but-equal doctrine invalid in the area of public education.

The 1954 Brown v. Board of Education decision declared that a classification based solely on race violated the 14th Amendment to the United States Constitution. The decision reversed the 1896 Plessy v. Ferguson ruling that had established the separate-but-equal doctrine. The Brown decision more than any other case launched the "equalitarian revolution" in American jurisprudence and signaled the emerging primacy of equality as a guide to constitutional decisions; nevertheless, the decision did not end state-sanctioned segregation.

Figure 3: The page on the left shows poor page setting. The page on the right shows optimized page setting, including optimized image placement, good headers, and well-marked paragraphs.

---

a total of eight possible. Participants in the optimized page setting condition correctly answered 5.32 comprehension questions on average (s.d. = 0.99). In contrast, participants in the poor page setting condition correctly answered 5.08 questions on average (s.d. = 1.31). A paired-samples t-test revealed no reliable differences across conditions for reading speed, $t(19) = 0.41$, $p = 0.69$, or comprehension, $t(19) = 0.96$, $p = 0.35$.

Mental Workload (NASA-TLX): Participants showed no reliable differences in the Task Load Index between reading the poor page setting documents (mean = 56.02) and the optimized page setting documents (mean = 50.33), $t(19) = 1.41$, $p = 0.17$.

Preference: 90% of the participants preferred the optimized page setting format. In contrast, 10% preferred the poor page setting format. A Wilcoxon Z test showed a reliable preference for the optimized page setting layout, $Z (N=20) = 3.58$, $p = 0.002$.

Results from this study showed that the quality of the page setting format influenced neither reading performance nor comprehension, despite the fact that participants often had to read around a photograph in the poor page setting documents. All but two participants chose the optimized page setting layout as their favourite. One participant said the positioning of the pictures in the middle of a line was good because it 'broke up the long lines and made it seem shorter.' Both participants, however, said the optimized page setting layout looked better when it was shown alongside the poor page setting at the end of the study.

4 New Approaches for Measuring Aesthetics [Instead of Performance]

These two studies demonstrate that some improvements in document typographic quality do not reliably improve user reading speed and comprehension performance, and may not even be explicitly noticed by users. Current measurement tests, which are based on performance and on subjective reporting of workload, are not sophisticated enough to test for improvements that most typographers agree on. How can we test more controversial typographic features?

Research on aesthetics is becoming more common in human-computer interactions as the field shifts its focus from creating usable products to creating desirable products. Sykes & Brown [2003] demonstrated that it is possible to measure arousal during video game play by examining pressure on the gamepad buttons. Reijneveld et al. [2003] used a non-verbal subjective rating of emotions to detect differences while individuals sat in different office chairs. Ward & Marsden [2003] measured the physiological indicators of galvanic skin response, heart rate, and blood volume pressure while individuals performed information searching tasks. Branco et al. [2005] measured facial muscle differences while participants performed word processing tasks.

Our goal is to develop a measure that is sensitive to improvements in aesthetics by extending two earlier methodologies. Our first measure is based on a body of research that shows that a good mood improves people's performance during creative cognitive tasks [Isen 1993].

Alice Isen et al. [1987] have demonstrated that participants who are put in a good mood before performing certain cognitive tasks perform better than participants who are not put in a good mood first. Participants can be placed in a good mood by receiving a small gift, such as a candy bar, or by watching five minutes of a humorous video. After being induced into a good mood, participants performed better on creative cognitive tasks, such as the candle task [Duncker 1945] and remote associates task [Mednick 1962], compared to participants who were not put in a good mood.

If a candy bar or humorous video can induce a good mood, can good typography induce a similar kind of good mood? We expect that after reading documents that contain good typography, participants will perform better on the tasks that Isen used to measure creative cognition.

The next two studies use creative cognitive tasks as the dependent measure. Half of the participants read with good typography and half read with poor typography. Our hypothesis is that the participants in the good typography condition will perform better on cognitive tasks than the participants in the poor typography condition. If our hypothesis is true, it suggests that good typography may elevate mood.

4.1 ePeriodicals Candle Task Cognitive Measure Study

Participants in this study read text that either had high-quality typography or poor-quality typography. All participants used special software on a Tablet PC that enabled them to read a full issue of *The New Yorker* magazine. The candle task was used as the measure of aesthetics.

AN APPENDECTOMY ON THE BAKERLOO LINE

BY GRAHAM CHAPMAN

D ear Sirs,
I've had letter after letter after letter since you published one particular query that asked, "What should I do about my appendix on the Bakerloo Line?" Well, "Miss N.." I can

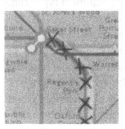

and ask for one. Remember, the stations marked with an "O" are interchange stations. Stations marked with a star are closed on Sundays, and also remember to pick up a plastic bucket for the guts.

Then study your map and find the brown line clearly marked "Bakerloo" in the key. Select a station appropriate to the severity of the inflammation. For mild or grumbling appendicitis, you could start at Lambeth North—being careful not to change at Waterloo—and have comfortably incised your abdomen and exposed the inflamed organ by the time you are between Marylebone and Kilburn Park. You will then have the time it takes you to reach Willesden Junction to complete the excision. And the six minutes between there and Wembley Central gives you plenty of time to be

AN APPENDECTOMY ON THE BAKERLOO LINE

BY GRAHAM CHAPMAN

D ear Sirs,
I've had letter after letter after letter since you published one particular query that asked, "What should I do about my

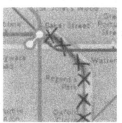

later on. I have set out some details that may help you in this sometimes irksome chore.

First, find yourself a Tube Map, issued free by London Transport, or go to your nearest Underground station and ask for one. Remember, the stations marked with an "O" are interchange stations. Stations marked with a star are closed on Sundays, and also remember to pick up a plastic bucket for the guts.

Then study your map and find the brown line clearly marked "Bakerloo" in the key. Select a station appropriate to the severity of the inflammation. For mild or grum-

Figure 4: The New Yorker with optimized (top) and poor (bottom) typography.

Participants: Twenty participants (10 male, 10 female) with normal or corrected vision participated in this study and received a compensation of Microsoft software. All participants classified themselves as occasional readers of The New Yorker. We used a between-participants design, in which we assigned 10 participants to the poor typography condition and the other 10 participants to the optimized typography condition. The data from one participant in the poor typography condition was discarded because she was familiar with the candle task.

Materials: ePeriodicals are electronic versions of print magazines. Each page is designed to fit perfectly on a 768×1024 native resolution Tablet PC in portrait orientation without scrolling. People turn pages (page up and page down) by pressing a tablet hardware button. People can also use a tablet pen to navigate directly to the table of contents or any article. In this study, we used the content from the January 5th, 2004 edition of *The New Yorker*, including the text, images, and advertisements that were used in that edition of the print magazine. The page layout differed from that of the print magazine to accommodate the size of the Tablet PC screen.

We created two versions of the ePeriodical. As shown in Figure 4, the optimized typography version used the New Yorker font with ClearType and good hyphenation and justification. The poor typography version used the bitmap version of the Courier font and included an extra two points of space between each word. Although the text looked terrible, users had no trouble reading the text – and the content was exactly the same in the two conditions.

Procedure: We gave each participant a brief tutorial about the ePeriodical user interface. The tutorial explained how to use the tablet hardware buttons to move to the next page or the previous page, and how to navigate to the table of contents and to any article. Participants could choose to read anything they wanted to read from this ePeriodical. We asked the participants to read for 20 minutes.

After the reading session, we gave the participants the candle task. In this mood-detecting task, we gave participants a box full of tacks, a candle, a match, and a corkboard, which was affixed to a wall. Their task was to attach the candle to the corkboard in such a way that the wax wouldn't drip all over the place when lit. They had 10 minutes to solve the task. We considered the task to be correctly solved if a participant emptied the tacks from the box, tacked the box to the corkboard, and placed the candle inside the box. All other solutions were considered incorrect.

4.2 Results

Candle task. We found that 4 of 10 participants correctly solved the candle task in the optimized typography condition. In contrast, 0 of 9 participants correctly solved the task in the poor typography condition. This is a reliable difference, $\chi^2(1) = 2.47$, $p = 0.04$. We propose that the typographic difference between poor and optimized typography drove the difference in the creative cognitive task. This finding is very similar to Isen's finding that a small gift or humorous video improved performance in creative cognitive tasks. This result indicates that typographic differences can also impact mood.

4.3 ePeriodicals Remote Associates Cognitive Measure Study

To examine whether we could replicate the above results by changing the creative cognitive task that is used, we replaced the candle task with the remote associates task, which is another cognitive task that Isen has shown to be influenced by positive mood. One advantage of the remote associates task compared to the candle task is that it can be used in within-participant studies, though this study uses a between-participant design.

In the remote associates task, we gave participants three words, such as *water*, *skate*, and *cream*, and then asked them to think of a word that created a common compound with each of the three words. In this example, the correct answer is *ice*. Participants saw the three items on a computer screen for up to 15 seconds, and then pressed a keyboard button as soon as they knew the answer. After the participants pressed the button or 15 seconds had elapsed, we prompted them to type their response. We collected the reaction time and the accuracy data from this test.

All other details of the study are identical to the first study. The same experimenter gave 20 new participants the same instructions about how to use an ePeriodical.

4.4 Results

Remote associates test: We found that the participants who viewed the optimized typography succeeded at 52% of the trials, at an average speed of 6395ms. Participants who viewed the poor typography succeeded at 48% of the trials, at an average speed of 6715ms. Although the means are in the predicted direction, neither the accuracy, $t(18) = 1.15$, $p = 0.27$, nor the speed differences, $t(18) = 0.42$, $p = 0.68$, are statistically reliable.

In summary, we conducted two studies using cognitive measures, which produced findings that suggest that more aesthetic typography can create greater positive feelings. When we induced a positive mood in the participants, they performed better on the candle task. However, the remote associates task did not show a statistically reliable difference.

5 Facial Muscle Activation

Another approach to measuring the emotion of readers is to measure changes in facial expressions by using facial electromyography (EMG). By placing tiny sensors over certain facial muscles, one can measure the minute changes in the muscles' electrical activity, which reflects changes in muscle tension. Facial EMG studies have found that activity of the corrugator muscle, which lowers the eyebrow and is involved in producing frowns, varies inversely with the emotional valence of the presented stimuli and reports of mood state; and activity of the zygomatic muscle, which controls smiling, is positively associated with positive emotional stimuli and positive mood state [Cacioppo et al. 1992; Dimberg 1990]. These effects have been found in passive viewing situations with various protocols and media, such as photos, videos, words, sounds, and imagery [Hazlett & Hazlett 1999; Larsen et al. 2003].

Increases in zygomatic EMG and decreases in corrugator EMG tend to indicate a positive emotional response. The orbicularis oculi muscle EMG controls eye smiling and is also positively associated with positive mood state. Some research has suggested that because this muscle is less subject to voluntary control than the zygomatic muscle, it may more truly reflect actual felt emotion [Cacioppo et al. 1992]. In task performance research, activity of the corrugator muscle provides a sensitive index of the degree of exerted mental effort [Waterink & van Boxtel 1994] and increases with the perception of goal obstacles [Pope 1994]. Several studies

Figure 5: Participant with facial EMG sensors.

have demonstrated that the corrugator EMG can reflect the computer user's tension and frustration [Scheirer et al. 1999; Hazlett 2003; Branco et al. 2005].

5.1 Page Setting Facial Muscle Activation Study

In this study, we compared the activation of facial muscles while participants read articles with optimized page setting and poor page setting. During the experiment, continuous emotional response data were collected from the corrugator (frown) muscle EMG and the zygomatic (smile) EMG.

Participants: 25 participants (13 male, 12 female) with normal or corrected vision participated in this study and received compensation of $90.

Materials: The page setting documents were the same as the documents that we used in the page setting reading speed study. We presented documents on a Sony Vaio laptop with a 15-inch display running 1400×1050 resolution. We continuously measured facial EMG by placing Rochester miniature Silver/Silver Chloride surface electrodes over the left zygomaticus major and corrugator supercilii muscles. We followed recommended guidelines for preparing the skin and placing the electrodes [Tassinary et al. 1989]. The raw EMG signals were amplified and filtered by using two Psylab (Contact Precision Instruments) bioamplifiers and processing system. EMG detection bandpass was set at 30Hz–500Hz, and the analogue EMG signal was digitized at 1000Hz.

Procedure: This study used a repeated measures design. We asked subjects to read six two-page articles: three in poor type and three in optimized type. The poor and optimized conditions were alternated for each participant, and the articles were counterbalanced between participants. After we attached the EMG sensors and a quiet baseline period had passed, the participants began reading the series of six articles. During the reading, the facial EMG measures were collected continuously.

5.2   Results

Reading speed and comprehension: Like the page setting reading speed study, there were no reliable differences in either reading speed or comprehension.

Corrugator EMG: We rectified the EMG values and calculated the 100ms data points. Because we were interested in the more subtle background effects of the typography, we filtered out extreme values of the EMG data series that were greater than 1.5 standard deviations (determined by pilot testing) above the series mean. These extreme EMG values were due to movement or other extraneous factors. Two participants' EMG data were not valid due to technical problems, which left us with 23 valid data series in the EMG statistical analyses. The corrugator mean value for the poor page setting documents was 11.59 microvolts; the mean value for the optimized page setting documents was 11.08 microvolts, which resulted in a mean difference of 0.51 microvolts (s.d. = 1.10). The corrugator muscle had reliably greater EMG when participants read the poor page setting documents, $F(1,22) = 4.90$, $p = 0.04$. This data showed that people used their frown muscles more while reading the text with the poor typography.

Zygomatic EMG: The zygomatic mean value for the poor page setting documents was 16.34 microvolts; the mean value for the optimized page setting documents was 15.89 microvolts, which resulted in a mean difference of 0.45 microvolts (s.d. = 4.83). This difference was not reliable, $F(1,22) = 0.22$, $p = 0.65$.

5.3   OpenType Facial Muscle Activation Study

This study expanded on the results of the first facial muscle activation study, which showed corrugator differences for the page setting documents. This study investigated EMG differences when participants read the documents with and without OpenType features. The difference between documents with vs. without OpenType is more subtle than the difference between page setting documents. In the OpenType reading speed study, we did not find a difference between the OpenType conditions, either in reading speed and comprehension or in document preference. In contrast, in the page setting reading speed study, we found a difference in document preference for the page setting documents.

In this study, we measured the orbicularis oculi (eye smile) muscle instead of the zygomatic muscle (both are associated with positive emotions) because we failed to find any zygomatic muscle differences in the page setting facial muscle activation study.

Participants: 25 participants (13 male, 12 female) with normal or corrected vision participated in this study and received compensation of $90.

Materials: The OpenType documents were the same documents as the ones we used in the OpenType reading speed study. The equipment and settings were the same as the ones we used in the page setting facial muscle activation study.

Procedure: The procedures were the same as the procedures we used in the page setting facial muscle activation study, except that we placed the EMG sensors on each participant's corrugator and orbicularis oculi muscles.

5.4 Results

Reading speed and comprehension: As with the OpenType reading speed study, there were no reliable differences in either reading speed or comprehension.

Corrugator EMG: One participant's EMG data was not valid due to technical problems, which left us with 24 valid data series in the EMG statistical analyses. The corrugator mean value for the no OpenType documents was 13.80 microvolts; the mean value for the OpenType documents was 12.56 microvolts, which resulted in a mean difference of 1.23 microvolts (s.d. = 2.83). The corrugator muscle had reliably greater EMG when participants read the no OpenType documents, $F(1,23) = 4.56$, $p = 0.04$.

Orbicularis oculi EMG: The orbicularis oculi mean value for the no OpenType documents was 10.35 microvolts; the mean value for the OpenType documents was 9.45 microvolts, which resulted in a mean difference of 0.90 microvolts (s.d. = 3.82). This difference was not reliable, $F(1,23) = 1.34$, $p = 0.25$.

The two facial muscle activation studies have demonstrated that we can detect subtle typographic differences by measuring the corrugator muscle. The corrugator muscle was more active when participants read the poor typography documents. The corrugator EMG decreases with increases in positive emotional state, and increases with increases in negative emotional state, tension, and mental effort. It is not clear from these studies which of these factors was associated with the type differences that we noted. The fact that we did not find differences with either of the positive emotion EMG measures – the zygomatic or orbicularis oculi facial muscles – does not help clarify the associated factors, because these measures are known to have a higher activation threshold [Larsen et al. 2003], and we are measuring very subtle effects.

6 Conclusions

The goal of this project was to develop new measures of subtle aesthetics differences for any domain. We have described two new measures and examined their application to detecting subtle typographic differences. These measures detected reliable differences, where classic measures of reading speed and comprehension failed to detect any differences. The first measure was based on Isen's findings that mood inducers, such as receiving a small gift or watching a humorous video, caused people to perform better on creative cognitive tasks, such as the candle task and remote associates task. In the first ePeriodical cognitive measure study, we manipulated typographic quality and demonstrated the same performance benefit that Isen found, which indicates that optimized typography has similar mood-improving powers as a small gift or humorous video does. In the second ePeriodical cognitive measure study, we did not find the same advantage in the remote associates task that Isen found, but we are still optimistic about exploring other creative cognitive tasks.

The second measure involved measuring the differences in facial muscle activation. In the facial muscle activation studies, EMG on the corrugator muscle successfully detected differences on both the page setting documents and the OpenType documents. The corrugator activation was greater for the poor typography condition in both studies, which indicates that participants experienced a greater level of frustration, disapproval, tension, or mental effort while reading documents that contain poor typography.

Our expectation is that these measures are generally useful for detecting subtle aesthetic differences in any field, and are not particular to typographic differences. Moving forward, we plan to use these measures to detect differences where we don't have a predetermined expectation for the outcome.

7 Future Work

Future research should incorporate these practical measures into a theoretically sound model of emotion. Right now, we cannot say if the good typography conditions induce a more positive emotion in the reader, or whether poor typography conditions require more tension or effort to read. Also, our six studies tapped into the overall positive and negative dimensions of emotion only. Future work might fruitfully investigate more specific emotional characteristics of typography.

We want to see aesthetic and emotional research become as commonplace as usability research and other performance measures. We prefer to use less intrusive physiological measures than an electrode attached to the skin. For example, the sensors could be hidden in chairs [Anttonen & Surakka 2005], or thermal imaging could be used to detect corrugator differences from a distance [Puri et al. 2005].

Acknowledgements

Special thanks to Michael Duggan for designing the page setting and OpenType stimuli, to Tracy Premo who ran the ePeriodical studies, and to Radoslav Nickolov and Steven Kim for helping create the ePeriodicals that contained optimized and poor page settings.

References

Anttonen, J. & Surakka, V. [2005], Affect and Intimacy: Emotions and Heart Rate while Sitting on a Chair, *in* G. van der Veer & C. Gale (eds.), *Proceedings of SIGCHI Conference on Human Factors in Computing Systems (CHI'05)*, ACM Press, pp.491–9.

Boyarski, D., Neuwirth, C., Forlizzi, J. & Regli, S. H. [1998], A Study of Fonts Designed for Screen Display, *in* C.-M. Karat, A. Lund, J. Coutaz & J. Karat (eds.), *Proceedings of the SIGCHI Conference on Human Factors in Computing Systems (CHI'98)*, ACM Press, pp.87–94.

Branco, P., Firth, P., Encarnacao, L. M. & Bonato, P. [2005], Faces of Emotion in Human–Computer Interaction, *in* G. van der Veer & C. Gale (eds.), *CHI'05 Extended Abstracts of the Conference on Human Factors in Computing Systems*, ACM Press, pp.1236–9.

Bringhurst, R. [2004], *The Elements of Typographic Style*, Hartley and Marks Publishers.

Cacioppo, J. T., Bush, L. K. & Tassinary, L. G. [1992], Microexpressive Facial Actions as a Function of Affective Stimuli: Replication and Extension, *Psychological Science* **18**(5), 515–26.

Dillon, A. [1992], Reading from Paper vs. Screens: A Critical Review of the Empirical Literature, *Ergonomics* **35**(5), 1297–326.

Dimberg, U. [1990], Facial Electromyography and Emotional Reactions, *Psychophysiology* **27**(5), 481–94.

Duncker, K. [1945], On Problem Solving, *Psychological Monographs* **58**(270). The American Psychological Association.

Dyson, M. C. & Kipping, G. J. [1998], The Effects of Line Length and Method of Movement on Patterns of Reading from Screen, *Visible Language* **32**(2), 150–81.

Gugerty, L., Tyrrell, R. A., Aten, T. R. & Edmonds, K. A. [2004], The Effects of Sub-pixel Addressing on Users' Performance, *ACM Transactions on Applied Perception* **1**(2), 81–101.

Hazlett, R. L. [2003], Measurement of User Frustration: A Biologic Approach, *in* G. Cockton, P. Korhonen, E. Bergman, S. Björk, P. Collings, A. Dey, S. Draper, J. Gulliksen, T. Keinonen, J. Lazar, A. Lund, R. Molich, K. Nakakoji, L. Nigay, R. Oliveira Prates, J. Rieman & C. Snyder (eds.), *CHI'03 Extended Abstracts of the Conference on Human Factors in Computing Systems*, ACM Press, pp.734–5.

Hazlett, R. L. & Hazlett, S. Y. [1999], Emotional Response to Television Commercials: Facial EMG vs. Self-report, *Journal of Advertising Research* **39**(2), 7–23.

Isen, A. M. [1993], Positive Affect and Decision Making, *in* M. Lewis & J. M. Haviland (eds.), *Handbook of Emotions*, The Guilford Press, pp.261–77.

Isen, A. M., Daubman, K. A. & Nowicki, G. P. [1987], Positive Affect Facilitates Creative Problem Solving, *Journal of Personality and Social Psychology* **52**(6), 1122–31.

Larsen, J. T., Norris, C. J. & Cacioppo, J. T. [2003], Effects of Positive and Negative Affect on Electromyographic Activity over Zygomaticus Major and Corrugator Supercilii, *Psychophysiology* **40**(5), 776–85.

Larson, K., van Dantzich, M., Czerwinski, M. & Robertson, G. [2000], Text in 3-D: Some Legibility Results, *in* M. Tremaine (ed.), *CHI'00 Extended Abstracts of the Conference on Human Factors in Computing Systems*, ACM Press, pp.145–6.

Mednick, S. A. [1962], The Associative Basis of the Creative Process, *Psychological Review* **69**(3), 220–32.

Pope, L. K. & Smith, C. A. [1994], On the Distinct Meanings of Smiles and Frowns, *Cognition and Emotion* **8**(1), 65–72.

Puri, C., Olson, L., Pavlidis, I., Levine, J. & Starren, J. [2005], StressCam: non-contact measurement of users? emotional states through thermal imaging, *in* G. van der Veer & C. Gale (eds.), *CHI'05 Extended Abstracts of the Conference on Human Factors in Computing Systems*, ACM Press, pp.1725–8.

Reijneveld, K., de Looze, M., Krause, F. & Desmet, P. [2003], Understanding What to Design through Empathy and Emotion: Measuring the Emotions Elicited by Office Chairs, *in Proceedings of the 2003 International Conference on Designing Pleasurable Products and Interfaces*, ACM Press, pp.6–10.

Scheirer, J., Fernandez, R. & Picard, R. W. [1999], Expression Glasses: A Wearable Device for Facial Expression Recognition, *in* M. E. Atwood (ed.), *CHI'99 Extended Abstracts of the Conference on Human Factors in Computing Systems*, ACM Press, pp.262–3.

Sykes, J. & Brown, S. [2003], Affective Gaming: Measuring Emotion through the Gamepad, *in* G. Cockton, P. Korhonen, E. Bergman, S. Björk, P. Collings, A. Dey, S. Draper, J. Gulliksen, T. Keinonen, J. Lazar, A. Lund, R. Molich, K. Nakakoji, L. Nigay, R. Oliveira Prates, J. Rieman & C. Snyder (eds.), *CHI'03 Extended Abstracts of the Conference on Human Factors in Computing Systems*, ACM Press, pp.732–3.

Tassinary, L. G., Cacioppo, J. T. & Geen, T. R. [1989], A Psychometric Study of Surface Electrode Placements for Facial Electromyographic Recording: I. The Brow and Cheek Muscle Regions, *Psychophysiology* 26(1), 1–16.

Tinker, M. A. [1963], *Legibility of Print*, Iowa State University Press.

Ward, R. D. & Marsden, P. H. [2003], Physiological Responses to Different Web Page Designs, *International Journal of Human–Computer Studies* 59(1–2), 199–212.

Waterink, W. & van Boxtel, A. [1994], Facial and Jaw-elevator EMG Activity in Relation to Changes in Performance Level During a Sustained Information Task, *Biological Psychology* 37(3), 183–98.

Aesthetic and Symbolic Qualities as Antecedents of Overall Judgements of Interactive Products

Sascha Mahlke

Centre of Human–Machine Systems, Berlin University of Technology, Jebensstraße 1 – J2–2, 10623 Berlin, Germany
Email: *sascha.mahlke@zmms.tu-berlin.de*

Quality aspects of an interactive system that address user needs that go beyond users' instrumental needs are one important area for user experience research. Two categories of non-instrumental qualities seem to be important: aesthetic and symbolic aspects. In an explorative study the role of different dimensions of non-instrumental quality and their influence on overall judgements, like beauty or goodness of an interactive product, were studied. Four digital audio players were used to get information on users' perception of instrumental and non-instrumental quality perceptions as well as overall judgements. The results show the importance of various non-instrumental quality aspects and point out the need for further research.

Keywords: user experience, aesthetics, hedonics, usability, evaluation.

1 Introduction

In their introduction to the recent special issue of Behaviour & Information Technology on 'Empirical Studies of the User Experience', Hassenzahl & Tractinsky [2006] mention three important areas for user experience research: non-instrumental quality aspects, the role of emotions and the experiential character of the user experience. In this paper, I will focus on non-instrumental qualities as one important aspect of the user experience. Non-instrumental qualities can be described as quality aspects of an interactive system that address user needs that go beyond tasks, goals and their efficient achievement. In an early attempt to define user experience of interactive products, Alben [1996], for example, identified beauty (i.e. aesthetics) as one important non-instrumental quality aspect of technology.

1.1   Dimensions of Non-instrumental Quality

Over the last years, various dimensions of non-instrumental quality aspects were discussed. Gaver & Martin [2000] argued for the importance of a whole range of specific non-instrumental needs, such as surprise, diversion, or intimacy, to be addressed by technology. Jordan [2000] argued for a hierarchical organization of user needs and claimed that along with the functionality and usability of the product, different aspects of pleasure, i.e. physio-, psycho-, socio- and ideo-pleasure are important to enhance the user's interaction with it.

Rafaeli & Vilnai-Yavetz [2004] presented a model that suggests that artefacts need to be analysed according to three conceptually distinct aspects: instrumentality, aesthetics and symbolism. Aesthetics and symbolism represent two categories of non-instrumental quality. Aesthetics refer to the sensual experience a product elicits, and the extent to which this experience fits individual goals and spirits. On the other hand, symbolism refers to the meanings and associations that are caused by the products. Tractinsky & Zmiri [2006] applied this approach to the domain of websites.

In another study, Lavie & Tractinsky [2004] focused on visual aesthetics of websites. They found that users' perceptions consist of two main dimensions, which they termed 'classical aesthetics' and 'expressive aesthetics'. The classical aesthetics dimension pertains to aesthetic notions that emphasize orderly and clear design and are closely related to many of the design rules advocated by usability experts. The expressive aesthetics dimension is manifested by the designers' creativity and originality and by the ability to break design conventions.

Hassenzahl [2001] introduced the concept of hedonic quality. He assumes that two distinct attribute groups, namely pragmatic and hedonic attributes, can describe product character. Therefore, a product can be perceived as pragmatic if it provides effective and efficient ways to achieve behavioural goals. On the other hand, it can be perceived as hedonic if it provides stimulation by its challenging and novel character or identification by communicating important personal values to relevant others [Hassenzahl 2004]. Summarizing he subdivides hedonic qualities into the two dimensions of stimulation and identification.

In the area of product design further interesting approaches exist. Veryzer [2000] summarized the broad literature on visual aspects of product design and their influence on consumer behaviour. He compared different models concerning the processing of product design and how users respond to it. Creusen & Schoormans [2005] claim several roles of product appearance. Next to the functional and ergonomic product values that are described as instrumental quality aspects, they discuss the aesthetic and symbolic product value as important quality dimensions. They define aesthetic value as pertained to the pleasure derived from seeing the product, without consideration of utility. Symbolic value can be described as the ability of a product's appearance to communicate messages, e.g. it may look cheerful, boring, friendly, expensive, rude, or childish.

Crilly et al. [2004] present an integrative approach to qualities of product design and summarized various aspects in three categories: semantic interpretation, aesthetic impression and symbolic association. This distinction relates to the aspects of instrumentality, aesthetics and symbolism introduced by Rafaeli & Vilnai-Yavetz [2004] in some way, but they are described in more detail and are connected to product design features. Semantic interpretation describes the proportion of the product's value that is attributed to its utility. Contrast, novelty and order as well as subjective concinnity that may be regarded as the extent to which the design appears to make sense to the viewer in respect to the consumer's personal, cultural and visual experience are aspects of aesthetic impression. Self-expressive symbolism is described as associated with products that allow the expression of unique aspects of one's personality. Otherwise, categorical symbolism is associated with products that allow the expression of group membership, including social position and status

Recapitulating, in most of these approaches two distinct categories of non-instrumental qualities are differentiated. On the one hand, aesthetic aspects are discussed. These contain most of all visual aspects of product appearance, but can also imply other sensual experience like haptic or auditory aspects of product use, as for example discussed by Jordan [2000] in his definition of physio-pleasure. The other category refers to a symbolic dimension of product appearance. The concept of hedonic quality discussed by Hassenzahl [2001] or the aspects of socio- and ideo-pleasure introduced by Jordan [2000] fit into this category.

Although, there is a broad discussion of non-instrumental quality aspects and their application to design, only a few validated approaches for quantitatively measuring them exist [Hassenzahl 2001; Lavie & Tractinsky 2004]. This fact complicates further research on their importance and interplay with other aspects of the user experience.

1.2 Non-instrumental Qualities' Interplay with Further User Perceptions

In some experiments the interplay of non-instrumental quality perceptions with other dimensions was studied. Some authors focused on the relation to usability assessments and overall judgements. Tractinsky et al. [2000] studied the connection between aesthetics and usability and reason that users' aesthetic judgement before using an interactive system affects their perceived usability even after usage of the system. Lindgaard & Dudek [2003] found a more complex interplay between these two constructs.

Mahlke [2002] studied the influence of user's perceived usefulness, ease of use, hedonic quality and visual aesthetics on the intention to use specific websites. He found that the instrumental quality aspects, i.e. usefulness and ease of use, show a main contribution to the overall judgement, but that also the non-instrumental qualities of the system, i.e. hedonic quality and visual aesthetics, play an important role. Hassenzahl [2004] studied the interplay between usability and hedonic quality in forming overall judgements. He used two overall judgements, i.e. beauty and goodness. He found that judgements of beauty are more influenced by user's perception of hedonic quality, while judgements of goodness – as a more general evaluative construct – are affected by both hedonic quality and usability. In Tractinsky's [2004] published review to this paper, he argued that Hassenzahl views beauty as a high-level evaluative judgement that weights certain low-level product

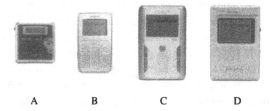

A   B   C   D

Figure 1: Digital audio players used in the study.

qualities, but only some of these product qualities were integrated in the study. Still the question remains, which influences further non-instrumental quality aspects have on forming high-level evaluative judgements of interactive products, like beauty or goodness.

To summarize the following research questions arise from these theoretical considerations:

- Which dimensions of non-instrumental qualities are important for interactive product experiences?

- What is their influence on overall judgements, like beauty or goodness of interactive products?

2   Method

An explorative study was conducted to answer these research questions. Four digital audio players were chosen for the study because we think this is a typical domain where the user's product experience is of great importance for product choice and usage behaviour. Thirty individuals (fifteen women and fifteen men) participated in the study. They were between 20 and 30 years old, most of them students at Berlin University of Technology. Experience with digital audio players in general was low. The four digital audio players presented in Figure 1 were used in the study. All were from the same manufacturer, so we did not have to deal with the influence of brand in this case. Nonetheless, players differed in terms of various design aspects.

All participants tested each product in the study. Presentation order was randomized. Four short tasks were given to the participants for each player. We combined some questionnaire methods to measure instrumental and non-instrumental qualities as well as overall judgements. Participants filled out a survey that assessed ratings on the quality dimensions after accomplishing the tasks for one player. Based on Davis et al. [1989] we investigated two instrumental qualities, i.e. usefulness and ease of use. Furthermore, we assessed non-instrumental quality perceptions on several dimensions. Hassenzahl's [2004] scales on stimulation and identification were used to represent the symbolic category. To gain information on the aesthetic category we used the two dimensions of classical and expressive aesthetics developed by Lavie & Tractinsky [2004] and the items proposed by Jordan

		Player				
		A	B	C	D	
Usefulness		2.7	3.1	3.9	3.6	$p < 0.001$
Ease of use		1.7	2.0	3.3	2.9	$p < 0.001$
Symbolic quality	Identification	2.8	3.6	3.3	3.0	$p < 0.01$
	Stimulation	2.8	3.9	3.5	2.8	$p < 0.001$
Aesthetic quality	Visual: classic	2.6	3.7	3.7	3.0	$p < 0.01$
	Visual: expressive	2.3	3.5	3.0	2.3	$p < 0.001$
	Haptic	3.3	4.1	3.6	2.7	$p < 0.001$
Goodness		2.6	3.1	3.7	3.0	$p < 0.01$
Beauty		2.8	4.3	3.9	2.6	$p < 0.001$

Table 1: Quality perceptions and overall judgements for the four players (mean values; ratings were between 6 as best and 0 as worst; significances on differences between the systems).

[2000] to measure physio-pleasure. Furthermore, participants rated beauty and goodness of the products overall on a one-item scale.

3 Results

First, results regarding the differences on instrumental and non-instrumental quality dimensions as well as overall judgements for the four conditions are presented. Thereafter, a regression analysis of the overall judgements of goodness and beauty based on the quality perceptions is described.

3.1 Quality Perceptions for the Four Players

Quality perceptions and overall judgements differed with respect to the four players (see Table 1). On all dimensions differences were significant for the four conditions. Player A was rated worst on most of the dimensions and obtained the worst overall ratings. Player B was rated highest on the non-instrumental quality dimensions, but received lower ratings for its instrumental qualities. Overall judgements for this player were the highest for beauty, but only medium for goodness. The opposite was found for Player D. Instrumental qualities were rated good to medium, while non-instrumental qualities were rated worse. Overall judgements are worst for beauty, but medium for goodness. Player C received good ratings for its instrumental and non-instrumental qualities. Therefore, the overall judgement regarding goodness is best.

3.2 Correlations of Quality Perceptions and Overall Judgements

The regression analysis of the overall judgements (see Table 2) shows that the overall judgement of goodness depends on most of the quality dimensions that were surveyed in this study. Ease of use has a main influence, but also identification, haptic and visual expressive quality as well as the usefulness of the system show significant influence. Moreover, the overall judgement of beauty only depends on non-instrumental qualities. First of all, the visual classical and haptic quality, but also identification are significant antecedents of the beauty of interactive products.

		Overall judgements	
		Goodness	Beauty
Usefulness		0.20 *	
Ease of use		0.33 **	
Symbolic quality	Identification	0.24 **	0.18 *
	Stimulation		
Aesthetic quality	Visual: classic		0.29 **
	Visual: expressive	0.20 *	
	Haptic	0.21 **	0.26 **
	R^2	0.67	0.45

Table 2: Regression analysis of overall judgements (β values and significances: ** $p < 0.01$, * $p > 0.05$).

4 Discussion

Only few empirical studies on the role of non-instrumental qualities in interactive system design exist. The results of this study demonstrate the importance of non-instrumental qualities for users' experience of technology. Especially, the cases of Player B and D show in which way instrumental and non-instrumental qualities interact. While Player B received poor ratings for its instrumental qualities, the higher ratings regarding aesthetic and hedonic aspects led to a medium overall judgement. The opposite was found for Player D. Here, poor non-instrumental qualities were compensated by better instrumental qualities.

Two categories of non-instrumental qualities were derived from the literature: aesthetic and symbolic aspects. The results on their importance for the overall judgements of goodness and beauty show, that both of them have significant influence. In detail, the concepts of identification and the three aspects of aesthetic quality showed significant importance. The concept of stimulation had no significant influence on neither of the overall judgements.

These results lead to one question that remains open. It is the question if the two categories and the dimensions used in this study are sufficient to assess non-instrumental quality perceptions as part of the user experience. In the literature, a lot of different conceptual approaches exist to structure the various possible aspects of non-instrumental quality, but no unified model exists. It also seems that it depends on the domain of an interactive product which dimensions are important. It is likely that haptic quality will be less important for a software tool than for a handheld product. Another problem concerns the measurement of these dimensions. As mentioned before only a few validated approaches exist to assess non-instrumental qualities. More work is needed on that topic.

Another issue for future research refers to the interplay of instrumental and non-instrumental qualities with emotions. First, there is a lot of literature that contradicts various new aspects of the user experience to instrumental quality aspects without differentiating between non-instrumental qualities and emotions. I think this distinction is important. The important reason is that emotions can be influenced by non-instrumental qualities as well as by instrumental aspects [Mahlke 2005, in press]. Regarding the interplay of these three components of the user experience various questions are still unanswered.

In which way can practitioners profit from these results? One consideration that seems clear is to integrate non-instrumental qualities in the evaluation process of interactive products. As I showed, first methodological approaches are available to do so. More research is necessary to learn how to consider these aspects in the design phases. Although, the results of this study must be seen as preliminary, they gave first hints for the further study of non-instrumental qualities as one important part of the user experience.

Acknowledgements

This research was supported by the German Research Foundation (DFG) as part of the Research Training Group 'Prospective Engineering of Human–Technology Interaction' (no. 1013). Special thanks to Creative Labs GmbH for supporting the study on digital audio players.

References

Alben, L. [1996], Quality of Experience — Defining Criteria for Effective Interaction Design, *Interactions* **3**(3), 11–5.

Creusen, M. & Schoormans, J. [2005], The Different Roles of Product Appearance in Consumer Choice, *Journal of Product Innovation Management* **22**(1), 63–81.

Crilly, N., Moultrie, J. & Clarkson, P. J. [2004], Seeing Things: Consumer Response to the Visual Domain in Product Design, *Design Studies* **25**(6), 547–77.

Davis, F. D., Bagozzi, R. P. & Warshaw, P. R. [1989], User Acceptance of Computer Technology: A Comparison of Two Theoretical Models, *Management Science* **35**(8), 982–1003.

Gaver, B. & Martin, H. [2000], Alternatives: Exploring Information Appliances Through Conceptual Design Proposals, *in* T. Turner & G. Szwillus (eds.), *Proceedings of the SIGCHI Conference on Human Factors in Computing Systems (CHI'00)*, CHI Letters **2**(1), ACM Press, pp.209–16.

Hassenzahl, M. [2001], The Effect of Perceived Hedonic Quality on Product Appealingness, *International Journal of Human–Computer Interaction* **13**(4), 481–99.

Hassenzahl, M. [2004], The Interplay of Beauty, Goodness, and Usability in Interactive Products, *Human–Computer Interaction* **19**(4), 319–49.

Hassenzahl, M. & Tractinsky, N. [2006], User Experience: A Research Agenda, *Behaviour & Information Technology* **25**(2), 91–7.

Jordan, P. W. [2000], *Designing Pleasurable Products*, Taylor & Francis.

Lavie, T. & Tractinsky, N. [2004], Assessing Dimensions of Perceived Visual Aesthetics of Web Sites, *International Journal of Human–Computer Studies* **60**(3), 269–98.

Lindgaard, G. & Dudek, C. [2003], What is the Evasive Beast We Call User Satisfaction?, *Interacting with Computers* **15**(3), 429–52.

Mahlke, S. [2002], Factors Influencing the Experience of Website Usage, *in* L. Terveen & D. Wixon (eds.), *CHI'02 Extended Abstracts of the Conference on Human Factors in Computing Systems*, ACM Press, pp.846–7.

Mahlke, S. [2005], Understanding Users' Experience of Interaction, *in* N. Marmaras, T. Kontogiannis & D. Nathanael (eds.), *Proceedings of the 2005 Conference of the European Association of Cognitive Ergonomics (incorporating the 10th Conference on Cognitive Science Aspects of Process Control)*, National Technical University, Athens, pp.243–6.

Mahlke, S. [in press], Studying User Experience with Digital Audio Players, *in Proceedings of the 5th International Conference on Entertainment Computing*, Lecture Notes in Computer Science, Springer.

Rafaeli, A. & Vilnai-Yavetz, I. [2004], Instrumentality, Aesthetics and Symbolism of Physical Artifacts as Triggers of Emotion, *Theoretical Issues in Ergonomics Science* **5**(1), 91–112.

Tractinsky, N. [2004], A Few Notes on the Study of Beauty in HCI, *Human–Computer Interaction* **19**(4), 351–7.

Tractinsky, N. & Zmiri, D. [2006], Exploring Attributes of Skins as Potential Antecedents of Emotion in HCI, *in* P. Fishwick (ed.), *Aesthetic Computing*, MIT Press, pp.405–22.

Tractinsky, N., Katz, A. S. & Ikar, D. [2000], What is Beautiful is Usable, *Interacting with Computers* **13**(2), 127–45.

Veryzer, R. W. [2000], Design and Consumer Research, *Design Management Academic Review* **1**(1), 1–16.

Involvement in Listening to Music from a Computer: The Effects of Pre-Existing Mood

Kari Kallinen, Timo Saari, Niklas Ravaja & Mikko Salminen

Helsinki School of Economics, Center for Knowledge and Innovation Research, Tammasaarenkatu 3, PO BOX 1210, Finland

Email: *{kari.kallinen, timo.saari, niklas.ravaja, mikko.salminen}@hse.fi*

We examined the effects of autobiographically induced mood states on involvement when listening to emotional music from a computer in 48 subjects. We found that pleasant mood and music elicited higher involvement in listening to music than unpleasant mood and music. We also found that, in connection with the arousal dimension of emotion the interaction between mood and music supported the mood congruency theory: arousing music elicited higher involvement after high-arousal mood than after low-arousal mood, whereas in regard to sedating music the reverse was true. However, in regard to emotional valence, we found that pleasant music elicited higher involvement regardless of the positive or negative mood of the listener, thus supporting the idea that generally people listen to music to get into a good mood. The results are of importance, given that listening to music using computers and portable devices has increased rapidly, and given the uses of music in multimodal contexts, such as in computer games.

Keywords: mood, music, emotions, involvement.

1 Introduction

Listening to music has become fully embedded in daily life. People listen to music, for example, to relax and to get themselves into a good mood, as well as background music in connection with a wide range of everyday activities, such as doing housework or driving a car [Sloboda et al. 2001]. Portable devices and computers are expanding the uses of music in everyday life. However, there is a scarcity of studies on listening to music from a computer. There are also few studies on the interactive effects of emotional quality of music and mood prior music listening on involvement into music.

When perceiving information (e.g. music) via media and communication technology (e.g. stereos, TVs, or portable CD players) people have a feeling of presence. In presence, the mediated information becomes the focused object of perception, while the immediate, external context, including the technological device, fades into the background [Biocca & Levy 1995; Lombard et al. 2000]. Thus, from one perspective, presence can be seen as psychological immersion, which refers to the degree of involvement and attention to stimuli [Witmer & Singer 1998]. In the present paper we were especially interested in examining in which degree the mood states prior listening to music, and the emotional quality of the music, moderate the involvement in listening to music from a computer.

According to a dimensional view of emotions, large amounts of variation in emotions can be located in a two-dimensional space, with coordinates of valence and arousal [Lang 1995; Larsen & Diener 1992]. The valence dimension refers to the hedonic quality of an affective experience and ranges from unpleasant to pleasant. The arousal dimension refers to the perception of arousal associated with such an experience, and ranges from very calm or sleepy at one extreme to very excited or energized at the other.

It is well recognized that the pre-existing mood and emotional tone of media stimuli moderate the involvement in media stimuli (e.g. music, see Branscombe [1985] and Kallinen & Ravaja [2004]). According to selective-exposure theory, individuals are motivated to make media choices in order to regulate their affective state (i.e. to maintain excitatory homeostasis [Zillmann & Bryant 1985]). For example, people often listen to music to maintain a good mood or to alter a negative mood towards a more positive one [Sloboda et al. 2001]. Thus it could be expected, that people prefer and get more immersed into a pleasant music rather than an unpleasant music. In addition to mood and music *per se*, it is also reasonable to expect that a pre-existing mood may interact with the emotional tone of music in predicting involvement. According to the mood congruency hypothesis, individuals preferentially process emotional stimuli that are congruent in emotional tone with their current mood state [Rusting 1998]. Thus it could be expected, that when in pleasant mood (i.e. after pleasant induction) people would get more involved in pleasant music than in unpleasant music, and when in highly aroused mood (i.e. after high-arousal induction) people would get more involved in high-arousal music than low-arousal music, for example.

In sum, the focus of the present paper was to examine the effects of mood and music on involvement in listening to music. In view of the aforementioned considerations, we expected that pleasant mood induction and music would elicit higher level of involvement than unpleasant induction and music (Hypothesis 1). On the basis of the mood-congruency hypothesis, we also expected that, when in pleasant moods, people would perceive pleasant music, and when in high-arousal mood, people would perceive high-arousal music as more immersive as compared to unpleasant and low-arousal music (Hypothesis 2a); in contrast, when in unpleasant moods unpleasant music, and when in low-arousal moods low-arousal music, would be expected to be perceived as more immersive (Hypothesis 2b).

2 Methods

2.1 Subjects and Materials

Forty-eight subjects with varying educational backgrounds participated in the study in return for two movie tickets. The subjects were 21 men and 27 women ranging from 21 to 51 years of age (mean = 25).

Mood was induced by autobiographical memories varying in affective valence and arousal. There was one mood induction for each of the following emotion categories: high-arousal pleasant (i.e. joy), low-arousal pleasant (i.e. relaxation), high-arousal unpleasant (i.e. fear), and low-arousal unpleasant (i.e. depression).

We chose 8 one-minute long pieces from the classical music repertoire on the basis of ratings in our earlier studies [see, for example, Kallinen 2005], which differed in terms of valence (i.e. pleasant, unpleasant) and arousal (i.e. high, low). Correspondingly to the emotional dimensions in mood inductions, there were two pieces of music for each of the following emotions: high-arousal pleasant (i.e. 'Final' from Saint Saëns' Carnival of Animals and 'Vivace' from Haydn's, Piano concerto in D), low-arousal pleasant (i.e. Bach's Inventio No. 8 in F and Marini's Passacaglia), high-arousal unpleasant (i.e. from the beginning of Borodin's Symphony No. 2 and from the beginning of Mussorgsky's 'Night on the Bare Mountain', and low-arousal unpleasant (i.e. from the beginning of the first part of Beethoven's Symphony No. 4 and from the beginning of the 'Romanze' from Schumann's, Symphony No. 4).

2.2 Measures

Involvement was assessed using a self report measure consisting of the following four items: 'When I listened to music, I felt clear and concentrated'; 'It would have been difficult to stop listening to music'; 'While and after listening to music I noticed that I have lost my sense of time and location'; 'When I listened to music, I felt I was intensely absorbed in it'. Each of the items was rated on a 7-point scale, ranging from 1 (very untrue for me) to 7 (very true for me). The sum of the 4 items was used as an index of involvement. The scales were presented on a computer screen. Mean reliability of the scale (in 32 measurements) was acceptable ($\alpha = 0.77$, s.d. = 0.06 [see Nunnaly 1978]).

Continuous psychophysiological recordings during the inductions were used to validate the success of mood inductions. The valence dimension of emotion was assessed by zygomaticus major (ZM, cheek, an index of positive emotions) and corrugator supercilii (CS, brow, an index of negative emotions) muscle regions. The arousal dimension of emotion was assessed by interbeat intervals (IBIs), which decreases when arousal increases (i.e. higher heart rate) and increases when arousal decreases (i.e. slower heart rate). The psychophysiological signals and data reduction were recorded using Psylab measuring devices and data collection software (Contact Precision Instruments, London, UK). Standard procedures were used as reported thoroughly for example in Kallinen & Ravaja [2004].

2.3   Procedure

After a brief description of the experiment, the participant was asked to write a description of an event or a situation that evoked each of four emotions – joy (delight), relaxation, fear, and depression – most powerfully in his or her own life. We emphasized to the participants that the success of the experiment depended on the truthfulness of his or her descriptions.

The participant was then seated in a comfortable armchair. Each of the 8 music pieces was paired with different mood inductions so that there were a total of 32 different trials (8 pieces × 4 inductions). Each trial (and an additional practice trial) consisted of:

1. a 15s mood induction period; and

2. a presentation of music.

The participant was instructed that the targeted emotion would be displayed on the computer screen, after which he or she should:

1. read the appropriate description of an emotional event/situation written by him or her,

2. indicate that he or she was ready using the keyboard, and

3. create a vivid image of personally experiencing and participating in the event/situation for 15s.

After each trial of induction and music, the participant rated his or her involvement in music using the four 7-point scales. The 32 trials were presented in a random order to each participant.

2.4   Data Analysis

The data on the involvement ratings were pooled over the individual two pieces representing the same emotion (i.e. high-arousal pleasant, low-arousal pleasant, high-arousal unpleasant, and low-arousal unpleasant). Data were then analysed by the General Linear Model (GLM) Repeated Measures procedure in SPSS, with four, i.e. valence of music (pleasant, unpleasant), arousal of music (high, low), valence of induction (pleasant, unpleasant), and arousal of induction (high, low) as within-subjects factors.

3   Results

3.1   Manipulation Check

The GLM Repeated Measures analysis indicated that IBIs were shorter (i.e. higher HR) during the high-arousal mood inductions compared to the low-arousal mood inductions (means 875.34ms and 897.93ms, respectively), $F(1,44) = 39.65$, $p < 0.001$. The GLM Repeated Measures analysis also showed that zygomatic EMG activity was higher during the positive mood compared to the negative mood inductions (means 9.60 and 7.13, respectively), $F(1,44) = 30.02$, $p < 0.001$. The analysis also showed that corrugator supercilii activity was higher during the negative mood inductions compared to the positive mood inductions (means 16.68 and 10.05, respectively), $F(1,44) = 40.48$, $p < 0.001$.

3.2 Involvement Ratings

The GLM Repeated Measures analysis revealed significant main effects for valence of induction, $F(1,47) = 11.02$, $p = 0.002$, and valence of music, $F(1,47) = 11.09$, $p = 0.002$, in predicting involvement ratings. Involvement ratings were higher after pleasant than after unpleasant induction (means 15.42 and 14.77, respectively), and after pleasant than after unpleasant music (means 15.65 and 14.55, respectively). Significant Valence of Induction × Valence of Music, $F(1,47) = 6.72$, $p = 0.013$, Valence of Induction × Arousal of Music, $F(1,47) = 5.51$, $p = 0.023$, and Arousal of Induction × Arousal of Music, $F(1,47) = 11.21$, $p = 0.002$, interactions were also found in predicting involvement ratings. As illustrated in Figure 1 (top panel), pleasant music elicited higher involvement ratings than unpleasant music after both pleasant and unpleasant induction, even though the difference between involvement ratings after pleasant and unpleasant music was bigger after pleasant induction than after unpleasant induction. As also illustrated in Figure 1, high-arousal music elicited higher involvement ratings than low-arousal music after pleasant (middle panel) and high-arousal (bottom panel) inductions, whereas the opposite was true after unpleasant and low-arousal inductions.

4   Conclusions

In the present paper, we examined the effects of pre-existing mood, as elicited by autobiographical memories, and emotional music on involvement in listening to music from a computer. The results showed that:

1. the mood induction procedure was successfully validated with psychophysiological measurements, and

2. both pre-existing mood and the emotional quality of music exerted an influence on the involvement on listening to music.

As expected (Hypothesis 1), pleasant music and mood induction elicited higher involvement in music listening than unpleasant music and mood induction.

The results gave only partial support for our Hypotheses 2a and 2b, which stated that people would be more involved in music listening when the emotional tone of the music is similar to their mood state prior listening (e.g. pleasant-pleasant or unpleasant-unpleasant; high-arousal – high arousal or low-arousal – low arousal, for example). We found that when in high-arousal mood, subjects were more involved in listening to high-arousal than low-arousal music, whereas when in low-arousal mood, they were more involved in listening to low-arousal than high-arousal music. Thus the results gave support for the mood-congruency theory, which states that individuals preferentially process emotional stimuli that are emotionally congruent with their current mood state. However, in connection with the pleasantness dimension of emotion this view was only partially supported. We found that subjects were more involved in listening to pleasant music, regardless

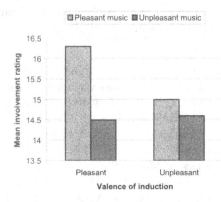

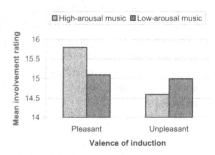

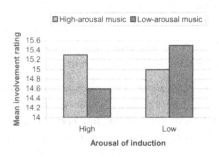

Figure 1: Involvement ratings after pleasant and unpleasant induction as a function of valence (top panel) and arousal (middle panel) of music. Involvement ratings after high- and low-arousal induction as a function of arousal of music (bottom panel).

of their negative or positive mood prior listening, even though the involvement was especially strong after the pleasant (i.e. congruent) mood state. Thus the results seem to also support the view that generally people tend to listen to music to maintain or get into a good mood.

In summary, the present investigation showed that affect derived from pre-existing mood and music varying in affective valence and arousal exerted an influence on self-reported involvement. We know no other experiment that has systematically investigated the interactive effects of pre-existing mood and music in connection with involvement. The results are of importance:

1. given that music is one of the most commonly used media but yet under explored in connection with subjective presence,

2. information of the relationships with pre-existing mood and emotional tone of music may be very valuable for using music in media contexts, and

3. the portable devices (such as CD player and mobile phones) and other new technologies (such as an Internet) are expanding the uses of music in everyday life.

The information on pre-existing mood and music on involvement can be used, for example to adapt the characteristics of music, to facilitate psychological effects such as engagement on a media, and thus possibly increase enjoyment, for example.

References

Biocca, F. & Levy, M. [1995], *Communication in the Age of Virtual Reality*, Lawrence Erlbaum Associates.

Branscombe, N. [1985], Effects of Hedonic Valence and Physiological Arousal on Emotion: A Comparison of Two Theoretical Perspectives, *Motivation and Emotion* 2(2), 153–69.

Kallinen, K. [2005], Emotional Ratings of Music Excerpts in the Western Art Music Repertoire and their Self-organisation in the Kohonen Neural Network, *Psychology of Music* 33(4), 373–93.

Kallinen, K. & Ravaja, N. [2004], Emotion-related Responses to Audio News with Rising Versus Falling Background Tone Sequences, *Musicæ Scientiæ* **Special Issue 2003–2004**, 85–110.

Lang, P. J. [1995], The Emotion Probe: Studies of Motivation and Attention, *American Psychologist* 50(5), 372–85.

Larsen, R. J. & Diener, E. [1992], Promises and Problems with the Circumplex Model of Emotion, *in* M. Clark (ed.), *Review of Personality and Social Psychology*, Vol. 13, Sage Publications, pp.25–59.

Lombard, M., Reich, R., Grabe, M. E., Bracken, C. & Ditton, T. [2000], Presence and Television: The Role of Screen Size, *Human Communications Research* 26(1), 75–98.

Nunnaly, J. [1978], *Psychometric Theory*, McGraw-Hill.

Rusting, C. L. [1998], Personality, Mood and Cognitive Processing of Emotional Information: Three Conceptual Frameworks, *Psychological Bulletin* **124**(2), 165–96.

Sloboda, J. A., O'Neill, S. A. & Ivaldi, A. [2001], Functions of Music in Everyday Life: An Exploratory Study using the Experience Sampling Method, *Musicæ Scientiæ* **5**(1), 9–32.

Witmer, B. G. & Singer, M. J. [1998], Measuring Presence in Virtual Environments: A Presence Questionnaire, *Presence: Teleoperators and Virtual Environments* **7**(3), 225–40.

Zillmann, D. & Bryant, J. [1985], Affect, Mood and Emotion as Determinants of Selective Exposure, *in* D. Zillmann & J. Bryant (eds.), *Selective Exposure to Communication*, Lawrence Erlbaum Associates, pp.157–90.

Interface Affect and Familiarity: Some Implications for Designing the Interaction

Elizabeth Uruchurtu, Roger Rist & Lachlan MacKinnon[†]

School of Mathematical and Computer Sciences, Heriot-Watt University, Riccarton Campus, Edinburgh EH14 4AS, UK

Tel: *+44 131 451 3287*

Email: *{ceeeu,rjr}@macs.hw.ac.uk*

[†] *School of Computing and Creative Technologies, University of Abertay Dundee, Kydd Building, Dundee DD1 1HG, UK*

Tel: *+44 1382 308 601*

Email: *l.mackinnon@abertay.ac.uk*

While learning is increasingly understood as the result of a complex interaction having both cognitive and affective components, to date there is not comprehensive, empirically validated theory that addresses both aspects to support the construction of technologies that interact with learners in challenging new ways. This paper reports on a study carried out to explore the extent to which interface affect influences learning performance and whether familiarity with the interface style influences such affect, also how those variables relate to the learner's cognitive style. A clear relationship is determined between interface affect, being the reaction of a student to the style of an interface, and the learning outcomes achieved through the use of that interface. Little interaction was however observed between these variables and cognitive style. This suggest that certain features of the interface design and ultimately the adaptive behaviour of a learning system can be matched to the user's characteristics to promote positive affect and effective learning.

Keywords: interface affect, familiarity, cognitive style, interface design, Web-based learning.

1 Introduction

Over the past few years, research and development of Web-based learning has increasingly moved towards an individual, technology-based, learning centred model aiming at providing the learning experience that best suits each individual. In order to progress towards personalizing the interaction, an important issue seems to be the analysis of individual differences that impact the modelling dimensions underpinning adaptive learning systems.

As part of this research, key cognitive characteristics of learners have been identified and their implications for the design of the interface, as well as their relationship with learning performance analysed [Uruchurtu et al. 2005]. Previous results showed no clear relationship between cognitive style and learning outcomes; interestingly however, a relationship was observed between interface affect, being the reaction of a student to the interface design, and the learning outcomes achieved through the use of that interface. These results, supported by findings from a range of disciplines, advance our understanding of the human brain not only as a cognitive information processing system, but as a system in which affective functions and cognitive ones are interrelated [Fijda 1993; Norman 2002; Picard et al. 2004]. Learning is therefore increasingly understood as the result of a complex interaction of structures and processes having cognitive and affective aspects. Research has been carried out to lay the foundations for a better understanding of the role of affective states in learning. Particular attention has been paid to motivation and to the development of technologies for affect perception and emotion recognition [Picard et al. 2004], but to date there is no comprehensive, empirically validated theory of emotions that addresses learning. There is a clear need for further evidence to support the construction of technologies that interact with learners in new ways from a holistic approach that includes affective as well as cognitive aspects. This research aims to identify some of the parameters that influence interface affect and to explore their relationship with the learners' cognitive skills and performance.

2 The Case for Affect

It has been suggested that emotional experience is built up from a small set of basic emotions such as happiness, sadness, fear, anger and disgust [Oatley 1992]. For Fijda [1993] this approach is unsatisfactory because the concepts used to label those elementary qualities are semantically decomposable. He suggests that only affect proper – the experience of pleasantness or unpleasantness – is both unanalysable and specific for emotion.

Emotions arise from encounters with events that are perceived as relevant for the individual. It is the notion of 'affect' that gives emotions their non-cognitive character: affect is not experienced as a feeling of pleasantness; rather the individual is aware of the pleasant or unpleasant nature of the emotion-eliciting event [Fijda 1993]. The appraisal of emotional events also includes a series of values on dimensions such as certainty-uncertainty, goal conduciveness, self-confidence, and controllability. This profile helps to differentiate types of emotions from one another. Emotions also signal the state of the individual's estimated coping ability – their 'felt state of action readiness' [Fijda 1993]. Different emotions tend to involve different types action readiness and strong correlations have been observed, for example, between fear and avoidance and between joy and approach. States of action readiness do not in the first place refer to inner feelings, but to sets of predictions of past and future appraisals and relational behaviours (e.g. in anger, negative evaluation of the event and/or future avoidance of the object), and of behaviour types that are likely to come forth (e.g. in anger, verbal aggression if the confrontation persists) [Fijda 1993]. Emotional experiences are thus objects of reflective judgement: past events help building a framework that influence the way individuals assess a particular situation, their affective reaction and consequent behaviour.

3   Cognition, Emotion and Interaction

Different emotional states induce different kinds of thinking: positive moods broaden the thought processes towards greater creativity in problem solving [Isen 2000; Norman 2002]; negative affect focuses the mind, leading to avoidant and defensive tendencies, closure to stimulation, and selective attention [Fijda 1993; Norman 2002]. Thus, if the interaction between learners and web-based learning materials produce an emotional reaction in the student, this response would influence their thinking process and, ultimately, their learning performance.

As previously argued, affect signals our coping ability and subsequent response to the current environment and this judgement is based on the reference context built by each individual from previous experiences. Similarly, it has been observed in previous studies [Davis & Wiedenbeck 2001] that different interfaces evoke different reference contexts, which in turn raise positive/negative affect towards the interaction. Emotional reactions and individual cognitive factors are therefore intertwined during the interaction: the more different an interface is with respect to the reference context the learner posses, the increased the cognitive load, the lower concentration on the task, and higher attention to the interaction. Taken to the extreme, curiosity is overloaded – too complex, too incongruent – which may lead to a sense of loss of control and lower motivation. Negative affect is therefore expected in this situation. On the contrary, the evoked reference context might raise positive affect and aid meaningful learning.

All this concepts together suggest that certain elements of the interface style elicit a sense of familiarity with the learning environment; this judgement being part of the emotional appraisal of the current situation.

3.1   The Case for Cognitive Styles

In education, the concepts of learning style and cognitive style have been explored extensively, and although these are used interchangeably, cognitive style refers to the 'individual's preferred and habitual approach to organizing and representing information' [Riding & Rayner 1998]. If cognitive styles are individual and non-changing, they could provide significant basis for designing personal interfaces. However, there is no clear evidence form previous research of a consistent relationship between cognitive styles and learning outcomes.   Findings from past studies [Graff 1999, 2003; Mckenzie et al. 1999; Riding & Cheema 1991; Riding & Grimley 1999] have been ambiguous and while some studies find a consistent relationship between style and learning, others find no effect. In addition, the multiplicity of classifications related to cognitive styles has led to a certain extent of confusion. In an attempt to integrate much of the earlier work in the field, Riding & Cheema [1991] concluded that many of the classifications used could be grouped into a number of learning strategies and two principal cognitive styles: Wholist-Analytic (WA) – the tendency of individuals to organize information in parts or as a whole; and Verbalizer-Imager (VI) – the tendency of individuals to represent information verbally or in mental pictures when thinking.

3.2 Interface Design

To provide a truly personal learning environment that may help to elicit the right mood for each individual, an adaptive approach is required. As Norman [2002] suggests, we should start building artefacts that change gracefully along with their users in a personal and pleasurable way. For this change to take place, the interaction model of an adaptive learning system has to be conceived as an active dialogue between the system and its users, one capable of inferring and evaluating the user's intentions and actions in order to exhibit a more cooperative behaviour. Since the dialogue between the user and the system is mediated by the interface, two issues become central: the construction and use of a suitable model of the user; and an interface design capable of demonstrating the adaptive behaviour expected from the system. To address these points, we have identified some key defining cognitive characteristics of learners and some instructional conditions that capitalize on these [Uruchurtu et al. 2005]. In order to accommodate the individual differences and their related instructional conditions, our research suggests that a learning system should exhibit an adaptive behaviour based on, at least, the following variables: sequence of instruction, content representation, content structuring, control strategy, and feedback.

4   A Case Study

As part of the development of an adaptive system based on the framework described previously, a prototype was developed. LearnInt was created using learning material from an online learning module on computer hardware and comprises two extreme interfaces: the first design is highly imager and wholist (W/I); the second one (A/V) is highly verbal and analytic [Uruchurtu et al. 2005]. These are the most unitary style combinations, ordered from 'extreme wholist' to 'extreme analytic' [Riding & Rayner 1998]. The salient feature in the design of the interfaces is the content's mode of presentation: one interface presents information verbally, and the other in terms of images and diagrams, including elements on the screen such as buttons and navigational aids. The sequence established in the original design of the learning material was observed; however, advance organizers were included for the wholists. An outline was placed for analytics so they are able to follow the sequence they consider best; for the W/I interface the sequence of the material is defined by the system in a linear approach. The hypertext structure is also different: the W/I interface is linear with no additional links or deeper levels of content, but with frame arrangements. In contrast, the A/V interface allows the students to proceed to any page, and further levels are used. Titles and headers are prominent in both designs

	W/I Interface		A/V Interface	
	Mean	S.D.	Mean	S.D.
Interface Affect ($\alpha = 0.832$)	5.83	1.51	5.83	1.60
Content ($\alpha = 0.849$)	5.67	1.78	5.78	1.75
Structure ($\alpha = 0.923$)	5.77	1.80	6.65	1.47
Presentation ($\alpha = 0.930$)	6.68	1.41	6.37	1.50
Navigation ($\alpha = 0.960$)	6.64	2.12	7.82	0.84
Layout ($\alpha = 0.864$)	5.87	1.84	6.73	1.41
Ease of Use ($\alpha = 0.900$)	6.50	1.66	6.99	1.48
Familiarity ($\alpha = 0.822$)	6.15	1.29	7.10	1.13

Table 1: User evaluation of the interfaces used.

since these help student understanding and give organization to the material. Other graphical components between the two interfaces: a larger, brighter combination of colours for the imager design, graphical/textual buttons on each screen, and a different layout in each case.

4.1 Evaluation

An experiment was carried out, aiming at exploring to what extent interface affect influences learning performance, also whether familiarity with the interface relates to such affect, and how those variables interact with the learner's cognitive style. For each interface style two topics were available: Combinational circuit design (Topic 1) and Relational circuit design (Topic 2). Participants – a sample of MSc students in Computing – were randomly assigned to one of the four possible treatments (2 designs × 2 topics). Measures were set as interface affect, user reaction to various aspects of the interface style, perceived familiarity with each interface, and learning performance. Data about interface affect, user reactions and familiarity were collected using a questionnaire with a nine-point Likert scale. Learning performance was registered in terms of information recall as measured by a test for each topic comprising 6 multiple-choice question with degrees of confidence. The participants' cognitive style was assessed using the VICS and E-CSA-WA test [Peterson et al. 2003]. Participants attended two sessions on two consecutive days. In the first session they carried out Task 1, next they answered the evaluation questionnaire, and then answered the exam for the first topic assigned. During the second session, participants carried out Task 2, answered its evaluation questionnaire, answered the exam about the corresponding topic and, finally, carried out the cognitive style test. It is important to note that the cognitive style test was left at the end in order to avoid that its results influenced the students' reactions.

4.2 Results

The sample consisted of 60 volunteers (average age = 26 years, max = 45, min = 22). The evaluation questionnaire consisted of eight sections as shown in Table 1. α coefficients for each section showed acceptable reliability of the sub-scales. The evaluation was positive towards both interfaces (Table 1).

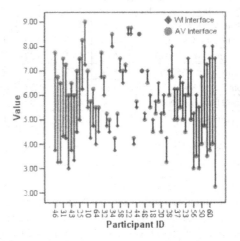

Figure 1: Differences in interface affect.

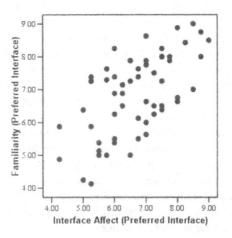

Figure 2: Significant relationship between interface affect and familiarity.

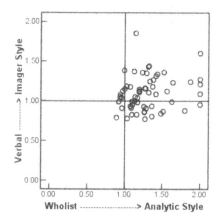

Figure 3: Distribution of participants according to their cognitive style.

In terms of individual results, most of the participants had a preferred interface (Figure 1). This is a key result from this study, since it demonstrates a difference in the user's interface affect. Differences in performance were also observed: 52 participants performed differently between the two interfaces, and 31 of them (~60%) performed better in their preferred interface. The correlation coefficient between interface affect and learning performance was 0.364, which is significant at the 0.01 level. Familiarity was significantly correlated with interface affect (0.510 at the 0.01 level) as shown in Figure 2.

It is important to note that although there were slight differences between groups of participants in terms of interface affect, learning performance and familiarity, F-tests indicated that there were no systematic differences across groups (i.e. differences were not due to the treatment they were allocated to).

The results obtained from the Cognitive Style test show that the participants in this study have a Verbal-Imager style between 0.89 and 2.0 suggesting an imager style preference ($n = 60$, mean = 1.304, s.d. = 0.297). Their Wholist-Analytic style was between 0.77 and 1.85, showing an analytic preference ($n = 60$, mean = 1.099, s.d. = 0.217). Their Wholist-Analytic style was between 0.77 and 1.85, showing an analytic preference ($n = 60$, mean = 1.099, s.d. = 0.217). The distribution of the participants according to their cognitive style is shown in Figure 3.

Table 2 shows the summary of the correlations obtained between the users' interface affect and performance in their preferred interface, and between these and their scores in the cognitive style test – both dimensions. As stated before a significant relationship was observed between interface affect and familiarity, also between interface affect and performance, and between familiarity and performance. Interestingly, users' Wholist-Analytic cognitive style is significantly correlated with familiarity (at the 0.01 level), while the Verbal-Imager dimension seems not to be related to the rest of the variables.

	Affect	Performance	Familiarity	WA Style
Interface Affect	1			
Performance	0.364 **	1		
Familiarity	0.510 **	0.375 **	1	
WA Cognitive Style	0.265	0.310	0.342 **	1
VI Cognitive Style	0.125	0.039	-0.032	0.202

Table 2: Correlation between main variables; ** significant at the 0.01 level.

5 Discussion

As expected, learners responded differently to each interface style, expressing different affect towards the interfaces used: 58 out of 60 participants expressed a more positive affect to either the W/I interface or the A/V one. Differences were also observed in the learning performance of the participants: 52 students performed differently between the two interfaces, and 31 of them performed better in their preferred interface. This suggests that students perform better in the interface to which they have a more positive affect.

As observed, interface affect is significantly related with the students' perceptions in terms of content structure, mode of presentation, navigation facilities, layout, and ease of use. Since perceived familiarity also interacts with interface affect, a relationship might be determined between these two concepts. The implications of these findings suggest that performance of individuals is superior when interface conditions lead to positive moods – this has been observed in previous studies [Isen 2000; Norman 2002]. These results also support findings from a range of disciplines that advocate the idea of the human brain as a system in which affective functions and cognitive ones are interrelated [Fijda 1993; Davis & Wiedenbeck 2001; Norman 2002; Picard et al. 2004].

The results from the VICS and E-CSA-WA test suggest an imager and analytic style preferences. The two dimensions in combination indicated that 30 students were Analytic-Imagers and 21 Analytic-Verbalizers; this distribution corresponds to scores previously observed [Uruchurtu et al. 2005]. In this experiment, just the Wholist-Analytic dimension correlated with familiarity, which might be explained by the fact that the great majority of the participants were of Analytic style. Nevertheless, a question remains as to why cognitive style did not interact with interface affect or learning performance. Further implications of the findings from this study suggest that components on which interface styles were designed accounted for differences in users' perceptions. Therefore, the adaptive variables suggested in this research stand as good candidates for providing adaptivity and eventually personal learning environments.

6 Conclusions

This paper describes a study carried out to evaluate the extent to which interface affect and familiarity influence learning performance under different interface conditions. Its results contribute to the knowledge base on interaction design with emphasis on how individual cognitive and affective characteristics should be considered for the provision of personal, adaptive learning environments. A sample of university students participated in the experiment, using the LearnInt system as test vehicle. The analysis of the data suggests that interface style does have an impact on learners' interface affect which seems to be mediated by perceived familiarity. In turn, interface affect have an impact on the student's learning performance. In terms of cognitive style, in this experiment just the Wholist-Analytic dimension correlated with familiarity. The evidence of this study, supported by previous research, suggests that impact of cognitive style in learning performance is still unclear. Conversely, the results indicate that certain features of the interface design and ultimately the adaptive behaviour of a learning system can be matched to the user's individual differences in order to promote positive interface affect and more effective learning. Further work is however required to investigate different and deeper levels of learning in this and other learning domains, also to incorporate advances in terms of emotion recognition and adaptive techniques to provide the behaviour expected from such a learning environment. The current findings clearly have important implications for the design of web-based learning systems as individuals seem to benefit from using personal, adaptive learning environments designed to match their characteristics and emotional responses.

Acknowledgements

This work is partially supported by the Mexican Secretariat of Education and the National Council of Science and Technology (CONACyT), Studentship 161398.

References

Davis, S. & Wiedenbeck, S. [2001], The Mediating Effects of Intrinsic Motivation, Ease of Use and Usefulness Perceptions on Performance in First-time and Subsequent Computer Users, *Interacting with Computers* **13**(5), 549–80.

Fijda, N. H. [1993], Moods, Emotion Episodes, and Emotions, *in* M. Lewis & J. M. Haviland (eds.), *Handbook of Emotions*, The Guildford Press, pp.59–74.

Graff, M. [1999], Cognitive Style and Hypertext Structures, *in* J. Hill, S. Armstrong, M. Graff, S. Rayner & E. Sadler-Smith (eds.), *Proceedings of the 4th Annual Conference of the European Learning Styles Information Network (ELSIN)*, pp.233–42.

Graff, M. [2003], Assessing Learning from Hypertext: An Individual Differences Perspective, *Journal of Interactive Learning Research* **14**(4), 425–38.

Isen, A. M. [2000], Positive Affect and Decision Making, *in* M. Lewis & J. M. Haviland-Jones (eds.), *Handbook of Emotions*, second edition, The Guildford Press, pp.417–35.

Mckenzie, J., Rose, S. & Head, C. [1999], A Study of the Relationship between Learning Styles Profiles and Performance on an Online Team-based Collaborative Learning Project, *in* J. Hill, S. Armstrong, M. Graff, S. Rayner & E. Sadler-Smith (eds.), *Proceedings of the 4th Annual Conference of the European Learning Styles Information Network (ELSIN)*, pp.313–32.

Norman, D. [2002], Emotion and Design: Attractive Things Work Better, *Interactions* **9**(4), 36–42.

Oatley, K. [1992], *Best Laid Schemes: The Psychology of Emotions*, Cambridge University Press.

Peterson, E. R., Deary, I. J. & Austin, E. J. [2003], The Reliability of Riding's Cognitive Style Analysis Test, *Personality and Individual Difference* **34**(5), 881–91.

Picard, R. W., Papert, S., Bender, W., Blumberg, B., Breazeal, C., Cavallo, D., Machover, T., Resnick, M., Roy, D. & Strohecker, C. [2004], Affective Learning: A Manifesto, *BT Technical Journal* **22**(4), 253–69.

Riding, R. & Cheema, I. [1991], Cognitive Styles: An Overview and Integration, *Journal of Educational Psychology* **11**(3-4), 193–215.

Riding, R. J. & Grimley, M. [1999], Cognitive Style, Gender and Learning from Multimedia Materials in 11-year-old Children, *British Journal of Educational Technology* **30**(1), 43–56.

Riding, R. J. & Rayner, G. [1998], *Cognitive Styles and Learning Strategies: Understanding Style Differences in Learning and Behaviour*, David Fulton Publishers.

Uruchurtu, E., MacKinnon, L. & Rist, R. J. [2005], User Cognitive Style and Interface Design for Personal, Adaptive Learning: What to Model?, *in* L. Ardissono, P. Brna & A. Mitrovic (eds.), *User Modeling 2005: Proceedings of the Tenth International Conference on User Modeling (UM2005)*, Vol. 3538 of *Lecture Notes in Computer Science*, Springer-Verlag, pp.154–63.

Connecting with Others

VideoArms: Embodiments for Mixed Presence Groupware

Anthony Tang[†], Carman Neustaedter[‡] & Saul Greenberg[‡]

[†] *Human Communication Technologies Laboratory, University of British Columbia, Vancouver, B.C., Canada*

Email: *tonyt@ece.ubc.ca*

[‡] *Interactions Laboratory, University of Calgary, Calgary, Alberta, Canada*

Email: *{carman,saul}@cpsc.ucalgary.ca*

Mixed presence groupware (MPG) allows collocated and distributed teams to work together on a shared visual workspace. Presence disparity arises in MPG because it is harder to maintain awareness of remote collaborators compared to collocated collaborators. We examine the role of one's body in collaborative work and how it affects presence disparity, articulating four design implications for embodiments in mixed presence groupware to mitigate the effects of presence disparity: embodiments should provide local feedback; they should visually portray people's interaction with the work surface using direct input mechanisms; they should display fine-grain movement and postures of hand gestures, and they should be positioned within the workspace. We realize and evaluate these implications with VideoArms, an embodiment technique that captures and reproduces people's arms as they work over large displays.

Keywords: consequential communication, embodiments, distributed groupware, gestures, mixed presence groupware, single display groupware.

1 Introduction

Large surfaces such as tabletop and whiteboards naturally afford collocated collaboration, allowing multiple people to work together over the shared display. As large digital displays become more ubiquitous, we anticipate they will offer a shared workspace for not only collocated people, but distant collaborators as well.

> *Imagine you are a member of a design team located in Calgary.*
> *You schedule a brainstorming session with your Vancouver-based*
> *counterparts on a new product idea. Your company has special meeting*
> *rooms in each city, connected by audio links and containing large*
> *digital stylus-based whiteboard displays. Groupware allows members*
> *of your Calgary team and the Vancouver team to concurrently draw*
> *ideas on the display wall using styli, which everyone sees in real time.*

This scenario describes *mixed presence groupware* (MPG), software that connects both collocated and distributed collaborators together in a shared space. Although hardware support for this MPG scenario already exists, we do not yet know how to design software to support this kind of activity in a fluid, seamless way. MPG systems are still in their infancy: to date, only a few research systems have investigated this arrangement of collaborators [Apperley et al. 2003; Everitt et al. 2003; Tang et al. 2005]. Yet simply providing technological support for MPG ignores a core problem called presence disparity: in MPG workspaces, some collaborators are physically present, while others are not. The result of this discrepancy is that collaborators tend to focus their energy on collocated collaborators at the expense of their distributed counterparts [Tang et al. 2005].

One reason for this asymmetric interaction is that collocated collaborators are seen in full fidelity, while remote participants are represented by only embodiments – virtual presentations of their bodies. Most commercial groupware systems reduce this virtual presentation to a telepointer (remote mouse cursor), which clearly cannot compete against the communicative power of a physical body. Presence disparity unbalances a collaborator's experience of the group: maintaining awareness, sensing engagement and involvement and communicating is much easier with collocated collaborators compared to remote collaborators.

In this paper, we explore the problem of designing embodiments for MPG. First, we develop an understanding of the role collaborators' bodies play in collaborative work by exploring three concepts – feedback and feedthrough, consequential communication, and gestures. From these, we articulate four design implications for MPG embodiments to mitigate presence disparity:

1. embodiments should be visible to both collocated and remote collaborators;

2. embodiments should be driven by direct input mechanisms and presented in high fidelity;

3. embodiments should capture and display fine-grained movements and postures; and

4. embodiments should be positioned in the context of the workspace.

Second, we apply these implications to design a prototype system called VideoArms. As we will see, VideoArms provides a rich embodiment by digitally capturing people's arms as they work over large work surfaces, where it overlays these arms on the remote displays. Finally, we present the results of a pilot study that support our current VideoArms design directions for embodiments in MPG.

2 Background: Bodies in Collaborative Work

The physical body plays a large role in collocated collaboration, helping to explicitly convey information, and providing a means for others to maintain an awareness of our workspace activities [Gutwin 1997]. For embodiments in mixed presence groupware to reduce presence disparity, we need to understand the particular communicative affordances bodies bring the collaborative process so that we can recreate them for remote collaborators.

This section reviews three concepts that give some insight to how bodies contribute to collaborative work [Pinelle et al. 2003]: feedback and feedthrough, consequential communication, and gestures. Although these concepts are well known in the computer-supported cooperative work (CSCW) community, they manifest themselves differently in mixed presence groupware. By reviewing these concepts and reflecting on their consequences in naïve MPG implementations, we derive four design principles for MPG embodiments.

2.1 Feedback and Feedthrough: Perceiving Ourselves and Others

We perceive our own actions and the consequences of our actions on objects as feedback, and we constantly readjust and modify our actions as our perceptions inform us of changes to the environment, or changes about our bodily position [Robertson 1997]. Our ability to perceive ourselves is important: without our ability to perceive our own bodies as physical objects in the world, threading a needle when blindfolded might otherwise be a painful experience.

In distributed groupware, feedback is echoed to other participants as *feedthrough*, the reflection of one person's actions on other users' screens [Dix et al. 1998]. In collaborative work it is important to be able to understand remote collaborators' actions and the effect they are having on the workspace. Within a distributed system, feedback and feedthrough play a dual role: feedback not only informs us of our own actions, but gives us insight to how our actions are being interpreted on the other side (the feedthrough).

In mixed presence groupware, one only needs to look at collocated collaborators to acquire full feedthrough. Because feedback and feedthrough are the same, the person doing the action also knows what the other person can see [Rodden 1996]. In contrast, one may see only partial feedthrough of a remote collaborator's actions. Because feedback and feedthrough may not be identical (e.g. due to network latency or other deficiencies in the system), the person performing the action (e.g. a gesture) can only intuit what remote collaborators might see. This dissimilarity between feedback and feedthrough for remote vs. local collaborators can introduce imbalance, confusion, and uncertainty in how people experience the interaction.

Figure 1: A bird's eye view of a physical workspace.

This imbalance between feedthrough and feedback suggests our first design principle for mixed presence groupware embodiments. *To provide feedback of what others can see, a person's embodiment should be visible not only to one's distant collaborators, but also to oneself and one's collocated collaborators.*

2.2   Consequential Communication: Watching Others Work

Our bodies are the source of *consequential communication*: information generated as a consequence of our activities in the workspace [Segal 1995]. A person's activity in the workspace naturally generates rich and timely information often relevant to collaboration. For instance, the way a worker is positioned, and the types of tools or artifacts being held and used tells others about that individual's current and immediate future work activities (e.g. Figure 1).

The graceful choreography of teamwork arises from the subtle role played by consequential communication. Segal [1995] found that pilots spend 60% of their time simply observing co-pilots' consoles while they were being manipulated. Further, he reports that pilots would often react smoothly to one another's actions without explicit verbal cuing. Similarly, Gutwin [1997] observed that 'participants would regularly turn their heads to watch their partners work' in small group interaction. Tang's [1991] reports of choreographed hand movements during group work over physical surfaces can also be understood in terms of consequential communication: by observing others' actions and activities in a shared workspace, one can fairly accurately predict others' future acts or intentions, thereby easily working with or around them. Consequential communication is an important conduit for maintaining an awareness of others, allowing us to monitor, understand and predict others' actions in the workspace without explicit action on their part [Gutwin 1997].

In mixed presence groupware, consequential communication between collocated vs. remote participants is out of balance, as people have different views of their collocated and remote participants. Collocated actions over the physical workspace allow others to observe individual atomic-level interactions with the workspace (e.g. reaching towards a stylus, fingers grasping the stylus, lifting the stylus, moving the stylus towards the display, touching its tip to the display, etc.), allowing them to predict future activities well. Indirect input devices (e.g. mice) can restrict consequential communication between collocated participants, since they can no longer see how bodies are attached to actions, or how actions are generated [Gutwin & Greenberg 1998]. For remote collaborators, one's ability to observe others depends directly on the embodiment's abstraction and fidelity. Yet virtual environments typically tend away from atomic-level interactions, often representing activities at a coarser level (e.g. a mouse pointer changes into a pen representing a mode change from pointing to drawing, or a pen suddenly appearing in an avatar's empty hand). This abruptness makes remote participants' actions less predictable.

MPG embodiments need to have a comparable range of expressiveness and fidelity compared to their corporeal counterparts if they are to provide parity in the consequential communication that is conveyed. The embodiment must capture appropriate information, and present it in an interpretable way: the closer an embodiment's presentation relates to the activities of the participant, the easier those activities are to interpret. This brings us to our second implication for the design of MPG embodiments. *To support consequential communication for both collocated and distributed participants, people should interact through direct input mechanisms, where the remote embodiment of how the input device is manipulated is presented at sufficient fidelity to allow collaborators to easily interpret all current actions as well as actions leading up to them.*

2.3 Gestures: Facilitating Intentional Communication

Gestures are intentional bodily movements and postures used for communicative purpose [Bekker et al. 1995; Kirk et al. 2005]. Gestures provide participants with a spatial and kinetic means to express their thoughts, reinforcing what is being done and said in the workspace. Gestures are a frequent consequence of how bodies are used in collaborative activity: Tang [1991] observed that 35% of hand activities in a physical workspace were gestures intended to engage attention and express ideas. Because intentional gesturing is so frequent, hindering the process – by not giving participants the ability to view or to produce gestures effectively – may negatively impact collaborative activities in mixed presence groupware.

Two classes of gestures facilitate the communication of ideas and coordination in group work: pure communicative acts, and those that relate to the workspace and its artifacts. Pure communicative gestures, which arise from a person's natural communicative effort, are used by both the speaker and listener for fluid interaction. People use such gestures to facilitate both speech production [Krauss et al. 1995], and interpretation [Riseborough 1981]. Gestures can also convey semantic information above and beyond speech alone (e.g. deictic gestures), and some replace speech entirely (e.g. yes or no via thumbs-up or thumbs-down). Similar gestures are also used to help coordinate conversational turn-taking (e.g. putting up one's hand to express a desire to speak, or gesturing at the next speaker).

The communicative value of these pure communicative gestures relies on our ability to produce gestures by animating our bodies, and upon others being able to see these gestures in detail. In mixed presence groupware, while collocated collaborators see these gestures in detail, remote participants do not. This leads to our third implication for the design of MPG embodiments: *To support bodily gestures, remote embodiments should capture and display the fine-grained movement and postures of collaborators. Being able to see these gestures means people can disambiguate and interpret speech and actions.*

Workspace-oriented gestures relate directly to the collaborative workspace and the artifacts contained within. These gestures typically refer to objects or locations in the workspace, or clarify verbal communication by illustration over the workspace [Harrison & Minneman 1994]. Bekker et al. [1995] identify three workspace-oriented gestures: kinetic (movement that illustrates an action sequence), spatial (movement that indicates distance, location or size), and point (pointing at a person, object or place, where targets may be concrete, abstract, denoting an attitude, attribute, effect, direction or location) – often referred to as a deictic reference. Bekker et al. [1995] also observed that gestures were often combined into *sequences*. For example, one common sequence in design activities is a *walkthrough*: a succession of kinetic gestures illustrating how something might be used. Since collaborators will often combine atomic-level gestures in novel sequences to express ideas, attempting to support remote gesturing by providing 'canned' gestures would be cumbersome.

Further, Bekker et al. [1995] highlighted the importance of the design role of gestures: those that relate to design activity, such as referring to objects, persons or places, showing distances, enacting the interaction between user and product, etc. This role shows that a gesture's semantic information is often heavily related to the context in which it is produced. For instance, gestures in the workspace often refer to objects or locations in the workspace (e.g. 'I think this should be this big').

In mixed presence groupware, collocated collaborators see exactly how these gestures are enacted over the workspace. Yet workspace-oriented gestures of remote participants are often shown via a telepointer: a crude surrogate where information fidelity is lost. Alternatively, gestures of remote collaborators are often seen in a video stream outside the workspace, which removes much of the meaning conveyed by the gestures. Thus, our fourth implication for the design of MPG embodiments is that: *To support bodily gestures as they relate to the workspace context, remote embodiments should be positioned within the workspace to minimize information loss that would otherwise occur.*

This discussion of gestures reinforces our second implication recommending direct input mechanisms. Since the ability to freely use gestures is important for fluent speech production, smooth interaction in MPG is necessarily best facilitated by un-tethered input devices (pens, touch surfaces) that interact directly with the display surface. This leaves people free to both gesture and work directly over the work surface. Tethering users to input devices such as keyboards or mice inhibits users from gesturing as a part of their communicative effort.

In closing, we should mention that our review does not consider the role of eye contact for interpersonal communication, and eye gaze for knowing where others are focusing their attention [e.g. Ishii & Kobayashi 1993]. Instead, we have reviewed

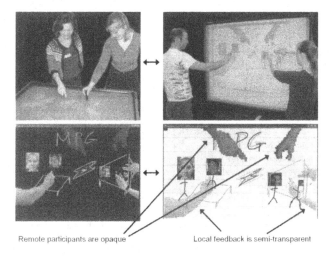

Remote participants are opaque   Local feedback is semi-transparent

Figure 2: A sample MPG session using VideoArms.

three concepts revealing how bodies – particularly the visible aspects of the body from a top-down view (Figure 1) – facilitate the collaborative process. Furthermore, we have suggested why these lead to presence disparity problems in mixed presence groupware, and recommend how this disparity can be mitigated through careful embodiment design. In the next section, we put these design principles to practice in building VideoArms, an MPG embodiment.

3   VideoArms: A Video-based MPG Embodiment

VideoArms is a prototype video embodiment mixed presence groupware system that visually recreates the part of the body normally seen over the workspace: people's arms. In this section, we give an overview of our VideoArms system, briefly explain its relationship with other similar systems and how it addresses each of our design principles. We then briefly describe its implementation.

VideoArms digitally captures collaborators' arms as they work over the workspace using a video camera, and redraws the arms at the remote location. Figure 2 illustrates a sample session. Two connected groups of collaborators (Figure 2, top) each work over different touch-sensitive surfaces. Each surface runs the same custom MPG application, allowing all participants to simultaneously see, sketch and manipulate artifacts within a common workspace. Figure 2 (bottom) gives a close up of what these participants can see when using the VideoArms embodiment in this MPG application:

1. collaborators see their own arms as local feedback, rendered semi-transparently;

2. each group sees the solid arms of remote participants in 2.5-dimensional fidelity (the system captures and reproduces colour-based depth-cues); and

	Local feedback of embodiment	Direct input mechanism	Rendering of fine-grain movement	Workspace-embedded embodiments
Agora [Kuzuoka et al. 1999]		✓	✓	✓
ClearBoard [Ishii & Kobayashi 1993]		✓	✓	✓
Designer's Outpost [Everitt et al. 2003]		✓		✓
Facetop [Stotts et al. 2004]	✓		✓	✓
LIDS [Apperley et al. 2003]	✓		✓	✓
Roussel [2001]			✓	✓
TeamWorkstation [Ishii & Kobayashi 1993]	✓		✓	
VideoDraw [Tang & Minneman 1991a]		✓	✓	✓
VideoWhiteboard [Tang & Minneman 1991b]		✓	✓	✓
WSCS-II [Miwa & Ishibiki 2004]		✓	✓	✓
VideoArms	✓	✓	✓	✓

Table 1: How various video-based embodiment techniques address the four design implications of MPG embodiments.

3. remote arms are painted to preserve the physical body positioning relative to the workspace.

Both physical and video arms are synchronized to work with the underlying groupware application, where gestures and actions all appear in the correct location.

Figure 2 also reveals communicative aspects of the embodiment. In this MPG setting, participants can simultaneously gesture to the full, expressive extent of arms and hands. The system neither dictates nor implies any sort of turn-taking mechanism, and captures workspace and conversational gestures extremely richly. Finally, users are not tethered to particular locations in the workspace: using touch and pens to interact with the groupware application, users are free to physically move around the workspace as they see fit.

3.1   Related Systems

The VideoArms metaphor captures and presents the workspace from a bird's eye view of the workspace, cf. 'through the glass' metaphor from earlier work [Ishii & Kobayashi 1993; Tang & Minneman 1991b]. From this perspective, the arms are the primary indicators of a collocated collaborator's presence (as in Figure 1). While VideoArms builds upon concepts of other non-MPG systems that integrate video feeds of remote collaborators within the workspace, it differs in several respects:

1. VideoArms' design is an attempt to solve the problem of presence disparity unique to MPG using the design implications described earlier;

2. VideoArms facilitates distortion-free composition of multiple video feeds and the evaluation of more abstract presentation techniques;

3. VideoArms is intended to support multiple collaborators at a site, allowing collaborators to see and interpret fine-grained activities of remote collaborators: most other systems assume only a single person per site.

Table 1 summarizes how embodiment techniques offered in other systems only partially address our four MPG design implications.

VideoDraw [Tang & Minneman 1991a], VideoWhiteboard [Tang & Minneman 1991b], TeamWorkstation and ClearBoard [Ishii & Kobayashi 1993] were all intended to connect a pair of distance-separated collaborators, each of whom could draw in a shared workspace. These systems used analog cameras to transmit both the images of the collaborators (their arms and bodies in VideoDraw and VideoWhiteboard, and their faces in TeamWorkstation and ClearBoard) and the contents of the workspace. While effective for their purposes, these systems suffered from two major limitations:

1. people were not able to manipulate each other's physical drawing marks (although later versions of ClearBoard addressed this problem using transparent digital displays); and

2. the analog video mixing technology limited the number of sites that could be composited without significant image degradation.

Facetop is a digital video-based system intended to support two remotely located extreme programmers that uses a ClearBoard-like metaphor [Stotts et al. 2004]. Roussel [2001] uses a chroma-key technique to address the image degradation issues. While both systems are excellent for two remote collaborators, the techniques do not adequately support collocated consequential communication due to the physical separation of the gesturing area and input area.

LIDS uses a fully digital system to recreate VideoWhiteboard for distributed PowerPoint presentations [Apperley et al. 2003]. LIDS captures the image of a person working in front of a shared display using consumer-grade cameras, and transforms this image via background subtraction and posturing techniques into a frame containing the digital shadow of the person. Three images are then overlaid to create the scene: the digital shadow, the PowerPoint slide, and another overlay that captures digital annotations. Similarly, the Distributed Designer's Outpost [Everitt et al. 2003] also captures digital shadows via rear-projection; however, the low fidelity of the shadows is only useful for showing another person's presence and very coarse gestures. As with VideoWhiteBoard, both approaches use shadows, which provide considerably less detail than full fidelity images – a desired feature according to users of Distributed Designer's Outpost.

Most of the preceding examples were designed to support collaboration between distributed individuals (instead of groups). With MPG, we explicitly design for collaboration between distributed sites with multiple individuals [Tang et al. 2005]. Only three of the systems were designed to support MPG explicitly: Agora [Kuzuoka et al. 1999], Distributed Designer's Outpost [Everitt et al. 2003] and WSCS-II [Miwa & Ishibiki 2004]. Agora builds on the analog approaches of ClearBoard and VideoWhiteboard to support two dyads, sharing the same limitation that physical artefacts cannot be manipulated in remote locations. WSCS-II's approach produces a shared virtual space, thereby allowing participants who are not actively engaged in the task to be embodied. In contrast, our focus is primarily in a shared work surface, and the active participants on the surface.

Figure 3: The image on the left is colour-segmented to find the skin-colour pixels (middle). The two images are then combined to produce the VideoArms image on the right.

While VideoArms builds on these prior approaches, it explicitly addresses the problem of presence disparity in MPG by supporting our four design implications:

- Local participants know what remote people see because their own embodiments are shown as semi-transparent feedback.

- Because the body is used as an input device that works directly on the touch sensitive surface, VideoArms supports consequential communication. Other collaborators (whether collocated or remote) can easily predict, understand and interpret another's actions in the workspace as one reaches towards artefacts and begins actions. Because collaborators are not tethered to input devices, their actions are direct and in the workspace context.

- Rich gestures (coupled with conversation and artifact manipulation) are well supported because the remote arms are displayed in rich 2.5-dimensional fidelity and a reasonable (although not ideal) framerate (~12 fps) that proved acceptable for interpreting gestural meanings.

- Task-related gestures are easily interpreted because they are placed in the context of the workspace.

3.2   Implementation Details

In this section, we show how all of the above design implications are realized by describing the key implementation details of VideoArms.

VideoArms uses inexpensive web cameras hand-positioned approximately two meters in front of the display to capture video images of collaborators. The software extracts the arms (and other bare-skinned body parts) of collaborators as they work directly over the displayed groupware application (see Friedland et al. [2005] for a more robust implementation). Transmitted images are processed at the remote workstation to appear as an overlay atop the digital workspace. To provide local feedback, VideoArms overlays the local person's video on the work surface. To avoid image degradation (and thus facilitate scaling to multiple sites), VideoArms extracts and composites onto the workspace image only a person's body parts (such as one's arms): all other background visuals are removed.

Frames captured by the camera are processed, transmitted and displayed in a four step process (Figure 3). First, pixels matching skin colour (based on a Mahalanobis distance calculated against a sample of 10 or more skin sample pixels) are identified. Morphological opening is applied to this skin mask to produce a silhouette mask (Figure 3, middle). Second, this mask is combined with the original image (Figure 3, right). Third, the image is transmitted to all clients using UDP packets for quick delivery. Finally, standard raster graphics compositing techniques are used to paint the image on the groupware work surface.

VideoArms uses Python, the .NET Framework, the Intel Performance Primitives library, the Python Imaging Library, and the Python numarray open source libraries. On a Celeron 2.4GHz, video frames are processed at 320×240 resolution at 25 frames per second, and overlaid across a 640×480 groupware workspace. While further optimizations are possible, our primary intention was to develop a system suitable to test our ideas rather than to produce a production-level implementation [see Friedland et al. 2005].

4 Initial Experiences from an Exploratory Study

We conducted an exploratory study with pairs and groups of four to understand whether our approach to embodiment design had merit in terms of mitigating presence disparity. At this early design stage, we were interested in an initial validation of our design implications for mixed presence groupware embodiments. This exploratory study was aimed to be observational and fairly broad-brush, designed so that we could look for large effects and critical incidents:

- What problems would participants have with VideoArms?

- Would participants make use of the ability to gesture freely? Would they continue to gesture even if there was a voice link, and were these gestures intended for remote collaborators, collocated collaborators or both?

- Would consequential communication occur across the link?

In essence, our larger goal was to see if a richer, video-based embodiment of remote collaborators could mitigate the effects of presence disparity on the collaborative process as they worked on their natural activities. We also recognized that VideoArms might be an imperfect instantiation of our design implications, so our lesser goal was to look for specific design flaws and to iterate over our design.

4.1 The Study

Pairs and groups of four completed a series of collaborative workspace tasks (directed puzzle completion and a design task) using a custom mixed presence groupware application on two large displays (one table, one upright whiteboard) running across a remote link. The puzzle completion task was designed so that participants had asymmetric knowledge about how the finished puzzle should look (and therefore had to cooperate with one another to complete the task). With groups of four, one participant on each side of the link had knowledge of the finished puzzle, but these participants were restricted to directing the other participants in completing the puzzle (they were not allowed to directly work on the puzzle themselves). The design task allowed participants to freely sketch their ideas on the workspace (similar to a standard whiteboard), and asked them to design a photograph print dialogue.

These tasks are modified forms of the follower+director task from [Gutwin 1997] and the design task from [Tang 1991].

Participants worked over a custom-built MPG application on two different large displays. To simulate remote collaboration, displays were located in separate rooms. The first was a rear-projected, touch sensitive SMARTBoard, which has a 167.6cm screen (diagonal). The second was a similarly sized but horizontally mounted and front-projected DVIT display. The DVIT display could support two simultaneous touches, but the SMARTBoard could not. To prevent this technical difference from affecting the results of the study, the study software interpreted only one touch per board. Each group of participants was split in two: for groups of two, one participant worked in front his or her own display; similarly, groups of four were split into two pairs, and each pair worked in front of a shared display.

Using a partial within-subjects design, participants completed the puzzle completion tasks alternately with VideoArms, and then with telepointers only. Some groups had a voice link, some did not (to understand how voice affected gesture interpretation). Finally, groups of four completed the design task with only VideoArms. We videotaped the sessions, and collected field notes detailing the kinds of gestures that were used with the different embodiment techniques, and the kinds of interaction patterns that were evident.

We recruited 22 paid participants from the university computer science student population. We chose users familiar and comfortable with computers, and asked that they come in pairs (and in four cases, groups of four).

Finally, to expedite the calibration process, participants wore yellow dishwashing gloves to use with VideoArms (their bright, uniform colour facilitated easy extraction of arm images). While VideoArms was designed to pick up skin tones, we took this shortcut for two reasons:

1. we could calibrate the system for glove colour ahead of time (instead of recalibrating for each group); and

2. our primary interest was not the computer vision algorithm used to extract skin features, but on the collaborative aspects of the system – we did not expect the use of gloves to affect the outcome.

Indeed, if VideoArms proves worthwhile, we anticipate that computer vision specialists could rework our implementation to generate far more efficient implementations and faster calibration methods [Friedland et al. 2005].

4.2 Major Findings

We saw a consistent, constant mix of natural gesturing behaviour and consequential communication regardless of the embodiment (VideoArms vs. telepointers). However, the nature of the gestures was far more varied and natural with the VideoArms embodiment. Consequently, VideoArms was able to engage participants across the link in a far richer way regardless of the group size. This section reports on these observations of participant behaviour with illustrative vignettes from the sessions. We caution again that this is an exploratory study. Our claims are somewhat tentative due to the modest number of participants; however, we stress that the behaviours observed across our participant groups were fairly consistent, and thus suggestive of generalizable behavioural patterns.

Consistent use of gestures. Participants used a wide variety of natural and easily interpreted static and motion-based gestures with VideoArms. With pairs, gestures often acted as audio substitutes. For example: waving to say hello, or 'push it that way', or 'bring it this way', an a-okay, a hold gesture (open hand with fingers apart), an open-handed wave as an error signal, or a thumbs-up to signal that something was correct. Across all groups, the variety of VideoArms gestures observed was fairly extensive. Beyond kinetic, spatial and pointing gestures [Bekker et al. 1995], we observed deixis (referential gestures relating to speech), as well as illustrations (gestures clarifying speech). The following session transcript illustrates how participants appropriated VideoArms for two-handed gestures – something that was impossible in the telepointer condition:

> *(L and M are on opposite sides of the link.)*

> **L:** *With her left hand, L points to an artefact that M should grab. Once M has touched the artefact, L points to where M's artefact should go with her right hand. L then grabs her own artefact with her left hand and moves it in place (still pointing with her right hand), checking to see if M has moved hers to the right place.*

> **L:** *Satisfied that M has moved it to the right place, L retracts her right hand, and makes a full-arm clapping motion.*

Because the fidelity of VideoArms was low (compared to real life), participants generally exaggerated the nature of these gestures both in speed and in size – a direct response to the local feedback of the embodiment (i.e. the feedback was not 'keeping up' to the speed of the gesture, or the gesture was too subtle to be seen).

Rich gestures used as part of the collaborative process. VideoArms provided a remarkably useful communications medium for participants. Participants were able to fluidly gesture and integrate those gestures into their interactions with collocated and remote participants. Further, these gestures were more varied and natural (accompanying speech) than those expressed with the telepointers:

> *(J & K are collocated, and separate from B & C.)*

> **J:** *'Okay, K, move yours over to here.' J points at a location.*

> **B:** *In the meantime, B on the other side has directed C to move her artefact to a certain spot.*

> **J:** *J sees that C has not moved it exactly to the right position. 'C, could you guys move it closer to right over here', J makes a jabbing motion with her finger, as if she could push C's hand to the right position.*

With the telepointer-based embodiments, many of the gestures were motion-based, including waving (to indicate presence or to garner attention), directed thrusting

Figure 4: Participants spent a lot of time watching each other. On the left, H watches her colocated partner W's activities. On the right, D also watches W carefully via VideoArms.

to indicate a location, and so forth: artificially impoverished versions of real-life gestures. Most interestingly, we occasionally observed collaborators 'incorrectly' pointing with their hands instead of using the telepointer embodiment. This meant that those gestures would not be seen by remote collaborators. It also suggests that gestures are most naturally performed using the physical body – something that VideoArms supports by design.

Watching is an integral part of the collaborative process. Participants spent a considerable amount of time observing their partners (whether collocated or remote) to understand the state of the activity, regardless of the type of embodiment (Figure 4). In the puzzle task, directors would watch to ensure their partners had grabbed the correct artefact, or had positioned the artefact in the correct location. When directors detected an error (e.g. if the follower grabbed the wrong artefact or had moved it to the wrong location), directors would redirect followers to the correct artefact or location. Followers would reciprocally watch directors' actions to determine which artefact to pick up.

If an embodiment supports consequential communication, we should also expect to see users correcting the actions of others in the workspace. Of note, we saw many instances of correction occurring across the link in the groups of four conditions. This means that participants were sufficiently engaged with remote participants to suggest corrections instead of waiting for the mistake to be noticed. The previous vignette illustrates an instance of this occurrence.

5   Discussion and Conclusions

Based on the results from our observational study, we believe that our design principles are appropriate starting points for embodiments in mixed presence groupware. We saw evidence that VideoArms helped to mitigate presence disparity by promoting more varied yet natural communication across the link.

Participants used VideoArms to gesture in the workspace. We observed deixis, and a wide variety of natural gestures with VideoArms, which persisted in the presence of a voice channel and a collocated collaborator. Importantly, gestures were not replicated for remote participants: a single gesture was generally sufficient to communicate to both collocated and remote participants. Participants also made use of VideoArms by carefully watching the arms of others in the workspace, lending support to the importance of consequential communication. Furthermore, we also observed instances of error-correction across the link, facilitated by consequential communication. By increasing the level and style of engagement across the link, VideoArms helped to mitigate presence disparity.

Further iteration on VideoArms is required to make it a practical embodiment system. As a prototype system, VideoArms had two limitations:

1. poor image quality; and

2. impractical camera placement.

VideoArms' colour segmentation technique produced on-screen artifacts, leaving images not clear and crisp enough for participants. More robust implementations are available [e.g. Friedland et al. 2005; Wilson 2005]. Second, the placement and use of cameras poses practical problems: with a vertical display, a collaborator's body sometimes occluded the camera's view of his or her arms. As a consequence, participants sometimes worked with their arms uncomfortably outstretched so that remote collaborators could see. In spite of these shortcomings, we saw very convincing evidence of VideoArms' utility as a communication medium. We predict that collaborators would likely make even further use of a better implementation.

The first generation of groupware systems succeeded by making the impossible possible: by letting people share views of their computer display, they gained the ability to work in real time over computer artifacts. As groupware moved on to successive generations, attention was increasingly moved to the fine-grained nuances of communicating through technologies [Pinelle et al. 2003]: subtleties in how people maintained awareness of one another's actions in the workspace [e.g. Gutwin 1997; Gutwin & Greenberg 1998], the role of gestures [e.g. Bekker et al. 1995; Krauss et al. 1995; Tang 1991], eyegaze [Ishii & Kobayashi 1993], feedthrough [Dix et al. 1998], consequential communication [Segal 1995], etc.

Our research continues the quest to programmatically capture, transmit and display much of the rich information that makes up the collaborative process. In doing so, we make three primary contributions:

First, we suggest that careful embodiment design can mitigate the presence disparity problem in mixed presence groupware, and offer four implications for their design grounded in a theoretical understanding of how people socially interact over a workspace. We explain why embodiments should incorporate feedback, consequential communication and gestures to mitigate the presence disparity problem, hoping to guide those designing MPG embodiments and technologies.

Second, we contribute VideoArms as a method: a video-based embodiment technique for supporting collocated and distributed collaboration around large displays. We recognized the intellectual roots of VideoArms in its predecessor systems, showing VideoArms' method extends previously presented concepts to the MPG setting, while recognizing the varied design choices of these earlier systems.

Third, we present early observations and a critique of VideoArms, for we expect future researchers not only to build on our successes but to try to overcome our failures. We believe that VideoArms is a reasonable first step for a workspace-focused MPG group because it presents the parts of the body that appear within the workspace context. Yet we recognize that eye contact and body positioning, which have been found to be important to collaboration [Ishii & Kobayashi 1993] are not supported at all. Similarly, we point out technical limitations of VideoArms: it is currently a working proof of concept, and as such there is still room for better performance. Issues such as frame rate, image extraction, camera positioning, skin colour calibration, latency, and so forth need to be fixed and improved.

VideoArms is best considered as a first serious solution to solving the presence disparity problem in MPG. We believe we have forwarded MPG research into a space where we can begin to understand embodiment design, and the tradeoffs between different embodiment types within MPG collaboration.

6 Acknowledgements

We thank members of the Interactions Lab for their intellectual support, and NSERC for financial support.

References

Apperley, M., McLeod, L., Masoodian, M., Paine, L., Philips, M., Rogers, B. & Thomson, K. [2003], Use of Video Shadow for Small Group Interaction: Awareness on a Large Interactive Display Surface, *in* R. Biddle & B. Thomas (eds.), *Proceedings of the Fourth Australasian User Interface Conference (AUIC 2003)*, Australian Computer Society, pp.81–90.

Bekker, M. M., Olson, J. S. & Olson, G. M. [1995], Analysis of Gestures in Face-to-face Design Teams Provides Guidance for How to Use Groupware in Design, *in* G. Olson & S. Schuon (eds.), *Proceedings of the Symposium on Designing Interactive Systems: Processes, Practices, Methods and Techniques (DIS'95)*, ACM Press, pp.157–66.

Dix, A., Finlay, J., Abowd, G. & Beale, R. [1998], *Human–Computer Interaction*, second edition, Prentice–Hall.

Everitt, K. M., Klemmer, S. R., Lee, R. & Landay, J. A. [2003], Two Worlds Apart: Bridging the Gap Between Physical and Virtual Media for Distributed Design Collaboration, *in* V. Bellotti, T. Erickson, G. Cockton & P. Korhonen (eds.), *Proceedings of SIGCHI Conference on Human Factors in Computing Systems (CHI'03)*, *CHI Letters* **5**(1), ACM Press, pp.553–60.

Friedland, G., Jantz, K. & Rojas., R. [2005], SIOX: Simple Interactive Object Extraction in Still Images, *in* S. Kawanda (ed.), *Proceedings of the Seventh IEEE International Symposium on Multimedia (ISM'05)*, IEEE Computer Society Press, pp.253–60.

Gutwin, C. [1997], Workspace Awareness in Real-time Distributed Groupware, PhD thesis, Department of Computer Science, University of Calgary.

Gutwin, C. & Greenberg, S. [1998], Effects of Awareness Support on Groupware Usability, *in* C.-M. Karat, A. Lund, J. Coutaz & J. Karat (eds.), *Proceedings of the SIGCHI Conference on Human Factors in Computing Systems (CHI'98)*, ACM Press.

Harrison, S. & Minneman, S. [1994], A Bike in Hand: A Study of 3-D Objects in Design, *in* K. Dorst, H. Christiaans & N. Cross (eds.), *The Delf Protocols Workshop: Analyzing Design Activity*, John Wiley & Sons, pp.205–18.

Ishii, H. & Kobayashi, M. [1993], Integration of Interpersonal Space and Shared Workspace: Clearboard Design and Experiments, *ACM Transactions on Office Information Systems* **11**(4), 349–75.

Kirk, D., Crabtree, A. & Rodden, T. [2005], Ways of the Hands, *in* H. W. Gellersen, K. Schmidt, M. Beaudouin-Lafon & W. Mackay (eds.), *Proceedings of ECSCW'05, the 9th European Conference on Computer-supported Cooperative Work*, KluwerAcad, pp.1–21.

Krauss, R., Dushay, R., Chen, Y. & Rauscher, F. [1995], The Communicative Value of Conversational Hand Gestures, *Journal of Experimental Social Psychology* **31**(6), 533–52.

Kuzuoka, H., Yamashita, J., Yamazaki, K. & Yamazaki, A. [1999], Agora: A Remote Collaboration System that Enables Mutual Monitoring, *in* M. E. Atwood (ed.), *CHI'99 Extended Abstracts of the Conference on Human Factors in Computing Systems*, ACM Press, pp.190–1.

Miwa, Y. & Ishibiki, C. [2004], Shadow Communication: System for Embodied Interaction with Remote Partners, *in* J. Herbsleb & G. Olson (eds.), *Proceedings of 2004 ACM Conference on Computer Supported Cooperative Work (CSCW'04)*, ACM Press, pp.467–76.

Pinelle, D., Gutwin, C. & Greenberg, S. [2003], Task Analysis for Groupware Usability Evaluation: Modelling Shared-workspace Tasks with the Mechanics of Collaboration, *ACM Transactions on Computer–Human Interaction* **10**(4), 281–311.

Riseborough, M. G. [1981], Physiographic Gestures as Decoding Facilitators: Three Experiments Exploring a Neglected Facet of Communication, *Journal of Nonverbal Behavior* **5**(3), 172–83.

Robertson, T. [1997], Cooperative Work and Lived Cognition: A Taxonomy of Embodied Actions, *in* J. Hughes, W. Prinz, T. Rodden & K. Schmidt (eds.), *Proceedings of ECSCW'97, the 5th European Conference on Computer-supported Cooperative Work*, Kluwer Academic Publishers, pp.205–20.

Rodden, T. [1996], Populating the Application: A Model of Awareness for Cooperative Applications, *in* M. J. Tauber, B. Nardi & G. C. van der Veer (eds.), *Proceedings of the SIGCHI Conference on Human Factors in Computing Systems: Common Ground (CHI'96)*, ACM Press, pp.88–96.

Roussel, N. [2001], Exploring New Uses of Video with VideoSpace, *in* M. R. Little & L. Nigay (eds.), *Engineering for Human–Computer Interaction: Proceedings of the 8th IFIP International Conference (EHCI 2001)*, Vol. 2254 of *Lecture Notes in Computer Science*, Springer-Verlag, pp.73–90.

Segal, L. D. [1995], Designing Team Workstations: The Choreography of Teamwork, *in* P. Hancock, J. Flach, J. Caird & K. Vicente (eds.), *Local Applications of the Ecological Approach to Human–Machine Systems*, Vol. 2, Lawrence Erlbaum Associates.

Stotts, D., Smith, J. & Gyllstrom, K. [2004], Support for Distributed Pair Programming in the Transparent Video Facetop, *in* C. Zannier, H. Erdogmus & L. Lindstrom (eds.), *Proceedings of XP Agile Universe 2004*, Vol. 3134 of *Lecture Notes in Computer Science*, Springer, pp.92–104.

Tang, A., Boyle, M. & Greenberg, S. [2005], Understanding and Mitigating Display and Presence Disparity in Mixed Presence Groupware, *Journal of Research and Practice in Information Technology* **37**(2), 71–88.

Tang, J. C. [1991], Findings from Observational Studies of Collaborative Work, *International Journal of Man–Machine Studies* **34**(2), 143–60.

Tang, J. & Minneman, S. [1991a], Videodraw: A Video Interface for Collaborative Drawing, *ACM Transactions on Office Information Systems* **9**(2), 170–84.

Tang, J. & Minneman, S. [1991b], VideoWhiteboard: Video Shadows to Support Remote Collaboration, *in* S. P. Robertson, G. M. Olson & J. S. Olson (eds.), *Proceedings of the SIGCHI Conference on Human Factors in Computing Systems: Reaching through Technology (CHI'91)*, ACM Press, pp.315–22.

Wilson, A. [2005], PlayAnywhere: A Compact Tabletop Computer Vision System, *in* P. Baudisch, M. Czerwinski & D. Olsen (eds.), *Proceedings of the 18th Annual ACM Symposium on User Interface Software and Technology (UIST'05)*, ACM Press, pp.83–92.

Supporting Crime Scene Investigation

Chris Baber, Paul Smith, Sandeep Panesar, Fan Yang & James Cross

Electronic, Electrical and Computer Engineering, The University of Birmingham, B15 2TT, UK

Tel: *+44 121 414 3965*

Email: *c.baber@bham.ac.uk*

In this paper, we describe the design and development of mobile technology to support crime scene investigation. We briefly review the crime scene investigation processes, arguing that it is highly distributed. We then propose the use of a simple case-based reasoning (CBR) system to support some aspects of this activity, and a wearable computer to assist in data collection. The includes a user trial by practising crime scene investigators, and concludes with discussion of future work.

Keywords: crime scene investigation, case-based reasoning, wearable computers.

1 Introduction

The work presented in this paper forms part of a larger investigation into 'shared awareness'. However, it should be noted that the notion of 'shared awareness' is not unproblematic and has been defined in a variety of ways across a variety of the domains in which human-computer interaction operates. Shared awareness could encompass knowing the location of colleagues, e.g. whether they are (or have been) at a particular location, are en-route etc. The increasing reliability of Global Positioning Systems (GPS) means that tracking of vehicles is fairly straightforward, and presenting such data on a map is common across many emergency services. Thus, providing 'awareness' of people's location is already a feature of many commercial applications (at least as far as tracking vehicles is concerned). However, knowing where someone is might be less useful than knowing what they are doing. For a crime scene manager, for instance, knowing that one person is collecting evidence at a scene, another en route, and a third completing paperwork could be useful to determine to whom to allocate incoming work. At one level, it becomes a simple matter to add information to the location data to reflect such global activities, and these data could be collected by the crime scene investigator reporting their status, e.g. through radio to a control room. The logical extension of this concept (and our point of departure) is to develop specific indices of activity and to collect such data implicitly as the person performs their activity. Previous work [Baber et al. 2005a] has demonstrated how a GPS combined with a simple sensor (in this case a metal detector) could provide data to a control room and display a person's location and their activity (e.g. switching on the detector to check an object, indicating that the object is metal etc.). In this manner, search activity can be performed collaboratively between a control room operative and a person in the field. The work we report develops this concept to allow multiple sources of information to be collected during the search. This could support sharing of the awareness of the search of a crime scene for people who are able to connect to the relevant server, in the form of a real-time view of the scene (perhaps superimposed on a photograph or map or sketch of the scene) to show what actions are being performed and where exhibits have been recovered.

A second issue relates to the fact the crime scene investigation is almost always a longitudinal activity – the evidence is collected and then analysed, and the analysis interpreted. These steps takes time, are performed by different individuals, and proceed in a fairly linear sequence. There is much interest in UK Police Forces in shortening the time between collection of an exhibit and the identification of an individual associated with that exhibit; this could be supported through having the analysis capability at the scene, i.e. the 'lab-on-a-chip' concept, or through sending digitized material, such as finger-marks, to be analysed. We assume that digitization will be commonplace in the very near future, and that transmission of material between the crime scene and other sites will be supported. In this manner, it will be possible for the crime scene manager to view the collection of evidence or for a forensic scientist to offer advice to the crime scene investigator or for the results of analysis to be collected and returned in parallel with search.

Thirdly, it might be useful to know who has interacted with exhibits over time. This is the basis of evidence tracking and, as we shall see below, is a topic that is receiving much interest in the form of developing and deployed commercial systems. Linked to this notion could be the presentation of who performed particular exhibit collection at different locations in the search of a scene (this is particularly significant in the recovery of exhibits from large areas, and could be equally well applied to accident investigation). Having some indication of 'who did what, when and where' could allow a particular search activity to be 'replayed' for the purposes of briefing or at exhibit hand-over. In addition, if one could identify particular patterns in which exhibits and incidents tend to co-occur (or, indeed, individuals and activities) then it is possible, over time, to build up an awareness of associated features. In the past, such patterns may well have made up the local knowledge held by officers in a particular patch; with the expansion of the police force, the increase in quantity of crime, and changes in specialization has come a fragmentation of such knowledge and an challenge to provide means of allowing a sharing of such knowledge (over and above briefings which take place away from the scene).

These three aspects are intended to illustrate the general notion of 'shared awareness' being used in this project:

1. allowing a person's location and activity to be viewed by others;

2. sharing digital material and interpretations;

3. providing people with an historical perspective on the collection of evidence.

Taken individually, these are similar to much of the work in the Computer-supported Cooperative Work (CSCW) domain. We would claim some unique features of our work, such as the mobility of the operators and the requirement to collect relevant information as implicitly as possible.

2 Crime Scene Investigation

Broadly speaking, crime scene investigation begins with an incident that can be interpreted as criminal, proceeds through examination of a scene, to the selection, collection and analysis of evidence, and to relating the evidence to a Case that can be answered. In terms of this latter stage, Toulmin [1958] proposed that criminal prosecution could be viewed as a form of argumentation (although his model of developing arguments could apply to other domains). In this model, a claim is supported by data. In the domain of crime scene investigation, the collection of data (exhibits) is usually the province of crime scene investigators, and needs to be conducted in as objective and unbiased a manner as possible. This means that the definition of a claim is performed separately (and subsequent to) collection of data. In order to ensure acceptance of the relationship between claim and data, there is a need to demonstrate the integrity and reliability of the data: this is termed the warrant. If there is any concern over the warrant, then the legitimacy of either data or claim can be called into question. In an adversarial legal system, such as in the UK, presentation of forensic analysis will often invite attempts to discredit the manner in which the exhibit was collected or analysed (warrant) as much as the nature of the exhibit itself (data) or the interpretation presented (claim). This structure of data-claim-warrant can be thought of as a recursive sequence in which material is gathered and developed into a more detailed argument. In order to test the resulting argument, it might be necessary to engage in rebuttal activity, which would require additional backing or qualifiers to the original structure. If one assumes that, ultimately, crime scene investigation is concerned with producing an 'argument', then it follows that the various steps that Toulmin [1958] proposes could be associated with the investigative process. What makes the process different for this paper is that likelihood that each step could be performed by different individuals. The investigation of a scene of crime involves several distinct agents, each performing different investigation, analysis and recording functions. For this reason, one can consider crime scene investigation to be 'distributed'.

Within the distributed cognition literature, several authors point to the concept that objects can be considered as 'resources' that support particular forms of action [Flor & Hutchins 1991; Hutchins 1995; Hollan et al. 2002]. Thus, for crime scene investigation, a window-pane might (to an experienced scene of crimes officer)

Focus	State	Goal	History	Plan	Possibility
Environment	Visual inspection	Retrieve exhibits	Recall similar scene	Follow procedure	Objects and surfaces hold evidence
Surface	Visual inspection or chemical treatment	Search, analyse, record	Recall likely surfaces to check	Apply technique	Surfaces hold fingerprints, DNA, fibres etc.
Object	Visual inspection	Search, analyse, record	Recall likely objects	Collect and record	Contain evidence or serve as evidence
Sample	Chemical treatment	Search, collect samples, record	Database of samples	Analyse and record	Evidence can be obtained from sample
Results	Results produced by analysis	Results in the form of graphs and numbers	Database of results	Record and interpret	Results can be interpreted probabilistically
Individual	Identified by specific features	Match results to features	Database of features	Compare	Match can be interpreted probabilistically
Report	Collation of material	Produce coherent case	Updating of collection	Compile results etc.	A case can be made on the basis of the evidence

Table 1: Relating focus of attention to abstract information structures.

support actions relating to the collection of evidence, e.g. sweat secretions might be left by a person resting their forehead against the window when looking into a house could potentially yield DNA, or finger-marks might be left on the window by someone attempting to open it. From this perspective, the environment and the objects it contains can be considered as resources for the actions surrounding crime scene investigation, and the recovered objects can be considered as resources for the actions surrounding forensic analysis (although, of course, forensics apply equally to the crime scene). What is necessary, in this context, is for the objects to be identified as potential resources. In addition to the environment and objects serving as resources for action, Suchman [1987] pointed out that the procedures that people apply to given activities can also be considered as resources. In the context of crime scene investigation, procedures govern the collection of evidence and ensure that accusations of bias or contamination are minimized. However, it is possible that the application of particular procedures will depend on the nature of the investigation – so it is feasible that some procedures might not be followed, because there is no apparent evidence to which they can be applied. When a procedure is being followed, it constrains and influences the manner in which actions are to be performed.

From this perspective, resources for action will influence the activity of the person in a particular environment. In order to translate from a theoretical position to the specification of designs, Wright et al. [2000] suggest a 'resource model'. This model aligns resource types with interaction strategies. The resource type is assumed to be a representation of an abstract information structure, which could cover the goals of the person, the plans being put into effect, the possibilities that objects have for performing actions, the history of previous actions performed by the person or with the objects, the state of the objects and the perceived action-effect relationship of the state of the objects. Each abstract information structure can be represented in a variety of ways, e.g. in the form of written or graphical information, in the state of objects, in the mental model held by the person etc. The interaction strategies cover particular forms of activity, such as plan following or construction, goal matching etc. Table 1 relates what might be termed the scene of crime officers focus of attention to the abstract information structures proposed by Wright et al. [2000].

Table 1 provides an initial assessment of the crime scene investigation in terms of the Focus of activity during the identification and collection of exhibits, and links these to Abstract Information Structures. From this table, we propose a basic set of requirements can be defined, in terms of the classes of activity that will need to be supported. For this work, we propose that it is necessary to support activity related to 'Plan', in terms of supporting evidence management; to support activity related to the 'History' and 'Goal' of investigation, and in particular, to provide support based on previous experience; and to support activity related to 'State' and 'Goal' in a manner that allows inspection of the scene to be performed without interruption, so that the CSI can maintain attention on the processes involved in exhibit collection.

3 Collecting Evidence and Developing Arguments

From Table 1, an initial class of activity relates to the evidence management to support 'Plan'. At present, there are three commercially available evidence management systems in the UK. The basic concept is to allow the transfer of evidence from crime scene to laboratory to court to be performed reliably, i.e. so as to record where the evidence is and who has handled it, and to update records pertaining to that evidence. The SETS (Single Evidential Tracking System – see http://www.compucorp.co.uk/sets) can be used at the crime scene and supports recording of Scene of Crime details, Modus Operandi, offences, found exhibits, and Forensic Science Service submissions. Anite's SOCRATES system – see http://www.aniteps.com/products/evidence_management.asp – is a suite of evidence tracking and management systems that not only record information from the crime scene and tracks evidence, but also manages workflow and Submissions. LOCARD – see http://www.locard.co.uk/index.html – uses a bar-code reader (interfaced with a laptop computer) to read in the bar code (printed on all evidence bags) so that all future reference to a particular item of evidence can be linked to this ID.

All the commercial systems have been designed to link with some of the Police Computer Systems, such as Holmes 2. It is interesting to note how the systems have approached the problem from slightly different angles. Whilst they support the digital representation and tracking of evidence, the manner in which a digital identifier is assigned to an item of evidence differs between systems, e.g. LOCARD directly pairs the evidence bag with its digital identifier through the use of bar-codes. Furthermore, the manner in which the system supports the overall activity of managing crime scene investigation differs, e.g. SOCRATES provides support for managing the workflow of several different forms of investigation, e.g. scene of crime, fingerprint etc.

Near-future developments appear to be directed at shortening the time between material being collected and analysed, and a suspect identified. To this end, there are several projects that use digital imaging to capture finger-marks or footwear marks, and then use these images for analysis. The advantage of such approaches is that the material is digitized and can be sent wirelessly to the analyst. Alternatively, the analysis could be performed at the scene itself, i.e. using 'lab-on-a-chip' concepts.

In this paper, we explore a concept system to support CSI. The intention is to develop technology that both fits with contemporary trends while also signalling potential developments to support shared awareness. To this end, we consider distributed cognition, case-based reasoning, wearable computers and shared awareness.

4 Case-based Reasoning

From table one, a second class of activity we wish to support is the use of previous experience in 'History' and 'Goal'. From an organizational perspective, changes in working practice means that CSIs now have much wider areas of coverage than previously and these tend to shared with colleagues who may work out of different offices. An obvious consequence of this move is that there is less likelihood of continually working in a small area and gaining 'local' knowledge of all the crimes that happened over the past few years. Leaving aside the question of whether the sheer amount of 'volume crime' can allow an individual to remember all cases, this raises an interesting question of how one might allow CSIs to share relevant experience. To consider this issue, we turn to Case-based Reasoning.

The premise of Case-based Reasoning is that instances of similar experiences can be grouped according to specific attributes. A typical example concerns the operation of a computer help-desk: customers call in with particular symptoms and are offered advice of actions to take. If there are ten cases which involve 'attribute X' and it was found that 'action y' solved the problem, then the next time 'attribute X' is presented, 'action y' can be offered. What is interesting about CBR is the notion that the pairing of attributes to actions is done automatically, i.e. there is no requirement for a human operator to type a query, and the manner in which the associations are drawn, i.e. the reasoning, arises through quite simple algorithms that are applied to the attributes. Thus, rather than defining the structure of the data or the manner in which attributes can be associated, CBR essentially allows associations to 'grow' with additional cases. The reasoning methods can vary from the fairly basic, such as correlation of cases in terms of specific attributes; to more complex, such clustering of cases by attribute and then finding the nearest neighbours to particular cases, or through the application of inductive algorithms to differentiate cases. Previous applications of CBR to crime-scene have been used to support the indexing of photographs [Pastra et al. 2003]. In our work, the main focus is less on the reasoning and more on the issue of creating 'cases'.

In our application (see Figure 1), each 'case' is added as a new line in spreadsheet of cases (in Excel), with the attributes being defined as columns. Adding a 'case' involves writing a defined data sentence that involves basic attributes that define the exhibit (see below). Within Excel, it is a simple matter to define macros

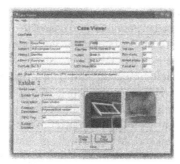

Figure 1: Case viewer.

that perform basic operations of these cases. For example, one can select the cases according to a specific attribute or set of attributes. Thus, if a new entry contains <location = car_park>, <incident = car_break_in> and <date = 30/01/06>, then it is possible to return cases with the same incident in the same location over the past few weeks. Of course, defining the algorithm that can return useful information will be a matter of further research. The point we are making in this paper is that it is possible to use CBR as a means of defining patterns in information collected, and to define simple rules to return sets of cases that may be of interest.

5 A Wearable Computer to Support CSI

The third class of activity identified in table one related to collecting exhibits without interruption. We have already claimed that the actions involved in finding material, collecting the material, analysing the material and then interpreting the analysis are performed by several people in several places in support of several goals using different representations. The representations need to be 'reliable, information, efficient, clear, accurate and malleable.' [Nemeth 2003]. These requirements can be taken further into functional requirements [Seagull et al. 2003]:

1. provide a common reference for communication;

2. provide a 'communal memory';

3. provide support for collaboration;

4. provide a mechanism for multiple manipulation of objects;

5. support flexible content-reconfiguration.

In addition to these requirements, we feel that it is essential for the technology to provide a means of supporting activity that does not interfere with current patterns of work and activity, e.g. if a computer system was introduced that required the scene of crime officer to continually stop ongoing activity in order to type information into the computer, this could interrupt their procedures. Furthermore, issues of contamination mean that it is necessary to make sure that any equipment taken into a crime scene has not be previously exposed to other scenes. In terms of requirements, we propose 'Seamless integration with current practice' and 'Minimal risk of contamination' to be added to the above list.

The notion that technology can fit into a distributed cognition view of CSI means that we wish to develop something that allows the user to focus as much as practicable on the scene itself, and for interaction with the scene to (in effect) serve also as the interaction with the computer. Thus, having identified an item of interest, the CSI could take a photograph of the item *in situ*, and then provide a verbal description of the item, or when an item is placed in an evidence bag (in order to become an exhibit), the ID of the evidence bag could be captured along with any further description. In essence, each item becomes a 'case' (in CBR terms) that can be tagged with photograph, ID of the evidence bag, location (say from GPS), verbal descriptions etc.– all of which can be collected without the CSI stopping the ongoing activity in order to complete forms. In this manner, the scene and items it contains remain the 'resources for action', with the CSI acting upon them (rather than switching attention between the scene and the computer, or other recording medium).

6 Designing a Prototype

The design for the MsSAM prototype followed standard human-centred design practice. In other words, a task analysis and series of field explorations were conducted. The initial task analysis was reported in Smith et al. [2005]. These lead to a set of requirements for a system to support contemporaneous logging of evidence during recovery. In addition to studying the activity of CSI, we have also been developing a theory, based on Distributed Cognition that relates evidence recovery to the notion that items at the crime scene represent resources for action, in terms of identification, recovery, and analysis [Baber et al. in press].

Whilst it is relatively easy to conceive of ways in which information can be collected and digitized, there remains a need to maintain focus on the actual work of the crime scene investigator. In this aspect, it is useful to draw an analogy with electronic patient records and evidence recovery and crime scene reports. Nygren et al. [1992] showed, patient records do not only contain data – they also, by the physical state of the records show how often the patient has been seen, or by the signatures on the forms who has provided treatment, or by the use of pencil or pen whether comments are definite or not. The point is that the patient records are both containers of information and means of representing additional information. It is likely that the evidence bags used in crime scene investigation, and the accompanying paperwork, could function in a similar manner. This means that simply replacing physical objects with digital versions might solve some problems, but introduce new ones. Tagging evidence bags goes some way to retaining the physicality of evidence bags, but more work is needed to understand how the forms and other records are used within the system. We link the wearable computer concept to that of Case-based Reasoning considered above. In order for the system to be useful, we feel that the entry of information to define each 'case' needs to be done in such a way as to be more or less implicit in the actions of the investigator; rather

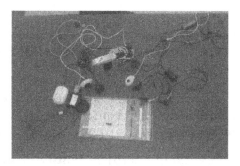

Figure 2: Prototype laid out on desk.

than having to complete forms or provide written descriptions (which would detract from the primary tasks of searching for and retrieving evidence), we use on-body technology to automatically log activity, and for this to be linked to the provision of feedback that can act as performance-support.

The prototype is built on a PC104 embedded PC board, and has SVGA out, two serial ports, on-board LAN and four USB ports. It is fairly small, measuring 170mm×40mm×100mm. The main unit is a 166MHz Pentium class chipset (expandable to up to 3.4GHz). The processor runs Windows XP and the application is written in C#. A Micro-optical head-mounted display can be used (with its own power source and data converter). A Fortuna Global Positioning System (GPS) is used for tracking the users' location. The RFID reader is a Texas Instrument unit (RI-STU-BB27-03). The RFID reader and GPS are connected to the serial ports. The USB ports are used by an Intel VGA web-cam, a microphone and headset, and a three-button mouse. The right mouse button is used to handle image capture and description, i.e. click the right mouse button once to preview the image, again to capture the image (which then prompts the user to speak a description) and then again to complete the recording of the description. The left button is used to start recording of scene descriptions. When the RFID tag is read, the user is prompted to provide a description of the item and its location (and then click the left button to end recording). Descriptions can be interpreted using Microsoft speech recognition modules, running from C# or can be stored as .wav files. The components are laid out on the desk in Figure 2.

The concept of use is as follows: on encountering an item that could be interpreted as evidence, the CSI takes a photograph of the item *in situ*, and provides a short description of both the item and the location. The description and location will be recognized through speech recognition, but additional 'voice-notes' can be added and stored as .wav files. The item will then be retrieved and placed in an evidence bag. As the bag is picked up, its RFID is read and the user is prompted to provide a name for the item. In this manner, a single item will have associated with it a photograph, an RFID code, and spoken descriptions. In terms of the user interface (viewed through the HMD), the user only needs to be able to preview images prior to capture. Thus, the user interface is simply a table showing each of the components of the data sentence required by the CBR system, e.g. {Date, Time, Location, Crime (from Crime Report), User Id, Image id, RF id, Description (from speech recognition), .wav file (for any associated speech)}.

The x3 is towards the top of the picture; the sensors (RFID, camera and GPS) are to the right; the user interface (headset and head-mounted display) are to the left. The evidence bag and blood swab, in the centre of the picture, are tagged with RFID chips to provide unique identification.

7   Preliminary Evaluation by Subject Matter Experts

Having developed a working prototype, an initial evaluation was conducted using undergraduate students [Baber et al. 2005b]. The MsSAM prototype was compared to the conventional practice of writing out evidence labels and logs. In a paper-based system, there is a need to record the same information more than once, e.g. the information recorded on the evidence labels is the same as that recorded in the log, and for the information to be entered from paper into a computer back at the office. In order to make the experiment a reasonable reflection of actual practice (even though we were using non-experts in this trial), we presented participants with three items to recover. In the paper condition, evidence labels and a log were completed; these included entering date, time, location, investigator ID and a brief description of the item. In the MsSAM prototype condition, date, general location and ID are captured automatically. The user can take a photograph of the item, and is prompted to provide verbal descriptions of the item and its precise location. Basically, the MsSAM system supported significantly faster performance, and led to more detailed descriptions of items (as measured by the number of words in a description). However, it is not obvious that similar results will result if the system is used by Subject Matter Experts, and so an additional trial was conducted at CENTREX[1].

7.1   Participants

This study involved five experienced Crime Scene Investigators (2 female, 3 male). The length of service ranged from 14 months (a recently appointed CSI) to 25 years (a recently retired CSI), although the median was around 9 years experience.

7.2   Procedure

The participants received an initial overview of the MsSAM system and an explanation of the study. They were told that they were required to complete evidence logs for three items provided to them, and that they were to complete these logs in as much detail as they deemed necessary. They were not placed under any time pressure. The experiment was run as a within-subjects design because it was felt that variations in approach might affect results. Thus, having the same people complete both conditions (counter-balanced to minimize order effects) could reduce possible contamination of results by approach.

The Scene involved a set of three items to be recovered in an office, i.e. a 3″ floppy disc, a business card, a screwdriver. Each item had to be described and then

---

[1] CENTREX is the UK Training Centre for scene of crime and forensic investigations within the Police Force.

	Time (MsSAM)	Time (Paper)	Words (MsSAM)	Words (Paper)
Study 1: Students	3.30	5.20	9.70	16.70
Study 2: CSIs	3.08	5.02	10.80	13.70
Difference	0.22	0.18	–1.10	3.00

Table 2: Comparison across studies.

placed in an evidence bag. In the paper condition, a label was completed for each evidence bag and a report of exhibits collected was written. The order in which items were retrieved was left to the discretion of participants. While this is a fairly crude version of the CSI task, it does (we feel) provide sufficient grounds for comparison of conditions and does reflect the aspects of information recording that is performed.

As far as possible, the approach that participants took to completing the paper forms was left to their own discretion. Completing the MsSAM system does assume a linear sequence of:

1. Take photograph of item *in situ.*

2. Provide a name for the item.

3. Pick up evidence bag and (when the RFID is read).

4. Enter a description of the location of the item.

5. Enter a description of the item.

7.3 Results

The study produced two sets of results: Performance Time and Word Count.

Performance time is defined as the time taken to completely enter details of all three items. For the MsSAM prototype, the mean time was 3.08 ($\pm$0.8) minutes, and for paper the mean time was 5.02 ($\pm$0.6) minutes. A paired t-test revealed that the difference in times was significant ($t(4) = 2.865$, $p < 0.05$). This suggests that, as with the earlier trials, there is a significant performance advantage for the MsSAM system.

In terms of word count, the mean number of words entered to describe the item and location was 10.8 words, while for the MsSAM prototype the mean number of words was 13.7. Again, a paired *t*-test revealed significant difference between conditions ($t(14) = 3.514$, $p < 0.005$). This suggests that the CSI producing longer descriptions when speaking than when writing.

Before concluding this section, it is instructive to contrast the results from the experienced CSIs with the students used in the earlier study (see Figure 2).

The differences between students and CSI performing the tasks are marginal to say the least. This is probably a reflection of the relative simplicity of the tasks used. However, it is interesting to note that a population of experienced computer users (i.e. engineering students) are no better than people who have had less experience of this sort of technology. The implication is that the prototype does not appear to lead to impairment on performance (as defined by the paper condition).

7.4　Conclusions

The study suggests that CSIs can use the MsSAM prototype and that performance may be superior to that of paper and manual recording. This finding is interesting because many of the current evidence management systems are attempting to computerize the paper forms, i.e. requiring CSIs to type rather than write information (although in the case of a 'digital pen', the information is written on paper and then uploaded to a computer). These developments see the primary challenge as being the digitization of paper-forms. In our work, we see the challenge as the creation of digital information from CSI activity.

Response to the system was generally positive. The main feeling seemed to be that anything that took the burden of paperwork from the job was worth looking at. One participant commented that he felt that the system would allow all of his attention to be on search and retrieval of evidence rather than having to interrupt this activity to complete forms.

8　Discussion

In this paper, we have considered the manner in which shared awareness can be supported by on-body technology and case-based reasoning (CBR). The aim is to provide a means by which CSIs can collect exhibits and to have a record of their activity created as they perform their activity. In this way, the completion of written labels for exhibits and report forms to log a search could be replaced by a digital representation. The possibility of including photographs as part of the record, and the potential use of speech recognition have been responded to very favourably by the CSIs we have spoken to and demonstrated the system to. Taking this information, via wireless Local Area Network (WLAN) provides a means by which people can collaborate on their work. Previous work has demonstrated this concept, and this represents a possible next step for the current work.

Creating the attributes of 'cases' for CBR means that it is possible to provide feedback to CSI at the scene, on the basis of automatically generated patterns of examples. This could, for example, highlight incidents within a particular area or could indicate similar types of incident over a defined time period. The fact that such patterns arise from submitting a 'case' (which has been automatically created as the result of particular search activities) provides a means of sharing the experiences of colleagues – records of previous searches can be linked to current activity. The aim is not, of course, to eliminate communication between CSIs but to flag-up possible patterns of incidents, exhibits and activity that they might previously not have considered.

By linking exhibit collection to location, by incorporating imaging as an integral part of this process, and by considering patterns of attributes (through CBR), we are approaching a view of shared awareness in which multiple sources of information (much of which will be generated automatically) can be shared by people working on crime scene investigation. Of the many challenges this raises, one of the most interesting (in terms of human-computer interaction) relates to the ways in which such information can be displayed and interacted with. Our belief is that having an image of the scene, and overlaying the location and activity of CSIs, together with the location and subsequent results of analysis of exhibits, provides an interesting starting point for such a system and this is currently under development [Cross et al. 2003].

Acknowledgements

The work reported in this paper is supported by a grant from the Engineering and Physical Sciences Research Council (EPSRC GR/S85115 MsSAM: Methods to Support Shared Analysis for Mobile Investigators).

References

Baber, C., Cross, J. & Houghton, R. J. [2005a], Distributed Collaboration in a Remote Search Task: Comparison of Datalink and Audio Communications, *in* P. D. Bust & P. T. McCabe (eds.), *Contemporary Ergonomics 2005*, Taylor & Francis, pp.64–8.

Baber, C., Smith, P., Cross, J., Hunter, J. & McMaster, R. [in press], Crime Scene Investigation as Distributed Cognition, *Pragmatics and Cognition* .

Baber, C., Smith, P., Cross, J., Zasikowski, D. & Hunter, J. [2005b], Wearable Technology for Crime Scene Investigation, *in Proceedings of the 9th International Symposium on Wearable Computers (ISWC 2005)*, IEEE Computer Society Press, pp.138–43.

Cross, J., Baber, C. & Woolley, S. I. [2003], Layered Annotations of Digital Images for Data Collection in the Field, *in Digest of Papers of the 7th International Symposium on Wearable Computing*, IEEE Computer Society Press, pp.154–9.

Flor, N. & Hutchins, E. L. [1991], Analyzing Distributed Cognition In Software Teams: A Case Study Of Team Programming During Perfective Software Maintenance, *in* J. Koenemann-Belliveau, T. G. Moher & S. P. Robertson (eds.), *Empirical Studies of Programmers: Fourth Workshop*, Ablex, pp.36–64.

Hollan, J., Hutchins, E. & Kirsch, D. [2002], Distributed Cognition: Toward a New Foundation for Human–Computer Interaction, *in* J. M. Carroll (ed.), *Human–Computer Interaction in the New Millenium*, Addison–Wesley, pp.75–94.

Hutchins, E. [1995], How a Cockpit Remembers its Speeds, *Cognitive Science* **19**(3), 265–88.

Nemeth, C. [2003], How Cognitive Artifacts Support Distributed Cognition In Acute Care, *in Proceedings of the Human Factors and Ergonomics Society 47th Annual Meeting*, Human Factors and Ergonomics Society, pp.381–5.

Nygren, E., Johnson, M. & Hendrickson, P. [1992], Reading the Medical Record. I. Analysis of Physicians' Ways of Reading the Medical Record, *Computer Methods and Programs in Biomedicine* **39**(1-2), 1–12.

Pastra, K., Saggion, H. & Wilks, Y. [2003], Extracting Relational Facts for Indexing and Retrieval of Crime-scene Photographs, *Knowledge-based Systems* **16**(5-6), 313–20.

Seagull, F. J., Plasters, C., Xiao, Y. & Mackenzie, C. F. [2003], Collaborative Management of Complex Coordination Systems: Operating Room Schedule Coordination, *in Proceedings of the Human Factors and Ergonomics Society 47th Annual Meeting*, Human Factors and Ergonomics Society, pp.1521–5.

Smith, P., Baber, C., Wooley, S., Cross, J. & Hunter, J. [2005], A Task Analysis of Crime Scene Investigation, *in* P. D. Bust & P. T. McCabe (eds.), *Contemporary Ergonomics 2005: Proceedings of the International Conference of the Contemporary Ergonomics (CE 2005)*, CRC Press, pp.331–5.

Suchman, L. A. [1987], *Plans and Situated Actions — The Problem of Human–Machine Communication*, Cambridge University Press.

Toulmin, S, E. [1958], *The Uses of Argument*, Cambridge University Press.

Wright, P. C., Fields, R. E. & Harrison, M. D. [2000], Analysing Human–Computer Interaction as Distributed Cognition: The Resources Model, *Human–Computer Interaction* **15**(1), 1–41.

Interaction for Me

The Beam Cursor: A Pen-based Technique for Enhancing Target Acquisition

Jibin Yin & Xiangshi Ren

Kochi University of Technology, 185 Miyanokuchi Tosayamada town, Japan

Tel: *+81 887 57 2209*

Fax: *+81 887 57 2220*

Email: *088402e@gs.kochi-tech.ac.jp, ren.xiangshi@kochi-tech.ac.jp*

URL: *http://www.gs.kochi-tech.ac.jp/088402e/, http://www.info.kochi-tech.ac.jp/ren/*

In this paper we introduce a novel interaction technique that improves target acquisition in pen-based interfaces. This technique is called Beam Cursor. The Beam Cursor exploits the sliding motion and dynamically updates the effective width of targets on screen according to the original location of the pen-tip, such that even if the pen-tip lands in the vicinity of a target the target can easily be selected. We also provide reports on two controlled experiments which were performed to evaluate the Beam Cursor in both 1D (dimension) and 2D target selection tasks on the pen-based interface. The experimental results indicate that the Beam Cursor is modelled on and predicted by Fitts' Law and that it is governed by the effective width of the targets. Results also show that the Beam Cursor significantly outperforms the Point Cursor and the Bubble Cursor [Grossman & Balakrishnan 2005].

Keywords: slide touch, beam cursor, Fitts' Law, graphical user interface, target selection.

1 Introduction

Target selection is a very common task of many graphical user interfaces (GUIs). As the number of selectable user interface elements increases the selection task becomes

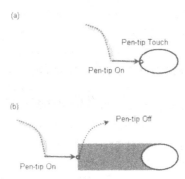

Figure 1: The ellipses illustrate targets. (a) The Slide Touch strategy: the pen-tip initially lands outside the target then slides towards the target; when the pen-tip touches the target the target is selected. (b) The Beam Cursor: the pen-tip lands on the screen surface then slides towards the desired target and the target is pre-selected and contained within a 'beam' (shaded area) which is emitted from the cursor in the direction of the target; when the pen-tip is lifted the target is selected.

more complex, so that studies aimed at improving target selection have become essential and very significant. Hence, many researchers have proposed various techniques that attempt to enhance target selection. At present, mobile computing devices such as PDAs, Tablet PCs and whiteboards are used widely. However, with few exceptions [Guan et al. 2004; Ren & Moriya 2000], most of these new techniques have been designed for mice. But the selection of targets using a stylus pen has some specific and unique characteristics which do not apply to the mouse interface. Two examples are, the lifting and pressing of the pen-tip and the sliding of the pen tip across the screen surface. Obviously, selection techniques that are suitable for mouse interfaces do not necessarily suit the special characteristics of stylus pens. Conversely, it seems equally obvious that the optimal performances of each of these significantly different devices will be achieved by significantly different kinds of operations, techniques and graphic elements.

Therefore, we present the Beam Cursor, a new selection technique which is based on the Slide Touch strategy [Ren & Moriya 2000], which is tailored for pen-based interfaces. Ren & Moriya studied several selection task techniques for pen-based interfaces and drew the conclusion that the Slide Touch strategy (Figure 1a) outperformed the other five selecting task techniques that they tested. In this technique, the pen-tip initially lands outside a target then slides towards the target; when the pen-tip touches the target the target is selected. The Beam Cursor enhances this technique by adding a virtual target size to the normal physical target size. The virtual target size feature means that the Beam Cursor dynamically updates the effective region of targets. When the pen-tip touches the screen surface, the Beam Cursor uses the initial contact point as a reference point, and divides the total space in which all targets reside into regions, so that there is just one target inside each region. When the pen-tip slides towards a target and enters the effective region of the target, the target is pre-selected and is contained by the beam (transparent red shading) which is 'emitted' from the cursor. When the pen-tip is taken off the screen surface the target is selected. (Figure 1b)

In the following sections, we will review previously published research reports dealing with pointing facilitation. We will then discuss the design and implementation of the Beam Cursor, evaluate the performance of the Beam Cursor in two experiments, and show that the Beam Cursor's performance can be modelled by Fitts' Law. We will conclude by discussing some implications for user interface design and also future work.

2 Related Work

2.1 Expanding Target or Reducing Distance

Fitts' Law [1954] is commonly used to predict the time it takes to move a mouse pointer from one location to another.

$$MT = a + b \log_2 \left(\frac{A}{W} + 1 \right)$$

According to Fitts' Law, the cursor movement time (MT) increases linearly with the Index of Difficulty (ID), which relies on the logarithm of the distance moved (the amplitude, A) and the width of the target (W). The two constants, a and b, are determined empirically and depend on cognition, motor preparation time and on hand-eye coordination. With respect to Fitts' Law, there are two simple ways to reduce the difficulty of a pointing task: increasing the target width or reducing the amplitude.

Regarding the virtual target size, a target has an effective width which can be defined as the effective area of a target which has been expanded beyond it's physical graphical width. One approach to improving target acquisition is to increase the target's width. McGuffin & Balakrishnan [2002] closely examined the degree to which Fitts' Law modelled actions aimed at selecting expanding targets in one-dimensional tasks. They found that Fitts' Law accurately models the performance of such actions, and that movement time is primarily governed by the final expanded size of the target. This result held even when the targets began expanding after most of the movement towards the target (90%) was complete. McGuffin & Balakrishnan's study examined selection of a single object with no surrounding objects, so the influence of distraction due to movement of neighbouring objects was not examined.

Kabbash & Buxton [1995] investigated the use of area cursors. The basic idea is that an area cursor has a larger active region or hotspot for target selection, rather than a single pixel hotspot as in standard cursors. Kabbash & Buxton showed that by setting W to be the width of the area cursor, selection of a single pixel target could be accurately modelled using Fitts' Law. Thus, very small targets would have a much lower index of difficulty when selected by an area cursor. However, a problem of ambiguity arises when the desktop environment is densely populated with targets, as multiple targets could fall inside the area cursor at one time. Grossman & Balakrishnan [2005] proposed the Bubble Cursor which improves upon area cursors by dynamically resizing its activation area depending on the proximity of surrounding targets, so that only one target is selectable at any time. The evaluation results prove that the Bubble Cursor significantly reduces target acquisition times in both simple and complex multi-target environments.

A way to reduce A (the amplitude) is to bring the target closer to the cursor. Bezerianos & Balakrishnan [2005] developed the vacuum technique which can bring distance targets closer to the widget's centre in the form of proxies that can be manipulated in lieu of the original. This technique is suitable for large screens. An alternative is to jump the cursor to the target. Guiard et al. [2004] proposed a selection technique called Object Pointing. In this technique the cursor never visits the empty regions of graphical space. It jumps from one selectable target to another. Object Pointing was found to be considerably faster than regular pointing in a 1D reciprocal pointing task. However in a 2D environment, it was shown that the degree to which object pointing outperformed regular pointing was dependent upon the density of the targets.

There have been a number of efforts to facilitate pointing by dynamically adjusting the control display (CD) gain. Worden et al. [1997] implemented 'Sticky Icons' by decreasing the mouse control-display gain when the cursor enters the icon. Control-display gain determines the mapping between physical mouse movement and resultant cursor movement. In this way, the user must move the mouse further to escape the boundary of the icon, effectively making the icon larger without using extra screen space. Worden et al.'s evaluation showed Sticky Icons to be efficient for selecting small targets. In a technique called *semantic pointing*, Blanch et al. [2004] showed that performance could be predicted using Fitts' Law, based on the resulting larger W and smaller A in motor space. Once again, however, problems arise when multiple targets are presented as the intervening targets will slow the cursor down as it travels to its destination target.

2.2   Selection Techniques for Pen-based Interfaces

Although many target selection techniques have been proposed as described above, the corpus of relevant literature is lacking in studies of selection techniques for pen-based interfaces. Ren & Moriya [2000] and Guan et al. [2004] are the exceptions. Ren & Moriya compared pen-based selection techniques and their characteristics, and proved that the proposed Slide Touch strategy is the best of the six techniques. Slide Touch is where the target is selected at the moment the pen-tip touches the target for the first time after landing on the screen surface. The experimental results show that it is particularly useful in situations where the target is isolated or where targets are arranged sparsely. Guan et al. presented the *Zoom Selector* which pre-selects, enlarges and relocates the targets covered by a transparent round circle into a large pie sector to enhance the target's acquisition. The evaluation results indicate that the Zoom Selector outperforms the normal click method when used for small targets. It is suitable for small target acquisition or situations where targets are arranged densely.

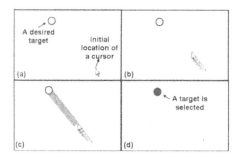

Figure 2: (a) A pen-tip lands on screen surfaces and its initial location is recorded; (b) the pen-tip slides to the desired target; (c) when the cursor enters the effective region of a target the target is contained by a transparent red beam emitting from the cursor; (d) the pen-tip lifts from the screen surface then the target is selected.

3   Beam Cursor Design and Implementation

The Beam Cursor is an interaction technique that enables quick access to targets on areas of a pen-based display. The Beam Cursor employs the *sliding* action of the stylus pen and dynamically updates the effective width of the target according to the contact point of the pen-tip and the layout of the surrounding targets, thus enhancing the target's acquisition. When the pen-tip lands on the screen and slides towards a target, the target is included in a 'beam' which is 'emitted' from the cursor. This means that the target is pre-selected as the stylus approaches and it is selected when the pen-tip is lifted from the screen surface (see Figure 2).

In designing the Beam Cursor, we explicitly sought to address Slide Touch, which is the inspiration of the Beam Cursor.

Slide Touch [Ren & Moriya 2000] is the technique whereby the target is selected at the moment the pen-tip touches the target for the first time after landing on the screen surface. It is a very useful selection technique for pen-based interfaces. However, the technique requires the pen-tip to touch the target which is to be selected before selection can be affected. The Beam Cursor combines the virtual target concept and the Slide Touch strategy to enhance target acquisition. That is, every target is allocated an effective width which is bigger than its physical width. The following section discusses how the effective width is allocated to each target.

Regarding virtual target size, every target has an effective width based on its physical width in motor space. During the actual process of target selection, the user can first determine the target to select. Aiming at the desired target, the Beam Cursor allocates the effective regions of all the targets to enable the desired target to occupy a much bigger effective region. A simple algorithm is used to continuously update the effective regions of targets (see Figure 3).

- When the pen-tip lands on the screen surface, the contact point is recorded as the reference point.

- Taking that point as the centre point, the Beam Cursor divides the total space

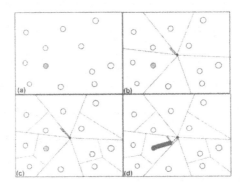

Figure 3: (a) There are many targets in the screen, where the solid blue target is the goal target; (b) When pen lands on screen surface, the initial point is recorded as reference point, which is used as a centre point to divide the screen into n sectors (to clear demonstrate the principle, n is set at 6 in the figure 3. At fact, Beam cursor sets n at 15.). The targets in the same sector constitute a group. (c) Targets in the same group are allocated effective regions according to the Voronoi diagram principle. (d) When a cursor slides into a certain sector the target that is closest to it is pre-selected.

into n (Based on an informal test *n* is set at 15) equal sectors. The targets in the same sector constitute a group.

- Targets in the same group are allocated effective regions according to the Voronoi diagram principle. So when a cursor slides into a certain sector the target that is closest to it is pre-selected.

Based on this algorithm the pen-tip can land on any possible position in the vicinity of the target to enable it to have a much bigger effective region. The pen-tip then to travel a very short distance to enter the effective region of the desired target. Even if the pen-tip lands on a position imprecisely, a slight movement towards the target affects pre-selection of the desired target. When the cursor enters the effective region of a target the target is contained by a transparent red beam emitting from the cursor. This acts as a reinforcing visual cue to the user, showing that the desired target is indeed pre-selected by the cursor, thus reducing the cognitive load of the user and eliminating any uncertainty about which target will be selected when the pen is removed.

With respect to 'abort' of a selection task, the selection task can be cancelled by withdrawing the pen-tip to its initial location area.

4 Experiment 1

The Beam Cursor not only enlarges the effective width of the target but also dynamically updates it, based on the pen-tip's initial landing point on the screen surface. From previous work on expanding targets [McGuffin & Balakrishnan 2002; Zhai et al. 2003], it was found that users were able to take advantage of the larger expanded target width even when expansion occurred after 90% of the distance to the target had already been traveled. It was also shown that overall performance could be modelled accurately by Fitts' Law by setting W to the expanded target width. So we would expect that Fitts' Law would hold in situations where the effective width of targets dynamically changes when selecting targets. However, the Beam Cursor has a few specific properties that make it difficult to directly apply Fitts' Law to model it.

1. Once the pen-tip lands on the screen surface, the effective width of the target changes.

2. Before capturing a target, the Beam Cursor should be slid towards the target for a very short distance.

It is important to empirically determine if Fitts' Law holds for Beam Cursors. This is the first goal of Experiment 1.

Even if the Fitts' Law is shown to model the Beam Cursor performance accurately, this does not necessarily mean that the Beam Cursor provides a significant advantage over Point Cursors. Furthermore, the Beam Cursor enhances target acquisition by enlarging the effective width of targets. And, based on the principle of allocating the effective region to the intended target, the Beam Cursor expands the effective width of the target the user wants to select while shrinking other targets. So we wondered whether the performance is governed by the effective width rather than the actual width of the target. In other words, selecting a target with an actual width W and an effective width EW with a Beam Cursor should be equivalent to selecting a target with an actual width of EW with a regular Point Cursor. Thus, the second goal of Experiment 1 is to determine whether performance is governed by and makes maximum use of the effective width.

To answer these questions in a systematic manner, we begin by studying the Beam Cursor performance in the simplest possible pointing task: 1D target acquisition. We compare the Beam Cursor with the Point Cursor in Experiment 1.

4.1 Apparatus

The hardware used in Experiment 1 was the Fujitsu Tablet PC running Microsoft Windows XP. It weighed 1.48kg, and was 210.432mm (W) × 157.824mm (H). The spatial resolution of the screen was 0.2055mm pixel^{-1}. The software for the experiment was developed using Sun Microsystems Java.

4.2 Participants

Ten subjects (all male) who had all had previous experience with computers were tested for the experiment. The average age was 22.3. All subjects had normal or 'corrected to normal' vision with no colour blindness, were right handed, and used the pen in the right hand.

4.3 Procedure and Design

The task was a reciprocal 1D pointing task in which subjects were required to select two fixed targets back and forth. The targets were arranged as solid circles, keeping a distance between them along the horizontal axis. The target to be selected was coloured green, and the other target was red. In reality, if there were only two targets

Figure 4: The setup of the 1D reciprocal pointing experiment. The green circle is the target to be selected. The red circle is the next goal target. Blue circles are placed to control the *EW/W* ratio. Note: *EW* is an approximate value, which is gotten based on the effective width allocation principle of Beam Cursor.

on the screen, the effective width of targets in a Beam Cursor interface would be very big. The subject would only have to move the stylus pen a very short distance to select the target. Thus, to simulate the realistic target acquisition scenario some distracter targets were placed around both goal targets such that their effective widths (*EW*) were controlled. Distracters were rendered as blue solid circles (see Figure 4). Subjects were instructed to select between the two targets alternately. They were told to emphasize both accuracy and speed. When the subject correctly selected the target she or he would hear a beep sound and the targets would swap colours, which was an indication that the subject had to now move towards and select the other target which was now green.

The design of the experiment was as follows: crossed cursor technique (*CT*) × amplitude (*A*) × width (*W*) × effective width (*EW*). A full crossed design resulted in 54 combinations of *CT* (Point Cursor, Beam Cursor), *A* (288, 576, 864 pixels), *W* (12, 24, 36 pixels), *EW* (48, 96, 144 pixels). Each subject had a total of 27 combinations (3 amplitudes × 3 target widths × 3 target effective widths) appearing in random order (partial counterbalancing) for each technique. Each combination consisted of 5 selection attempts (i.e. 4 reciprocal movements between the 2 targets). At the start of the experiment, for each cursor technique, subjects were given a warm-up block of attempts to familiarize them with the task and conditions. Each subject performed the experiment in one session lasting approximately 30 minutes, depending on each subject's proficiency in selecting the targets. The session was broken up according to cursor technique. Whenever the subject felt tired she or he was allowed to take a rest.

4.4 Results

An ANOVA (analysis of variance) with repeated measures was used to analyse performance in terms of movement time, error rate and subjective preference. Post hoc analysis was performed with Tukey's honestly significant difference (HSD) test.

4.4.1 Selection Time

The analysis showed that there was significant difference between the Point Cursor and the Beam Cursor in selection time, $F(1,19) = 14.62$, $p < 0.005$. The overall mean selection times were 945 milliseconds for the Point Cursor and 701 milliseconds for

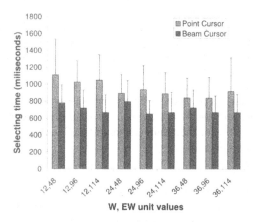

Figure 5: The mean selection time by W, EW values for both cursors.

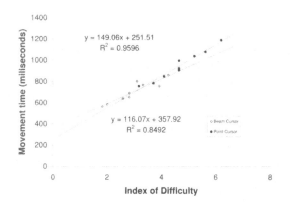

Figure 6: Line regression of target distance against movement time.

the Beam Cursor. A repeated measures analysis of variance also showed a significant main effect for W, $F(2,57) = 63.11$, $p < 0.001$; EW, $F(2,57) = 106.54$, $p < 0.001$; and A, $F(2,57) = 94.86$, $p < 0.001$. As Figure 5 illustrates, performance of the Beam Cursor is dependent on EW rather than W whereas performance of the Point Cursor depends on W.

Figure 6 plots the movement time as a function of the index of difficulty (ID). For the Point Cursor, we define ID as $\log_2(A/W + 1)$, while for the Beam Cursor, $\log_2(A/EW + 1)$. Linear regression analysis showed that the Point Cursor fits the Fitts' Law equation with $r^2 = 0.9596$ and the Beam Cursor fits the Fitts' Law equation with $r^2 = 0.8492$. Here the r^2 value is a little low, which is due to the fact that the effective width of targets is an approximation based on the allocation principle of the effective width in Experiment 1. This means that selection using the Beam Cursor can not only be modelled using Fitts' Law, but selection is just as fast as if the target had an actual width of *EW* and a Point Cursor were being used.

4.4.2 Error Score

The analysis of mean error score shows that there was no significant difference between the Point Cursor and the Beam Cursor. Overall error rates were 3.08% for the Point Cursor and 3.51% for the Beam Cursor, all well within the typical < 4% range seen in target acquisition studies.

4.4.3 Subjective Preference

There was a significant difference between the Point Cursor and the Beam Cursor in subjective preference, $F(1,18) = 8.00$, $p < 0.05$. Subjects gave the Beam Cursor a significantly higher rating than the Point Cursor. Several mentioned that they found the Beam Cursor gave them a more comfortable wide selection region for targets, especially for small targets.

5 Experiment 2

Experiment 1 determined that the Fitts' Law can model the Beam Cursor and predict the selection time in 1D reciprocal pointing tasks. The experimental results show that Fitts' Law can model and predict the Beam Cursor. It also shows that selection performance is governed by the effective width of targets rather than their physical width. In Experiment 1, the Beam Cursor significantly reduced selection time, which further indicates that increasing the effective width of targets does enhance target acquisition.

However, the experiment on 1D targets is an easy and abstract scenario contrasting to actual user interfaces. So we wondered whether the Beam Cursor delivers the same advantages with complex 2D situations. In the second experiment, we explore the Beam Cursor's performance in a more realistic environment with multiple 2D targets with various target widths and layout densities.

If the space surrounding targets is bigger, the effective width of targets will be bigger. In Experiment 2 we will probe this further. And we include the Bubble Cursor [Grossman & Balakrishnan 2005] which is discussed in the related work section. This technique is perhaps more promising than other existing techniques for improving target acquisition. In the previous work on the Bubble Cursor, it is found that, taking mice as the input device, the Bubble Cursor significantly decreases selection time. So we wondered if the Bubble Cursor offers the same advantage when a stylus pen is the input device? In other words, we wanted to know whether the technique that is suitable for mice is also as suitable for stylus pens. Since the Beam Cursor is a direct extension of the Slide Touch strategy, there is no reason to expect it to perform *worse* than Slide Touch. This was confirmed in pilot studies, and as such we did not include Slide Touch in our experimental comparison.

5.1 Apparatus

The apparatus was the same as in Experiment 1.

5.2 Participants

Ten subjects (all male) who had all had previous experience in computers were tested for the experiment. The average age was 21.4 years. Four of them were test subjects in Experiment 1. All subjects had normal or 'corrected to normal' vision with no colour blindness, all were right handed, and all used the pen in the right hand.

5.3 Procedure and Design

This experiment tested 2-dimensional and multiple target display arrangements. The selection task was serial in contrast to the simple reciprocating movement required for Experiment 1. The target to be selected was green and the others were pale red.

In this experiment, subjects were required to select the green target which appeared randomly among a number of pale red targets on the display. When a selection performance was finished, that green target would change to red and another target would become green indicating that it is the new target. This design required the user to jump in any direction on the screen, not just horizontally as in Experiment 1.

Subjects needed to finish multiple sets of selection tasks. For each set of selection tasks, the number and the width of targets on the screen were different. When the experiment began, the subject saw a green target. The time for the task was recorded from the moment the first green target was selected. Each interval for the two selection actions was recorded. This allowed us to analyse the time of each selection and the total time of all the selection tasks. A successful selection resulted in a beep sound. If no beep sound was heard, it meant that an error had occurred. The feedback we provided was the same as in Experiment 1. When a target was preselected it would be contained by a transparent red beam emitted from the cursor.

The design of the experiment was as follows: crossed cursor technique (CT) × width (W) × density (D). A full crossed design resulted in 27 combinations of CT (Beam, Point, Bubble), W (12, 24, 36 pixels), D (6, 12, 30). For each of the 3 techniques, 9 combinations (3 target widths × 3 target densities) appeared in a random order. Each subject had a total of 144 attempts (3 widths × (6 + 12 + 30) densities). At the start of the experiment, subjects were given a warm-up session for each cursor technique to familiarize them with the task and the conditions. Each subject performed the experiment in approximately forty minutes, depending on individual proficiency. The experiment was broken up according to cursor technique. Whenever the subject felt tired she or he was allowed to take a rest.

5.4 Results

5.4.1 Selection Time

A repeated measures analysis of variance showed that there was a significant interaction between the three cursor techniques in selection time. The post hoc Tukey (HDS) test showed that the Beam Cursor was faster than both the Point Cursor and the Bubble Cursor $F(2,27) = 6.11$, $p < 0.01$. No significant interaction was found in selection times between the Point Cursor and the Bubble Cursor. The overall mean selection times were 158 seconds for the Beam Cursor, 199 seconds for the Point Cursor and 188 seconds for the Bubble Cursor (see Figure 7). The results clearly show that the Beam Cursor can improve target acquisition in complex

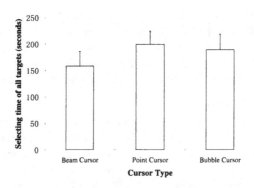

Figure 7: The overall mean selection time for the three cursor techniques.

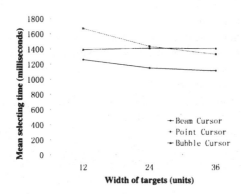

Figure 8: The mean selection time for targets of different target widths.

2D experimental circumstances. The fact that there was no significant interaction between the Point Cursor and the Bubble Cursor is due to the different experiment apparatuses. On a pen-based interface and using a stylus pen, the Beam Cursor significantly surpasses the Bubble Cursor [Grossman & Balakrishnan 2005]. That is, in the experimental circumstances of a pen-based interface, the constant lifting of the pen-tip, limits the advantage of the Bubble Cursor. The results also indicate that the selection targets using a stylus pen has its own specific characteristics and that selection techniques that suit mice are not necessarily suitable for stylus pens.

Target width: A significant difference in selection time was observed between the three cursor techniques for each target width, 12, 24 and 36 pixels, $F(2,27) = 142.59$, $F(2,27) = 98.6$ and $F(2,27) = 63.28$, $p < 0.001$. This means that significant differences in selection times remained when the target width was varied. As seen in Figure 8, with the target width increasing the selection

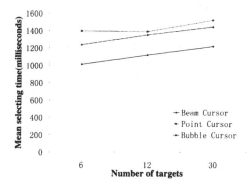

Figure 9: The mean selection time for targets in layouts with different target densities.

time did not significantly decrease for the Beam Cursor. This is due to the fact that the Beam Cursor is governed by the effective width of targets, not the physical width of the target.

Target density: A significant difference in selection time was observed between the three cursor techniques for each target density, 6, 12 and 30, $F(2,27) = 30.9$, $F(2,27) = 81.65$ and $F(2,27) = 99.41$, $p < 0.001$. This means that significant differences in selection times remained when the target density was varied. As seen in Figure 9, when the target density was small the difference between the Beam Cursor and the Point Cursor became more significant. This was due to the fact that, when the target density was small, the void space among the targets became wider and the effective width of targets increased. So, for the situation in which targets are placed tightly together, the Beam Cursor probably has a little advantage in selection time.

5.4.2 Error Score

The analysis of the mean error score showed that there was no significant difference between the Beam Cursor, the Point Cursor and the Bubble Cursor. Overall error rates were 2.81% for the Beam Cursor, 3.55% for the Point Cursor and 2.21% for the Bubble Cursor, all well within the typical < 4% range seen in target acquisition studies.

5.4.3 Subjective Preference

There was a significant difference between the Beam Cursor, the Point Cursor and the Bubble Cursor in subjective preference, $F(2,27) = 6.58$, $p < 0.01$. The post hoc Tukey (*HSD*) test showed that the Beam Cursor and the Bubble Cursor were both better than the Point Cursor. No significant interaction was found between the Beam Cursor and the Bubble Cursor.

6 Discussion and Conclusion

The article proposes an interactive technique called Beam Cursor, which enables the quick selection of targets on pen-based interfaces. The Beam Cursor employs the sliding motion and dynamically updates the effective width of targets according to the initial contact point of the pen-tip and the layout of the surrounding targets. The aim is to enhance target acquisition. We then described the methods and results of Experiment 1 and Experiment 2 respectively.

Experiment 1 verified that the Beam Cursor can be modelled and predicted by Fitts' Law using the one dimension reciprocal pointing task. We compared the Beam Cursor with the Point Cursor. The evaluation results show that Fitts' Law can model the Beam Cursor and predict the selection time. Selection performance is governed mainly by the effective width of targets, not by the physical width of targets. The Beam Cursor outperforms the Point Cursor for the different E/EW ratio.

Experiment 1 is a simple abstract experimental circumstance. Experiment 2 further evaluates the effectiveness of the Beam Cursor on target acquisition. In the second experiment we introduced a current promising selection technique, the Bubble Cursor. We evaluate the three selection techniques under the condition of different target densities and different target widths. The experimental results indicate that the Beam Cursor is better than both the Point Cursor and the Bubble Cursor. There is no significant difference between the Point Cursor and the Bubble Cursor.

Pen devices have specific interactive characteristics: e.g. the lifting and pressing of the pen-tip and the ability to slide the pen-tip on the screen surface. When contrasted with the normal click of a mouse, the unsteadiness of the pen tip can make the press and click action inaccurate. This unsteadiness makes it difficult for users to hit a precise point on a target. According to our observations, it is very common for the pen tip to make contact within a larger range near but outside the target because of the touch screen's slipperiness and the pen tip's vibrations. Therefore, allowing some tolerance in the initial location of the pen-tip and providing a simple means of adjustment via a hand movement which approaches the target would appear to greatly decrease the effect of an imprecise touchdown as well as decreasing the cognitive load of the user. That is why the Beam Cursor exploits the *sliding* motion.

Virtual targets means that every target has an effective width based on its physical width in its relation to the motor space surrounding it. Actually, selection techniques, such as the area cursor [Kabbash & Buxton 1995] and the Bubble Cursor [Grossman & Balakrishnan 2005], expand the target width to enhance selection performance. In other words these techniques make full use of the void space around the targets in motor space. The Bubble Cursor employs the Voronoi diagram to increase target size in motor space to the maximum. However, the Beam Cursor allocates the effective region to targets giving priority to the desired target. The goal of this allocation principle is to endow a much bigger effective region to the desired target. As seen from the experimental results, the Beam Cursor indeed reduces the selection time.

We also found the Beam Cursor to be better than the Bubble Cursor, one of the more promising selection techniques in the literature. However, we must be careful before drawing too many conclusions about the relatively poor performance of the Bubble Cursor in our experiment. The Bubble Cursor is able to enhance selection performance where mice are used as input devices. We compared the Beam Cursor with the Bubble Cursor in the pen-based interface, and found that this environment limits the advantage of the Bubble Cursor to some extent. This indicates that selection techniques designed for mice are probably not suitable for stylus pens.

Another characteristic of the Beam Cursor is that it enhances target acquisition without changing the position and size of targets, unlike some other selection techniques [Guan et al. 2004; Zhai et al. 2003], The Beam Cursor dynamically updates the effective width of targets without altering the arrangement of items on the screen.

The effective width determines the selection performance of the Beam Cursor and the void space around targets governs their effective width. So even if a target is very small but its surrounding void space is wide, its effective width is still big and its Index of Difficulty (*ID*) with regard to selection is quite small. Obviously, the Beam Cursor does not yield any benefit for target selection on a screen where the targets are laid side to side because there is almost no void space among the targets and the effective width of targets is almost equal to their physical width.

The positive results from our experiments suggest that the Beam Cursor could be a beneficial addition to user interfaces. We can develop a plug-in to incorporate the Beam Cursor into user interfaces. This would be very appropriate to exploit 'selection' mode. We can design an appropriate command to allow switching between the Beam Cursor and the Point Cursor. For example, we can set a command button on the taskbar; when the user wants to select targets by Beam Cursor, she or he would just click the command button to activate the Beam Cursor. Or it may be activated by setting this command as an item in the pop-up menu which is also convenient for the user.

References

Bezerianos, A. & Balakrishnan, R. [2005], The Vacuum: Facilitating the Manipulation of Distant Objects, *in* G. van der Veer & C. Gale (eds.), *Proceedings of SIGCHI Conference on Human Factors in Computing Systems (CHI'05)*, ACM Press, pp.361–70.

Blanch, R., Guiard, Y. & Beaudouin-Lafon, M. [2004], Semantic Pointing: Improving Target Acquisition with Control-display Ratio Adaptation, *in* E. Dykstra-Erickson & M. Tscheligi (eds.), *Proceedings of SIGCHI Conference on Human Factors in Computing Systems (CHI'04)*, ACM Press, pp.519–25.

Fitts, P. M. [1954], The Information Capacity of the Human Motor System in Controlling Amplitude of Movement, *Journal of Experimental Psychology* **47**(6), 381–91.

Grossman, T. & Balakrishnan, R. [2005], The Bubble Cursor: Enhancing Target Acquisition by Dynamic Resizing of the Cursor's Activation Area, *in* G. van der Veer & C. Gale (eds.), *Proceedings of SIGCHI Conference on Human Factors in Computing Systems (CHI'05)*, ACM Press, pp.266–71.

Guan, Z., Ren, X., Li, Y. & Dai, G. [2004], Zoom Selector: A Pen-based Interaction Technique for Small Target Selection, *IPSJ Journal* **45**(8), 2087–97.

Guiard, Y., Blanch, R. & Beaudouin-Lafon, M. [2004], Object Pointing: A Complement to Bitmap Pointing in GUIs, *in* W. Heidrich & R. Balakrishnan (eds.), *Proceedings of Graphics Interface 2004*, A. K. Peters, pp.9–16. http://www.graphicsinterface.org/proceedings/2004/.

Kabbash, P. & Buxton, W. [1995], The 'Prince' Technique: Fitts' Law and Selection using Area Cursors, *in* I. Katz, R. Mack, L. Marks, M. B. Rosson & J. Nielsen (eds.), *Proceedings of the SIGCHI Conference on Human Factors in Computing Systems (CHI'95)*, ACM Press, pp.273–9.

McGuffin, M. & Balakrishnan, R. [2002], Acquisition of Expanding Targets, *in* D. Wixon (ed.), *Proceedings of SIGCHI Conference on Human Factors in Computing Systems: Changing our World, Changing Ourselves (CHI'02)*, *CHI Letters* **4**(1), ACM Press, pp.57–64.

Ren, X. & Moriya, S. [2000], Improving Selection Performance on Pen-based System: A Study of Pen-based Interaction for Selection Tasks, *ACM Transactions on Computer–Human Interaction* **7**(3), 384–416.

Worden, A., Walker, N., Bharat, K. & Hudson, S. [1997], Making Computers Easier for Older Adults to Use: Area Cursors and Sticky Icons, *in* S. Pemberton (ed.), *Proceedings of the SIGCHI Conference on Human Factors in Computing Systems (CHI'97)*, ACM Press, pp.266–71.

Zhai, S., Conversy, S., Beaudouin-Lafon, M. & Guiard, Y. [2003], Human On-line Response to Target Expansion, *in* V. Bellotti, T. Erickson, G. Cockton & P. Korhonen (eds.), *Proceedings of SIGCHI Conference on Human Factors in Computing Systems (CHI'03)*, *CHI Letters* **5**(1), ACM Press, pp.177–84.

Assisting Target Acquisition in Perspective Views

Yangzhou Du[†], Olivier Chapuis[†], Yves Guiard[‡] & Michel Beaudouin-Lafon[†]

[†] *LRI & INRIA Futurs, Bât 490, Université Paris-Sud, 91405 Orsay, France*
Email: *{du, chapuis, mbl} @lri.fr*

[‡] *Mouvement et Perception, CNRS & Université de la Méditerranée, 13288 Marseille Cedex 9, France*
Email: *yves.guiard@univmed.fr*

This article introduces an interaction technique designed to assist target acquisition in flat documents that are visualized in perspective. One reason to allow camera tilts in graphical interfaces is that perspective views provide users with a gradual variation of scale, allowing them to see local detail in the context of a general overview. Our analysis, however, shows that the non-linearity of scale variation in a perspective view jeopardizes the acquisition of very remotely located objects. We introduce and experimentally evaluate a solution in which:

1. viewing angle is automatically coupled with tilt angle; and

2. the tilt is constrained so that the virtual camera stays at a constant altitude and remains pointed to a fixed spot on the document.

Our results show that with our enhanced perspective navigation technique targets are easy to reach even for extremely high levels of difficulty. Target acquisition time obeys Fitts' Law and performance becomes as rapid as with the familiar pan and zoom technique.

Keywords: Fitts' Law, target acquisition, multi-scale pointing, multi-scale navigation, perspective view.

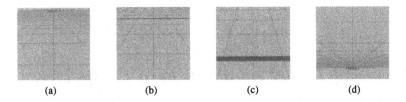

(a)	(b)	(c)	(d)

Figure 1: Performing a pointing task in our PV navigation interface. (a) Being at first too far away to be displayed, the target can only be shown as a symbolic beacon. (b) The target is now visible as a 1-pixel thick line but it is still difficult to click. (c) The target is near enough to be clicked. (d) The clicked target has disappeared, and the next target is at the other end of the document, so the user tilts the camera in the opposite direction.

1 Introduction

Considerable efforts have been made over the last two decades to devise satisfactory interfaces for viewing exponentially increasing amounts of information through limited screen displays. Multi-scale interfaces now allow users to interact with information objects at different scales [Furnas & Bederson 1995; Guiard & Beaudouin-Lafon 2004]. Notable instances of these multi-scale interfaces are those using the bi-focal [Tzavaras & Spence 1982], the fish-eye [Furnas 1986], and the pan and zoom [Perlin & Fox 1993] technique. The last technique is the most widely used nowadays in the field of interactive information visualization.

With all the above mentioned techniques, the viewing direction is always oriented perpendicular to the document plane. By contrast, this paper will focus on the case in which the user is allowed to freely tilt the camera relative to the document plane. Our aim is to develop novel multi-scale document-navigation techniques that exploit perspective viewing (PV). Figure 1 depicts what was seen by participants in the target acquisition experiment with PV to be reported below. Not only was camera tilting permitted, but the user could navigate the document while viewing it in perspective – of interest here is the case of interactive perspective viewing.

Starting from a local perpendicular view, our participants were to reach and click a very remote target, a narrow red strip located a large distance away in a linearly arranged document but in a known (upward or downward) direction. By tilting the virtual camera upward (Figure 1a), the target could be made to enter the view but, being at first located too far away, it could be displayed only as a beacon (the text string 'TARGET'), which provided a rough indication of the target location, in keeping with the semantic-zoom principle of Bederson & Hollan [1994]. The next step was to move to the target by horizontally translating the tilted camera relative to the document (or, in an equivalent description, by dragging the document relative to the tilted camera) until it became not just visible (Figure 1b) but large enough for cursor selection (Figure 1c). As soon as a successful mouse click was recorded by the system, the target jumped to another remote place and the camera had to be tilted in the opposite direction (Figure 1d) – thus, we used the so-called reciprocal version of Fitts' [1954] task, with the camera having to be tilted up and down and translated back and forth to perform the task.

A PV interface exhibits the valuable property of presenting the viewer with a smooth transition from the local detail to a global overview that shows remote regions of the document, as emphasized by Mackinlay et al. [1991]. The perspective view obtained by camera tilting involves a continuous gradient of visualization scale: the farther an item in the document, the lower its visualization scale. Compared with the standard zooming technique, which conserves a uniform scale all over the view, with scale varying over time, a navigation technique that exploits PV can vary the visualization scale over space too, with a whole range of scales displayed at the same time in the same view. When this technique is embedded into a visualization interface, the user is able to look at the global context without losing the current detail.

One noteworthy difference between the tilt-based navigation technique and the familiar zooming technique is that camera tilting is direction-specific whereas zooming is omni-directional. For example, the user will selectively tilt the camera upward to look for some item known to be located in the beginning of the document. By contrast, zooming-out means searching indistinctively in all directions of the document, even when the user knows in what specific region the search should proceed. Since a view has a limited number of pixels, the omni-directionality of the zooming-out operation has a cost. Namely, the document region that was of interest to the user just before the zoom-out inevitably shrinks out like everything else in the view. Unless the user has no idea whatsoever of the target location, a directional search seems preferable. Also, there are cases where losing the contents of the detailed view from which the navigation starts is problematic – for example the final selection of the target may well require reference to some information available in this detailed view. Thus there is reason to believe that PV has a potential for documents visualization, at least as a complement to the traditional zooming interface.

In a recent work [Guiard et al. 2006a], we have pleaded for the PV visualization of documents and reported a preliminary experimental evaluation of the efficiency of PV for large planar document navigation. Using a pointing task that could be very difficult (with indices of difficulty up to 15 bits, using Fitts' [1954] metric), we found that target acquisition with a simple PV technique was about as efficient as with the standard pan-zoom technique for tasks of moderate levels of difficulty. However, for extremely distant targets (a case to be possibly met in the case of extremely large documents) the PV interface with a bare implementation was no longer workable. We concluded that to handle this limitation of the PV technique, some artificial techniques need to be designed to assist navigation.

Below we present a detailed analysis of the target acquisition problem in a PV interface for very high levels of difficulty and introduce a practical solution. While the view angle (or the field of view) was fixed in our previous implementation of basic PV interface, in the assisting technique we propose it is now allowed to vary and it is actually coupled with tilt angle. In addition, a new kind of camera rotation is exploited, in which the camera travels at a fixed altitude while being constrained to remain oriented to a fixed point in document space. We will report an evaluation experiment showing that with these assisting techniques arbitrarily difficult pointing tasks can be performed in a PV interface, with the users' performance being similar to that obtained in the usual pan-zoom technique.

2 Related Work

In this section we review the main techniques described in the literature that have been devised to assist multi-scale document navigation.

To facilitate the browsing of large document in pan-zoom interface, Igarashi & Hinckley [2000] proposed the speed-dependent automatic zooming technique. As the scrolling speed increases, the system automatically adjusts the zoom level so that the velocity of the optical flow field keeps constant. To alleviate the focus-targeting difficulty under fisheye-view distortion, Gutwin [2002] presented a technique called speed-coupled flattening, which dynamically reduces the distortion level of a fisheye based on pointer velocity and acceleration. While discussing navigation in 3D, one may think of assisting navigation techniques that are sensitive to objects and the environment. These techniques base their camera control on the 3D world coordinate system and on sensing the surfaces of the objects in the scene. Khan et al.'s [2005] 'HoverCam', Zeleznik & Forsberg's [1999] 'UniCam', and Tan et al.'s [2001] navigation system are instances of this category. Arsenault & Ware [2002] have reported a study that helps to understand target acquisition with PV visualization. They isolate the observer's visual field of view (determined by a screen) from frustum field of view (determined by computer graphics geometry).

Our approach differs from the above in that we address PV navigation in the case of a *planar* surface, a case quite worthy of consideration given the ubiquity of planar documents in current interfaces, whether for desktops or hand-held devices. The assisting technique we discuss below addresses the pointing difficulty raised by scale implosion in PV visualization. To our knowledge, and to our surprise, there has been virtually no research directly relevant to this topic in the HCI field.

3 The Problem of Grasping Difficulty in Perspective Views

As mentioned earlier, we showed that a bare implementation of the PV concept does not accommodate pointing tasks over some threshold of difficulty [Guiard et al. 2006a]. Let us analyse this phenomenon in some detail. We are considering the case of a user allowed to click and drag a document with the screen cursor like, say, in Adobe Acrobat Reader. The new feature is that the drag operation can now be done on a document that is visualized in perspective. An important property of this setting is that the scrolling speed of the document, in its plane, now varies in a highly non-linear way depending on the location of the point that has been grasped. If the cursor has grasped the document at some near location, then very small scrolls will be obtained. However, given the non-linearity of the function, the same drag movement performed at farther locations in the view (hence involving another level of visualization scale) will have an effect on document scrolling that may differ by several orders of magnitudes.

Suppose the user tilts the camera until a very remote target item enters the view, and the beacon that land marks this item appears near the horizon. If the user places the screen cursor slightly above the beacon to drag the target closer, the target (in

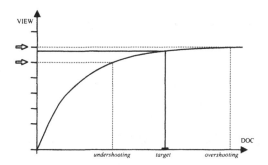

Figure 2: 1D illustration of the grasping error problem for very remote targets in PV (the dimension considered is the line covered by the camera focus as the user tilts the camera). The view-document mapping actually follows a function of the form $y = 1/x$.

fact along with the whole document) will travel at a tremendous speed and end at a huge distance on the opposite side of the observation point, meaning that the user will lose the target. Alternatively, if the user grasps the document with the screen cursor slightly below the beacon, the target beacon may squarely refuse to move at all. Last but not least, if the cursor grasps the documents exactly at the screen pixel that is land-marked by the beacon, a gentle drag may cause an undetermined effect between the previous two. The reason is because visualization scale in a PV interface varies in a highly non-linear way across the screen, leading to a scale implosion at some critical distance. One screen pixel in a PV display corresponds to a small document length for near regions and obviously to much larger document lengths for farther regions. If the screen pixel falls near the horizon, the corresponding length in document space may be huge, even infinite. As the resolution of document grasping for mouse-dragging cannot be finer than one screen pixel, the nonlinear variation of view-document mapping causes uncontrollable errors, as illustrated in Figure 2.

While discussing the overshooting problem in 3D space, it seems timely to recall the Point-of-interest navigation technique introduced by Mackinlay et al. [1990]. The key idea of these authors is to approach a point of interest (i.e. the target) logarithmically, by moving the same relative percentage of distance to the target on every animation cycle. This strategy, however, does not seem to be applicable in the case of a document viewed in perspective. Because of the highly nonlinear property of PV visualization, the initial aiming point may be far away from the real target and the target can be definitively lost in the very first animation cycle.

This problem, which we call the PV grasping problem, becomes particularly tricky when the index of difficulty (*ID*) exceeds 15 bits, using Fitts' metric (see Appendix 1 for a detailed mathematical explanation of this critical value). Due to the grasping error, the whole target-acquisition procedure becomes quite difficult or takes unexpectedly long time while dealing with tasks of higher levels of difficulty.

The definition of the *ID*, which measures the level of difficulty in Fitts' target-reaching paradigm [MacKenzie 1992], should be made explicit here:

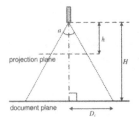

H	camera height
h	focal length
α	field of view, or viewing angle
D_c	covering distance

Figure 3: The virtual camera setup in the case of the classic zooming interface.

$$ID = \log_2\left(\frac{D}{W} + 1\right)$$

where D and W stand for target distance and target width, respectively. Fitts' Law states the empirical fact that in general the minimum time required for target-acquisition, or movement time (MT), varies linearly with the ID:

$$MT = a + b \times ID$$

The coefficients of this linear function, the intercept a and the slope b, can be used to quantify users' performance with a given interface. This allows us to run rigorous experiments to evaluate the usability of our new designs relative to the state of the art.

Please note that in this paper the ID is always calculated in the document plane, rather than in the view plane. This allows us to estimate the difficulty of the navigation task regardless of whether or not the target can be geometrically represented on the screen. As long as the target corresponds to less than one screen pixel, calling for a symbolic representation (the beacon), the difficulty of reaching it cannot be estimated in the view plane.

4 A Formal Analysis and a Solution

As already mentioned, the special difficulty of performing very high ID tasks with PV comes from the grasping error in the vicinity of the horizon. This section formally addresses the problem and then presents our solution. Note that we treat the problem in 1D space, along the line covered on the document by the camera focus as the user tilts the camera. The non-linearity concerns the longitudinal dimension of PV (in Figure 1, for example, only the vertical height, not the horizontal width, of grid squares decreases non-linearly with observation distance). First, let us define the concept of 'Visualization Scale' (S_v) as the ratio of object size in the documents and its projection size on the screen:

$$S_v = \frac{\delta_{doc}}{\delta_{prj}}$$

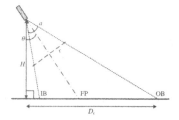

θ tilting angle of camera axis

r ½ projection screen size.

Figure 4: The virtual camera setup in the case of PV.

---

where δ_{doc} denotes the original size of the object on document plane and δ_{prj} denotes the size of its projection. Whereas S_v is a constant all over the projection plane in the perpendicular view of a usual zooming interface, it varies dramatically in PV. Figure 3 shows the pan-zoom situation where the camera is oriented perpendicular to the document plane and introduces a number of camera parameters. Note that D_c is a measure of how far the camera can see in the document, it is defined in the document plane from the camera location to the boundary point. Since the axis of the camera is perpendicular to the document plane, the relationship $\delta_{doc}/\delta_{prj} = H/h$ holds and the value of S_v is constant over the whole projection plane:

$$S_v = \frac{H}{h}$$

Now consider the ratio of S_v over D_c. This ratio reflects how the visualization scale varies with a distance covered by the camera during the navigation. In the situation of Figure 3, $D_c = H\tan(\alpha/2)$, we have:

$$\frac{S_v}{D_c} = \frac{1}{h\tan(\alpha/2)} \tag{1}$$

As h and α are constants, the above ratio is also a constant. Visualization scale is simply proportional to covering distance D_c during pan-zoom navigation. This is perhaps one of the valuable properties of the zooming technique that make the pan-zoom interface popular.

Figure 4 shows the case in perspective projection. As the axis of the camera is no longer perpendicular to the document plane, two boundary points in the area covered by the camera must be distinguished: the inner boundary (IB) and the outer boundary (OB). The axis of the camera intersects the document plane at the Fixation Point (FP).

In perspective projection, obviously, the visualization scale is no longer constant over the view. We will pay special attention to S_v at the point where OB is projected, because S_v changes here a lot more than at any other point, and actually the PV grasping problem mainly occurs here. In the case shown in Figure 4, the following equation depicts a local length δ_{doc} in the document plane that is projected to the screen plane:

$$\delta_{prj} = \delta_{doc} \cos(\theta + \alpha/2) \frac{r/\sin(\alpha/2)}{H/\cos(\theta + \alpha/2)} \frac{1}{\cos(\alpha/2)}$$

In the right hand side of this equation, δ_{doc} (a very short length at OB) is followed by three factors. The first factor is there because of the camera tilt. The second item scales the length by the distance ratio. The last one is due to the fact that the screen is a plane and the view direction is not exactly perpendicular to this plane. As a result, the value of S_v at OB is:

$$S_v = \frac{\delta_{doc}}{\delta_{prj}} = \frac{H \sin(\alpha/2) \cos(\alpha/2)}{r \cos^2(\theta + \alpha/2)}$$

As $D_c = H \tan(\theta + \alpha/2)$, the ratio of S_v and D_c becomes:

$$\frac{S_v}{D_c} = \frac{\sin(\alpha)}{r \sin(2\theta + \alpha)} \tag{2}$$

When the field of view α is a fixed value, this ratio depends on θ only. If the camera is tilted until $\theta + \alpha/2$ tends to $\pi/2$ (with OB becoming almost parallel to the document plane), the denominator of the right hand side of Equation 2 cancels and the visualization scale gets a huge value relative to covering distance D_c. This explains the PV grasping difficulty.

It would help if S_v could have a fixed linear relationship to D_c, as is the case with the pan-zoom technique, that is, like in Equation 1. To achieve this goal, the solution is just to set the right-hand side of Equation 2 to be constant. Thus, let us change the value of α so that the relationship below holds:

$$\sin(\alpha) = \sin(2\theta + \alpha)$$

It seems reasonable to impose limitations on the viewing angle $0 \leq \alpha \leq \pi/2$ and $\pi/2 \leq 2\theta + \alpha \leq \pi$. Thus, $\pi - \alpha = 2\theta + \alpha$, i.e.:

$$\alpha = \frac{\pi}{2} - \theta, \quad 0 \leq \theta \leq \pi/2$$

We have obtained a very simple relationship between α and θ. If α varies according to θ as described, we will obtain a fixed linear relationship between visualization scale and covering distance, like in the pan-zoom case. We call this strategy the automatic coupling of viewing angle and camera tilt. Note the important difference between the basic PV implementation and this new one: the field of view was originally fixed in any case but is now made to depend on the direction of view. In fact, this new strategy takes some similarity with a property of our visual perception. When people stand on an endless plain and cast eye on a very remote object, they will concentrate on the target and try to reduce the field of view (subjectively, of course). While it is actually implemented with our assisting technique, it amounts to a zooming-in effect associated with the camera tilt, since with constant screen size, reducing the field of view implies increasing the focal length.

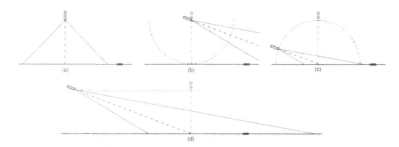

Figure 5: Three kinds of camera rotation with the strategy of coupling view angle to tilt angle. The target on document plane is represented as a thicker segment on the horizontal line. (a) An up-right view. (b) Panoramic rotation, showing the likely case of a missed target due to a tilting overshoot. (c) Hemispherical or 'lunar' rotation, showing the difficulty of visualizing the target because the distal boundary of the selection hardly moves at all. (d) Trans-rotation, which ensures that the target will be seen.

5 Choosing an Appropriate Type of Camera Rotation

Assuming we follow the strategy proposed above, the next question is about the location of the centre of camera rotation. Starting with an upright view of camera, (Figure 5a), we first chose a panoramic (i.e. camera-centred, Figure 5b) kind of rotation for our PV navigation technique, but we soon realized there was a serious shortcoming. The part of the document covered by the camera moved forward so quickly that the user most of the time missed remotely located targets. (Note this case does not appear very conspicuously in Figure 5b. It will become more and more remarkable when the target is located far from the observation.) We then turned to the 'lunar' (fixation-point centred) rotation, as shown in Figure 5c. Now, while the selection area was able to expand/stretch around the fixation point, the outer boundary OB in Figure 4 was never too far thanks to the reduced field of view, but camera height varied too much. Finally the most effective solution was a rotation around the fixation point coupled with the constraint that camera altitude is fixed, as shown in Figure 5d. We called this manipulation a *trans-rotation* of the virtual camera because this kind of rotation is a mixture of a translation and a rotation, one centred at the fixation point (FP).

Note that in the case of a FP-centred rotation, target distance should be redefined as that measured from FP to the target, rather than from the camera to the target. Thus, camera rotation will not change target distance and hence the *ID*, which will only change with a camera translation. Although these three kinds of camera rotation were described in our previous study [Guiard et al. 2006a], only the panoramic rotation was tested in the experiment. In the present study the trans-rotation was actually adopted and fully practised.

We discovered through experience that a trans-rotation had desirable properties for our PV interface. First, the selection area can be extended by tilting the camera direction at an infinite distance. This means the remote target can be reached, no matter how far it is. Second, as the fixation point in document space does not move, the current local focus is not lost during a camera tilt. Finally, since the altitude of

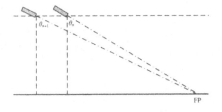

Figure 6: The camera tilt variation caused by one notch of mouse-wheel rotation.

the camera never changes during the search, the initial visualization scale will be restored as soon as the camera returns to a perpendicular orientation.

In order to facilitate the automatic coupling of viewing angle and tilt angle, another idea is to limit the maximum camera tilting angle θ within $\pi/2$ and to allow for a finer control when θ approaches $\pi/2$. The camera tilt being driven by mouse-wheel, we found it quite useful to introduce a non-linear mapping between mouse-wheel turning and camera tilting. The mouse wheel rotates in a discrete way, on a notch-by-notch basis. In our previous implementation with a bare, unaided PV interface, every notch in the wheel resulted in 5 degrees of rotation in camera. This caused the document region covered by camera to grow so quickly (following a tangent function in fact) that the region seen with one notch sometimes seemed to be disconnected from that seen with the preceding notch. In order to obtain visual consistency as is the case with a PZ interface, two successive covering regions should be varied in size proportionally. In the current design, when the mouse-wheel rotates forward or backward by one notch, we change θ so that $\tan(\theta)$ increases/decreases by 20%, i.e. $\tan(\theta_{n+1}) = 1.2\tan(\theta_n)$, as illustrated in Figure 6. In this way, the camera is able to cover fairly large distances within a finite number of notches – yet the tilting angle of the camera will never exceed $\pi/2$. In fact, the mapping of angles between the mouse-wheel and the camera has become nonlinear. This mapping, however, is unsuitable for small camera tilts – the rotation of the camera is too slow or it squarely stops (if the camera is upright). To remedy this, we use a linear mapping for $\theta < \pi/4$, with one wheel notch causing $\pi/36$ of rotation on the camera tilt. To summarize the above, the change of tilting angle with the notch variation is depicted by the equation:

$$\theta_{n+1} = \begin{cases} \theta_n + \pi/36 & \theta_n \leq \pi/4 \\ \tan^{-1}(1.2\tan(\theta_n)) & \theta_n > \pi/4 \end{cases}$$

With the above described auxiliary strategies, when the user continuously rotates the camera, the beacon will come closer and closer to the screen centre, an effect quite reminiscent of the effect of zooming-out. Then the user needs to translate the camera while rotating it back. When the camera is almost back to a perpendicular position, the beacon disappears because the target has become large enough that it can be visualized. So the whole procedure seems consistent with that of pan-zoom technique. Our experience is that a new user manages to master the technique within minutes.

6   User's Performance Evaluation

A formal evaluation experiment was run on a 2.8GHz PC with 512MB of RAM running Linux and X-Windows, using a 17-inch monitor with a 1280×1024-pixel resolution driven by a powerful video card. The program, created with Java3D, was run in an 800×800-pixel window. A screen shot of the document used for the experiment is offered in Figure 1, which shows a PV display.

The test was carried out with our enhanced PV navigation technique as well as with the familiar pan-zoom (PZ) technique, which provided a reference for comparison. The only input device was a standard optical wheel-mouse. Both in PV and PZ, the camera panning was driven by mouse moving. The camera zooming in PZ and tilting in PV were controlled by mouse wheel turning. The details of Fitts' pointing experiment in PZ interface can be found in Guiard et al. [2001].

Eight unpaid volunteers participated in the performance test. The experiment was divided into trials, each trial consisting of 6 movements (i.e. 7 successful target clicks). Four values of *ID* were chosen for the experiment (12, 17, 22 and 27 bits) each participants running four trials at each level of *ID*. The trial sequences were arranged pseudo-randomly according to Latin squares. There were a total of 16 trials per participant and per technique. Four participants started the session with PV and switched to the PZ technique, the other four ran the experiment in the reverse order. The participants were invited to have a rest between the two parts of the session.

Before the test, the participant was offered a few minutes of practice to familiarize with the new interface and the navigation techniques. When the participant felt confident, the formal test started, with the program recording all users' activities as well as all motions of the virtual camera. The recorded data were processed with the following rules. In each trial, the first two movements were ignored as warm up. Movement time (*MT*) was defined as the time elapsed between two successful clicks. Note that the program ignored unsuccessful clicks, just waiting until a target hit was recorded before presenting the next target. Since, therefore, the error rate was a forced 0%, we may now use *MT*, on its own, to estimate performance quantitatively.

Figure 7 shows the performance or the participants in our enhanced PV interface and in the standard PZ interface. The *MT* measures reported in our previous paper [Guiard et al. 2006a] for the unaided implementation of the PV navigation technique are also shown for comparison.

With the unaided PV technique, *MT* increased non-linearly with the *ID* up to a critical *ID* of 15 bits – beyond which the task was actually no longer workable. In contrast, the figure shows that with our enhanced PV technique extremely difficult pointing tasks, up to *ID* = 27 bits in the present test, could be successfully handled. It should be realized that applied to the case of a document formatted according to the norms of the IEEE proceedings, a task with an *ID* of 27 bits would mean reaching and selecting one particular text line located at a distance of 3 million pages.

For both the PZ and the enhanced PV conditions, *MT* varies linearly with the *ID*, in keeping with Fitts' Law. The linear equations of best fit are:

PZ: $\quad\quad MT = 0.437\,ID + 0.132 \quad r^2 = 0.9999$

Enhanced PV: $\quad MT = 0.423\,ID + 0.083 \quad r^2 = 0.9905$

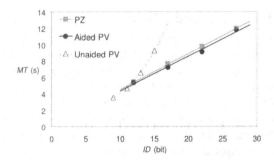

Figure 7: Movement time for the enhanced PV and the PZ techniques, plotted as a function of the *ID*. Also shown are the *MT* measures obtained with the unaided PV technique. *MT* is averaged over all participants.

The important implication of the finding that *MT* does obey Fitts' Law in our enhanced PV interface is that because time now increases linearly with *ID*, any target reaching task, however difficult, can be carried out – the upper limit of difficulty characteristic of unaided PV navigation has vanished.

The other point to be made from Figure 7 is that our enhanced PV navigation technique yielded a performance quite similar to that obtained with the usual PZ technique. In particular, the intercepts are very close and the curves are roughly parallel, with no obvious crossing point. In both cases, performance bandwidth (the inverse of Fitts' Law slope) is about 2.3 bits s^{-1}. A two-factor ANOVA run on *MT* with repeated measures on the *ID* factor (12, 17, 22 and 27 bits) and the technique factor (PZ vs. aided PV) confirmed the visual impression gained from the figure. Beside the trivial finding of a highly significant ID effect ($F(3,21) = 281.05$, $p < 0.0001$), neither the main effect of the technique nor the two-factor interaction was statistically reliable ($F(1,7) < 1$ and $F(3,21) < 1$, respectively).

7 Conclusion

We have described a novel multi-scale visualization techniques based on perspective viewing, the main merit of which is that it offers a gradual transition from local detail to remote view [Mackinlay et al. 1991]. With a basic, system-unaided implementation of the PV technique, we showed that it is almost impossible for users to perform a difficult pointing task (*ID* > 15 bits), because a severe accuracy problem arises for selecting an appropriate grasping point at very large distances in the document. We have offered a formal analysis of this problem and proposed a solution. First, we automatically couple viewing angle and tilt angle. To further facilitate navigation, we describe another two assistance techniques, one consisting of a nonlinear mapping between the mouse-wheel and the camera tilt, and the other based on a new kind of camera rotation, trans-rotation. Our evaluation data showed excellent pointing performance with the newly developed PV interface. *MT*s conform to the classical Fitts' Law, up to a considerable 27 bits, without any evidence that the technique will fail at higher levels of *ID*.

The technique we have described and evaluated in this study should be thought of as an optional resource for PV navigation rather than a permanent feature, because obviously reducing the viewing angle has a cost for the user. The trick we designed makes it possible to reach objects located in the documents at an extremely large distance from the current observation point (a case that needed to be considered as it may occasionally happen), but the shortcoming is that it sacrifices what is perhaps the fundamental advantage of PV – the possibility of seeing both the local detail and the global environment during navigation, just like in real-world vision where all surfaces are actually seen in perspective. Therefore the best way to implement our assistance technique is presumably in the form of an easily reversible mode within PV navigation.

In view of the considerable promise of PV visualization, we feel that efforts to improve PV navigation by means of appropriate assistance tricks like those we described in this paper are quite worth the while. From the moment the PV navigation technique has been cured of its specific weakness, that which we designate as the grasping problem for extremely high *ID*s, we may seriously contemplate proposing camera tilts as a basic facility for document navigation in graphical user interfaces. After all, introducing a camera tilting facility in interfaces simply means providing users with extended (translational *plus* rotational) control over the virtual-camera, an improvement relative to the current pan and zoom technique, which only exploits camera translations. Although quite simple conceptually and technically easy today, given the power of current tools like graphical cards and OpenGL programming, the change we recommend is likely to have diverse and far reaching consequences. Identification of these consequences is an intriguing problem tailored for human-computer interaction research. It will take time, demanding both formal evaluation experiments and user experience with realistic prototypes.

Our next step will be to compare, using the same experimental platform, our enhanced PV navigation technique with the best multi-scale visualization techniques that have been recently proposed, such as the Speed dependent automatic zooming technique (SDAZ) of Igarashi & Hinckley [2000] and the OrthoZoom technique of Appert & Fekete [2006]. In the present study, as has been traditionally the case in Fitts' Law studies, the pointing task was performed on an empty plane – a blank, if textured, document. We are now implementing a 3D visualization of a real large document which consists of the 150,000 verses of William Shakespeare's complete works [Guiard et al. 2006b]. We believe that asking people to find one particular line on a real text document rather than an abstract graphical strip on an empty plane makes up a more interesting and meaningful experimental task, as well as one that allows the experimental evaluation of new multi-scale document navigation techniques under more realistic conditions.

Acknowledgements

We gratefully acknowledge the generous financial support of the French Ministère délégué à la recherche et aux nouvelles technologies (ACI Masses de données, Micromegas Project).

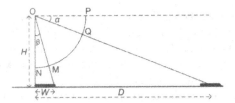

Figure 8: Elements of the grasping difficulty problem in PV.

Appendix 1

Here we explain why an *ID* of 15 bits seems to be a critical value when the grasping difficulty is raised indefinitely. Figure 8 shows the target projection with a tilted camera. The centre of the camera, *O*, is at a height *H*. For the sake of simplicity a spherical rather than planar screen is used (no essential difference will result). The view is represented as a quarter of circle *PQMN*. The direction *OP* being parallel to the document plane, *P* appears at the horizon in the view. When the target of width *W* is at a short distance, it is projected on the screen as arc *MN*. When the target is at a considerable distance *D* from the observation point, its projection size becomes smaller than one pixel, its beacon marking the single point *Q*.

Now suppose that the target is very far away, at a distance such that *PQ* exactly clips the highest pixel of the view. It will be difficult to grasp a target whose distance is farther than *D* because from the target to infinity everything will be mapped to this last pixel. If the screen cursor grasps this pixel to drag the target back, the mapped position of the mouse cursor in document space will be essentially undetermined.

Let us estimate the *ID* for this limiting case. The screen has a resolution of *R* pixels evenly distributed over arc *PQMN*. As *PQ* exactly clips one pixel, the angle between *OP* and *OQ* should be $\alpha = \frac{1}{R}\frac{\pi}{2}$. When the target has a maximum projection size, say *S* pixels (camera upright), there are *S* pixels on the arc *MN*, then $\beta = \frac{S}{R}\frac{\pi}{2}$. As $\tan(\alpha) = \frac{H}{D}$ and $\tan(\beta) = \frac{W}{H}$, we have:

$$
\begin{aligned}
ID &= \log_2\left(\frac{D}{W}+1\right) \\
&= \log_2\left(\frac{D}{H}\frac{H}{W}+1\right) \\
&= \log_2\left(\frac{1}{\tan(\alpha)\tan(\beta)}+1\right) \\
&= \log_2\left(\frac{1}{\tan(\frac{\pi}{2R})\tan(\frac{S\pi}{2R})}+1\right)
\end{aligned}
$$

It can be seen that this critical value of the *ID* depends on screen resolution *R* and the maximum projection size of target *S*. In a practical condition, *R* = 800 pixels and *S* = 10 pixels. By the above equation, we obtain an estimate of 14.7 bits for the critical *ID*.

References

Appert, C. & Fekete, J.-D. [2006], OrthoZoom Scroller: 1D Multi-scale Navigation, *in* R. Grinter, T. Rodden, P. Aoki, E. Cutrell, R. Jeffries & G. M. Olson (eds.), *Proceedings of SIGCHI Conference on Human Factors in Computing Systems (CHI'06)*, ACM Press, pp.21–30.

Arsenault, R. & Ware, C. [2002], Frustum View Angle, Observer View Angle and VE Navigation, *in* C. A. Vidal & C. Kirner (eds.), *Proceedings of the V Simpósio de Realidade Virtual – 2002*, Brazilian Computer Society, pp.15–25. http://www.ccom.unh.edu/vislab/PDFs/FrustumObserverViewAngle.pdf, last accessed 2006-05-30.

Bederson, B. B. & Hollan, J. D. [1994], Pad++: A Zooming Graphical Interface for Exploring Alternate Interface Physics, *in* P. Szekely (ed.), *Proceedings of the 7th Annual ACM Symposium on User Interface Software and Technology, UIST'94*, ACM Press, pp.17–26.

Fitts, P. M. [1954], The Information Capacity of the Human Motor System in Controlling Amplitude of Movement, *Journal of Experimental Psychology* **47**(6), 381–91.

Furnas, G. W. [1986], Generalized Fisheye Views, *in* M. Mantei & P. Orbeton (eds.), *Proceedings of the SIGCHI Conference on Human Factors in Computing Systems (CHI'86)*, ACM Press, pp.16–23.

Furnas, G. W. & Bederson, B. B. [1995], Space-scale Diagrams Understanding Multiscale Diagrams, *in* I. Katz, R. Mack, L. Marks, M. B. Rosson & J. Nielsen (eds.), *Proceedings of the SIGCHI Conference on Human Factors in Computing Systems (CHI'95)*, ACM Press, pp.234–41.

Guiard, Y., Bourgeois, F., Mottet, D. & Beaudouin-Lafon, M. [2001], Beyond the 10-bit barrier: Fitts' Law in Multi-scale Electronic Worlds, *in* A. Blandford, J. Vanderdonckt & P. Gray (eds.), *People and Computers XV: Interaction without Frontiers (Joint Proceedings of HCI2001 and IHM2001)*, Springer-Verlag, pp.573–87.

Guiard, Y., Chapuis, O., Du, Y. & Beaudouin-Lafon, M. [2006a], Allowing Camera Tilts for Document Navigation in the Standard GUI: A Discussion and an Experiment, *in* A. Celentano & P. Mussio (eds.), *Proceedings of the Conference on Advanced Visual Interface (AVI 2006)*, ACM Press, pp.241–4.

Guiard, Y., Du, Y., Fekete, J.-D., Beaudouin-Lafon, M., Appert, C. & Chapuis, O. [2006b], Shakespeare's Complete Works as a Benchmark for Evaluating Multiscale Document-navigation Techniques, *in* E. Bertini, C. Plaisant & G. Santucci (eds.), *Proceedings of BELIV06, a Workshop of the AVI 2006 International Working Conference*, ACM Press, pp.65–70.

Guiard, Y. & Beaudouin-Lafon, M. [2004], Target Acquisition in Multi-scale Electronic Worlds, *International Journal of Human–Computer Studies* **61**(6), 875–905.

Gutwin, C. [2002], Improving Focus Targeting in Interactive Fisheye Views, *in* D. Wixon (ed.), *Proceedings of SIGCHI Conference on Human Factors in Computing Systems: Changing our World, Changing Ourselves (CHI'02)*, *CHI Letters* **4**(1), ACM Press, pp.267–74.

Igarashi, T. & Hinckley, K. [2000], Speed-dependent Automatic Zooming for Browsing Large Documents, *in* M. Ackerman & K. Edwards (eds.), *Proceedings of the 13th Annual ACM Symposium on User Interface Software and Technology, UIST'00, CHI Letters* **2**(2), ACM Press, pp.139–48.

Khan, A., Komalo, B., Stam, J., G., F. & Kurtenbach, G. [2005], HoverCam: Interactive 3D Navigation for Proximal Object Inspection, *in* S. N. Spencer (ed.), *Symposium on Interactive 3D Graphics: Proceedings of the 2005 symposium on Interactive 3D Graphics and Games*, ACM Press, pp.73–80.

MacKenzie, I. S. [1992], Fitts' Law as a Research and Design Tool in Human–Computer Interaction, *Human–Computer Interaction* **7**(1), 91–139.

Mackinlay, J. D., Card, S. K. & Robertson, G. G. [1990], Rapid Controlled Movement Through a Virtual 3D Workspace, *Computer Graphics* **24**(4), 171–6.

Mackinlay, J. D., Robertson, G. G. & Card, S. K. [1991], The Perspective Wall: Details and Context Smoothly Integrated, *in* S. P. Robertson, G. M. Olson & J. S. Olson (eds.), *Proceedings of the SIGCHI Conference on Human Factors in Computing Systems: Reaching through Technology (CHI'91)*, ACM Press, pp.173–9.

Perlin, K. & Fox, D. [1993], Pad: An Alternative Approach to the Computer Interface, *in* J. Kajiya (ed.), *Proceedings of SIGGRAPH'93 20th Annual Conference on Computer Graphics and Interactive Techniques, Computer Graphics (Annual Conference Series)* **27**, ACM Press, pp.57–64.

Tan, D., Robertson, G. & Czerwinski, M. [2001], Exploring 3D Navigation: Combining Speed-coupled Flying with Orbiting, *in* J. A. Jacko, A. Sears, M. Beaudouin-Lafon & R. J. K. Jacob (eds.), *Proceedings of SIGCHI Conference on Human Factors in Computing Systems (CHI'01), CHI Letters* **3**(1), ACM Press, pp.418–25.

Tzavaras, I. & Spence, R. [1982], A Bifocal Display Technique for Data Presentation, *in* D. S. Greenaway & E. A. Warman (eds.), *Proceedings of Eurographics'82*, North-Holland, pp.27–43.

Zeleznik, R. & Forsberg, A. [1999], UniCam – 2D Gestural Camera Controls for 3D Environments, *in Proceedings of ACM Symposium on Interactive 3D Graphics*, ACM Press, pp.169–73.

Does Being Motivated to Avoid Procedural Errors Influence Their Systematicity?

Jonathan Back[†], Wai Lok Cheng[‡], Rob Dann[‡], Paul Curzon[‡] & Ann Blandford[†]

[†] *UCL Interaction Centre, UCL, Remax House, 31–32 Alfred Place, London WC1E 7DP, UK*
Email: *{j.back, a.blandford}@ucl.ac.uk*

[‡] *Department of Computer Science, QMUL, Mile End Road, London E1 4NS, UK*
Email: *pc@dcs.qmul.ac.uk*
URL: *http://www.dcs.qmul.ac.uk/research/imc/hum/*

Post-completion error (PCE) is a type of procedural error that occurs even when an individual has the knowledge required to perform the task correctly. After performing a 'task critical' step a PCE can occur if an individual forgets to perform a required 'related step' before starting a new task. Research has demonstrated that PCE is sensitive to external influences. For example, forgetting to collect the original document after making photocopies is more likely if an individual is thinking about 'other things' or is interrupted. Two gaming environments were designed to test the systematicity of PCE where participants were actively trying to avoid them. In both experiments a participant's score was reset to zero if a PCE occurred. Results showed that this penalty did not significantly influence the systematicity of the error within a gaming session. It was also found that the likelihood of PCEs occurring could be predicted by the intrinsic difficulty associated with performing the 'task critical' step or by an individual's ability to accurately remember information relevant to the task. This implies that even when individuals are motivated to avoid PCEs, user performance remains vulnerable to this error type. Within demanding environments, this vulnerability is likely to be more exposed.

Keywords: error, post-completion error, procedural error, motivation, priming, games.

1   Introduction

Errors are one measure of the quality of human performance. For example, Miller [1956] identified an important property of working memory by discovering that individuals make errors when recalling more than 7 (±2) unrelated elements of information. However, the everyday concept of error presupposes related goals that are cued by the environment. For example, when making coffee for a friend you do not have to recall whether they take sugar until the coffee has brewed. Moreover, the importance that an individual assigns to a particular goal may influence how the goal is performed. If the goal is critical to achieving a task then an individual may be motivated to ensure that performance is error free. This paper reports an empirical investigation into whether motivation within an engaging task paradigm can reduce the systematicity of a specific type of procedural error known as post-completion error (PCE).

The opportunity to make a PCE arises after the execution of a 'task critical' action that achieves a task. If an individual then forgets to perform a required procedural step before commencing a new task then a PCE occurs. Examples include forgetting to collect your change after buying chocolate from a vending machine, forgetting the original document after making photocopies, and forgetting to turn the gas off after cooking a meal. PCE is not associated with a lack of knowledge. This type of error can still occur when individuals have the required procedural knowledge to perform a task correctly. Norman [1981] identified that such 'slips' can be attributed to either a failure to perform necessary attentional monitoring, making an inappropriate attentional check, or forgetting. A PCE occurs when a step is forgotten. This is due to the post-completion step not being a necessary precondition to completing a task. PCEs are caused by a failure in prospective memory. Prospective remembering is the process and skill required to support the fulfilment of an intention to perform a specific action in the future. They are intentions that we can not put into effect at the time we form them [Ellis & Kvavilashvili 2000]. A critical aspect of success is not only recall of the content of the task but also retrieval at an appropriate moment for action. Consequently, there is a move towards understanding how the task environment influences working memory, attention and other cognitive functions.

It is not satisfactory to suggest specific error manifestations are a result of a generally high task performance error rate. It is now recognized that errors in routine interactive behaviour are not the product of some stochastic process, and that causal explanations of human error can be developed. Byrne & Bovair [1997] showed that PCE is sensitive to the working memory demands of the task environment. People make errors frequently, but do not make errors every time. Current experimental research on human error has successfully designed situations where certain types of errors can be provoked [Gray 2000]. This involves the development of procedures that ensure errors are not associated with a lack of procedural knowledge but occur due to the cognitive phenomenon being investigated (training trials ensure participants know what they are supposed to be doing). Recent research has identified various factors that affect the PCE rate such as, for example, dynamic visual cues [Chung & Byrne 2004]. It has also been shown that PCE

	Move your ship left and right using the arrow keys. Fire your gun using the space bar to shoot aliens.	
	Catch any astronauts falling from the sky, your ship will automatically bring out its catcher attachment.	
	Release astronauts over the yellow and black base.	
	Release aliens over the red and black prison.	
	Once you have released the astronaut, your ship will try to return to its normal state. After a couple of seconds, it will switch to look like the image on the left. When it is in this state, press G to switch back to gun mode.	
	Attempting to fire without pressing G will damage your weapon mechanism for a few seconds and cost you points!	

Figure 1: Space invaders instructions.

occurs in non-routine problem-solving situations [Li et al. 2005]. In an attempt to further examine the robustness of PCE, this paper reports on two experiments that investigated whether motivating a participant to avoid PCE in an engaging task environment influenced systematicity.

2 Experiment 1: Space Invaders

In the space invader game experiment[1] participants were required to shoot alien space ships, capture falling aliens, and rescue falling astronauts. A PCE is possible after rescuing an astronaut and then forgetting to change from rescue mode to shooting mode (see Figure 1, final instruction). The objective of the game is to obtain a place on the high score table. If a PCE is made, a player's score is reset to zero. Gamers are therefore likely to be motivated to avoid PCEs.

Data from twenty Queen Mary, University of London students was used for analysis[2]. A within-subjects experimental design was used. All participants undertook a training level. Participants were required to repeat the training level until they successfully rescued two astronauts without making any PCEs (onscreen prompts were provided for the first astronaut rescue only). Level one also required two astronaut rescues. It was possible that participants were still learning how to play so error data was not considered for analysis until a participant started level two. Levels 2–6 required four astronaut rescues per level (i.e. there were four PCE opportunities per level). Each level required all aliens to be destroyed and there was an increase in difficulty between levels (faster aliens that were harder to shoot).

---

[1] This game can be found at http://www.dcs.qmul.ac.uk/cs4fn/humanerror/pce/.

[2] Selected from a pool of 59 volunteers who played the game. 20 participants were selected on the basis that they completed training level and attempted Levels 1–5 (not enough participants attempted Level 6 for analysis).

Level	N	Mean (out of 4)	Std.Dev.
2	20	0.300	0.571
3	20	0.700	0.657
4	20	0.350	0.587
5	20	0.400	0.503

Table 1: PCE rates for Levels 2–5.

Results show that participants systematically forgot to change from rescue mode to shooting mode (by pressing G). The systematicity of this error was 10.9% (Levels 2–6). Table 1 shows the mean error rate and standard deviations for Levels 2–5 (data not normally distributed). A within-subjects analysis was performed (number of PCEs made per level). A Friedman's 'test of four related samples' (non-parametric) revealed that there was no significant difference associated with PCE rates (Friedman's $\chi^2 = 6.41$, d.f. = 3, $p > 0.05$). Despite participants being motivated to avoid PCE, the error remained systematic within a gaming session.

Further analysis showed that the error was not stochastic. It was found that the time it took to complete an astronaut rescue influenced the systematicity of the error. When no PCE was made the mean time taken to rescue was 3.74 seconds. However, when a PCE occurred the mean time was 4.60 seconds. A Mann-Whitney U non-parametric two independent samples test was performed (time taken to rescue: when a PCE occurs vs. when a PCE does not occur). If an astronaut rescue was more difficult / time consuming (either due to distance to 'yellow and black base', or avoiding alien fire) then this significantly increased the likelihood of a PCE (Mann-Whitney $U = 30233.5$, Wilcoxon $W = 253679.5$, $Z = -3.518$, $p < 0.001$). Implications are discussed in Section 4.

3 Experiment 2: Driving Game

In the driving game experiment [Cheng 2006] participants were required to capture cars of a specified colour (e.g. red) by moving the black police car (using the arrow keys). While in the process of capturing red cars participants were also required to remember specific details about cars of another specified colour (e.g. yellow) (see Figure 2). Details to remember included: the number of yellow cars, lane most frequently occupied by yellow cars (1–5), letters displayed on the roof of yellow cars, and whether a yellow car was seen before a car of any other colour when a new level was started (five levels in total). After a predetermined number of red cars were captured (dependent on level difficulty) a participant was required to: move to the kerbside (using the arrow keys), apply the handbrake (pressing 'D'), submit a report form about yellow cars (completing the form and clicking submit), and then release the handbrake (pressing the space bar) before attempting to move away from the kerbside (using the arrow keys). A PCE was possible after submitting a report if a participant forgot to release the handbrake before attempting to move away from the kerbside. If a PCE was made, a player's score was reset to zero. Specified

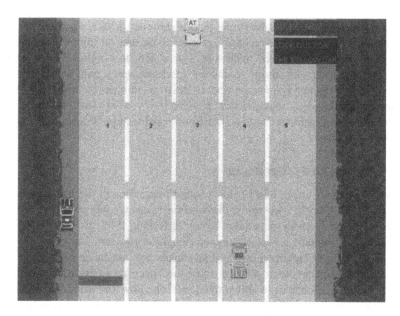

Figure 2: Driving game.

	N	Mean Error (out of 10)	Std.Dev.	Mean Answer Scores (out of 40)	Std.Dev.
Symbolic	30	0.970	0.765	17.73	3.051
Textual	30	0.570	0.626	18.13	2.662

Table 2: PCE rates and answer scores for driving game versions.

car colours changed when a level was completed. After participants successfully completed a training session, they were required to play a control version of the game where no PCE cue was provided. Following the control version two different versions of the driving game were played: one where a textual PCE cue was provided (press space to release brake), and one where a symbolic cue was provided (flashing handbrake light). The order in which a participant attempted cue game versions was counterbalanced.

30 Queen Mary, University of London students volunteered. A within-subjects experimental design was used. Participants were required to repeat the training level until they successfully completed the level without making any PCEs (prompts were provided for the first report submission only). Results showed that participants systematically forgot to release the handbrake before attempting to drive away from the kerbside (systematicity with symbolic cue = 9.7%, with textual cue = 5.7%). Table 2 shows the mean error rate alongside mean question answer scores. A Wilcoxon signed rank test determined whether the textual cue was significantly

better at preventing PCE than the symbolic cue (number of PCEs: textual cue game vs. symbolic cue game). Surprisingly, results show that the more salient textual cue was not significantly better (Wilcoxon $Z = -2.216$, $p > 0.05$). Further analysis showed that a participant's ability to answer questions was a good predictor of PCE rates (for both cue game versions: number of PCEs vs. number of correct answers). If participants found it easier to remember answers they were less likely to make a PCE. A Wilcoxon signed rank test found a significant relationship (Wilcoxon $Z = -8.249$, $p < 0.001$).

4   Discussion and Conclusions

Previous laboratory studies on PCE have found that although the frequency of the error can be lowered by providing just-in-time cues [Chung & Byrne 2004] or reducing working memory demands [Byrne & Bovair 1997; Li et al. 2005], the error remains systematic. Previous experimentation has not, however, explicitly tried to motivate participants in a way that makes the avoidance of PCE the most important task consideration. Results from the space invaders experiment show that motivating participants in this way does not allow the error to be avoided within a gaming session. Moreover, motivation did not even significantly reduce the frequency of the error between levels. This finding provides further support to the theory that a 'priming process' is needed to facilitate prospective remembering [Ellis & Kvavilashvili 2000] since being motivated to remember to do something is not sufficient.

Altmann & Trafton's [2002] activation based goal memory model suggests that cognition is directed by the most active goal retrieved at any given time (e.g. avoiding alien fire while rescuing an astronaut). If an individual needs to refocus attention to achieve a previously formulated goal (e.g. remembering to hit 'G' to activate the gun after rescuing an astronaut) then this old goal needs to undergo a 'priming process' to become active. Associative links can act as primers (e.g. remembering to clean your shoes may be triggered by an intention to leave for work). Space invader participants usually avoided making a PCE, but sometimes the associated link, remembering to hit 'G' to activate the gun after rescuing an astronaut, was not strong enough if a participant was expending extra effort to avoid alien fire while rescuing an astronaut. It was found that if it took longer than usual to complete an astronaut rescue then the likelihood of a PCE occurring significantly increased. This is a novel finding since previous research on PCE has not considered that the intrinsic difficulty of the 'task critical' step might provide a causal explanation for why PCEs occur. Findings remain consistent with Byrne & Bovair's [1997] working memory load theory.

The car driving experiment investigated whether the use of different cue types coupled with a participant's goal of avoiding PCEs influenced systematicity. Neither the textual nor symbolic cue allowed participants to avoid PCEs. Although the textual cue reduced the number of PCEs when compared to the symbolic cue, this difference was not significant. Interestingly, it was found that an individual's ability to remember information relevant to the task (in short term memory) could be used to predict the likelihood of PCEs. In this experiment the 'task critical' step was submitting a report. If the process of providing the report, i.e. remembering details about cars of a specific colour, was more difficult, then the strength of the associated link or 'priming process', i.e. remembering to release handbrake after submitting report, was lower and a PCE was more likely. This finding provides further evidence that the intrinsic difficulty of the 'task critical' step can be used as a causal explanation for PCE.

Designing engaging interaction environments might allow for more complex and consequently more useful interactions since a user may feel more confident, expressive, and motivated. Research presented within this paper has demonstrated the importance of minimizing the complexity associated with 'task critical' steps that are likely to be used for 'priming processes'. Future research should identify these steps and ensure that allowing more complex interactions do not compromise 'priming processes' causing more procedural errors.

Acknowledgements

Work conducted as part of the HUman error Modelling project (HUM), funded by EPSRC (GR/S67494 and GR/S67500). We are grateful to all participants in the studies reported here.

References

Altmann, E. M. & Trafton, J. G. [2002], Memory for Goals: An Activation-based Model, *Cognitive Science* **26**(1), 39–83.

Byrne, M. D. & Bovair, S. [1997], A Working Memory Model of a Common Procedural Error, *Cognitive Science* **21**(1), 31–61.

Cheng, W. L. [2006], Investigation into the Effects of Different Cues to Reduce Human Errors: Post-completion Errors, MSci Dissertation, Department of Computer Science, Queen Mary, University of London.

Chung, P. & Byrne, M. D. [2004], Visual Cues to Reduce Errors in a Routine Procedural Task, *in* K. Forbus, D. Genter & T. Regier (eds.), *Proceedings of the 26th Meeting of the Cognitive Science Society (CogSci2004)*, Lawrence Erlbaum Associates, pp.227–32.

Ellis, J. & Kvavilashvili, L. [2000], Prospective Memory in 2000, *Applied Cognitive Psychology* **14**(7), s1–s9.

Gray, W. [2000], The Nature and Processing of Errors in Interactive Behavior, *Cognitive Science* **24**(2), 205–48.

Li, S., Blandford, A., Cairns, P. & Young, R. M. [2005], Post-completion Errors in Problem Solving, *in* B. G. Bara, L. Barsalou & M. Bucciarelli (eds.), *Proceedings of the 27th Meeting of the Cognitive Science Society (CogSci2005)*, Lawrence Erlbaum Associates, pp.1278–83.

Miller, G. [1956], Human Memory and the Storage of Information, *IRE Transactions on Information Theory* **IT-2**(3), 128–37.

Norman, D. A. [1981], Categorization of Action Slips, *Psychological Review* **88**(1), 1–15.

Usefulness of Interactive Animations in Electronic Shopping

Fabio Nemetz & Peter Johnson

*Department of Computer Science, University of Bath,
Bath BA2 7AY, UK*

Tel: *+44 1225 384427 / 386811*

Email: *{F.Nemetz,P.Johnson}@bath.ac.uk*

In this paper, we first discuss one of the most cited problems that consumers face while making purchase decisions online, namely, the difficulty in judging the quality of products. We then propose the use of multimedia product experience in an environment that supports comparisons between alternatives. We present data from an experiment where 40 participants performed five shopping tasks. Our findings show that both multimedia product experiences and comparison tools have positive effects on the quality of decisions and on consumer satisfaction. Multimedia experience also affects learning in a positive way, while comparison tools support efficiency. Finally, we present implications for the design of e-shopping applications.

Keywords: multimedia, interactive animations, electronic shopping, electronic commerce, consumer decision-making, multimedia product experience

1 Introduction

The ability for e-stores to overcome the users' need to physically see a product in order to make a buying decision is critical to online shopping success [Alba et al. 1997]. Surveys like the GVU [1998] show that difficulty in judging the quality of products is the most cited reason for people not to shop online. In order to verify if this finding is valid, we conducted a small survey with 40 randomly selected participants asking why they do not shop (more) online – same multiple-choice question used in the GVU survey. The result (Figure 1) was very similar: the main problem consumers have when shopping on the Internet is that it is very hard to

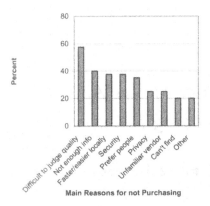

Figure 1: Main reasons for not purchasing (more) online, in descending order.

evaluate products. This is most critical for products that need to be experienced directly.

The basic purpose of our research is to investigate the effects of multimedia interaction in consumer decision-making, specifically on the evaluation of products. There are many questions to consider such as how to design effective and usable multimedia shopping environments that create the feeling of directly experiencing a product. Can interactive media technology reduce consumer's uncertainty and risk associated with shopping online? Does multimedia produce fewer or more choices that are effective? What is the effect on consumer's satisfaction? Does it improve consumer learning? This paper starts to address these questions in terms of the effects interactive animations have on decision quality, learning, efficiency and satisfaction.

The next section presents previous work, followed by related concepts and findings from the consumer behaviour field on why and how consumers learn about products. We then consider the use of multimedia to allow consumers to inspect products online, along with some considerations of its effects. An experiment to evaluate interactive product animations is then described, followed by results and discussion. We conclude by considering implications for design of e-shopping applications.

2 Previous Work

Surprisingly, given the growing importance of e-shopping, little is actually known about how to design applications that support consumer's evaluation of alternatives, particularly for products that normally need to be experienced directly [Smith et al. 2005]. Klein [1999] assessed the effects of media richness (video × pictures) and user control over judgements (beliefs, attitudes, persuasion) and learning. She found that media richness and user control had some positive effects on persuasion and attitudes, but no effects on learning. Häubl & Figueroa [2002] found a positive effect of 3D product presentations on users' intention to purchase products. Li et al. [2001] also found some positive effects of 3D presentations, except for products that needed to be touched during inspection (e.g. bedding material). These aforementioned studies [Häubl & Figueroa 2002; Klein 1999; Li et al. 2001] followed a preference model paradigm in which the consumer is faced with only one product and the intention is to study consumers' preference towards that particular product. This type of model is useful for persuasion purposes as in advertising. A different experiment [Häubl & Trifts 2000] that followed a choice model paradigm, in which the consumer has to choose one product when faced with a set of alternatives, asked participants to choose a product from several alternatives described by their attributes. The authors found that participants that were able to compare product attributes in tables produced better choices and were more efficient than participants who were not able to compare attributes. The limitation of this work was that only search attributes were presented, and there was no way for the consumer to experience the products.

The novelty of the present work is that it uses a choice model paradigm that puts the consumer in the centre of the decision-making process [Bazerman 2001] where she or he can inspect the products online, and, more importantly, uses functional inspections in that the consumer can interact with a model of the product, e.g. by pressing buttons.

3 Theoretical Background

One of the key issues in a purchase situation is the risk perceived by the consumer associated with a purchase. Perceived risk is defined as an assessment consumers make of the consequences of making a purchasing mistake as well as of the probability of such a mistake actually occurring [Spiekermann & Parachiv 2002]. From the three dimensions of risk [Cases 2002] – financial, performance and time – we are mostly interested in performance (functional) risk, which stands for the uncertainty that a product might not perform as expected in terms of its functional aspects and thus not deliver the benefits promised. Performance risk in e-shopping is closely related to the fact that the product is not (physically) present, and the consequence is that consumers find it difficult to judge its quality.

In trying to reduce perceived risk, one of the strategies employed by consumers is to learn more about the products they are interested in. People use different approaches to learning depending on the type of the product, which ultimately depends on the type of attributes it possesses.

There are several different ways to distinguish the various types of attributes of a product. One of the best known is Nelson's [1981] distinction between search and experience attributes. Search attributes are those that can be fully assessed prior to use, e.g. price of a car, colour of a chair, number of calories per serving of a yoghurt. On the other hand, experience attributes can only be assessed by using/trying out the product, e.g. taste of a chocolate bar, user-friendliness of a programmable VCR. Products have a mix of search and experience attributes; nevertheless it is possible to classify products into search products if their dominant attributes are search ones, and into experience products if their dominant attributes are experience ones [Klein 1998].

The distinction between search and experience products is directly related to the concept of perceived risk. When shopping online, as consumers do not have complete information about experience products, uncertainty is increased and consequently risk is perceived as being higher [Girard et al. 2002; Lowengart & Tractinsky 2001]. In contrast, less uncertainty is involved in shopping online for search products as consumers can easily assess the quality of the attributes. That explains why search products such as books and videos were the first to be sold successfully online [Lowengart & Tractinsky 2001]. Studies of perceived risk in e-shopping demonstrate that consumers do perceive search and experience goods as having different levels of risk [Jarvenpaa et al. 2000; Lowengart & Tractinsky 2001].

3.1   Learning about Products: Education × Experience

The findings from the literature on consumer behaviour suggest that consumers learn about products through education (indirect experience), such as advertising, and through direct experience, such as product trial [Hoch & Deighton 1989; Smith & Swinyard 1983]. Learning through education involves obtaining information through mechanisms such as advertising, contacting sales people, and the consumer's own directed effort to seek data. In contrast, learning through experience involves gaining knowledge through actual contact with products.

Hoch [2002, p.449] states that learning from 'experience is more engaging than education because it is more vivid and intentional'. Compared to education, Hoch argues that experience is more dramatic and intense, and acts on more than one of the senses, consequently it is more memorable. Learning from experience is driven by the self-identified goals of the consumer, and therefore more likely to be relevant and involving to the consumer [Hoch & Deighton 1989].

Consumers learn about a product prior to purchase to try to predict how well it will provide an expected performance [Daugherty et al. 2005; Osselaer & Alba 2000]. Direct experience enables consumers to anticipate the future consumption experience of a product better than an indirect experience [Li et al. 2001]. Direct experience is thought to cause consumers to have greater confidence in their product choices [Hoch & Deighton 1989]. Furthermore, Fazio & Zanna [1981] suggest that direct product experience is the optimal information source primarily because it is multisensory, customized to our information needs, and more credible than other indirect sources.

3.2   Is Direct Experience Always Superior?

Contrary to previous findings, Wright & Lynch [1995] found that direct experience is superior for experience attributes only, and indirect experience is superior for search attributes. For search attributes, consumers assume they posses a subjectively reliable inferential rule that links an observable aspect of the product with a desired attribute, benefit, or outcome (e.g. the power of the engine of a car). On the other hand for experience attributes, consumers perceive a far less reliable link between information available before use and the benefits or outcomes experienced later (e.g. a PDA advertised as being easy to operate). Claims about experience attributes cannot be verified before use, because they are a matter of individual sensory perception – in this case, product trial produces more reliable inferences than does exposure to indirect sources (e.g. advertising) [Wright & Lynch 1995].

The implications of these findings for e-shopping are that both direct and indirect experiences should be designed to support consumer's learning about experience and search attributes respectively.

4 Learning about Products in E-shopping: Multimedia Product Experience

One of the limitations of e-shopping is that it is not possible to experience the product directly, which hinders consumer learning about experience attributes. However, multimedia technology can be used to provide a simulation of the product where the consumer interacts directly with a representation of the product. This type of experience, referred to here as 'multimedia experience', can be classified as a third way of consumer learning, residing between indirect and direct experiences. The main goal of multimedia experience for consumers is to assess product performance prior to purchase [Klein 1998]; consequently it has the potential to reduce perceived risk.

It is important to make a distinction between multimedia and virtual experiences. Li et al. [2001, p.14] conceptualize virtual experience as being 'psychological and emotional states that consumers undergo while interacting with products in a 3D environment'. While similar to the effects of multimedia experience, virtual experience is concerned mostly with the use of 3D technology for visual inspection of products, whereas multimedia experience has a wider definition, focusing on human-computer interaction and the interactive environment rather than just on the visual aspects. In this way, 3D visualizations, as well as interactive animations and virtual reality, are examples or special cases of multimedia experience.

It has been suggested that when consumers rely only on direct experience, they are more likely to make bad judgements [Hoch 2002]. One possible solution for this problem is to facilitate comparisons among products [Muthukrishnan 1995].

In order to test the effects of multimedia on consumer decision-making, we designed and implemented an online shopping environment prototype where the presence of multimedia product experiences and comparison tools were manipulated systematically. This prototype was used for the experiment reported in the following sections.

5 Hypotheses

To understand the effects of multimedia and comparison tools in e-shopping, we designed and ran an experiment based on shopping tasks. In order to create a multimedia product experience, we used interactive product animations.

This section presents a set of hypotheses about how the dependent variables are affected by the presence of each of the two independent variables, multimedia product demonstrations (MM) and comparison tools (CT). In this paper we present results for the following dependent variables: effectiveness, learning, satisfaction and efficiency.

Each hypothesis is stated in terms of the expected difference, everything else being equal, between a scenario in which one of MM or CT is used in an online shopping trip for a complex decision-making and a scenario where it is not. By crossing the two levels of MM (No-MM, meaning absence of multimedia, and MM meaning presence of multimedia) and two levels of CT (No-CT meaning absence of comparison tools, and CT meaning presence of comparison tools), the four conditions of study are constructed. The control case in which neither is available to a shopper corresponds to a very basic online store. The hypotheses are:

H1. Effectiveness: the presence of (a) MM and (b) CT will increase the quality of the decisions – measured by the score on decisions for the tasks;

H2. Learning: the presence of (a) MM and (b) CT will improve learning – measured by an incidental-learning test;

H3. Satisfaction: The presence of (a) MM and (b) CT will make subjects feel more subjectively satisfied with the website – measured by a post-questionnaire using 7-point rating scales.

H4. Efficiency: (a) The presence of MM will make the interaction less efficient – (b) The presence of CT will make the interaction more efficient – measured by dividing the number of correct decisions by the total time spent in the tasks.

6 Experimental Design

A laboratory experiment was carried out to partially test the multimedia effect in an e-shopping environment. Participants used one version of an e-store where interactive product demos and comparators were manipulated. In this section, we describe the experiment and the results obtained.

6.1 Product Class Choice

Earlier studies comparing direct and indirect experience have indicated that a pre-requisite must be met in the selection of the product to be used in the test: the product must have salient attributes which can be evaluated by means of a trial [Smith & Swinyard 1983], where consumers assess some experience attributes through an inspection. This study uses digital cameras as the selected product, as it has an approximately equal balance of important search and experience attributes, making it a product with equal needs for direct and indirect experiences [Wright & Lynch 1995].

6.2 The Prototype

We designed and implemented a prototype e-store that sells 11 digital cameras, which are all of the same brand, so as not to introduce a confounding variable: brand preference. Each camera is described in terms of its search attributes (specifications, price, pictures of the camera) and experience attributes (how the camera works and pictures taken with it) along with expert reviews. To make the prototype as close as possible to a real e-shop, we re-used and adapted contents from websites that sell these cameras (see Acknowledgements).

Comparison of Specs: Similar Size

	DC280	DC215	DC215 Millenium	DC3400	DC240	DC5000	DC4800
General Data							
Price	£300	£200	£233	£266	£294	£385	£400
Weight	.75 lbs	.66 lbs	.66 lbs	.75 lbs	.7 lbs	1.011 lbs	.716 lbs
Height	3 in.	2.7 in.	2.7 in.	3 in.	3 in.	3.267 in.	2.72 in.
Width	2 in.	4.5 in.	4.5 in.	5.2 in.	5.2 in.	5.51 in.	4.72 in.
Depth	2 in.	1.7 in.	1.7 in.	2.1 in.	2 in.	3.503 in.	2.56 in.
Camera Size	Medium Size	Medium Size	Medium Size	Medium Size	Medium Size	Medium Size	Medium Size
Weatherproof	No	No	No	No	No	Yes	No
Resolution							
Megapixels	2.0	1.0	1.0	2.0	1.2	2.0	3.1
Pixels	1760 x 1168	1152 x 864	1152 x 864	1760 x 1168	1280 x 960	1760 x 1168	2160 x 1440
Resolution Modes	1760 x 1168 896 x 592	1152 x 864 640 x 480	1152 x 864 640 x 480	1760 x 1168 896 x 592	Best Better Good	1760 x 1168 896 x 592	2160 x 1440 1800 x 1200 1536 x 1024 1080 x 720

Figure 2: Comparing search attributes of the DC280 with cameras similar in size – not all attributes are shown in this figure. The images and data used are copyright Eastman Kodak Company, used with permission.

Figure 3: Interactive multimedia demos of the cameras side-by-side (comparison of experience attributes). The images are copyright © Eastman Kodak Company, reproduced with permission.

6.3 Independent Variables

The independent variables manipulated are:

1. Comparison tools (CT) – type of interactive decision aid that is designed to assist consumers in making in-depth comparisons among the alternatives [Häubl & Trifts 2000].

2. Interactive multimedia product demo (MM) – allows consumers to experience the product before making a purchase decision.

The study was a 2×2 factorial design. The two factors were manipulated between subjects.

The independent variable comparison tools can take on two values: No-CT, in which comparison tools are absent; and CT, in which comparison tools are present. In the CT conditions, participants are able to make several types of comparisons among alternatives. Search attributes, in this case price and specifications, can be presented in a table sorted by either price or resolution. It is also possible to select cameras to be compared by different criteria: price range, similar resolution or similar size (Figure 2). For the experience attributes, pairwise comparisons are provided: it is possible to select two cameras and inspect their functionalities side-by-side (Figure 3) through the interactive animations. Pairwise comparisons of pictures taken by different cameras are also provided.

In the No-CT conditions, it is only possible to examine information of one single camera at a time. It is expected that without the facilities provided by the comparison tools, the decision-making process will be more complex. The reason is that it becomes difficult to evaluate the different attributes. The cognitive effort is higher, because the consumer has to use a memory-based process to compare the different attributes of the different products.

It is important to note, though, that while the No-CT condition has less functionalities compared to the CT condition, exactly the same amount of information is provided for all cameras.

The independent variable interactive multimedia product demo can take on two values: No-MM, in which the products' demos are presented with static images and MM, in which consumers can interact with the product through interactive animations. So, in theory, in the No-MM conditions, the experience attributes are more difficult to learn – reading descriptions of the workings of the camera illustrated with some pictures. On the other hand, in the MM conditions, the experience attributes are presented in a more realistic mode, where it is possible to interact with a model of the camera, simulating the functional inspection of a real one. For example, in order to learn the various features of the camera, the user is guided to explore the different functionalities of the camera using a representation of the camera. The direct experience is simulated by a multimedia experience where product behaviours are triggered by actions such as clicking the shutter to take a picture.

To keep information constant, all steps included in the demonstrations have two versions: one static and non-interactive, using text and pictures, and one animated and interactive. So, every single step in a static demonstration has a counterpart in the dynamic one, and vice-versa.

6.4 Procedure

The experiment was conducted in an office at the department of Computer Science – University of Bath. 40 students from different areas (62.5% computer science, mean age = 21.35 years, s.d. = 2.81, all between 18 and 31 years of age, with 25 (62.5%) male and 15 (37.5%) female) took part in the experiment. They answered a call-for-volunteers message posted on the University Web-based notice board.

Upon arriving at the office, the participants were told that the purpose of the study was to evaluate a website. First, a profile questionnaire was filled in, capturing basic demographics, involvement and attitude towards Internet commerce and digital cameras. After that, a training session followed: participants were given a standard introductory 5 minute demonstration of the website to make them familiar with the system, strictly following scripts prepared in advance to alleviate biases. They were then asked to use the website for 3 minutes, and after that to perform five training tasks to check that they had acquired the basic skills needed to perform the real experimental tasks. Completed answers to the tasks were automatically collected together with the elapsed time.

The participants were tested individually and performed the same 5 tasks (shopping trips) using one of the four versions of the system (ten participants were randomly assigned to each of the four conditions). On average, it took each participant approximately 20 minutes (mean = 20.4, s.d. = 8.3) to solve all 5 tasks, for a total of more than 13 hours of experimental data. After a participant had completed the five tasks, that person proceeded to the learning test, to see what had been learned from the shopping session. Next, a satisfaction questionnaire was completed, and after that, a debriefing was given. All the sessions were video taped, allowing for further analysis.

6.5 Tasks

To assure robustness, different types of tasks were used. There were five complete tasks, typical for this kind of environment, presented in the same order to all subjects. Participants did not express their own preferences, but rather the requirements of a known third party (e.g. 'your friend, John'; 'the insurance company Delta'; 'the department of archaeology' – see below for one complete task). This decision to use a third-party task was made in order to achieve better measures of decision quality and accuracy [Frøkjær et al. 2000]. Of course the tasks of making decisions for one's self and for others are not identical, nor are they independent; however the assumption taken here is that these differences do not interact with the factors manipulated in this experiment. The main disadvantage of using self-preference measurements is that it is difficult to measure accuracy. As demonstrated in [Ariely 2000], it is perfectly valid to use third party tasks.

As an example, one of the tasks was:

'Your friend, John, has a Kodak camera and you know he's happy with the brand (he says he likes the quality of the cameras and the results he obtains with them). The last time you met him, he mentioned being interested in buying his first digital camera and asked for your advice. His budget is £200 and he also asked you to be sure it was an easy to use, simple camera that produces good quality pictures. Which camera would you recommend to John? Can you offer him a second choice?'

7 Results

ANOVAs treat comparison tools and multimedia as between-subject factors. All hypothesis tests are directional, so all reported significance tests are one-tailed. p values are significant if less than 0.05. Other values are considered non-significant.

7.1 Decision Quality

Decision quality is measured by effectiveness of the decisions. The tasks were formulated so as to include a 'dominant' alternative which is objectively better than any other in the choice set [Häubl & Trifts 2000], i.e. better on at least one attribute, and not worse on any attribute. For example, for a task that asks for two recommendations, as in the example above, one point is given for each correct recommendation in the correct order. So, a score of two is given if the participant

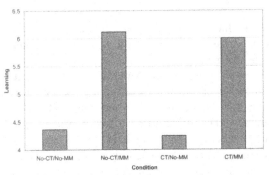

Figure 4: Mean score on learning by condition.

chooses the two best cameras in the correct order (best and second best). Half-point is given for correct recommendation but in the wrong order, and zero to a wrong recommendation. The final score in decision quality is the sum of the partial scores for the 5 tasks. It is important to note that the dominant alternative changes according to the criteria of the task (for instance, if two cameras have the same price, they will have different resolution, size, etc.).

A two-way (MM×CT) ANOVA was performed to determine the effects of MM and CT on participants' decision quality (Figure 4). From the results, we can reject the null hypothesis. There was a significant main effect of multimedia on decision quality, $F(1,36) = 3.34$, $p = 0.038$. Participants in the MM condition gave more accurate recommendations (mean = 7.92, s.d. = 1.127) than did participants in the No-MM condition (mean = 7.30, s.d. = 1.10). Hypothesis H1a is supported. The main effect of comparison tools is significant, $F(1,36) = 4.50$, $p = 0.020$. In general, participants in the CT condition made more accurate decisions (mean = 7.97, s.d. = 0.89) than did participants in the No-CT condition (mean = 7.25, s.d. = 1.27). This result supports H1b. The comparison tools × multimedia interaction was not significant, $F(1,36) = 6.25 \times 10^{-3}$, $p = 0.471$.

7.2 Learning

One important measure in consumer behaviour is consumer learning. Learning was measured by a test administered after all tasks were completed (the tests were marked by the experimenter). An example of a question is shown in Figure 5.

There was no significant effect for CT, $F(1,36) = 0.015$, $p = 0.452$, but MM, $F(1,36) = 2.852$, $p = 0.05$ was significant. Inspection revealed that participants in the MM conditions produced better scores (mean = 6.00) in the learning test than did participants in the No-MM conditions (mean = 4.31). There was no significant effect for the interaction between CT and MM, $F(1,36) < 0.001$, $p = 0.5$. Hence, H2a is supported, and H2b, not supported.

7.3 Satisfaction

To measure satisfaction, participants answered a questionnaire (Likert-scale with 7 points). Figure 6 shows the satisfaction component for each of the 4 conditions

The main feature(s) of the DC5000 (see picture) is/are (multiple choices):

A. pocket-size

B. zoom of 6x

C. robust, sturdy body

D. works as a web camera as well

E. highest resolution among the cameras

F. weather proof

G. don't know

Figure 5: Example question. The image is copyright © Eastman Kodak Company, reproduced with permission.

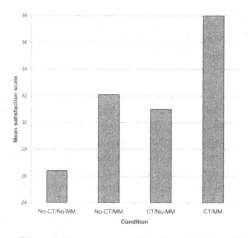

Figure 6: Mean score on satisfaction scale by condition.

(questions produced a score ranging from 6 to 42). An ANOVA test found a significant effect due to CT, $F(1,36) = 9.173$, $p = 0.002$ (higher satisfaction in the CT condition) and a significant effect due to MM $F(1,36) = 13.249$, $p < 0.0001$ (higher satisfaction in the MM condition). Both H3a and H3b are supported. No effect was found for the interaction: $F(1,36) = 0.223$, $p = 0.320$).

7.4 Efficiency

One argument against the use of animations is that they increase interaction time, and consequently decrease efficiency. For this study, we weighed the importance of time relative to effectiveness, using the concept of user efficiency (Figure 7), computed as (task effectiveness) /(task time) [Bevan 1995]. An ANOVA on user efficiency per condition revealed that the presence of CT was significant ($F(1,36) = 7.15$, $p = 0.005$). Participants in the CT condition were more efficient (mean = 862.89, s.d. = 311.73) than the ones in the No-CT condition (mean = 604.88, s.d. = 296.62).

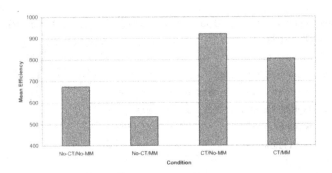

Figure 7: Efficiency by condition.

As for MM, its presence was not significant ($F(1,36)$ = 1.75, p = 0.097). There was no significant effect for the CT×MM interaction ($F(1,36)$ = 0.02, p = 0.450). Hypothesis H4a is not supported and H4b is supported.

8 Discussion

In summary, except for H2b and H4a, the hypotheses were supported.

The results support the notion that decision quality is strongly contingent upon product demonstrations and comparison tools. Both multimedia product demonstrations and comparison tools had a positive impact on effectiveness. The positive effect of multimedia product experience in decision quality relative to indirect experience supports the assumption of its proximity with direct experience [Hoch & Deighton 1989]. The positive effect of comparison tools is explained by the possibility of making in-depth comparisons, not only of search attributes, but also experience ones. It supports the findings by Häubl & Trifts [2000] in relation to search attributes.

The results for the learning test indicate that interactive multimedia animations lead to a greater retention of information about the products. Because the amount of information was kept constant across all conditions, it appears that the interactive animations provide an additional source of recall and recognition. This conclusion is consistent with the claim that multimedia increases the distinctiveness of a stimulus, thereby facilitating learning processes by increasing the accessibility of the stimulus in memory. The improvement MM produced in learning was quite significant: 40% for the No-CT conditions and 41.20% for the CT conditions.

Since for all conditions the learning test was incidental, it is possible to suggest that the interactive multimedia product demonstrations engaged subjects in processing information that was more conducive to learning [Anderson 2000; Hoch & Deighton 1989]. It seems that subjects using interactive animations process the product demonstrations in a more meaningful and deeper way. This finding also confirms the proximity of multimedia experience to direct experience.

As for CT, it did not produce the expected effect on learning; it seems that less cognitive overhead was not enough to produce a difference in learning. Or it was counter-balanced by the need to make decisions in a memory-based activity (in the No-CT condition) instead of stimulus-based activity (in the CT conditions).

The results showed that the presence of interactive animations (MM) had no effect on efficiency. Even though participants in the MM condition took more time to complete the tasks, they were not less efficient than the ones in the No-MM condition. This can be explained by the fact that they were more effective, i.e. their decisions were more accurate. On the other hand, comparison tools greatly improve efficiency due to the facilities in determining the relative merits of the alternatives. The lack of comparison tools forces the user to make comparisons using information she or he can remember, which decreases efficiency. This finding is an important one, supporting [Häubl & Trifts 2000], in the sense that it contradicts established knowledge about consumer behaviour that says that an increase in accuracy necessarily leads to a decrease in efficiency.

The results for subjective satisfaction show that consumers are more subjectively satisfied with both product demonstrations and comparison tools.

Finally, we did not see any interaction effect between the two independent variables, although it has been suggested in the literature that comparison facilities can alleviate the problems associated with experience alone [Hoch 2002; Muthukrishnan 1995].

9 Implications for Design

Nisbett & Ross [1980] claim that when a direct experience happens, doubts about the validity of the information are reduced and the personal relevance of the information is enhanced. Alba et al. [1997] argue that the move from indirect to more direct experiences increases the confidence a consumer will have in the correlation between the observed attributes and actual product benefits. Information becomes more useful in terms of their potential to predict satisfaction from subsequent consumption, therefore, reducing the risk of a bad decision. As pointed out by Klein [1999], when a consumer has greater confidence in her ability to predict satisfaction, she will learn more and have more confidence in what she learns. If we compare these findings with the ones from the present study, we can see that multimedia experience can potentially improve the evaluation of products online. The following implications for design arise from our research:

- Products with salient search and experience attributes should be presented by both indirect and multimedia experiences.

- Comparison tools are essential to support evaluation of alternatives.

- Comparison tools should support not only search attributes (e.g. technical specifications) but also experience attributes (e.g. product demos).

- Multimedia experience for products dominated by functional salient features should be designed to support behavioural inspection.

- Indirect experience, multimedia experience and comparison tools should be integrated in an environment that facilitates comparisons of any attribute.

- Multimedia experience should be designed to offer guided exploration of the product.

10   Conclusions and Future Work

Most of the work researching consumer behaviour in e-shopping is done by researchers in marketing, consumer behaviour and advertising, disciplines that view the whole shopping process in terms of marketers whose main goal is to sell more, to persuade, and ultimately increase profits. Previous research wants to know what makes a consumer decide whether or not to buy a product; and this is an appropriate dependent variable for research that benefit the companies [Bazerman 2001]. However it does not address issues related to supporting individuals make wiser purchase decisions. Our work takes a different perspective in the sense that it advances knowledge aimed at helping the consumer to benefit from better designs which will support improved decision-making. Ultimately, the goal is to maximize the consumer's expected benefit, by giving him enough information to take the optimum (or close to it) decision.

As in any laboratory study, the results of the present research need to be viewed in light of potential limitations that can affect overall reliability and validity. First, only one product category was studied. Even though digital camera is an appropriate product for the study of consumer behaviour, a cross-category investigation is still necessary before there can be any generalization of the findings. Second, the use of a student population always introduces questions about external validity, although the participants (mean age = 21.35 years, s.d. = 2.81) represent one of the age groups that is most active in e-shopping [GVU 1998]. Finally, even though the e-shopping application is realistic, it is based on cameras of the same brand, which restricts to a certain degree the decision-making process.

Nevertheless, we feel that this work represents a fundamental step towards an important area of HCI and electronic shopping. The results support the notion that decision quality is strongly contingent upon multimedia product demonstrations and comparison tools. Our findings not only inform designers on what type of product will most benefit from multimedia experience, but also quantify these benefits in terms of decision quality, learning, efficiency and satisfaction. Comparison tools support the basic task of evaluating alternatives; if not supported, effectiveness and efficiency for this task will decrease considerably. In future work we intend to address the issue of external validity, designing a follow-up experiment using a different class of products. We are also in the process of relating the outcomes of the reported study with the analysis of the video data.

Acknowledgements

Fabio Nemetz's PhD is funded by CAPES/Brazil.

References

Alba, J., Lynch, J., Weitz, B., Janiszewski, C., Lutz, R., Sawyer, A. & Wood, S. [1997], Interactive Home Shopping: Incentives for Consumers, Retailers, and Manufacturers to Participate in Electronic Marketplaces, *Journal of Marketing* **61**(3), 38–53.

Anderson, J. R. [2000], *Learning and Memory: An Integrated Approach*, second edition, John Wiley & Sons.

Ariely, D. [2000], Controlling the Information Flow: The Role of Interactivity in Consumers' Decision Making and Preferences, *Journal of Consumer Research* 27(2), 233–48.

Bazerman, M. H. [2001], Consumer Research for Consumers, *Journal of Consumer Research* 27(4), 499–504.

Bevan, N. [1995], Measuring Usability as Quality of Use, *Software Quality Journal* 4(2), 115–30.

Cases, A. S. [2002], Perceived Risk and Risk-reduction Strategies in Internet Shopping, *International Review of Retail, Distribution and Consumer Research* 12(4), 375–94.

Daugherty, T., Li, H. & Biocca, F. [2005], Experiential Ecommerce: A Summary of Research Investigating the Impact of Virtual Experience on Consumer Learning, *in* C. Haugtvedt, K. Machleit & R. Yalch (eds.), *Online Consumer Psychology: Understanding and Influencing Consumer Behavior in the Virtual World*, Lawrence Erlbaum Associates, pp.457–89.

Fazio, R. H. & Zanna, M. P. [1981], Direct Experience and Attitude-Behavior Consistency, *Advances in Experimental Social Psychology* 14, 161–202.

Frøkjær, E., Hertzum, M. & Hornbæk, K. [2000], Measuring Usability: Are Effectiveness, Efficiency, and Satisfaction Really Correlated?, *in* T. Turner & G. Szwillus (eds.), *Proceedings of the SIGCHI Conference on Human Factors in Computing Systems (CHI'00)*, *CHI Letters* 2(1), ACM Press, pp.345–52.

Girard, T., Silverblatt, R. & Korgaonkar, P. [2002], Influence of Product Class on Preference for Shopping on the Internet, *Journal of Computer-mediated Communication* 8(1). http://jcmc.indiana.edu/vol8/issue1/girard.html, last accessed 2006-05-08.

GVU [1998], Georgia Tech Graphics, Visualization & Usability Center's 10th WWW User Survey, http://www.gvu.gatech.edu/gvu/user_surveys/survey-1998-10, last accessed 2006-05-08.

Häubl, G. & Figueroa, P. [2002], Interactive 3D Presentations and Buyer Behavior, *in* L. Terveen & D. Wixon (eds.), *CHI'02 Extended Abstracts of the Conference on Human Factors in Computing Systems*, ACM Press, pp.744–5.

Häubl, G. & Trifts, V. [2000], Consumer Decision Making in Online Shopping Environments: The Effects of Interactive Decision Aids, *Marketing Science* 19(1), 4–21.

Hoch, S. J. [2002], Product Experience is Seductive, *Journal of Consumer Research* 29(3), 448–53.

Hoch, S. J. & Deighton, J. [1989], Managing What Consumers Learn from Experience, *Journal of Marketing* 53, 1–20.

Jarvenpaa, S. L., Tractinsky, N. & Vitale, M. [2000], Consumer Trust in an Internet Store, *Information Technology and Management* 1(1-2), 45–71.

Klein, L. R. [1998], Evaluating the Potential of Interactive Media Through a New Lens: Search Versus Experience Goods, *Journal of Business Research* **41**(3), 195–203.

Klein, L. R. [1999], Creating Virtual Experiences in the New Media, PhD thesis, Harvard Graduate School of Business Administration.

Li, H., Daugherty, T. & Biocca, F. [2001], Characteristics of Virtual Experience in Electronic Commerce: A Protocol Analysis, *Journal of Interactive Marketing* **15**(3), 13–30.

Lowengart, O. & Tractinsky, N. [2001], Differential Effects of Product Category on Shoppers' Selection of Web-based Stores: A Probabilistic Modeling Approach, *Journal of Electronic Consumer Research* **2**(4), 12–26.

Muthukrishnan, A. V. [1995], Decision Ambiguity and Incumbent Brand Advantage, *Journal of Consumer Research* **22**(1), 98–109.

Nelson, P. J. [1981], Consumer Information and Advertising, *in* M. Galatin & R. D. Leite (eds.), *Economics of Information*, Kluwer, pp.42–82.

Nisbett, R. & Ross, L. [1980], *Human Inference: Strategies and Shortcomings of Social Judgement*, Prentice–Hall.

Osselaer, S. M. J. V. & Alba, J. W. [2000], Consumer Learning and Brand Equity, *Journal of Consumer Research* **27**(1), 1–16.

Smith, R. E. & Swinyard, W. R. [1983], Attitude-Behavior Consistency: The Impact of Product Trial Versus Advertising, *Journal of Marketing Research* **20**(3), 257–67.

Smith, S. P., Johnston, R. B. & Howard, S. [2005], Vicarious Experience in Retail E-commerce: An Inductive Taxonomy of Product Evaluation Support Features, *Information Systems and E-business Management* **3**(1), 21–46.

Spiekermann, S. & Parachiv, C. [2002], Motivating Human-Agent Interaction: Transferring Insights from Behavioral Marketing to Interface Design, *Journal of Electronic Commerce Research* **2**(3), 255–285.

Wright, A. A. & Lynch, D. E. [1995], Communication Effects of Advertising versus Direct Experience When both Search and Experience Attributes are Present, *Journal of Consumer Research* **21**(4), 708–18.

Interactions in the Wild

Output Multimodal Interaction: The Case of Augmented Surgery

Benoît Mansoux[†‡], Laurence Nigay[†] & Jocelyne Troccaz[‡]

[†] *CLIPS-IMAG / équipe IIHM, 385 rue de la Bibliothèque, 38041 Grenoble cedex 9, France*

Tel: *+33 4 76 51 43 65*

Email: *benoit.mansoux@imag.fr*

[‡] *TIMC-IMAG / équipe GMCAO, Faculté de Médecine, 38700 La Tronche, France*

Output multimodal interaction involves choice and combination of relevant interaction modalities to present information to the user. In this paper, we present a framework based on reusable software components for rapidly developing output multimodal interfaces by choosing and combining interaction modalities. Such an approach enables us to quickly explore several design alternatives as part of an iterative design process. Our approach is illustrated by examples from a computer-assisted surgery system that runs in a specific environment (i.e. an operating room) and so needs adapted multimodal interaction. Our approach supports the exploration of several output multimodal interaction design alternatives with the surgeons.

Keywords: multimodal presentation, software components, computer-assisted surgery systems.

1 Introduction

In this paper we focus on the software development of output multimodal interfaces (from the system to the user) by describing a component-based framework, called ICARE, which allows the easy and rapid development of multimodal interfaces. Our approach relies on our previous work: the ICARE framework for input multimodal interfaces [Bouchet et al. 2004]. In this paper we explain the extensions to the existing ICARE framework for the case of outputs.

Our goal is to define a framework to enable rapid development of output multimodal interfaces and therefore more iterations as part of an iterative user-centred design method for achieving usable multimodal user interfaces [Myers et al. 2000]. Our application domain is computer-assisted surgery requiring adapted multimodal interaction for a specific environment, the operating room. We are using our framework for cost-effectively exploring several output multimodal interaction design alternatives with surgeons.

The structure of the paper is as follows: first, we present related work on development frameworks and tools for multimodality. Second we present our extensions of the ICARE framework for output multimodal interaction by outlining the conceptual model that includes elementary and modality dependent components as well as generic components (reusable components) for combining modalities (fission mechanism) and its implementation. We finally illustrate the approach by considering the design of the output interface of a computer-assisted kidney puncture system, PERM.

2   Related Work: Tools for Multimodality

Although several multimodal systems have been built, their development still remains a difficult task. The existing frameworks dedicated to multimodal interaction are currently few and limited in scope.

Existing tools mainly focus on input multimodality, either by addressing a specific technical problem including the fusion mechanism [Flippo et al. 2003; Nigay & Coutaz 1995], the composition of several devices [Dragicevic & Fekete 2004] and mutual disambiguation [Oviatt 2000; Flippo et al. 2003], or by being dedicated to specific modalities such as gesture recognition [Westeyn et al. 2003], speech recognition [Glass et al. 2004] or the combined usage of speech and gesture [Krahnstoever et al. 2002]. Going one step further than providing a particular modality or generic reusable mechanisms (i.e. fusion and mutual disambiguation mechanisms), Quickset [Johnston et al. 1997] defines an overall implementation architecture as well as the Open Agent Architecture (OAA) [Moran et al. 1997]. Quickset mainly focuses on input multimodality based on speech and gesture and has been applied to the development of map-based systems.

For outputs, several studies have been performed in the context of the conversational paradigm, also called intelligent multimedia presentation in which seminal work is presented in [André et al. 1993]. The system is designed here as a partner for the user (computer-as-partner [Beaudoin-Lafon 2004]): an output communicative act as part of a natural dialogue between the user and the system is made perceivable by a multimodal presentation. Moreover the main focus of such existing output multimodal frameworks is to automatically generate the output presentation, also called presentation planning systems, based on a speech act, a context such as the current available interaction resources and a user's profile. For example in the Embassi demonstrator [Elting et al. 2003], the architecture is based on OAA and includes a dedicated agent to achieve the combination of output modalities. Based on a speech act, the current context and the user's profile, Embassi generates multimodal presentations that are rendered by a dynamic set of distributed agents.

Focusing on the direct manipulation paradigm (computer-as-tools [Beaudoin-Lafon 2004]), very few tools are dedicated to the design and development of output multimodal interfaces. MOST (Multimodal Output Specification Tool) [Rousseau et al. 2004] is a recent framework for multimodal output interaction which focuses on automatic generation of multimodal presentation based on the interaction context defined as the triplet <user, system, environment>. MOST includes a rule-based selection mechanism for generating the multimodal presentation. MOST therefore defines a reusable framework for developing adaptive multimodal systems and its focus is not on the design of multimodality but more on adaptability by providing an editor for specifying the adaptation rules. A more closely related tool to our ICARE framework is CrossWeaver [Sinha & Landay 2003]: it is a prototyping tool dedicated to non-programmer designers. The created prototypes may involve several input modalities and two output modalities: visual display and text-to-speech synthesis. CrossWeaver divides the design process into three steps. First, the designer makes various sketches to form a storyboard. She/he also decides which combinations of input and output modalities will be available for each sketch and for transitions between sketches. Then, the user tests the prototype with the available input and output modalities. Finally, thanks to a log of the user's actions in the previous step, the designer can analyse how multimodality is handled by the user, and can quickly change the combination of modalities to adapt the interaction. Implementation of CrossWeaver is also based on OAA. As opposed to CrossWeaver, our ICARE framework is a development tool that enables cost-effectively modifications of modalities and combinations of modalities as part of an iterative design process.

To sum up, in comparison with existing frameworks and tools, our ICARE framework is dedicated to output multimodal interaction enhancing the sensory-motor capabilities of an interface by enriching it with innovative output modalities, such as augmenting a surgical tool with a mini-screen. The computer is not a partner as in intelligent multimedia presentation but a tool (computer-as-tools [Beaudoin-Lafon 2004]) for enhancing the task of the user. Moreover our focus is on design exploration by providing a tool enabling rapid development of several output multimodal interaction design alternatives. We currently do not address the problem of automatic adaptation but more the one of adaptable output interfaces. The extent to which interaction techniques and modalities can be successfully selected automatically remains the subject of debate within the HCI research community [Chalmers & Galani 2004]. Moreover, for the case of augmented surgery, our application domain, automatic adaptation is not suitable, even adaptable interfaces must still be experimentally validated.

As defined by Myers et al. [2000], in the general context of user interface software tools, tools for multimodal interfaces must aim to have a low threshold (easy to use) while providing a high ceiling (how much can be done with the tool). Additionally, in order to take account of the ever-widening world of modalities, the tools must be easily extendable, an extensibility that we address in our ICARE framework by considering a component-based approach.

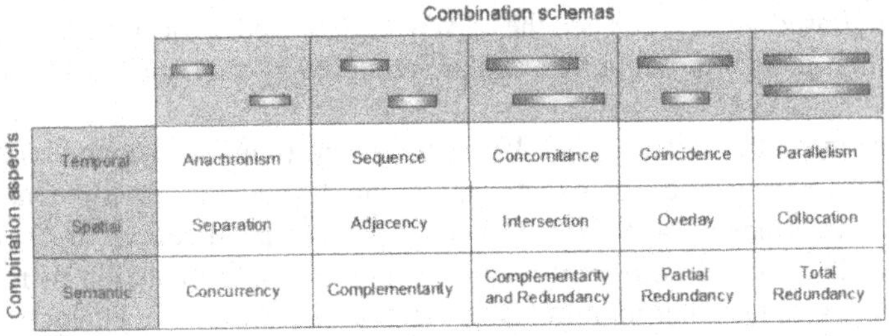

Combination schemas

Figure 1: The combination schemas applied to two combination aspects, the temporal and spatial ones. Figure from Vernier & Nigay [2000].

3 Output Modality and Multimodality

We define an input (from the user to the system) / output (from the system to the user) interaction modality as the coupling of a device d with an interaction language $L : < d, L >$ [Nigay & Coutaz 1997]. For outputs (from the system to the user), a physical device delivers information. Examples of physical devices include loudspeakers and screens. An interaction language defines a set of well-formed expressions (i.e. assembly of symbols according to some conventions) that convey meaning. The generation of a symbol, or a set of symbols, involves actions on physical devices. Examples of interaction languages include pseudo-natural language and graphical animation. Our definition of an output modality enables us to extend the range of possibilities for output multimodality that implies multiple output modalities. Indeed a system can be multimodal without having several output devices. A system using the screen as the unique output device is multimodal whenever it employs several output interaction languages: indeed one device and multiple interaction languages raises the same design and engineering issues as using multiple modalities based on different devices. Our definition of output multimodality is therefore system-oriented and a user-centred perspective may lead to a different definition.

Moreover in the face of such an increasing variety of interaction modalities we can no longer expect to model each output modality in all their diversity at the concrete level. In order to reason about modalities at a higher level of abstraction, a core model must be defined for characterizing the modalities. Such a core model for modality integration will greatly help designers and programmers by allowing them to reason at a higher level of abstraction than the level of a particular modality. This is necessary to be able to select them for an efficient multimodal presentation. Towards this goal, a first set of properties has been proposed in [Vernier & Nigay 2000] for characterizing the interaction language that we reuse in our ICARE framework.

Although each modality can be used independently within a multimodal system, the availability of several modalities in a system naturally leads to the issue of their combined usage. The combined usage of multiple modalities opens a vastly augmented world of possibilities in user interface design. Our framework is based on the CARE properties [Nigay & Coutaz 1997] for reasoning about multimodal interaction: These properties are Complementarity, Assignment, Redundancy, and Equivalence that may occur between the modalities available in a multimodal user interface. We define these four notions (CARE) as relationships between devices and interaction languages and between interaction languages and tasks. Vernier & Nigay [2000] extends the CARE properties to further characterize the combination. Our resulting composition space is organized along two axes. The first axis ranges over a set of combination schemas, as presented in Figure 1.

These schemas use the five Allen [1983] relationships to provide a means of combining multiple modalities into a composite modality. The second axis considers five aspects for characterizing a combination: 1-Time, 2-Space, 3-Articulatory, 4-Syntactic and 5-Semantic. The most studied aspect of combination is the semantic one presented in Figure 1, where one considers the meaning of the conveyed information along the modalities (complementarity and redundancy). The articulatory (device) and syntactic (language) aspects of a combination are based on the definition of a modality as the coupling of a physical device d with an interaction language L. Finally the last remaining aspects, temporal and spatial, are presented in Figure 1. Temporal aspects of the combination have been studied in the literature and are related to the guiding principle in [Reeves et al. 2004]: 'to ensure system output modalities are well-synchronized temporally (for example map-based display and spoken directions)'. For spatial aspects, in the context of computer-assisted surgery systems, we have studied the spatial continuity in interaction [Dubois et al. 2002].

4 ICARE for Multimodal Output

Based on the definitions of the previous section, we here present the extensions to the existing ICARE framework for output multimodality. We first describe the new aspects of the ICARE conceptual model for output multimodality and then focus on its implementation.

4.1 ICARE Conceptual Model for Output Multimodality

The ICARE framework for input multimodality [Bouchet et al. 2004] is based on components and includes elementary and combination components. We reuse these two types of components for output multimodality.

Elementary components define building blocks useful for defining an output modality. The two types of elementary components are the Device and the Interaction Language components. An ICARE Interaction Language component communicates with a Device component via events, in order to form an output modality. Such elementary components are the same as for inputs except for the characteristics that describe them. Examples of characteristics for an output interaction language component include transient or sustained, precise or vague, local or global and deformed or not, as defined by Vernier & Nigay [2000]. In Figure 2, we present the elementary components of two modalities of a game prototype that we have developed using ICARE. The goal is to complete a physical puzzle and the system helps the player to correctly orient the puzzle pieces. For providing the guidance information, the output modalities are graphics displayed on a localized mini-screen fixed to the puzzle piece as well as voice messages.

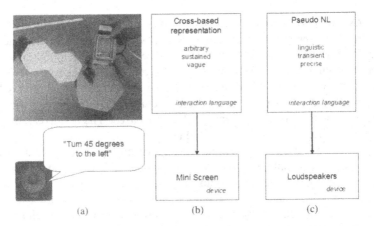

Figure 2: Examples of ICARE elementary components developed for a puzzle game. (a) A puzzle piece with a mini-screen that displays guidance information as two crosses, one mobile (the current orientation) and one static (the right orientation) (M1), while playing a pseudo natural language oral message (M2); (b) ICARE components for modality M1 = <cross-based graphical representation, mini-screen>; (c) ICARE components for modality M2 = <pseudo NL, loudspeakers>.

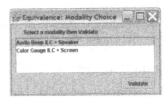

Figure 3: Modality selection window (part of a meta user interface).

Composition components are generic in the sense that they are not dependent on a particular output modality. Based on the CARE properties and the combination space (cf. Section 3), four combination components are defined. Such composition components for outputs are different than the ones defined for inputs: indeed while for multimodal inputs we classically define a fusion mechanism, for outputs one key design issue is a fission mechanism. Four composition components for outputs enable us to define a fission mechanism for a given presentation task.

The Redundancy component enables the parallel use of several equivalent modalities to present the same information. Redundant usage of modalities by forcing the user's perception reinforces the respect of two ergonomic criteria: observability and insistence. The Redundancy component receives an event and dispatches it to all the modalities linked to it. It corresponds to the case 'total redundancy' of Figure 1.

The Equivalence component, analogous to the Redundancy one, implies the use of equivalent modalities. Equivalence differs from Redundancy because the output modalities are not active at the same time. The Equivalence component receives an event and sends it to only one of its linked modalities. It implies a choice of modality done either by the user (adaptable system) or by the system (adaptive system). When done by the user, such a choice is specified by the user using input modalities as part of a meta user interface that enables the user to select the modalities amongst a set of equivalent modalities. Figure 3 presents a simple way of selecting an output modality by direct manipulation using a mouse. Multimodal input interaction can be defined for selecting the output modalities. As a conclusion our ICARE framework for inputs can be used for defining that meta user interface.

The Redundancy/Equivalence component mixes the Redundancy and Equivalence components behaviours. It corresponds to the Redundancy component where redundancy could be optional. This component allows the selection of one or more equivalent output modalities. In theory, this component is not necessary, but it makes the handling of equivalent modalities simpler. The Redundancy/Equivalence component receives an event and sends it to one or more modalities.

Finally, a Complementary component is used when a set of modalities is needed to convey information. Each modality carries a different piece of information. Complementary implies that the user combines the perceived data (fusion of perceived data) in order to interpret the conveyed information. But from a system point of view, the Complementary component performs data fission for output. The Complementarity component receives an event and sends a part of the information contained in this event to each modality. The application designer selects which part of information is sent to each modality. The complementary component implements the three cases 'complementarity', 'complementarity and redundancy' and 'partial redundancy' of Figure 1.

In Figure 4 we present an example of a Complementarity component as well as a Redundancy one for the game prototype of Figure 2. The ICARE diagram of Figure 4a describes a complementary use of two modalities, one for displaying the direction to turn the puzzle piece on the mini-screen while the exact angle is specified by an oral message. We could also decide using the same Complementarity component to display the direction and the angle on the mini-screen while repeating the angle by an oral message. In such a case, the Complementarity component is used for specifying a partial redundancy usage of the two modalities. The Redundancy component of Figure 4b implies a total redundancy: the guidance information is displayed on the mini-screen by two crosses while an oral message repeats the same guidance information in pseudo natural language way (i.e. 'Turn 45 degrees to the left').

4.2 ICARE Implementation Model for Output Multimodality

For implementing the ICARE components, since we extended our ICARE framework for multimodal input, we use the same component technology as for input: the JavaBeans technology. The properties of output modalities are class attributes which can be accessed/modified. The communication between ICARE components is based on the Java event model. To assemble two ICARE components, it is necessary that one component subscribes to events generated by the other component: we provide examples of subscribing in the following section.

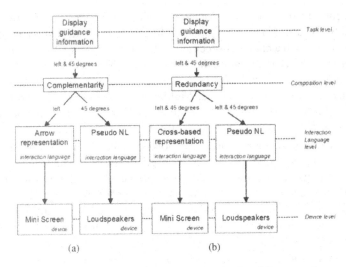

Figure 4: Examples of ICARE combination components developed for a puzzle game. (a) Two complementary modalities. (b) Two redundant modalities.

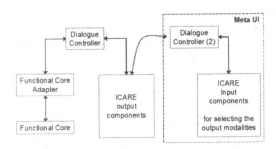

Figure 5: ICARE components within an ARCH software architecture and the meta user interface that enables the selection of equivalent modalities by the user.

As for input, the ICARE output components correspond to the two Interaction components of the ARCH software architectural model [UIMS 1992]. As shown in Figure 5, the Dialogue Controller defines the information to be presented (e.g. <turn 45 degrees left> in Figure 4) and corresponds to the task level. The ICARE components are then responsible for defining the multimodal presentation of the information. For the case of Equivalence and Redundancy/Equivalence components, a choice amongst the modalities must be performed as explained in the previous section (cf. Figure 3). If performed by the user, such a choice requires the definition of a meta user interface that includes a second Dialogue Controller (Dialogue Controller (2) in Figure 5) as well as ICARE input components for specifying the selection. The selection is then sent by the second Dialogue Controller to the ICARE output components.

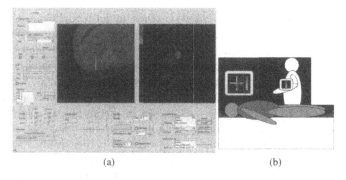

(a)   (b)

Figure 6: (a) The graphical interface of PERM, running on a PC. (b) The PERM setup with a desktop screen and a mini-screen.

So far, we have developed several ICARE output elementary components for the game prototype of Figure 2 as well as for the computer-assisted surgery system PERM that is described in the following section. For combination components, the four components described in Section 4.1 are developed. Moreover we recently started to address the temporal and spatial aspects of a combination, described in Figure 1. Control parameters must be added to the combination components, for example to specify that one modality is used first followed by the second one ('Sequence' case in Figure 1).

We currently manually assemble the ICARE output components as opposed to input ICARE components that are graphically assembled by direct manipulation in the ICARE graphical editor. When the output ICARE components will be inserted in the graphical editor, the developer/designer will graphically assemble the components without knowing the details of their implementations and from the resulting high level specification as in Figure 4, the code of the output multimodal UI will be then generated. So far we assemble the output components manually. We will explain the details of the manual assembling in the context of our PERM system.

5   Illustrative Example: The PERM System

We applied our ICARE approach for the development of the output interface of the Computer-assisted Surgery (CAS) system, PERM, a computer assisted kidney puncture, developed in collaboration with the Grenoble University Hospital. Our goal is to be able to quickly explore several design alternatives with the surgeon. PERM contains several phases corresponding to a predefined surgical protocol. It is a complex system and many parameters for different phases can be configured in the existing desktop user interface, represented in Figure 6a. We focus on the guiding task, which occurs during the surgical intervention. PERM assists the surgeon by providing in real time the position of the puncture needle according to a planned trajectory.

Since the desktop interface forces the surgeon to switch visual attention between the operating field and the guidance information displayed on screen, we decided to explore several design alternatives based on other output modalities such as sound and graphics on a mini-screen using our ICARE framework. While performing the puncture, few concepts are useful to the surgeon and include the real-time needle position and orientation and the planned trajectory. By using sound or by fixing a mini-screen onto the needle (Figure 6b) or on the surgeon's wrist, we can bring back important concepts within the operating field. A mini-screen is an innovative interaction device for CAS systems. As shown in Figure 6b, we can tie a mini-screen to the puncture needle. On the desktop screen, the whole set of guidance information (i.e. the needle position and orientation) is displayed. On the mini-screen, only the needle depth is displayed because it may be the most important piece of information at that time of the guiding task. Based on our design space for mini-screen organized along two dimensions, the usage of the mini-screen and the displayed information [Mansoux et al. 2005], various design solutions are defined. By developing the output interface with our ICARE framework, our goal is to quickly explore such design alternatives with a surgeon.

We have developed several ICARE elementary components for defining output modalities. Three output Device components are developed: the screen, the mini-screen and the microphone. We also developed several Interaction Language components: a colour gauge, a slider, a cross-based representation, a repeated sound in addition to the graphical presentation of the initial design that includes a 3D reconstruction and scanner images on top of which the performed trajectory is displayed (Figure 6a). We plan to develop more Interaction Language components before testing them with the surgeon. For example, a 2D colour gauge designed to fill the mini-screen will be developed. For exploring several design alternatives we will use our four composition components defined in Section 4.

In order to highlight the benefits of our approach (even though we are still assembling the components manually) we explain how we can easily change a modality in PERM and then how we can change a combination of modalities.

5.1 *Changing a Modality*

In PERM, once the needle is inserted into the patient's body from the planned entry point and with the right orientation, the surgeon must know how deep the needle is, according to the trajectory length. There are many ways to represent that ratio: needle depth / trajectory length. So far we developed three modalities. One modality is based on sound: a sound is repeated but the period of repetition is dynamic and based on the distance between the current location of the needle according to the target point. We adapt here the Doppler effect by varying the period of repetition instead of the amplitude of sound. The closer the needle is to the target point, the more frequently the sound is repeated (decreasing the period). Two other modalities are graphics displayed on the mini-screen tied to the needle. One graphical modality displays a colour gauge (Figure 7a) while the other one displays a slider (Figure 7b).

If we want to change the slider by the colour gauge, we need to replace one Interaction Language component by another and to connect the components again. The following few lines of code (pseudo Java) show how to create some components and to link them. Firstly, we create three components: one Device and two Interaction Languages.

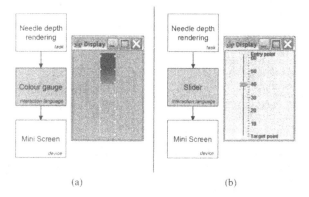

(a)   (b)

Figure 7: Two graphical modalities based on a mini-screen but with different interaction languages: (a) a colour gauge; (b) a slider.

```
MiniScreen myScreen = new MiniScreen ( . . . ) ;
ColourGauge aGauge = new ColourGauge ( . . . ) ;
Slider aSlider = new Slider ( . . . ) ;
```

Then we link two components: an Interaction Language with the Device.

```
aGauge.addListener ( myScreen ) ;
```

The MiniScreen is now listening to events coming from the ColourGauge. When the output components will be integrated in the graphical editor, the modification of a modality will be done graphically and the corresponding code will be automatically generated.

While changing a component in the ICARE assembling, it is possible that the developer needs to adjust the communication between the new component and the rest of the components. Adding extra code is sometimes needed to handle the new link. The following lines describe how to do it.

```
aSlider.addListener ( new ILListener ( ) {
    public void newData ( ICAREEvent e) {
        // non default behaviour
        // extra data processing added here
        . . .
        /* Create a new event with the transformed data. */
        ICAREEvent eNew = new ICAREEvent ( . . . ) ;
        myScreen.setData ( eNew ) ;
    }
} ) ;
```

In that specific case, the MiniScreen is not the listener of the interaction language any more. An anonymous Java class (of type ILListener) makes a bridge between the two components.

The example could appear as a simple change of graphical widgets because of the simple content carried by the modality. But an Interaction Language component conveys meaning and is able to adapt/transform the conveyed data. It is not limited to a simple widget and can be a more complex element such as a text-to-speech module.

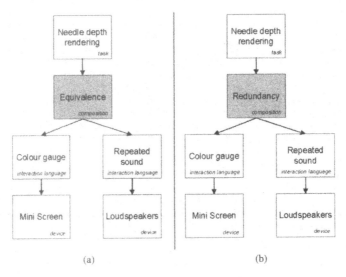

Figure 8: Switching from a configuration with (a) Equivalence to one with (b) Redundancy.

5.2   *Changing a Combination of Modalities*

Changing a combination of modalities is straightforward and easier than changing a modality because the combination components are generic ones. Changing a combination of modalities involves simply switching one combination component by another one. Figure 8 shows the only change needed between an equivalent configuration and a redundant one for two modalities. Configuring the internal behaviour of the composition component (i.e. setting its parameters) is the only additional task that the designer may need to do.

Changing the composition components is straightforward and will enable us to quickly explore several design alternatives with the surgeon. For example by simply considering the two graphical modalities (slider and gauge) and the sound modality, several design solutions can be cost-effectively experimented with the surgeon.

Moreover we also plan to study the adaptation of the modalities during the surgical intervention (i.e. the meta user interface of Figure 5). For example, because the sound is less precise than a graphical representation, we can anticipate that the surgeon may need to change the modalities during the different phases of the intervention:

- only the sound is active when the needle is not touching the patient's body;

- the sound and the colour gauge are used redundantly when the needle is inserted; and

- only the colour gauge is active when the needle tip is very near the target point (e.g. < 10mm).

For this example, a Redundancy/Equivalence component will be used and linked to both modalities. Nevertheless making the output multimodal interface adaptable by the surgeon requires further studies in order to provide the adequate input modalities: we plan to explore voice commands and a pedal press for changing the output modalities.

Another key issue for adaptability, not applicable in Computer-assisted Surgery (CAS) systems since the surgeon is an expert of the system, is to make observable the available modalities and forms of multimodality. Finally we exclude automatic adaptation (adaptivity as opposed to adaptability) for CAS systems. For example let us consider that the automatic adaptation of the output modalities for presenting guidance information to a surgeon in PERM. Again the change of modalities is made at the turning point between two surgical phases: for example when the needle is not touching the patient's body, guidance information with anatomical and pre-operative information is displayed on a monitor and as soon as the needle is touching the patient's body, only the pre-planned trajectory is displayed as crosses on a mini-screen attached to the puncture needle. Although the surgeon is trained to use the system, such automatic adaptation may be a surprise. Moreover a very small backward movement of the needle may imply to come back to the presentation on the monitor, making the output interface very unstable (back and forth between the monitor and the mini-screen). Automatic adaptation in PERM is not planned and we will experimentally study adaptation by the surgeon using voice commands or a pedal press.

6 Conclusion

In this paper, we have presented the extensions to our ICARE framework for developing output multimodal interfaces. The approach is based on reusable software components for rapidly developing output multimodal interfaces by choosing and combining interaction modalities. We illustrated the framework by considering the development of several design alternatives of PERM, a computer-assisted kidney puncture system. Before further enriching the ICARE framework (including a graphical editor for assembling the output components and a mechanism based on psychological knowledge to guide the selection of the components), our current work is to test the design solutions of PERM with a surgical team. Our goal is three-fold:

1. evaluate the usability of the modalities and of the setting with the mini-screen;

2. test the adaptation of the output modalities by the surgeon during the surgical intervention; and

3. evaluate the approach itself as a tool to quickly explore design alternatives with the surgeon.

Acknowledgements

Special thanks to J. Bouchet and M. Serrano for their help in developing the ICARE components and to Mr. G. Serghiou for reviewing the paper. This work is partly funded by the SIMILAR European FP6 network of excellence dedicated to multimodality (http://www.similar.cc).

References

Allen, J. F. [1983], Maintaining Knowledge about Temporal Intervals, *Communications of the ACM* **26**(11), 832–43.

André, E., Finkler, W., Graf, W., Rist, T., Schauder, A., & Wahlster, W. [1993], WIP: The Automatic Synthesis of Multimodal Presentations, *in* M. T. Maybury (ed.), *Intelligent Multimedia Interface*, AAAI Press, pp.75–93.

Beaudoin-Lafon, M. [2004], Designing Interaction, Not Interfaces, *in* M. F. Costabile (ed.), *Proceedings of the Working Conference on Advanced Visual Interface (AVI 2004)*, ACM Press, pp.15–22.

Bouchet, J., Nigay, L. & Ganille, T. [2004], ICARE Software Components for Rapidly Developing Multimodal Interfaces, *in* R. Sharma, T. Darrell, M. Harper, G. Lazzari & M. Turk (eds.), *Proceedings of the 6th International Conference on Multimodal Interfaces (ICMI'04)*, ACM Press, pp.251–8.

Chalmers, M. & Galani, A. [2004], Seamful Interweaving: Heterogeneity in the Theory and Design of Interactive Systems, *in* D. Gruen & I. McAra-McWilliams (eds.), *Proceedings of the Symposium on Designing Interactive Systems: Processes, Practices, Methods and Techniques (DIS'04)*, ACM Press, pp.243–52.

Dragicevic, P. & Fekete, J.-D. [2004], The Input Configurator Toolkit: Towards High Input Adaptability in Interactive Applications, *in* M. F. Costabile (ed.), *Proceedings of the Working Conference on Advanced Visual Interface (AVI 2004)*, ACM Press, pp.244–7.

Dubois, E., Nigay, L. & Troccaz, J. [2002], Assessing Continuity and Compatibility in Augmented Reality Systems, *Universal Access in the Information Society* **4**(1), 263–73.

Elting, C., Rapp, S., Mölher, G. & Strube, M. [2003], Architecture and Implementation of Multimodal Plug and Play, *in* S. Oviatt, T. Darrell, M. Maybury & W. Wahlster (eds.), *Proceedings of the 5th International Conference on Multimodal Interfaces (ICMI'03)*, ACM Press, pp.93–100.

Flippo, F., Krebs, A. & Marsic, I. [2003], A Framework for Rapid Development of Multimodal Interfaces, *in* S. Oviatt, T. Darrell, M. Maybury & W. Wahlster (eds.), *Proceedings of the 5th International Conference on Multimodal Interfaces (ICMI'03)*, ACM Press, pp.109–16.

Glass, J., Weinstein, E., Cyphers, S., Polifroni, J., Chung, G. & Nakano, M. [2004], A Framework for Developing Conversational User Interfaces, *in* R. K. Jacob, Q. Limbourg & J. Vanderdonckt (eds.), *Proceedings of the 5th International Conference on Computer-Aided Design of User Interfaces (CADUI 2004)*, Kluwer, pp.347–58.

Johnston, M., Cohen, P. R., McGee, D., Oviatt, S. L., Pittman, J. A. & Smith, I. [1997], Unification-based Multimodal Integration, *in* P. R. Cohen & W. Wahlster (eds.), *Proceedings of the 35th Annual Meeting of the Association for Computational Linguistics and of the 8th Conference of the European Chapter of the Association for Computational Linguistics*, Morgan-Kaufmann, pp.281–8.

Krahnstoever, N., Kettebekov, S., Yeasin, M. & Sharma, R. [2002], A Real-time Framework for Natural Multimodal Interaction with Large Screen Displays, *in* A. Waibel, W. Gao, E. Horvitz, S. Furui & J. Yang (eds.), *Proceedings of the 4th IEEE International Conference on Multimodal Interfaces (ICMI'02)*, IEEE Computer Society Press, pp.349–54.

Mansoux, B., Nigay, L. & Troccaz, J. [2005], The Mini-Screen: An Innovative Device for Computer Assisted Surgery Systems, *in* J. D. Westwood, R. S. Haluck, H. M. Hoffman, G. T. Mogel, R. Phillips & R. A. R. anf K. G. Vosburgh (eds.), *Medicine Meets Virtual Reality 13: The magical Next Becomes the Medical Now*, Vol. 111 of *Studies in Health Technology and Informatics*, IOS Press, pp.314–20.

Moran, D. B., Cheyer, A. J., E., J. L., Martin, D. L. & Park, S. [1997], Multimodal User Interfaces in the Open Agent Architecture, *in* A. R. Puerta & E. Edmonds (eds.), *Proceedings of the 2nd International Conference on Intelligent User Interfaces (IUI'97)*, ACM Press, pp.61–8.

Myers, B., Hudson, S. E. & Pausch, R. [2000], Past, Present, and Future of User Interface Software Tools, *ACM Transactions on Computer–Human Interaction* **7**(1), 3–28.

Nigay, L. & Coutaz, J. [1995], A Generic Platform for Addressing the Multimodal Challenge, *in* I. Katz, R. Mack, L. Marks, M. B. Rosson & J. Nielsen (eds.), *Proceedings of the SIGCHI Conference on Human Factors in Computing Systems (CHI'95)*, ACM Press, pp.98–105.

Nigay, L. & Coutaz, J. [1997], Multifeature Systems: The CARE Properties and Their Impact on Software Design, *in* J. Lee (ed.), *Intelligence and Multimodality in Multimedia Interfaces: Research and Applications*, AAAI Press, Chapter 9. http://iihm.imag.fr/publs/1995/IMMIChapNigay95.pdf, last accessed 2006-05-27.

Oviatt, S. L. [2000], Taming Recognition Errors with a Multimodal Interface, *Communications of the ACM* **43**(9), 45–51. Special Issue on Spoken Language Interfaces.

Reeves, L. M., Lai, J., Larson, J. A., Oviatt, S., Balaji, T. S., Buisine, S., Collings, P., Cohen, P., Kraal, B., Martin, J. C., McTear, M., Raman, T. V., Stanney, K. M., Su, H. & Wang, Q. Y. [2004], Guidelines for Multimodal User Interfaces Design, *Communications of the ACM* **47**(1), 57–9.

Rousseau, C., Bellik, Y., Vernier, F. & Bazalgette, D. [2004], Architecture Framework For Output Multimodal Systems Design, *in Proceedings of Australian Conference on Computer–Human Interaction (OzCHI 2004)*, CHISIG. http://www.limsi.fr/Individu/vernier/Publis/OZCHI04-LongPaper.pdf last accessed 2006-05-27.

Sinha, A. K. & Landay, J. A. [2003], Capturing User Tests in a Multimodal, Multidevice Informal Prototyping Tool, *in* S. Oviatt, T. Darrell, M. Maybury & W. Wahlster (eds.), *Proceedings of the 5th International Conference on Multimodal Interfaces (ICMI'03)*, ACM Press, pp.117–24.

UIMS [1992], A Metamodel for the Runtime Architecture of an Interactive System: The UIMS Tool Developers Workshop, *ACM SIGCHI Bulletin* **24**(1), 32–7.

Vernier, F. & Nigay, L. [2000], A Framework for the Combination and Characterization of Output Modalities, *in* P. Palanque & F. Paternò (eds.), *Interactive Systems. Design, Specification, and Verification: Proceedings of the 7th International Workshop, DSV-IS 2000*, Vol. 1946 of *Lecture Notes in Computer Science*, Springer-Verlag, pp.35–50.

Westeyn, T., Brashear, H., Atrash, A. & Starner, T. [2003], Georgia Tech Gesture Toolkit: Supporting Experiments in Gesture Recognition, *in* S. Oviatt, T. Darrell, M. Maybury & W. Wahlster (eds.), *Proceedings of the 5th International Conference on Multimodal Interfaces (ICMI'03)*, ACM Press, pp.85–92.

mSpace Mobile: Exploring Support for Mobile Tasks

Max L. Wilson, Alistair Russell, Daniel A. Smith & m.c. schraefel

IAM Research Group, School of Electronics and Computer Science, University of Southampton, Southampton SO17 1BJ, UK
Email: *{mlw05r, ar5, das05r, mc}@ecs.soton.ac.uk*

In the following paper we present a formative study comparing two Web application interfaces, mSpace Mobile and Google Local in supporting Web-based location discovery tasks on mobile devices while stationary and while on the move. While mSpace Mobile performed well in both stationary and mobile conditions, performance in Google Local dropped significantly in the mobile condition. We postulate that mSpace Mobile performed better because it breaks the paradigm of the page for delivering Web content, thereby enabling new and more powerful interfaces to be used to support mobility.

Keywords: mSpace Mobile, evaluation, mobility, mobile devices, performance, design, human factors.

1 Introduction

Increasing ubiquitous connectivity with the Internet for mobile devices such as PDAs and smartphones, via cellular networks and wifi-hotspots, means that progressively more Web-based information services are accessed from such devices while on the move. Mobile device access to the Web has motivated considerable research into dynamically re-presenting full size web pages more effectively for small screens [Baudisch et al. 2004; Kamba et al. 1996]. This work, however, has been mainly focused on viewing a *single* page (implicitly, while stationary), rather than on carrying out tasks *while mobile* which may require access, back and forth, to *multiple* pages to address even a simple query such as 'where is a Japanese restaurant near a cinema showing this film I wish to see?' In such mobile information foraging activities, the page-as-unit paradigm gets in the way of the information the person wishes to access, as people must scan through superfluous-to-task content on numerous pages to get at just the data they want.

mSpace Mobile (http://mSpace.fm/mobile) is an approach to support *mobile* Web-based planning and exploration activities on small screen devices that, using new Web protocols, eliminates the page as smallest information unit. This new approach allows us to use more effective UI techniques like focus+context zooming to support rapid exploration of an area of interest. This paper reports on the study we ran to compare mSpace Mobile with a current state of the art smartphone/PDA devices for carrying out these explorations and planning activities. The study considered both stationary and mobile performance in order to understand whether there were performance differences between the two interfaces in mobile activities in particular, and to begin to tease out from the comparison the interface attributes contributing to these differences. In the rest of this paper we describe the related work, mSpace Mobile itself and the formative study. In the discussion of the results, we are able to begin to use these findings to move towards design heuristics to support design for *mobile* information foraging activities.

2   Related Work

Beyond repackaging Web pages for small screens, visual UI research has looked at mechanisms to leverage focus+context displays to cope with small screens, the exemplar of which has been Bederson et al.'s [2004] DateLens work. Likewise, multimodal research has looked at controlling applications with touch and audio, eliminating video entirely, assuming the video channel is being used for other tasks [Pirhonen et al. 2002]. These examples however have not been concerned with interaction performance with the device while a person uses the interface *while mobile*. Earlier work on mobile systems in changing contexts has focused on applications like tour guide systems: how well the information adapts to location; how location awareness can be represented. The GUIDE system and its follow-on work using multi-modal interactions for the delivery of information on a location-aware device is an exemplar of this kind of work [Bornträger et al. 2003], while more recent work [Fujii et al. 2005; Kim et al. 2005] focuses on the effectiveness of more dynamically constructed, location aware tours. While changing context is an important aspect of mobile device interaction especially that which is focused on location discovery tasks, *mobility per se* and its effect on performance, is not a core part of design or evaluation in these systems.

Indeed, from what we can find, work on effect of mobility on task performance with mobile devices is recent, and has focused primarily on performance in target acquisition tasks. For instance, recent work has shown unsurprisingly that text entry on mobile devices is either slowed by being in motion or slows the walking speed of the user; increased text box size reduces the difficulty [Mizobuchi et al. 2005]. Similar work has shown that larger zones enabled by interactions like tap and drag are more effective than small scroll bar targets when moving with mobile devices [Mackay et al. 2005]; tap and drag is used where possible within the mSpace Mobile interface. Further work has evaluated screen tapping accuracy and frequency relative to gait phase and shown that the majority of tapping occurs most, and most

Figure 1: The left panel shows the mSpace Mobile interface. The right panel shows the overlays on areas of the interface: Section A – the columnar entity selector; Section B – the information box; Section C – a context graphic, in this case a map; Section D – an mSpace selector and Section E – an Interest list, in this case labelled Favourites.

accurately, in the latter phases that precede each new step; this is when the device hand is lowering away from the stylus [Crossan et al. 2005].

Beyond target acquisition performance, our interest has been to begin to look at the effect of interface attributes on ability to support and carry out more cognitively rich and yet mundane tasks such as planning activities. In our case we are interested in activities which involve a set of compound queries to complete a task – such as finding a restaurant near by a cinema that is showing a film of interest – *while mobile*.

3   mSpace Mobile: ZedPanes

mSpace Mobile (see Figure 1), rather than presenting information in a page, represents information as areas of information or domains, where each domain contains a set of associated dimensions.

A location domain, as an example, may have the dimensions Transport, Cuisine, Entertainment, Sites, Clean Public Toilets, and so on, whereas a film domain might have Actors, Producers, Countries, Genres. It is beyond the scope of this paper to describe how these dimensions are generated or populated. Suffice it to say that the data is from existing Web resources and uses next-generation Web protocols; an overview of the approach is available by Harris et al. [2004].

To facilitate interaction on mobile devices, mSpace uses a combination of a spatial, multicolumn display with a zoomable focus+context interface called ZedPanes as shown in Figure 1. The spatial layout of the multicolumn UI enables a person to select a dimension element like Japanese in the dimension Cuisine. The next column then lists the names of restaurants near the currently selected location as shown in the map pane, and the map reflects the positions of the restaurants in the list. Selecting any element in a dimension (Figure 1, Section A) also brings up information about that element (Figure 1, Section B). For instance, by selecting a particular restaurant, a description of the restaurant, its location, web site and menu if

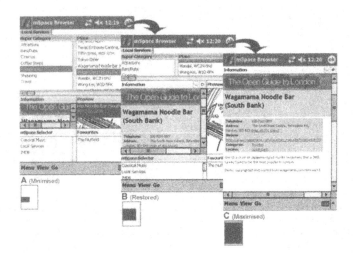

Figure 2: mSpace Mobile ZedPanes: A shows the default equal zoom level; B shows the info box expanded to the take up more of the screen but with other areas of the screen still visible; C shows the info box pane expanded to full screen. Any of the panes can be expanded or contracted in this way by a single click.

available is rendered. It is therefore easy for people to see the associated contexts of any selection and switch between them rapidly for comparison and contrast. Double tapping an item adds it to a pane for Finds pane (Figure 1, Section E, a feature not used in the study, below). Selecting an item in the Favourites list recovers its associated information. If a person wishes to focus on any particular pane to see it in more detail, ZedPanes enables that pane to be zoomed up two additional levels: focussed (where other panels are reduced) and full screen (Figure 2). In this way people have persistent control over area of interest and can readily switch focus among panes. ZedPanes has been inspired by Bederson et al.'s [2004] DateLens, expanding it such that where DateLens is restricted to zooming on tabular data like calendars, ZedPanes can support any number of nested hierarchical panes; each pane also has its own three-level zoom. The mSpace multi-paned display facilitates rapid domain exploration by enabling easy selection and focus on individual elements while maintaining persistent context.

4 Study

Our study is mainly a formative exploration of issues that affect carrying out discovery and planning activities with Web-based sources while mobile, and while using a mobile device. Our hypothesis is that the mSpace Mobile interface will perform better than state-of-the-art Web applications designed to support similar planning activities particularly when on the move. For our study we focused specifically on *location-based* discovery and planning tasks. By location-based, we mean activities that take place in a physical location, and by planning we mean building a sequence of related activities, for example finding information such as: cinemas playing a certain movie, then finding times of showings; finding restaurants within a certain distance to that cinema that will be open after the film finishes. Sequences of compound queries like these are natural (and necessary) for carrying out even simple plans: can we have dinner close to the theatre, for instance. By using a sequence rather than a discrete task, we considered we would be better able to explore why either interface performed better or worse in realistic scenarios.

As a context for stepping through a sequence, we built a scenario of an evening out (dinner and a movie), where the participants needed to find appropriate resources to support these activities. There were 6 activities in each scenario. The scenario started with an activity such as finding cinemas showing a given film 'near by' the starting location for the trial. Each following activity built on the previous step. For instance, from the cinema, participants were asked to find restaurants near it that feature a particular cuisine, and then of those, to find ones which also have take-out. Some tasks were completable within the main interface, by which we mean they could be completed without clicking to a remote webpage; others required clicking to an external website linked from the main interface as well as the information available in the main interface itself. Each scenario was balanced to have equivalent steps within the main interface and jumps out to external websites.

This focus on location-as-context let us compare mSpace Mobile with the popular Google Local (http://local.google.co.uk), a Web state of the art application with an interface that, like mSpace Mobile, supports discovery of entities like restaurants and cinemas (via keyword search), plots these locations on a zoomable map, lists the finds beside the map, and provides information about an entity when selected, including a link, when available, to that business's site, all in one view. Google Local also supports associated information discovery. Reviews of discovered locations, for example, are often made available within the context of a place plotted on a Google Local map.

While Google Local has not been optimized for mobile appliances such as phones, it is still useful and usable on a PDA. Our concern with this study, however, is *not* to carry out a head to head competition between mSpace Mobile and Google local, but to use the comparison as a way to tease out specific design attributes that may affect performance under two specific conditions: first, when actually moving and using the device, and second when carrying out a sequence of tasks rather than a single lookup.

5   Method and Apparatus

A 2×2 within-group repeated measures design was used: the two interfaces, mSpace Mobile and Google Local, were tested in two conditions, stationary and mobile. Exposure to each interface was counterbalanced. Stationary trials, however, always preceded mobile trials: we were keen to ensure comfort with the devices in a seated environment before we asked participants to walk about using them. The stationary condition was performed sitting in a chair in a private office.

For the in-motion condition, participants carried out their tasks while walking around a 60m indoor course. While we are interested in mobility's effects on 'real world' activities like carrying out planning on mobile devices while walking to catch a train, we opted to use an in-lab rather than in the wild, outdoor environment both for value of results and safety of participants. As found by Kjeldskov et al. [2004], the added time and complexity of carrying out in the field experiments is not outweighed by the value of the results returned. Indeed, their work shows that while many critical usability issues were found in both in lab and field studies (8 to 7 respectively) significantly more of what they class as 'serious' usability issues were discovered in the lab than in the field. Since our goal was primarily to discover whether or not there were significant differences in mobile performance between application interface designs, it seemed we would be able to make this determination, perhaps more effectively, without introducing undue complexity and safety issues of carrying out the study in the field. In order to simulate safely the kind of split attention to both the task and the environment a walker requires in a live environment, participants were therefore asked to navigate both around and between well-marked objects on the track. Simulated obstacles included a road crossing, where participants were required to take notice of the obstacle and stop. Similarly, participants had to walk between two closely located chairs; this requires users to realise a narrowing pathway. Finally, chairs were placed randomly on the ground, simulating the need to avoid objects such as posts and bins. Real obstacles included walking through doors and avoiding on-coming participants who were navigating the course in the opposite direction. Beyond the benefits of safety by using an indoor course (participants were not in danger of being hit by a car), the controlled environment supported close monitoring of participants and detailed recording of their actions. An equal number and kind of objects were used for both interfaces, but the course was adjusted for each UI to reduce learning effect.

For the study we sought participants who identified themselves as comfortable with using mobile devices, who used them regularly and who said that they did indeed carry out tasks with them while walking. The study included 6 men and 3 women ranging in age from 18 and 45, all experienced with computing technology and familiar with using PDAs. Thirty percent of participants regularly used a PDA; all however owned at least one portable device, such as a mobile phone and/or personal stereo. All reported experiences they characterized as 'regular' in using these portable devices (making calls, choosing music) while walking with them.

Before beginning, the participants were given training with both mSpace Mobile and Google Local. Each interface was run on the same iPaq hand-held PDA and used the same wireless network to access the Web data. The scenario was read aloud to the participants, one activity in the sequence at a time. When the first activity was completed, the next activity would be read out. Participants were given 10 minutes to complete the entire scenario, although 2 extra minutes were allowed for those close to completing the tasks: a pilot study had indicated that 6 minutes had been the maximum time necessary to complete the entire sequence. We captured the time to complete the full sequence on each interface. We also asked participants to think aloud as they worked. While one investigator read out the sequence for the

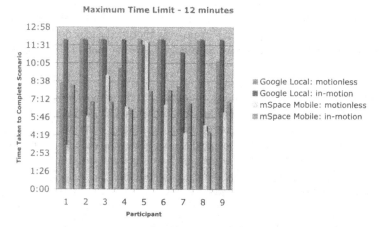

Figure 3: Graph showing the performance times of each participant in the four conditions.

participant, another investigator recorded observations. Each trial concluded with a semi-structured interview of the participant to solicit further comments about their experience of the interfaces in each condition.

6 Results

6.1 Quantitative Measures

Our hypothesis that mSpace Mobile would perform more effectively in each condition was borne out. Figure 3 shows the completion times for each participant in each condition and UI. The lines across the graph show the average completion time for each UI in each condition. Paired t-tests were used to evaluate the specific differences between the two dependent variables, the mobile and stationary conditions of each interface. As we were not interested in any effect between interfaces, paired t-tests (rather than ANOVA) were sufficient for a comparison of two means. mSpace Mobile performed significantly faster (30%, $t(8) = 6.5566$, $p < 0.0005$) than Google Local in the stationary condition; this increased to almost 40% faster, also significant ($t(8) = 12.2425$, $p < 0.0001$), in the in-motion condition. The difference between motion conditions in mSpace Mobile is not significant (6%, $t(8) = 0.5040$, $p = 0.6279$), whereas the performance drop in Google Local between conditions is greater (10%), but not quite significant ($t(8) = 2.2714$), $p = 0.0528$). The degree to which mSpace Mobile performed better in particular in the mobile condition, however, is a conservative value. Participants were halted after 12 minutes. This stopping value was used for subsequent statistical evaluation. Whereas all these participants in both stationary and mobile conditions with mSpace finished the tasks, 4 of 9 (44%) in the stationary and 7 of 9 (78%) in the mobile condition with Google Local did not complete the sequence by the 12 minute mark, near double the time needed to complete the sequence in either condition for mSpace Mobile. Even for a small sample size, the consistent degree of difference in terms of performance across participants and between the two interfaces, particularly in the in-motion condition, suggests that evaluating mobile devices both *in-motion* and with *sequential tasks* are an effective metric for assessing mobile UI performance.

6.2 Observations

The time required to load external pages requested from within Google Local had an effect on performance in both conditions. Each click in Google Local is a call out to the Web, which can increase interaction time, depending on network performance. In mSpace Mobile information associated with a selection, such as the next column entities, their map locations and information views is transported in smaller chunks and cached: calls to the network are reduced, overall interface response is faster.

While performance time for mSpace Mobile across conditions was largely similar, Google Local's performance dropped considerably from the stationary to the mobile condition. While network performance remained equivalent between conditions, it became apparent from observing participants that scrolling and text entry in Google Local took longer to carry out while mobile than while stationary; this supports the work done by Mizobuchi et al. [2005] and Mackay et al. [2005].

Participants commented on this difference themselves during interviews. We also noticed that participants frequently slowed their pace when entering text in Google Local, whereas there was less pace slowing observed with mSpace Mobile. One participant noted that target acquisition was challenging for selecting individual items within the columns of mSpace Mobile, though this did not seem to have a noticeable effect on their performance between the conditions. In cases where participants knew the location of something, they preferred Google Local for its text entry. For this reason, some participants said they would appreciate a text search box in mSpace Mobile as a complement to the UI (this has since been added). Overall participants said they preferred the direct manipulation of mSpace Mobile.

7 Discussion

From the above, several conditions emerge which contribute to effective performance when carrying out planning activities with mobile devices, particularly when on the move: persistent views of information, quick data transfer, reduced requirement for text entry, and reduced requirement for activities like scrolling that require both acquiring and holding a target – this later point reinforces the findings on mobile target acquisition [Crossan et al. 2005]. mSpace Mobile's emphasis on single tap selection and expandable panes reduces the need either for scrolling or text entry, contributing to improvement in performance by reducing the number of taps to the interface. While it is possible that walking amplified the scrolling and text entry problems to such an extent as to account for the considerable performance difference between conditions in Google Local, it may be that additional cognitive load factors come into play as a result of the cumulative delays caused to task completion by any one of these factors, reducing performance further. In contrast, the performance of mSpace Mobile remained fairly constant across conditions.

This finding suggests that mSpace Mobile's non-page paradigm for presenting Web data, with resulting reduced calls to the network, its largely persistent views of information in a domain, and its focus+context interface may reduce cognitive load and improve performance by improving recognition rather than recall in the interface, particularly when on the move. Further study will be needed to tease out these factors' effects

8 Conclusions

In this paper we have carried out a formative, exploratory study to consider the effects of being mobile on the ability to carry out sequential tasks like resource discovery and planning activities when accessing the Web via mobile devices. In contrast to typical mobile device Web viewers, we have proposed a non-page based paradigm for exploration of Web information. The approach foregrounds persistent domain overviews from which selections can be made utilizing direct manipulation techniques. To optimize screen space, the UI for exploration is a focus+context, multi-paned display. We have shown that first, when tested against Google Local, a Web application designed to support the kinds of location discovery tasks we tested, mSpace Mobile performed significantly better in both mobile and stationary conditions. Second we have shown that mobility – in this case walking – has a significant degradation effect on sequential task performance when using a traditional Web page-as-unit model.

These early findings point to interesting directions for designing devices to support network-dependent activities on mobile devices for both stationary and in-motion usability. It seems that, in general, better UI paradigms for access, exploration and planning are enabled when breaking the current page paradigm for delivering network-based content. In terms of design and evaluation heuristics, use-in-motion may be a significant factor for evaluating interaction design effectiveness for mobile devices. Likewise, testing for sequential rather than single task performance seems to be an important criterion for evaluating on-the-move interaction performance. We propose these criteria to be considered as a part of a potential taxonomy of design criteria for mobile devices the community may evolve.

Acknowledgements

Thanks to the EPSRC AKT project (GR/N15764/01), DTC Knowledge Fusion Project (C/N03751/8.14) and the School of Electronics and Computer Science, University of Southampton, for their support. Thanks also to Sacha Brostoff, Stephen Brewster and Alan Dix for their insights into the statistical analysis.

References

Baudisch, P., Xie, X., Wang, C. & Ma, W.-Y. [2004], Collapse-to-Zoom: Viewing Web Pages on Small Screen Devices by Interactively Removing Irrelevant Content, *in* S. K. Feiner & J. A. Landay (eds.), *Proceedings of the 17th Annual ACM Symposium on User Interface Software and Technology (UIST'04)*, *CHI Letters* 6(2), ACM Press, pp.91–4.

Bederson, B. B., Clamage, A. D., Czerwinski, M. P. & Robertson, G. G. [2004], DateLens: A Fisheye Calendar Interface for PDAs, *ACM Transactions on Computer–Human Interaction* 11(1), 90–119.

Bornträger, C., Cheverst, K., Davies, N., Dix, A., Friday, A. & Seltz, J. [2003], Experiments with Multi-modal Interfaces in a Context-aware City Guide, *in* L. Chittaro (ed.), *Human–Computer Interaction with Mobile Devices and Services: Proceedings of the 5th International Symposium on Mobile Human–Computer Interaction (Mobile HCI 2003)*, Vol. 2795 of *Lecture Notes in Computer Science*, Springer-Verlag, pp.116–30.

Crossan, A., Murray-Smith, R., Brewster, S., Kelly, J. & Musizza, B. [2005], Gait Phase Effects in Mobile Interaction, *in* G. van der Veer & C. Gale (eds.), *CHI'05 Extended Abstracts of the Conference on Human Factors in Computing Systems*, ACM Press, pp.1312–5.

Fujii, S., Takahashi, Y., Fukuoka, H., Ichikawa, T., Sakai, S. & Mizuno, T. [2005], Development of Ubiquitous Historical Tour Support System, *in* R. Khosla, R. J. Howlett & L. C. Jain (eds.), *Proceedings of the 9th International Conference on Knowledge-based Intelligent Information and Engineering Systems (KES 2005)*, Vol. 3681-4 of *Lecture Notes in Artifical Intelligence*, Springer, pp.412–7.

Harris, C., Owens, A., Russel, A. & Smith, D. A. [2004], mSpace: Exploring the Semantic Web: A Technical Report in Support of the mSpace Software Framework, Technical Report, University of Southampton.

Kamba, T., Elson, S., Harpold, T., Stamper, T. & Sukaviriya, P. [1996], Using Small Screen Space More Efficiently, *in* M. J. Tauber, B. Nardi & G. C. van der Veer (eds.), *Proceedings of the SIGCHI Conference on Human Factors in Computing Systems: Common Ground (CHI'96)*, ACM Press, pp.383–90.

Kim, J.-W., Kim, J.-Y., Hwang, H.-S. & Kim, C.-S. [2005], Location-sensitive Tour Guide Services Using the Semantic Web, *in* R. Khosla, R. J. Howlett & L. C. Jain (eds.), *Proceedings of the 9th International Conference on Knowledge-based Intelligent Information and Engineering Systems (KES 2005)*, Vol. 3681-4 of *Lecture Notes in Artifical Intelligence*, Springer, pp.908–14.

Kjeldskov, J., Skov, M. B., Als, B. S. & Høegh, R. T. [2004], Is it Worth the Hassle? Exploring the Added Value of Evaluating the Usability of Context-aware Mobile Systems in the Field, *in* S. Brewster & M. Dunlop (eds.), *Human–Computer Interaction — Mobile HCI 2004: Proceedings of the 6th International Symposium on Mobile Human–Computer Interaction*, Vol. 3160 of *Lecture Notes in Computer Science*, Springer-Verlag, pp.61–73.

Mackay, B., Dearman, D., Inkpen, K. & Watters, C. [2005], Walk 'n Scroll: A Comparison of Software-based Navigation Techniques for Different Levels of Mobility, *in* M. Tscheligi, R. Bernhaupt & K. Mihalic (eds.), *Mobile HCI '05: Proceedings of the 7th International Conference on Mobile Human Computer Interaction with Mobile Devices and Services*, ACM Press, pp.183–90.

Mizobuchi, S., Chignell, M. & Newton, D. [2005], Mobile Text Entry: Relationship Between Walking Speed and Text Input Task Difficulty, *in* M. Tscheligi, R. Bernhaupt & K. Mihalic (eds.), *Mobile HCI '05: Proceedings of the 7th International Conference on Mobile Human Computer Interaction with Mobile Devices and Services*, ACM Press, pp.122–8.

Pirhonen, A., Brewster, S. & Holguin, C. [2002], Gestural and Audio Metaphors as a Means of Control for Mobile Devices, *in* D. Wixon (ed.), *Proceedings of SIGCHI Conference on Human Factors in Computing Systems: Changing our World, Changing Ourselves (CHI'02)*, *CHI Letters* **4**(1), ACM Press, pp.291–8.

Place and the Experience of BLISS

Darren J. Reed & Peter Wright

Science and Technology Studies Unit, Department of Sociology, University of York, York YO10 5DD, UK
Tel: *+44 1904 433047*
Email: *djr14@york.ac.uk*

Department of Computer Science, University of York, York YO10 5DD, UK
Tel: *+44 1904 432741*
Email: *pcw@cs.york.ac.uk*

This paper builds on earlier work that understands the design of bus information panels as rooted in a landscape of human experience. It turns the mundane activity of waiting at a bus stop into a problematic space of emotion and volition by understanding the dialogic relationship between human and technology. It does this by developing a novel approach to interaction design, which combines a theoretical framework, which reveals the rich experience and 'felt life' of technology, with an empirical analysis of bus information. By imagining a series of conversation-like dialogues, based in a Conversation Analytic (CA) sensitivity to the achievement of meaning in sequence [Condor & Antaki 1997], it generates a series of experience narratives that provide for a critical analysis of the information presentation. It uses this to engage with the idea of place as a layered feature of the bus stop.

Keywords: experiential narrative, real-time bus information.

1 Introduction

A positive experience is key to recruiting new people to bus services [Reed & Wright to appear]. Part of this experience involves the taking on of the passenger role, through a process of becoming. 'Becoming' in this context refers to a transformation of values and identity. What needs to happen for the government to succeed in its stated aims of increasing bus passengers is more than just persuading or coercing people to get on a bus every so often, rather it involves people becoming the kind of people who value and enjoy using buses as part of their lives. In order to understand how such a transformation might be brought about its important to understand people's experiences of bus use and what it takes to become a bus user in this strong sense. We can think of 'becoming a passenger' as a matter of career, in terms of a taking on and then repeated performance of the role. Integral to this process are contingent moments of activity and perception, in the initial experiences of the bus stop, that themselves are prefigured by the person's history.

In our previous writings on user experience [McCarthy & Wright 2004], we looked at the general relationship between person and technology. We argued that the relationship between self and meaning is a matter of continual dialogue with the 'other' – whether this is construed as a person, people or things – through which the person recognizes, develops and confirms a sense of self. For McCarthy & Wright's then, self and technology are in a dialogical relationship; technology can either enhance or impede the resolution, or unity, of becoming [ibid.].

In this paper we focus on the bus stop as a physical space, and ask whether it can be seen also as a 'place', that carries a sense of personal and cultural meaning, instead of a mere punctuation of travel from place to place. Place, as we will explain, denotes a positive experience of space. In this analysis we imagine the bus stop as place through a novel combination of theory and empirical analysis of a real time bus information and management system, based upon a two-year investigation comprising interviews, observation and reflection-based study of the installation of the system.

BLISS – the Bus Location and Information SubSystem – broadcasts predicted and scheduled arrival times of individual buses on passenger information panels (or PIPs) at bus stops. The system also influences bus running times by manipulating traffic light timings and provides service information to bus managers. This aspect is meant to provide more consistent running times and the ability to formulate better timetables. This system is representative of the government's transport and environment strategy to recruit new bus passengers through the provision of Real Time Information (RTI) at bus stops [Lyons et al. 2001] (see also Stradling et al. [2000]). The design of these information communication technologies (ICTs) assumes the value and neutrality of information [McLaughlin et al. 1999], and is meant to provide for journey flexibility through choice.

There has been a move to understand the needs of passengers as users [Shaw 2004], however there is as yet little work into the waiting passenger's experience. One example is seen in the work of Evans [2005], who looks to understand the sense of safety at a bus stop as contributing to the processes underlying social exclusion and inclusion of older people. He relates this to physical and material properties of bus stops, such as lighting, the condition of the walkways leading to the bus stop and whether the level of the curb allows for access to the bus. Evans' work does two things: first it stands as an example of avoiding negative experience through design, second it relates this to the physical location and properties of a bus stop.

Beyond thinking of the bus stop as a physical space, we can also think of it as a *place*. Evans' combination of experience and space moves some way toward a richer understanding of the merely functional aspects of the bus stop, towards a nuanced, individual and relational understanding; One that recognizes real people with genuine concerns who make sense of their experiences through active engagement, interpretation and reflection. McCarthy & Wright [2004] provide a means to extend this analysis to include broader experiences, premised upon individual's past experiences and their expectations, which fits with the government's aim to enhance the public's experience of bus travel by reducing uncertainty through technology; that itself is premised upon a prospective and retrospective rationale. By providing predictive information about buses that have not yet arrived, and hence ensuring a sense of certainty, the expectations of passengers can be managed and assured. Previous experiences of poor bus services will be replaced by a positive experience and people will be attracted to travelling on buses.

One question that has not been asked is how passenger experience might be affected, improved, or indeed worsened by ICT provision and design. We focus here on the information panels, by imagining the rich experience of a naïve 'passenger-in-waiting' in the context of the bus stop. In this way we look to understand the role of technology in the realization of the bus passenger identity and specifically in the way it provides for or impedes a sense of place. We do this through McCarthy & Wright's [2004] theoretical framework of experience.

2 A Theory of Experience

McCarthy & Wright formulate the route to understanding rich experience in terms a framework of four 'threads' of experience – the sensual, the emotional, the compositional and the spatio-temporal – and six sense making processes – anticipating, connecting, interpreting, reflecting, appropriating, and recounting. They point out that threads of experience 'are not fundamental elements of experience. Rather they are ideas to help us think more clearly about technology as experience' [ibid. pp.79–80]. The term threads conveys a sense of being interwoven.

We will use these elements as a template to open up and think about the rich experience of standing at a bus stop, which is normally understood as a banal situation. We imagine the experience of a naïve passenger with no or little experience of catching a bus, and the process of becoming a passenger. Which is understood not only in the sense of becoming a regular bus user, but also in the deeper sense of it being a personal identity statement and value system.

3 Experience of Technology and Place

As technology becomes more pervasive, ubiquitous and embedded in our physical environment, human–computer interation (HCI) researchers have begun to open research discourses to new perspectives from human geography, architecture and the built environment. McCullough [2004] in his analysis of ambient technologies develops a concept of interaction spaces that leans on architectural discourse as well as interaction design and social psychology. Augé [1995] develops the concept non-place and a number of researchers have also developed a distinction between space and place from work in human geography [e.g. Tuan 2001]. For Dourish [2001], spaces are characterized by physical properties; places are characterized by social properties [ibid. p.89]. When we conceive of place, we are interested in 'activities', 'emergent practices' and 'communities of practice' [ibid. pp.90–1].

When we think about a bus stop as a space, we are drawn to think of it as having a specific geographic location, geometric dimensions, and physical features such as perspex sides and metal roof. When we think of it as a place, we are drawn to think about the activities that occur there, and the commonly accepted norms of behaviour that coalesce around and are part of the understanding of those who successfully take on the role of passenger in waiting. Space and place are not unrelated, however – activities and practices are prompted and contained and afforded by the physical character of space – indeed it is the dialogical character of the relationship between space and place that is most interesting. If we apply a dialogic notion of individual experience we can ask questions about the mutual elaboration of space, place and person.

Understood as relational and dialogic, the transformation (or lack of it) from space to place (or to use Augé's term non-place to place) is revealed as experiential, and can be detailed through the experiential framework. That is as temporal, sensual, emotional, reflexive, and part-and-parcel of personal histories and lived lives. Questions about technologies in space and place provide for – in the first instance – a design critique: is it a space, or is it a place? This leads on to questions about how technology might support a construction of a sense of place from space. As Dourish puts it, once we realize that place is a matter of interaction, we realize that 'place can't be designed, only design for' [Dourish 2001, p.91]. But more importantly in the case of the BLISS system, a reorientation to the transformation of space to place allows for an understanding of passenger identity in relation to the bus stop in that 'a sense of place and a sense of personhood dialogically constitute each other' [McCarthy & Wright 2005, p.921]. Interaction with technology should be seen at the 'level of personhood' and we can ask to what extent 'technologies extend or diminish spaces of possibilities' [ibid. p.924].

An often-referenced example of technology that is pertinent to standing at a bus stop is the use of a personal music device. 'MP3 users create tailored music collections and listening preferences, and use their players to manage space – by creating bubbles of familiarity in unfamiliar spaces and by creating zones of comfort in crowded spaces' [ibid. p.922]. The idea of 'bubbles of familiarity' is useful when we talk about public information sources. We might ask to what extent do electronic information signs create bubbles of familiarity? The experience at a bus stop is part of a longer experience. Walking to the bus stop and getting on the bus top and tail bus stop dwelling, but so too do the experience of home and work. Bus professionals talk about a continuity of experience from bus stop waiting to bus travel. The extent to which the information signs diminish continuity of experience is an important question.

4   Method

A description of an experience tends to be monological because the motivation is usually one of intelligibility and consistency. However a dialogical account is more conversation like, it doesn't deal in absolutes and it draws the reader into a relationship with the words. With a wish to characterize our writing as dialogical, we suggest a novel generative and presentational method we call experiential narrative. This is used to describe, analyse and critique, interactions with electronic information signs, and explicate the theory. In this way we aim to be reflexive about our own practices of writing about experience [Schön 1991].

The fieldwork for the study involved interviews with key stakeholders (bus operator, system developer, procurer and bus passengers), as well as reflection at bus stops that involved observation and discussion (and included the taking of photographs and shooting of video). This empirical insight was combined with the McCarthy & Wright experience framework to produce a series of experiential narratives in which a person who has never used the buses before is imagined in the situation of the bus stop.

The method incorporates dialogue in the writing of experiential narratives by contrasting different narrative sections (diagrams, story narrative, academic quotation and commentary) and in this way draws the reader into a dialogue with and between the sections. By doing this it aims to maintain an element of reader creativity as they too are drawn into the experience.

We present four experiential narratives: In the first, our imagined naïve passenger Dave goes to a bus stop that does not have an electronic information display. We use this narrative to introduce the experiential threads and sense-making processes in the theoretical approach. The remaining narratives relate to a single day in which Dave travels to and from work by Park and Ride bus (Narratives 2 and 4) (which involves driving a car to an out of town location and then boarding the bus); at lunchtime he looks to journey to and from his home by bus only (Narrative 3). Each example is based upon collected empirical data, and observational reflection on the part of the researcher.

5 Experiential Narrative 1

Dave had seen people standing at bus stops of course, bitter, stony faced people, huddled together, peering longingly down the road, but he'd not been on a bus for years. He far preferred the warmth and comfort of his car, enclosed and protected from the elements in his own private surroundings. His conscience about having two cars in the family had got the better of him though, and now he was left with two choices, either cycle or catch the bus.

'The sensual thread of experience ... is concerned with our sensory engagement with a situation, which orients us to the concrete, palpable, and visceral character of experience.' [McCarthy & Wright 2004, p.80]

Dave was cold and wet; the rain had chosen precisely the moment he stepped out of the door to join forces with the strong wind. He arrived at the bus stop only to find several 9.00 am commuters waiting ...

Coming to rest in the physical and material space of the bus stop punctuates Dave's transit from home to work, two places where he felt comfortable. The car drive had been another comfortable place, a personal place where he felt in control, able to act how he liked. The interior space an expression of himself, with his work-bag on the passenger seat, his tapes in the glove compartment.

Arriving at the stop has a history in the 'relationship between anticipation and actuality' – prefigured as much by needed shelter as the novelty of walking to the bus stop. At the same time, a small achievement has been made; he's arrived at the stop. Almost immediately there is space for reflection: a sense of completion, a moment of relief and release of anxiety, part of the emotional thread of experience,

'The emotions at work in an experience belong to a self engaged in a situation and concerned with the movement of events toward an outcome that is desired or disliked.' [ibid. p.83]

The transition from movement to resting deepens the potential for 'connecting' with sensual experiences, encased, as Dave is, in a bounded and intimate space, forced to stop and accumulate time. Simply stopping allows for an appreciation of bodily self, now partially sheltered from the elements; Close proximity to others brings immediate sights, sounds and smells.

To begin with Dave stands at a slight distance to the 'stony faced', but then when another person arrives he shuffles forward closer to group of people, the guy in the suit with strong after-shave, the two teenagers, both wearing single earpieces so they can chat and listen to music at the same time. The sound and smell of traffic ruffles his hair. He feels anxious with the proximity of others.

These emotions are 'the colour shot through the experience that holds all aspects of the experience together' [ibid. p.83]. Early, late, bad day, good day, happy, sad, all now taint the experience; all potentially brim over into the socially shared environment.

The space is populated and animated by others, each chained to the place of waiting – other people, other thoughts, other relations, and other accountabilities. Each constrained by the shared task of becoming, each alone in their thoughts and emotions, each having to keep them in check.

'The compositional thread is concerned with the relationships between the parts and the whole of an experience. ... In an unfolding interaction ... it refers to the narrative structure, action possibility, plausibility, consequences, and explanations of actions ... Attention to the compositional thread evokes questions: what is this about? What has happened? ... What will happen next? Does this make sense? What would happen if?' [ibid. p.87].

Physical orientation is primary: where does the person position himself or herself in this restricted domain? Is there a queue? Where does it begin and end. Could the arrangement of bodies hold a secret code?

Once Dave had figured out where to stand, that didn't offend anyone, but was still sufficiently sheltered from the rain, it dawned on him that the only thing left to do was wait – he wasn't very good at waiting.

Essentially 'waiting' has a relationship to the past and to the future. Prefigured in anticipation; projected in consequence. Waiting is located in a narrative of movement, of objective, and of uncertainty, that is itself only the prologue to the unfolding drama. Crucially, however, waiting is by definition neither forward nor backward in the narrative, neither progression, digression nor regression.

For Dave the composition of the bus stop experience includes 'reflecting':

Has the bus gone, he wonders, how would I know? He looks around; there are three other people at the stop, 'they look relaxed, there must be a bus on its way'.

'An intense emotional engagement can make our sense of time change. A frustrating experience can leave us perceiving space as confined and closeting. ... Time may speed up or slow down, pace may increase or decrease, spaces may open up or close down.' [ibid. p.91]

The spatio-temporal thread is key to the bus stop experience. Assured and relaxed the passenger in waiting may experience no temporal and spatial abnormalities; all is as it should be. For Dave uncertainty colours his reasoning: time becomes 'experientially dense' [Flaherty 1999] stretching the minutes, the bus stop increasingly cramped with people.

'In our construction of the spatio-temporal aspect of an experience, we may distinguish between public and private space; we may recognize comfort zones and boundaries between self and other, or between present and future.' [McCarthy & Wright 2004, p.91]

We can see these ideas in the arrangement of passengers in space. The bus stop's physical signs and timetables not only contain, arrange and orient the physical space, they also sanction a small-scale Brownian motion of passengers as they weave and collide in their confinement, motivated by a sense of individual ownership of the information.

The narrative of becoming a passenger starts before reaching the bus stop through the 'framing' [Goffman 1974] of expectation. Deliberate framing can occur in at least two ways: through the utilization of a schedule (a printed list of times), the planning of a journey and a delimiting of expectation of bus stop experience; or through a common sense and shared notion of 'headway' or frequent interval bus service, a discursive mechanism used to promote, characterize and demarcate expectation by bus operators.

Dave had heard that the bus he was trying to catch was supposed to be 'every eight minutes', but here he was, and he is sure that he's been here for more than eight minutes. He wished he hadn't tried the bus, how much warmer, calmer and in control he would be, if he was in his car right now.

Research into perception based upon models of waiting time, asserts that people tend to over estimate the amount of time that they are waiting for a frequent interval bus [Avineri 2004]. What this research doesn't do is take account of the emotional and experiential reasons for this. The question becomes, how does the introduction of the electronic information signs affect this experience of waiting.

The experience framework contains four threads: the sensual, the emotional, the compositional, and the spatio-temporal; and a number of sense-making processes: connecting, framing, interpreting, reflecting, appropriating, and recounting. Our second, third and fourth narratives relate to a single day, in this way we can speak to how one set of experiences relates to another.

6 Experiential Narrative 2

Dave feels a moment of hesitation as he locks his car, why doesn't he just drive into town, like he always has done. The cold presses on him and he takes one last look at his car, and then turns toward the lit bus stop, some twenty meters away. At first he feels alone in the enormous car park, but then he realizes that there is actually a mass of people getting out of their cars, and converging on the bus stop. Convinced it's a race, he weaves and twists through the parked cars.

There's seems to be a bus waiting, but also a large queue. Alone in a crowd, he considers returning to his car and driving into town; at least it was warm, and there wouldn't be all these people.

The information displayed at Rawcliffe Bar is 'predicted arrival time' and clock time. The PIP is dynamic, with the digits changing continually.

Predicted time relates directly to the geographical location of the bus stop; through the satellite tracking element of BLISS the position of a specific bus is combined with a temporal calculation of the speed of the last three buses running the route, to produce an estimation of how many minutes it will take the bus to reach the stop. The predicted arrival time is updated every thirty seconds as information is relayed about the buses position. If the bus encounters a traffic delay that was not experienced by the previous three buses (and hence not part of the algorithmic calculation) the predicted time will stall or may even ascend. Equally, on the occasion of a faster than previously seen bus, the predicted time will suddenly descend, showing a lower predicted time. The changes are apparent because the predicted times are comparable to the clock. Reading the sign, a person is drawn into the continual narrative.

'Nine minutes till the next bus, good'. He tries to gauge how many people get on a bus. Well at least I could get the next one. He feels immediately reassured, and strikes up a conversation with the woman standing behind him, 'that weather, eh ...'.

Dave stamps his feet a little, and entertains himself by watching the other people. He glances up at the sign 'eight minutes, great, oh and there's another one a few minutes later'. Calculating ten minutes into town and then five minutes walk. He'll be on time for his appointment.

'Only six minutes, brill. What happened to seven, I wonder?' Dave tries to count the number of people ahead of him. When he next looks up, the sign has changed again,

Happy at first that the first bus is about to arrive, he becomes more convinced that there are too many people in the queue. He looks at the second bus, 'twelve

minutes, another twelve minutes in the cold'. Dave tries to think back over the times of the second bus 'wasn't it fifteen minutes, eight minutes ago?' Edging slowly forward bumping into the person in front as the person behind nudges him; Dave holds his breath as he gets nearer and nearer the bus entrance.

When the second time does not seem to follow the first the reader is drawn into questioning the content, the information display as a tool is made visible: Why should there be a disparity between predicted time and clock time? Why should the time go up? Perhaps the bus is running late, perhaps it has broken down. We see here the clearest example of the compositional thread of experience spoken about by McCarthy & Wright, but in this case the necessity to engage creatively is forced on the reader to make sense of what they are reading. In phenomenological terms these are moments of breakdown [Winograd & Flores 1986], wherein the device is made visible. What it is doing, how it does it, are brought to mind, and the passenger is drawn into a critical relationship to the device.

The point is not so much the variance in time, this can be explained a way by the ebb and flow of the traffic, the point is the minutia of calculation that the reader is drawn into: counting down the minutes, calculating the results, all increasing the density of the moments. A phenomenon liable to intensify the concentration and lead to a lengthening of the subjective experience according to Flaherty [1999].

The relevance of the PIP is in good part a consequence of its dynamic nature. Like a continual textual narrative, it is never complete. As the assumed parallel relationship between the times is broken and the predicted times become independent of one another, the contingencies of individual buses are called upon to detail the disparate text. One bus must be moving, while another is 'stuck in traffic' or some such imagined explanation.

In the case of a delayed bus, this temporal dynamic is transformed into geographical reflection: where might the bus be delayed? What local arrangements of traffic and road might be causing the bus to move slower than normal? A dialogue between time and space is transformed into one about time and place.

Finally sitting on the bus Dave is momentarily relieved, but then realizes that he doesn't actually know where to get off. However as the bus drives through the town, he sees familiar sights and places – almost, he reflects, for the first time. When he reaches the town centre and gets off the bus, he is already thinking about the coming day.

7   Experiential Narrative 3

Encouraged by his success in the morning, Dave decides to go home and back during his lunch break. This time doing it all by bus; he wouldn't have to use the car at all to get to work. He knew that the 415 went near to his house and stopped near his work (he'd been sat behind it in his car enough times).

He only had an hour but he'd seen a new information sign on the bus stop near work. He could make his home in about seven minutes by car, so it can't take much longer.

The experience of the PIP is already framed in expectation, based upon Dave's earlier experience, and the fact that he had driven past the sign on previous days. Anticipation colours the expectation of the PIP.

Dave is the only person at the stop and he stands directly below the sign. The text on the sign radiates yellow, '7 Designer Outlet P&R 10min'. The description is familiar to him; he lives just a mile past the out of town shopping mall; but the bus doesn't go far enough. He needs the 415, that passes his house.

'18,22, ... 42, ... ah, 415', well at least he's at the right bus stop. He returns to his position under the glowing sign. Previously he had no idea that the bus stop had a name, but there it was 'Imphal barracks'. He spent some time trying to figure out what it meant, the army barracks was just up the road, but 'Imphal'?

Bus stops are individual, they are located in a unique geographical location, a space. But when they are named, even if that only refers to the street that they are on they takes on a more personal character. It reminds us that the geographical location is within a place, an area of the town, a community even. In a small way, the passenger identity is enriched through ownership, 'this is *my* bus stop'.

The clock pulses and changes, the information counts down, '10min', '8min', '3min' 'DUE'; the number seven bus arrives and the information disappears, only to be replaced by another line reading '7 Designer Outlet P&R 10min'. What about the 415? Dave thinks.

Dave is drawn into a relationship with the information. The ticking down, the disappearing and appearing information, create a dynamic temporally anchored narrative, but it is limited to the next two buses. Pivotal is the moment when one line of information is replaced another; a momentary expectation is quashed each time the 415 does not appear.

Dave becomes more and more agitated. How often does the 415 run he wonders. Why doesn't the sign show information about it? What about all the other buses listed?

Information is always specific and fragmentary and unfinished. There is always the possibility of identifying gaps. This incompleteness can become personal when viewed through an emotion of need.

After half an hour Dave decides that he is never going to get home and back in time. He walks back to his office, feeling annoyed.

8 Experiential Narrative 4

In the evening, our character Dave journeys from his work to the Park and Ride car park. The bus stop at museum gardens is in the centre of our northern town. Only Park and Ride buses stop at it. Unlike other bus stops there is no shelter; waiting passengers queue single file along a thin sidewalk. This emphasizes the number of people. This northern UK town is popular with day visitors, and commuters report deep frustration that they travel during rush hour.

Dave is already nervous about catching the bus home, given his experiences at lunchtime. He can see a queue stretching into the distance as he approaches what he thinks is the Park and Ride bus stop. If only he had asked the bus driver this morning where the right stop was. The bright yellow sign reads '2 P&R 6min', but Dave is unsure which Park and Ride service he needs. Just above the electronic display is a graphic that reads '2 Park and Ride Green Line'. '2'? 'Green' what does that mean? Above that is the text 'Rawcliffe Bar'. He decides to see if there is any more information written on the stop. He tries to avoid eye contact with the first five people at the front of the queue.

Neither the destination nor the location of the stop is immediately apparent from the electronic content. This particular style of PIP combines electronic content with printed graphics and it is possible with a little guess work to piece together what '2 P&R 6mins' means, by first assuming that the graphics all refer to one service, and therefore that 'Rawcliffe Bar', the number '2' bus and the 'Green Line' are all the same route. Assuming one knows that the Park and Ride service is called Rawcliffe Bar, the number 2 has the correct destination.

It might seem that having the location of the bus stop printed physically is more logical – given that the bus stop is not going to be moved. But somehow this feels less actively informing, rather more like a street sign, than an interactive resource. It requires that the reader reasons and reflects; it requires an assumption of intertextual continuity [Fox 1995]. Also the information sign, in this case, faces away from the queuing passengers. This means if people queue away from the sign in the direction of the traffic (the normal rule for queuing), they cannot see the information count down. Information and lack come into play again.

After what seems an age, Dave finally gets on a bus. He tries looking out the window at the familiar sights, but can find no interest in them. All he wants to do is get back to his car, turn on the stereo and drive home.

The bus stop is just a point in space; bus stop as place on the other hand denotes identity, ownership and the like. The bus passenger role is heterogeneous, commonalities of riding a bus are diluted into reasons for catching the bus: commuter, tourist, shopper, traveller, all embody sets of values, and all become an 'in-group' in relation to one-another. Becoming a passenger is not a simple matter of observable activity, but one of identity, utility and possibly priority. Getting to and from work is instrumental; having a day visiting as a tourist is pleasurable. Surely, workers should be able to get on the bus first!

Place is also layered and relational to other places. This might simply be about being located in a 'good' area or a 'bad' area. Where the bus stop is in relation to the town (outside, inside) says something about belonging to the town. Where the bus stop is located is important with regard to the competing character of a town: is the town a place of work, or of play? Certainly the PIPs are drawn into these relationships, if they show information for certain routes and not others, if they are positioned on certain bus stops and not others.

9 Discussion

The experiential narratives and comments are inspired by real instances and real-time reflection on the part of the researcher, in combination with bus stop interviews and discussions with groups of passengers. The conversation-like structure, wherein our character is seen to interact with the displays over a sequence of moments, is there to provide a sense of temporal revealing and also an underlying structure for the separate textual segments. By imagining the created narratives as occurring in sequence, we get a sense of how the experiences build over time.

9.1 Space, Place and PIPs

A bus stop sanctions a geographical position on a street where a bus is expected to stop and pick up passengers. In its simplest manifestation it is a single point, denoted by a pole fixed in the ground, usually with some form of flag-like sign. Bus stops with shelters – typically a structure with three sides and a roof in the UK – form an enclosed space around this single point and have the effect of creating an inside and an outside for the bus stop. This is when we might start to talk about a bus stop being characterized by space. Being 'inside' the shelter allows for an attribution of waiting passenger (and hence authority to get on the bus first), and is contrasted to non-passengers 'outside' the shelter. Thought of in these ways, the space qualifies a sense of identity in terms of what is other. Once 'inside' there are all sorts of expectations in play in terms of norms of behaviour and the like.

Like other bus stop apparel, the PIPs help to inform a space. At a typical shelter in the study, the single-sided information panels are positioned at one end of the shelter, facing in the direction of the traffic. This underlines the 'edge' of one side of the bus shelter, and interestingly provides additional cues about how to queue. We saw a deviant case in Narrative 3 that proves the point: When the sign faces in the opposite direction, to read the PIP passengers would have to queue with their backs to the oncoming traffic. The person at the end of the queue would be nearest the approaching bus. Moving to the front of the queue to read the information is a morally accountable matter.

In the majority of cases, the PIPs face the queuing people, and interestingly this adds to the identity of bus passenger. Especially in the arrangement of the shelter the information is contained and projected only to the shelter population. There is almost a sense of ownership: the information is for the waiting passengers and not, for example, the bus driver. With ownership comes identity, and with identity an expectation of conforming to a set of norms. A clear example of this, portrayed in the fourth experiential narrative, was when the researcher observed the sign. It was quite clear that there was a level of indignation at the possibility that the researcher was a passenger attempting the jump the queue. On most occasions, observing the signs, taking photographs etc. was observably looked on as curious. What could you be doing watching the sign, if you didn't intend to get on a bus?

We can already see the geometric space becoming a meaningful place, in terms of identity and ownership. Other aspects that further a sense of familiarity and belonging include the inclusion of a name for the bus stop (typically based on a side road or recognizable location, such as an army barracks). This naming provides for an individual identity for the bus stop and in turn an ownership on the part of a person: '*my* bus stop is called ...' Incidentally this is a feature that has always been in place, contained in written bus timetables, and known by seasoned travellers. Having a named bus stop makes this knowledge available to the neophyte.

This name also presents a particular character. One bus stop in the study is called 'East Cottages' which gives the impression of a rural area, even though it is actually in a suburb. How much better this name is to the one in Narrative 2, 'Imphal', which is confusing even to a person familiar with the area.

We might not say that a name says something about a bus stop, but also that having a bus stop with a PIP attached says something about the area in which the bus stop is located. Especially early in the proliferation of the information signs, an installed PIP conveys a sense of priority and worth. In turn, the passenger whose bus stop has an installed PIP might feel that they are valued above other passengers. All of this is fine as long as the information displayed is relevant to the individual bus passenger. The initial sense of worth can be undermined when if is found that the bus that *goes to where the person lives* for example is not included. The system was first installed on buses running from an out of town parking facility to an in town bus stop. The personal information is obscured by the anonymity of the service, which aims to help move a large number of people between the town and their car.

A similar point might be made about destination names. A sense of ownership is more likely when there is a named destination. Instead on the route into town, the destination is the nominal 'city centre', even if there is a single stop. An example is apparent in Narratives 2 and 4: The bus stop to catch the return bus is called 'Museum Gardens', but on the way into the town the destination is denoted as 'city centre'. Not only did our imagined character not know where to get off in the morning, he didn't know where to get on in the evening. This instantiates a lack of continuity. The destination on the return journey in this case is of course the out of town car parking facility, which is called Rawcliffe Bar. While it is only a staging post in the person's journey, it is at least named (largely because there are five 'Park and Ride' services and there needs to be some way to differentiate between them).

9.2 *Relevance and Reliance*

The earlier point about which buses are included in the information leads us to the issue of relevance. This too can be thought of as a dialogue between space and place. In spatial terms we can think of the physical relevance of the signs. The typical shelter arrangement brings the queuing person into a physical relationship to the sign. It stands over the person, facing them, bright and difficult to ignore. Of course a person can look away, find other things in their environment (or outside of it) to look at. The person is always drawn back to the information periodically as their eye line moves. There is a certain relevance here that is purely spatial. In some sense this relevance is imposed. Whether the information is relevant or not, the PIP is part of the environment. Indeed in the case where the content does not include the required bus, the sign still has meaning [Bolter & Gromala 2003]. Being spatially engaged with irrelevant information is a source of negative emotion.

In the second narrative, the content itself was seen to draw the reader into a conversation-like relationship – due in part to there being relevant information, but also in that there were problems presented as needing solutions.

As we said in an earlier paper, this interaction does not tend toward knowledge and a development of passenger expertise, because the unpredictability of the buses is fore-grounded and made central to this and every next experience of waiting at a bus stop. On each and every future occasion, assuming similar fluctuations in the progression of the predicted arrival time, the person will be drawn into the meaning of the information in terms of the contingencies of the bus in traffic. Put another way this could be seen as a form of reliance that promotes and necessitates a competence in understanding PIPs, not buses.

10 Conclusion

One question is whether experiential narratives can be adapted to function as a tool for designers. One way this might be done is to reformulate them as experience scenarios. We might then ask questions such as, what makes for a good as opposed to a bad experience scenario? What sort of scenario might it be and where in the design process might it be utilized? And possibly most importantly, how does one go about creating an experiential narrative that functions as a scenario? Key to these questions is what a scenario is and how it is utilized.

Rizzo & Bacigalupo [2004] detail a heuristic model of scenarios in which scenarios 'show a critical potential to enable forms of creative design that do not aim at solving specific problems but rather at shaping new activities that could not exist without the artefact or system being designed' [ibid. p.158]. They detail a range of scenarios supported by different configurations of narrative elements (point of view, main characters, context and mood, artefacts and agencies, conflicts and interactions, resolutions) [ibid. p.154], which support different aspects and roles within the design process. These range from *activity scenarios*, based on preparatory fieldwork early in the design process, through *mock-up scenarios* that match envisaged design with user activities, to *integration scenarios*, that imagine the effect of a finished design on the institution in which it is to be situated. However a common feature, and indeed instrumental advantage is the way the narratives within scenarios represent meaning in a determinative way,

'Narratives are representations that impose an interpretation over the sensible world, structure experience, organize memory, and give reality a unity that neither nature nor the past possess so clearly.' [ibid. p.153]

This is advantageous when generating design responses. So for example, activity scenarios, which are like our experiential narratives, are 'grounded and built on' ethnographic data. These are allowed to generate fictional narratives of 'concrete use episodes, from standard practices to routines taken to the extreme' and therefore 'a deep understanding of how people organize their current activities.' [ibid. p.155]

The way that our experiential narratives differ from this description is in the extent to which the grounded data and generated narrative produce single and imposed interpretations. This is a dynamic that Gaver & Martin [2000] call the balance between 'concreteness' and 'openness' when producing design prototypes. The dialogic mentality maintains that openness or unfinalizability is key to understanding experience; tools that are sensitive to these contingencies should themselves retain openness. The way this is achieved in our experiential narratives is in the structuring of varying elements that provide for differing authorial voices (see Ashmore [1989] for a use of this technique in academic writing).

Criticality and creativity can be seen as the consequence of the experience narratives that we have developed; rather than present the designer (or have the designer create) a concrete interpretation, experiential narratives encourage continual reinterpretation, but at the same time are grounded in the real world.

We have imagined an experiential account of a real time system called BLISS. We have done this by combining a theory of technology with passenger interviews and empirical observation and reflection, and presented it in a narrative structure of analysis and story telling. Through a focus on small moments of experiential conversation-like interactions the aim was to open up the experiential landscape of standing at a bus stop, so that designers could engage with the finely detailed elements of what is a mundane activity.

The technology is experienced; it rests in a web of sensual, emotional, reflectional, temporal and spatial experiences. Thinking in terms of experience allowed us to consider briefly the first experiences of PIP content in a variety of sites. Specifically we highlighted the notion of place, and started to consider how the technology might better provide for a transformation of space to place.

The study is situated in a broader investigation of temporality and trust in buses. The bus operator has a clear understanding of how to improve their service that includes a quest for 'value-added-ness' for passengers. This includes new, clean and spacious buses, but also improved facilities such as information provision. Encouraging potential passengers to feel as though the bus stop is more a place that a space is one way that this relationship can be developed.

References

Ashmore, M. [1989], *The Reflexive Thesis*, Chicago University Press.

Augé, M. [1995], *Non-places: Introduction to an Anthropology of Supermodernity*, Verso Books.

Avineri, E. [2004], A Cumulative Prospect Theory Approach to Passenger Behavior Modeling: Waiting Time Paradox Revisited, *Journal of Intelligent Transportation Systems: Technology, Planning, and Operations* **8**(4), 195–204.

Bolter, J. D. & Gromala, D. [2003], *Windows and Mirrors. Interaction Design, Digital Art, and the Myth of Transparency*, MIT Press.

Condor, S. & Antaki, C. [1997], Social Cognition and Discourse, *in* T. A. van Dijk (ed.), *Discourse as Structure and Process*, Vol. 1 of *Discourse Studies: A Multidisciplinary Introduction*, Sage Publications.

Dourish, P. [2001], *Where the Action Is: The Foundations of Embodied Interaction*, MIT Press.

Evans, G. [2005], Accessibility and User Needs in Transport Design, *in* R. Coleman & A. Macdonald (eds.), *Proceedings of Include 2005, International Conference on Inclusive Design*, Helen Hamlyn Research Centre, Royal College of Art. http://www.hhrc.rca.ac.uk/events/include/2005/proceedings/pdf/evansgraeme.pdf.

Flaherty, M. G. [1999], *Watched Pot: How We Experience Time*, New York University Press.

Fox, N. J. [1995], Intertextuality and the Writing of Social Research, *Electronic Journal of Sociology* **1**(2). http://www.sociology.org/content/vol001.002/fox.html.

Gaver, B. & Martin, H. [2000], Alternatives: Exploring Information Appliances Through Conceptual Design Proposals, *in* T. Turner & G. Szwillus (eds.), *Proceedings of the SIGCHI Conference on Human Factors in Computing Systems (CHI'00)*, *CHI Letters* **2**(1), ACM Press, pp.209–16.

Goffman, E. [1974], *Frame Analysis. An Essay on the Organization of Experience*, Northeastern University Press.

Lyons, G., Harman, R., Austin, J. & Duff, A. [2001], Traveller Information Systems Research: A Review and Recommendations for Transport Direct, Transportation Research Group. http://www.dft.gov.uk/stellent/groups/dft_mobility/documents/page/dft_mobility_503909.pdf.

McCarthy, J. & Wright, P. [2004], *Technology as Experience*, MIT Press.

McCarthy, J. & Wright, P. [2005], Technology in Place: Dialogics of Technology, Place and Self, *in* M. F. Costabile & F. Paternò (eds.), *Human–Computer Interaction — INTERACT '05: Proceedings of the Tenth IFIP Conference on Human–Computer Interaction*, Vol. 3585 of *Lecture Notes in Computer Science*, Springer, pp.914–26.

McCullough, M. [2004], *Digital Ground: Architecture, Pervasive Computing and Environmental Knowing*, MIT Press.

McLaughlin, J., Rosen, P., Skinner, D. & Webster, A. [1999], *Valuing Technology: Organisations, Culture and Change*, Routledge.

Reed, D. & Wright, P. [to appear], Experiencing BLISS when Becoming a Bus Passenger, Accepted to appear in the proceedings of Designing Interactive Systems 2006 (DIS'06).

Rizzo, A. & Bacigalupo, M. [2004], Scenarios: Heuristics for Action, *in* D. J. Reed, G. Baxter & M. Blythe (eds.), *Proceedings of ECCE-12: 'Living and Working with Technology'*, EACE, pp.153–60.

Schön, D. A. [1991], *The Reflective Practitioner. How Professionals Think in Action*, Avebury.

Shaw, S. [2004], The Design of Transport Systems: Discussion paper, Transport Research and Consultancy, London Metropolitan University. http://www.aunt-sue.org.uk/PDF% 20Versions/Design%20of%20Transport%20Systems,%20Discussion%20Paper.pdf, last accessed 2006-05-28.

Stradling, S. G., Meadows, M. L. & Beatty, S. [2000], Helping Drivers Out of their Cars. Integrating Transport Policy and Social Psychology for Sustainable Change, *Transport Policy* **7**(3), 207–15.

Tuan, Y. F. [2001], *Space and Place: The Perspective of Experience*, University of Minnesota Press.

Winograd, T. & Flores, F. [1986], *Understanding Computers and Cognition: A New Foundation for Design*, Ablex. From 1988, an Addison–Wesley publication.

Factors Contributing to Low Usage of Mobile Data Services: User Requirements, Service Discovery and Usability

Stavros Garzonis & Eamonn O'Neill

Computer Science Department, University of Bath,
Bath BA2 7AY, UK

Fax: *+44 1225 383 493*

Email: *{S.Garzonis,eamonn}@cs.bath.ac.uk*

There is evidence that most users do not exploit the capabilities offered by mobile data services. We propose that in addition to user requirements and usability, service discovery adds an extra dimension that may explain this lack of use. We conducted a 3-way evaluation study which combined expert evaluation, a diary study and cooperative evaluation to investigate the factors affecting low usage of data services. The task of selecting the appropriate service to solve everyday problems was demonstrated to be difficult using existing mobile services. The results indicated that service discovery plays a central role in determining user satisfaction and performance.

Keywords: service discovery, mobile data services, usability evaluation.

1 Introduction

Although mobile telephony has pervaded many people's lives, its widespread use is still restricted to two main services: voice calls and text messaging. The availability of mobile data services has been increasing in the last few years, but according to Strategy Analytics predictions [Taylor 2006], SMS will remain the dominant data application globally for 2006, accounting for 56% of end user spend on mobile data services. Second most popular services are downloads of ringtones, games and wallpapers or 'Person-to-application' SMS. This leaves information retrieval services with very low usage. This paper reports a study that investigated the reasons for this lack of usage of mobile data services.

Many researchers have explored the usability issues of mobile devices, many of which arise from limited input and output capabilities. First, the small physical size of mobile phones typically restricts the input to a small set of physically small buttons. This might have been adequate when phones were used only for voice calls but the increasing functionality of phones has encouraged alternative input methods. The original multi-tap method for texting through the 9 button keypad has been augmented by predictive text algorithms [e.g. Silfverberg et al. 2000], optimization of character placement [e.g. Gong & Tarasewich 2005] or number of keys [e.g. MacKenzie 2002] and most recently in PDAs and smartphones with stylus input [e.g. Kristensson & Zhai 2005] and miniature QWERTY keyboards [e.g. Clarkson et al. 2005]. Other approaches include gestures on the surface of the device [Pirhonen et al. 2002], gestures with the device in three dimensional space [Patel et al. 2004] and device tilting for typing [Wigdor & Balakrishnan 2003]. All these methods have indeed improved input efficiency but have mixed results in other aspects of usability, such as learnability and satisfaction. Secondly, the physical limitations of mobile displays limit the amount of information that can be conveyed. Techniques that have been applied to overcome this are the use of sound [Brewster 2002], rendering and restructuring the content that would normally appear in larger displays [Lemlouma & Layaida 2005] or cloning the small display on nearby bigger displays [Miyahara et al. 2005].

However, these studies do not entirely explain why people would use the same, perhaps unusable, devices in the same distracting environments for text messaging or voice calls but not for data services. One possible explanation could be based on user requirements. If the demand for voice calls and text messages is strong enough to tolerate these problems, people will still use them. On the other hand, if frustration overcomes the benefits of using data services, people will refuse to use them. This threshold is related to the question that any user may ask herself: 'Is it worth using?'. In marketing terms this is referred as 'perceived value' of a product or service. Although the perceived value of mobile data services is also influenced by factors such as financial costs and marketing techniques, these are outside the scope of this paper.

Identifying user requirements and designing usable interactions have long been acknowledged for their role in successful software design. Although these two factors still apply to designing successful mobile data services, there is one significant difference when compared to conventional software design for the desktop environment. On a desktop PC, a user is typically aware of most of the services that are provided by the PC. These often take the form of applications that the user has personally installed. In contrast, in the mobile environment, users may often be unaware of the services that are available through their handset or even how to find them. Services come with different labelling, structures, content and initiation processes. For example, to download games on the Orange UK network, one uses 'Orange Multi Media services' (http://www.orange.co.uk/multimedia/), while with Vodafone UK one uses 'Vodafone Live!' (http://vodafone-i.co.uk/live/) and in each of these cases, this is just the first step to accessing a game.

This lack of standardization is similar to the vast and unregulated services that one can find on the Internet. However, interacting with a PC in order to discover such services is more tolerable. Users can find their desired service by applying a variety of techniques, such as browsing, using search engines or following indices of services. However, these explicit user actions are harder to perform through the limited interaction methods of the mobile device. Therefore, our hypothesis is that the process of service discovery on mobile devices will be a major factor contributing to low usage of data services. If this is true, awareness of the available services, their approximate content and the procedure for invoking them will play a central role in the level of usage of the services. We define this knowledge as the *Service Awareness* that any user has at any given moment. Although this awareness can be raised through formal and informal advertising (e.g. word of mouth), our concern is with how context-aware systems could address service awareness more dynamically.

Furthermore, with the growth of smartphones with greater hardware capabilities and software adaptability, services are more likely to become contextually available. Thus, a service may be available or unavailable depending upon the current context. Aspects of context that may determine service availability include personal, spatial and temporal dimensions. Different services will be available to different people in different places and at different times. There is an extensive literature around context aware computing [e.g. Chen & Kotz 2000; Dey 2001; Barkhuus & Dey 2003] that describes computing systems that can sense and adapt to the dynamically changing environment of the user. The development of context awareness and the contextual availability of services through mobile phones has the potential to render service awareness even more problematic. For example, one might have access to a local voting service upon entering a local forum or the ability to print or exchange documents in ad hoc manners depending on the availability of other devices. In these cases, changes of location, social and technical context affect the availability of a service. This would make it even more difficult for a user to maintain awareness of what services are available to him at a particular time in a particular place. To encourage usage of these services, users' awareness of contextually available services must be supported.

In the next section we present related work in the field of mobile evaluation. In the section following, we describe a study that we conducted by combining three evaluation approaches, aiming to investigate reasons for the lack of usage of mobile data services. We then present the results of our study, grouped around three themes: user requirements, service discovery and usability.

2 Evaluating Mobile Services

We are specifically interested in the evaluation of mobile services and not of client applications. Our distinction between service and application draws on Microsoft's definition of a service being 'a software-based functionality provided by network servers' [Microsoft 2002]. We view the application as the software running on the handset and the service as the functionality provided between that application and the server. The focus of this study is not on application attributes such as font size or button functionality but on service requirements, discovery and usability.

In a survey conducted from 2000 through 2002, Kjeldskov & Graham [2003] report that only 41% of mobile-human interaction research involved any evaluation of system designs. These usability evaluations are usually focused on aspects such as devices' limitations [Brewster 2002], applications' user interfaces [Pirhonen et al. 2002] or the architecture of prototype systems [Cheverest et al. 2002]. They tend not to focus on the underlying structure of existing and wide-spread services.

Furthermore, there are no specific evaluation methods for mobile devices, with the exception perhaps of the Heuristic Walkthrough [Vetere et al. 2003]. This was an attempt to combine Heuristic Evaluation and Cognitive Walkthrough but it was found inadequate during its evaluation [Vetere et al. 2003]. In the absence of specialized evaluation methods, most researchers apply traditional HCI usability evaluation approaches.

Moreover, the literature is divided regarding the appropriate setting in which to conduct evaluations of mobile applications and services. While desktop environments are typically relatively stable (e.g. level of ambient noise, illumination, device availability), the context of mobile use is bound to be more unpredictable and more attention demanding. In the Kjeldskov & Graham [2003] survey, 71% of the mobile evaluations were performed in lab settings. Some researchers [e.g. Kjeldskov & Skov 2003] have attempted to replicate mobile conditions in the laboratory, where data collection and variable control is easier. On the other hand, others have argued that only field evaluations can identify issues relating to the true context of use where the user's attention may be divided among many things other than interacting with the device [Kjeldskov et al. 2004]. In an attempt to clarify the debate around lab vs. field evaluation for mobile phones, Kjeldskov et al. [2005] compared four different evaluation methods: cooperative field and lab evaluations, heuristic walkthrough and rapid reflection. The service that was evaluated was a location-aware mobile guide supporting the use of public transportation. They found that field and lab evaluations had considerable overlap in the 'critical' and 'serious' usability problems they picked up. Field evaluation only fell short in 'cosmetic' problems, which did not impede performance. In another study comparing 5 different lab-based evaluation techniques, Kjeldskov & Stage [2004] reported that seated participants found more 'cosmetic' usability problems than walking participants. In a review [Garzonis 2005] of the comparison between field and lab evaluations, we have argued that overall, typical lab conditions are better for device-centric usability studies.

In the study reported here, we used a range of evaluation methods and aimed to combine the advantages of both lab and field techniques.

3 The 3-Way Study

The study was a combination of expert evaluation, diary study and field cooperative evaluation. Each of these three approaches addressed some or all of the factors we identified as contributing to the lack of usage of mobile data services: user requirements, usability and service discovery. In this section, we describe the aims and procedure of each part of the study.

3.1 Expert Evaluation

An expert evaluation was conducted with two goals in mind. First, it focused on mapping the current data services provided through the main mobile web portal of one of the leading global mobile network providers in order to inform task selection for the cooperative evaluation study and to identify the optimum path and completion time for each task. Secondly, the expert evaluation was used to identify specific usability problems.

The evaluator had knowledge of established evaluation methods and was familiar with the mobile device used. However, he was not experienced with the use of mobile Internet or the content of the particular set of data services under investigation. The evaluation was done on a Nokia 6600 handset while pen and paper were used for keeping notes. It lasted approximately 1 hour, with 2 further hours spent on follow-up analysis.

Adopting a cognitive walkthrough approach, the evaluator browsed through the services and developed realistic scenarios, which he then executed using the phone in order to discover the optimum solution. The steps to the optimum solution form the optimum path which was recorded in a form of a 'mindmap'. The scenarios reflected potentially everyday situations in order to engage users in the subsequent cooperative evaluation. They were designed to cover a range of 5 different data services: sports information, 2 types of directory information, travel information and the 'Find & Seek' service. The lats is a location-aware service designed to provide maps and/or points of interests based on proximity to the user. The optimum paths of the tasks ranged from as shallow as 4 screens to as deep as 11 screens. They included specific parts of the services that were identified by the evaluator as liable to cause confusion. This provided the opportunity to validate the evaluator's findings against the results of the cooperative evaluation study. The easier and shallower tasks were included to counterbalance the study.

3.2 Diary Study

A 3-day diary study was conducted primarily to elicit information regarding user requirements for mobile services and secondly on service discovery. We designed our diary study drawing on related work by Rieman [1993]. The diary study gives an insight into peoples' ideas, problems and solutions in their own environment. It may be viewed as an informal equivalent of participatory design [Rieman 1993] and can inform future experimental designs.

There were 12 participants involved; 7 women and 5 men, aged from 24 to 36 (mean = 27.7, s.d = 3.6). They all had strong computer science backgrounds with 10 of them having considerable experience in HCI (at MSc or PhD level). Rating their mobile phone usage from 1 to 5 (1: less than once a week, 5: many times per day), they produced a mean of 4.1 (s.d. = 1.4). They were spread among 5 different major network providers and have been using a mobile phone for at least 4 years.

The procedure was explained to them in advance and they confirmed they had fully understood it. One question was emailed to the participants every day and they were asked to answer it during the day along with any questions they had received on previous days. Hence, on the first day, they had one question to consider. On the second day, they had two questions to consider, and on the third day, they had all three questions to consider. Therefore, the first question was most favoured in terms of time spent to answer and the third was least favoured. This was done for two reasons. First, the first question was the most open-ended and it would be compromised if it was given along with the rest of the questions. Similarly, the second question would be compromised by the third question. Secondly, the last question addressed our secondary goal of investigating what services users actually want. We therefore aimed for richer data on the first two questions, which addressed our primary goal of investigating users' preferences for service discovery techniques.

On the first day the participants were asked to use their imagination as to how their phone could help them in various situations throughout the day. Although we did not want to restrict the users' imagination, we advised them not to be totally unrealistic (e.g. 'I want my phone to fly' or 'to brew coffee'). Otherwise, the participants were free to 'invent' any service that could support their daily interactions and activities. This question aimed to capture users' needs regarding mobile applications. In particular, we were interested to see if and how often any ideas on context-aware services would come up before we introduced the notion to the participants with the second question.

The second question introduced the users to context-awareness by asking them what they would want their phones to be able to sense and what kinds of services could exploit that to their advantage. This question aimed to elicit information on what types of context aware services are most wanted in order to allow comparison with such existing services.

On the last day they were asked for their ideas about service discovery. The term 'service initiation' was used in order to avoid confusion with the more technologically-oriented term 'service discovery', as it is often used to mean devices-discovering-devices.

Each day of the diary study, the participants were asked to attempt to answer the question(s) early in the morning and then keep it/them in mind for the duration of the day. When they had an idea in relation to one of the questions, they were instructed to note it down along with information regarding their location, their main or parallel task(s) at the time, their social context and the time of the day. This was intended to help us to infer the potential context of use of the proposed service. At the end of each day, they were instructed to aggregate the findings of the day and expand on their ideas if necessary. They were allowed to expand on previous ideas but they were asked to keep the original script intact. For example, one participant could add details of an idea he had the first day but on the second's day sheet. Thus, the original wording of the idea was preserved in question's 1 sheet.

3.3 Cooperative Evaluation

3.3.1 Background

The third part of the study was a cooperative evaluation, which was based on work by Wright & Monk [1991]. They have developed the think-aloud method by adopting an approach where the participant is told to think of him or herself as a co-evaluator of the system. The participant is not only asked to 'think aloud' but more specific questions are asked and the evaluator encourages the participant to provide commentary. Although this involves the risk of the evaluator biasing the participant in his views about the system, if performed carefully, cooperative evaluation can evoke rich user data. Wright & Monk [1989] argued that evaluators need to look for two types of evidence of usability problems: critical incidents and breakdowns. Critical incidents occur when the participant is deviating from the optimum path to the task solution. Breakdowns were introduced by [Winograd & Flores 1986] and can be identified 'as any point at which the user's comments indicate that the system has become part of his or her subjective experience' [Wright & Monk 1991]. In other words, breakdowns occur when the participant is focusing on the technological medium instead of the task at hand.

Users' comments about the system and the identification of critical incidents aid breakdowns [Wright & Monk 1991]. Cooperative evaluation can provide useful data on the user's mental model. When these mismatches between the user's and designer's mental models of the system are taken into consideration, they can inform redesign of the system to better match users' perception of the service structure.

An alternative to cooperative evaluation is the use of retrospective verbal protocol. In this type of evaluation, the users do not interrupt the task execution for comments but are instead debriefed after the task. One of the main benefits of this approach is that they can expand as much as they want, without compromising their performance. However, the post hoc commentary produced after task completion misses the more intuitive user reactions to the system. Also, users partially forget past interactions and reconstruct them, providing inaccurate information. We chose to apply cooperative evaluation followed by a post-test questionnaire due to time constraints and because performance was secondary to user comments on mobile data services.

The setting was in a busy café with the participant and the evaluator sitting at a table, having coffee. We chose to do a field evaluation as the lab is a particularly unnatural setting for use of mobile phone evaluation [Kjeldskov et al. 2004]. Although mobile devices can be used in almost any setting, when interacting with them demands higher cognitive load, people attempt to reduce other cognitive distractions such as walking [Kaikkonen et al. 2005]. Hence, we chose a setting where the participants were seated. Other distractions such as ambient noise and social presence were present, providing a level of ecological validity. At the same time, having the participants seated facilitated data collection and more closely resembled a lab evaluation, mitigating the Achilles heel of field evaluation in identifying cosmetic problems.

3.3.2 Procedure

As with the expert evaluation, the cooperative evaluation used the main mobile web portal of a leading network provider. The users' actions and interaction with the evaluator were recorded by video and audio and by the evaluator's taking notes. For each task that the users were asked to perform, an optimum solution path had been identified through the expert evaluation. In the cooperative evaluation, the users' actions were recorded and compared to the optimum solution path. A critical incident was identified whenever a user deviated from that path. We extended the analysis to look not just at the initial deviation but also at the users' subsequent actions.

Figure 1: The phone with the camera attached.

Figure 2: The cooperative evaluation setting.

There were twelve participants, 6 women and 6 men, aged from 23 to 36, average age 27.8 (s.d. = 3.5). These were the same twelve participants who took part in the diary study apart from one substitution, as one participant had to be discarded due to a technical problem. This means they had the same strong computer science and HCI background, very frequent mobile phone usage but only 17% of them regularly used the phone for data services.

The phone used was a Nokia 6600 handset attached to a lightweight L-shaped wooden base with a web camera (PC Line) attached to the other end (Figure 1). The camera captured the mobile screen and the buttons just above the keypad (the keypad was not needed to complete the tasks). The camera had a built in microphone and was connected by a cable to a notebook computer resting on the table (Figure 2). A video camera was placed about 3 metres away from the table, capturing users' hand movements, body posture and facial expressions.

Participants who were not familiar with the phone were given a short tutorial on the buttons' functionality. To familiarize themselves with the device, they were asked to send a text message. Afterwards, they were presented with the instructions of the cooperative evaluation on the screen of the notebook computer. Each scenario was read to them before they attempted it and was visible on the screen throughout the process. This was to ensure that participants could revisit the question in case they lost focus or partially forgot their goal. There were 9 scenarios and each participant was randomly allocated to 3. The scenarios included finding walking directions (e.g. 'Find the nearest Chinese restaurant' or 'Find the nearest pharmacy'), and retrieving information regarding sports (e.g. 'Find when is the next F1 race'), weather (e.g. 'Find out how the weather is going to be tomorrow in Bristol') and entertainment (e.g. 'Find a cinema around you that shows movie Star Wars III').

4 Results

We analysed the results in three categories: user requirements, service discovery and interaction usability. Although these categories are strongly linked and sometimes have considerable overlap, they follow the logical course of actions to achieve a particular goal. First, the user forms the intention to reach that goal using her mobile device. Then she has to discover or recall the appropriate service and finally she interacts with that service to achieve the desired goal.

4.1 What People Need

As mentioned, one of the main goals of the diary study was to determine whether context aware services were required by users. In the first question of the diary study, 67% of the users came up with at least one idea for a context-aware service. If we exclude the participants who were 'using their phone only for calls and texts', who produced no ideas throughout the study, this number comes up to 80%. In total, 23% of the ideas produced by users throughout the study were context-aware related.

As participants provided multiple ideas on different days, the data can be organized in two ways: the ideas that were proposed by most participants (popularity) and the ideas that came up most frequently regardless of the participant (frequency).

The most popular idea, produced by 33% of the participants, was a context-aware service related to bus or train notification systems. The common theme included user notification about the actual location of the vehicle and the expected time of its arrival. The second most popular ideas, produced respectively by 25% of the participants, were related to voice instructions, automatic mobile profile switching (e.g. from 'silent' to 'outdoors') and trigger related events (i.e. notification of specific suggestions/actions only in the appropriate context). It is interesting to note that 3 out of the 4 most popular ideas were for context-aware services. Overall, 57% of the ideas were context-aware.

The most frequent idea however was not context aware. It represented 12% of all ideas and was related to voice or sound instructions and dictation. Second most frequent (6%) were ideas related to data synchronization, profile switching and bus/train live information. Table 1, summarizes the findings on ideas' popularity and frequency.

Some further data regarding user requirements could be derived from user comments during the cooperative evaluation. Some of them were noted by the evaluator during the evaluation and the post-test questionnaire. However, the audio recordings were partially irretrievable due to hardware malfunction and therefore the comments do not have sound statistical value. For example, we know that at least 75% of the participants explicitly stated their dissatisfaction with the network connection speed. However, they do not represent the entire sample since some of the audio record was missing.

Idea	Frequency %	Popularity %
Voice Instructions	11.59	25.00
Bus/train Dynamic Information	5.80	33.33
Synchronization	5.80	16.67
Profile Switching	5.80	25.00
Contextual Triggers	4.35	25.00

Table 1: Most frequent and popular ideas.

4.2   What People Can Discover

In this study, the term service discovery is limited to the action of choosing the appropriate data service among a set of services available to the network subscribers. When connected to the data service network, this set of services is visible as a grid of icons on the phone display. Connection could be achieved via one of the soft buttons on the starting screen, or through the phone menu, under the label 'Services'. The rest of the phone menu items (e.g. Camera, Messages) were considered as applications and not services. Although sometimes more than one service could lead to one of the desired goals, we define as optimum the service that requires the least steps to achieve the goal. All of these optimum services are on the top level of the menu and thus they can be accessed by just one click, or two clicks when not connected to the server. The time needed for an expert to access the optimum service ranges from 0 to 25 seconds, depending on the task.

The analysis of the cooperative evaluation indicated that overall, in 92% of the trials the participants interacted with the optimum service. Only 33% used the branded shortcut on the starting screen in their first attempt to connect to the server. The rest spent on average 6.4 minutes (s.d. = 6.1) and went through 18 pages (s.d. = 16.9) simply to connect to the server. The number of pages they viewed before arriving at the desired service was 9.4 (s.d. = 10.9) on average, which is 500% more than the optimum. On average they chose 1.8 services per task (s.d. = 1.5) or 1.7 (s.d. = 1.2) without repetitions. They also spent 3.1 minutes (s.d. = 4.0) to reach the service they considered as most appropriate. If the participant failed to complete the task, we counted as most appropriate the last service she or he used. The time spent was as much as 1403% more than the optimum time needed. A service was counted twice if the participant gave up on that service only to return back to it after having selected other services. Table 2 summarizes the results that indicate service discovery performance.

Overall, 82% of the tasks were completed successfully and 95% of them were achieved through the optimum service. However, on average 1.7 services (s.d. = 1.4) were chosen in the process. In 53% of the successful tests, the participants finished the task by making use only of the optimum service.

Measure to Service Discovery	Absolute Value	s.d.	Increase from Optimum (%)
Pages to Service Discovery	9.43	(10.93)	500.18
Services selected per task	1.84	(1.49)	84
Minutes to Service Discovery	3.13	(4.04)	1403

Table 2: Measures to service discovery.

Measure to task completion	Absolute value	s.d.	Increase from Optimum (%)
Pages to task completion	22.15	(15.33)	213
Minutes to task completion	8.24	(5.45)	499

Table 3: Measures to task completion.

4.3　What People Can Use

The results presented here cover user interaction during both service initiation and service usage. Times and number of pages visited were counted from the beginning of the interaction until the completion of each task. We argue that this count of pages visited is a more appropriate measure than just a deviation from the optimum path (i.e. critical incident). User performance is more accurately measured by the number of the extra pages they visited.

The minimum number of pages the participant needed to visit in order to complete the task defined the optimum depth of the solution. The 'Options' button of the handset would bring up a menu of potential actions and it was counted as one extra page even if the participant chose to exit the menu without selecting any of these actions. Selections that were cancelled before the new page was loaded were not counted.

The optimum depth of the solutions was on average 7.1 (s.d. = 2.4). However, the average number of pages visited by the participants was 22.1 (s.d. = 15.3), including repetitions and server error pages. This is as much as 213% more browsing than the optimum. Excluding the server error pages and the repetitions caused by these errors, the average number of pages visited was 21.1 (s.d. = 14.9) and the browsing was 198% of optimum. The optimum path was followed in only 3.6% of the tasks and only by 2 participants. The time needed to complete the tasks was 499% more than the optimum. Table 3 summarizes the results that indicate service usage performance.

One of the most common confusions was the 'Options' button (left soft button). 88% of the users misunderstood its function. Also, all of the participants who used the 'Search' function within a service were expecting a text box but were faced with lists of options. These same usability issues were brought up during the expert evaluation. The two most persistent flaws were poor labelling and vague error messages.

5 Discussion

We have argued that the low usage of mobile data services is influenced by three major factors: user requirements, service discovery and usability. The results of the 3-way study suggest that all three factors did indeed have an influence.

First, in terms of user requirements, we noticed that the most popular and most frequent ideas for services are not currently available to consumers. More than 50% of the ideas produced were about context-aware services and only 10% of the ideas proposed services that are currently provided. None of the suggested services included the most widely advertised existing services, such as news, sports, ringtones and pictures. An interesting observation is that most of services proposed addressed everyday problems, such as efficient commuting, avoiding embarrassment in social situations and facilitating navigation.

Service discovery proved to be exceptionally difficult, even when this simply meant having to choose from a static set of 12 services. It is clear that this will be even more complicated if the public is introduced to contextually available services. The results of this study indicated that the struggle of choosing the appropriate service exceeded the struggle of completing the task. Participants visited 500% pages more than needed to find the optimum service when for the overall task the respective number was 213%. Similarly, they spent 1403% more time than was needed for service discovery and 499% more for task completion.

These results also indicate that participants faced major difficulties in interacting with the device. Although they were experienced mobile users, they found it particularly difficult to interact with the data services. This is also backed up by the frequency and sometimes intensity of user comments of dissatisfaction during the evaluation. One of the strongest findings was that most participants explicitly stated during the evaluation that they would not use it in real life. Unfortunately, the malfunction of the microphone stop us from having the exact number of these comments. Among other interesting comments were 'I'd rather ask someone on the street' or 'I'd wait until I got to my PC'. There were even some who made very negative comments, such as 'I hate it', 'it's absolutely useless' or 'can I swear on camera?'.

There are also strong indications that the structure of most of the services does not match the users' mental models. The optimum path was followed in only 3.6% of the tasks and only by 2 participants. In most cases, task completion was hindered by deeply nested options with ambiguous labelling. For example, 'Nearest Bookmakers' was under 'More Sports', while 'Essential Services' was one level down from 'Tattoo & Piercing'. In another example, labels such as 'Pinpoint me' and 'Find me now' strongly suggested that the service would display the user's location. However, upon selecting them, users were asked manually to input their location in order to see the relevant map. Even then, they had to go through 6 more steps (including purchase confirmation and a terms and conditions page) to get the map. The labelling problem was reported both from the expert evaluation and from user comments.

Furthermore, although this study did not aim to take into account the financial cost of accessing the services, interesting data resulted from the cooperative evaluation. Users intuitively and explicitly weighed their overall satisfaction about their experience against the money they would have to pay to access these data services. Although they were not personally being charged in the study, they were reluctant to accept charges during the interaction (e.g. 25p for a map) and expressed their concern with comments like 'It's wasting my time and my money...', 'Will it charge me again? ', even '...this would be costing me money, wouldn't it? So I'd be getting a bit pissed off at this stage'.

One of the limitations of the study reported here is the small number of participants. The statistical power of the results is sometimes brought into question by a large standard deviation. Although this suggests relatively large differences in the participants' performance, it is also indicative of the differences in the strategies they followed. Some users always preferred to try the 'Search' option first, while others followed exploratory learning. We might to assume that a population of more mixed background and experiences would apply an even greater variety of strategies. In this sense, the homogeneity of our sample becomes a strength of the study as it highlights the need for inclusive systems' design.

Although concurrent verbal protocol is known to increase performance time, it does not account for an increase of as much as 500%. Besides, the number of extra pages that the users visited for each task is supporting the argument that they would also need much more time to complete the task.

Although all the equipment was thoroughly tested and functioned properly in the pilot study, an unpredictable fault made part of the audio recording irretrievable. This did not cause insuperable problems nor did it jeopardize the validity of the data reported here. We did lose some data on user comments which we are confident were of similar nature to the recorded data, since the evaluator was also taking notes.

Finally, the quality of service (QoS) could have further decreased user satisfaction. The error rate was one error every 13.5 minutes with 34 errors occurring in 7.8 hours of testing. On one occasion, one set of tasks had to be cancelled as the server did not respond 7 times in 14 minutes and the latency was very poor. Later we found out that this was due to exceptionally high number of requests to the server. QoS would have been better over a 3G network rather than the GPRS network that was used, but increased bandwidth does not always bring faster download times as service providers often take advantage of increased bandwidth to make the content richer.

6 Conclusion and Future Work

This study was motivated by the observation that mobile data services remain unused by the majority of mobile phone users. A combination of expert evaluation, diary study and cooperative evaluation was used to investigate the factors responsible for this lack of usage. Our prediction was that apart from the usual suspects of user requirements and usability, service discovery would also share this responsibility.

This prediction was indeed verified from the study results. Participants needed 1403% more time than optimum and 500% more pages to visit in order to initiate the service they considered as most appropriate for the task. These numbers are greater than the respective 500% extra time and 213% extra browsing that they needed to complete the tasks.

In our future work we aim to explore the concept of service awareness; an approach we consider will be particularly useful if services are to become contextually available. The mobile devices' limitations on interaction and the dynamic availability of the services will hinder the process of service discovery. Context-aware systems could provide some assistance in raising service awareness but there are multiple interaction, social and technological issues that need to be considered.

References

Barkhuus, L. & Dey, A. [2003], Is Context-aware Computing Taking Control Away from the User? Three Levels of Interactivity Examined, *in* A. K. Dey, A. Schmidt & J. F. McCarthy (eds.), *UbiComp 2003: Ubiquitous Computing (Proceedings of the Fifth International Conference on Ubiquitous Computing)*, Vol. 2864 of *Lecture Notes in Computer Science*, Springer-Verlag, pp.159–66.

Brewster, S. A. [2002], Overcoming the Lack of Screen Space on Mobile Computers, *Personal and Ubiquitous Computing* 6(3), 188–205.

Chen, G. & Kotz, D. [2000], A Survey of Context-aware Mobile Computing Research, Technical Report TR2000-381, Dartmouth College, USA.

Cheverest, K., Mitchell, K. & Davies, N. [2002], Exploring Context-aware Information Push, *Personal and Ubiquitous Computing* 6(4), 276–81.

Clarkson, E., Clawson, J., Lyons, K. & Starner, T. [2005], An Empirical Study of Typing Rates on Mini-QWERTY Keyboards, *in* G. van der Veer & C. Gale (eds.), *CHI'05 Extended Abstracts of the Conference on Human Factors in Computing Systems*, ACM Press, pp.1288–91.

Dey, A. K. [2001], Understanding and Using Context, *Personal and Ubiquitous Computing* 5(1), 4–7.

Garzonis, S. [2005], Usability Evaluation of Context-aware Mobile Systems: A Review, Paper presented at 3rd UK-UbiNet Workshop. http://www.bath.ac.uk/comp-sci/hci/UK-Ubinet%20Files/Garzonis/ukubinet05_S.Garzonis.pdf, last accessed 2006-05-09.

Gong, J. & Tarasewich, P. [2005], Alphabetically Constrained Keypad Designs for Text Entry on Mobile Devices, *in* G. van der Veer & C. Gale (eds.), *Proceedings of SIGCHI Conference on Human Factors in Computing Systems (CHI'05)*, ACM Press, pp.211–20.

Kaikkonen, A., Kekalainen, A., Cankar, M., Kallio, T. & Kankainen, A. [2005], Usability Testing of Mobile Applications: A Comparison between Laboratory and Field Testing, *Journal of Usability Studies* 1(1), 4–17.

Kjeldskov, J., Graham, C., Pedell, S., Vetere, F., Howard, S., Balbo, S. & Davies, J. [2005], Evaluating the Usability of a Mobile Guide: The influence of Location, Participants and Resources, *Behaviour & Information Technology* 24(1), 51–65.

Kjeldskov, J. & Graham, C. [2003], A Review of Mobile HCI Research Methods, *in* L. Chittaro (ed.), *Human–Computer Interaction with Mobile Devices and Services: Proceedings of the 5th International Symposium on Mobile Human–Computer Interaction*

(Mobile HCI 2003), Vol. 2795 of *Lecture Notes in Computer Science*, Springer-Verlag, pp.317–35.

Kjeldskov, J. & Skov, M. B. [2003], Creating a Realistic Laboratory Setting: A Comparative Study of Three Think-Aloud Usability Evaluations of a Mobile System, *in* M. Rauterberg, M. Menozzi & J. Weeson (eds.), *Human–Computer Interaction — INTERACT '03: Proceedings of the Ninth IFIP Conference on Human–Computer Interaction*, IOS Press, pp.663–70.

Kjeldskov, J. & Stage, J. [2004], New Techniques for Usability Evaluation of Mobile Systems, *International Journal of Human–Computer Studies* **60**(5-6), 599–620.

Kjeldskov, J., Skov, M. B., Als, B. S. & Høegh, R. T. [2004], Is it Worth the Hassle? Exploring the Added Value of Evaluating the Usability of Context-aware Mobile Systems in the Field, *in* S. Brewster & M. Dunlop (eds.), *Human–Computer Interaction — Mobile HCI 2004: Proceedings of the 6th International Symposium on Mobile Human–Computer Interaction*, Vol. 3160 of *Lecture Notes in Computer Science*, Springer-Verlag, pp.61–73.

Kristensson, P.-O. & Zhai, S. [2005], Relaxing Stylus Typing Precision by Geometric Pattern Matching, *in* R. St. Amant, J. Riedl & A. Jameson (eds.), *Proceedings of the 10th ACM International Conference on Intelligent User Interface (IUI 2005)*, ACM Press, pp.151–8.

Lemlouma, T. & Layaida, N. [2005], Content Interaction and Formatting for Mobile Devices, *in* A. Wiley & P. R. King (eds.), *Proceedings of the 2005 ACM Symposium on Document Engineering (DocEng'05)*, ACM Press, pp.98–100.

MacKenzie, S. [2002], Mobile text entry using three keys, *in* O. W. Bertelsen, S. Bødker & K. Kuuti (eds.), *Proceedings of NordiCHI 2002*, ACM Press, pp.27–34.

Microsoft [2002], Glossary of Networking Terms for Visio IT Professionals, http://www. microsoft.com/technet/prodtechnol/visio/visio2002/plan/glossary.mspx, last accessed 2006-05-09.

Miyahara, K., Inoue, H., Tsunesada, Y. & Sugimoto, M. [2005], Intuitive Manipulation Techniques for Projected Displays of Mobile Devices, *in* G. van der Veer & C. Gale (eds.), *CHI'05 Extended Abstracts of the Conference on Human Factors in Computing Systems*, ACM Press, pp.1657–60.

Patel, S. N., Pierce, J. S. & Abowd, G. D. [2004], A Gesture-based Authentication Scheme for Untrusted Public Terminals, *in* S. K. Feiner & J. A. Landay (eds.), *Proceedings of the 17th Annual ACM Symposium on User Interface Software and Technology (UIST'04)*, *CHI Letters* **6**(2), ACM Press.

Pirhonen, A., Brewster, S. & Holguin, C. [2002], Gestural and Audio Metaphors as a Means of Control for Mobile Devices, *in* D. Wixon (ed.), *Proceedings of SIGCHI Conference on Human Factors in Computing Systems: Changing our World, Changing Ourselves (CHI'02)*, *CHI Letters* **4**(1), ACM Press, pp.291–8.

Rieman, J. [1993], The Diary Study: A Workplace-oriented Research Tool to Guide Laboratory Efforts, *in* S. Ashlund, K. Mullet, A. Henderson, E. Hollnagel & T. White (eds.), *Proceedings of INTERCHI'93*, ACM Press/IOS Press, pp.321–6.

Silfverberg, M., MacKenzie, I. S. & Korhonen, P. [2000], Predicting Text Entry Speed on Mobile Phones, *in* T. Turner & G. Szwillus (eds.), *Proceedings of the SIGCHI Conference on Human Factors in Computing Systems (CHI'00)*, *CHI Letters* 2(1), ACM Press, pp.9–16.

Taylor, P. [2006], Mobile Consumer Applications Outlook 2006, Report 2751, Strategy Analytics. http://www.strategyanalytics.net/default.aspx?mod=ReportAbstractViewer&a0= 2751, registration required.

Vetere, F., Howard, S., Pedell, S. & Balbo, S. [2003], Walking through Mobile Use: Novel Heuristics and their Application, *in* S. Viller & P. Wyeth (eds.), *Proceedings of Australian Conference on Computer–Human Interaction (OzCHI 2003)*, Information Environments Program, University of Queensland, pp.24–32.

Wigdor, D. & Balakrishnan, R. [2003], TiltText: Using Tilt for Text Input to Mobile Phones, *in Proceedings of the 16th Annual ACM Symposium on User Interface Software and Technology, UIST'03*, *CHI Letters* 5(2), ACM Press, pp.81–90.

Winograd, T. & Flores, F. [1986], *Understanding Computers and Cognition: A New Foundation for Design*, Ablex. From 1988, an Addison–Wesley publication.

Wright, P. C. & Monk, A. [1989], Evaluation for Design, *in* A. Sutcliffe & L. Macaulay (eds.), *People and Computers V (Proceedings of HCI'89)*, Cambridge University Press, pp.345–58.

Wright, P. C. & Monk, A. F. [1991], A Cost-effective Evaluation Method for Use by Designers, *International Journal of Man–Machine Studies* 35(6), 891–912.

Mind, Body, and Spirit

Exploring the PieTree for Representing Numerical Hierarchical Data

Richard O'Donnell, Alan Dix[†] & Linden J. Ball[‡]

[†] *Computing Department,* [‡] *Psychology Department, Lancaster University, Lancaster LA1 4WA, UK*

Email: *a.dix@lancaster.ac.uk*

URL: *http://www.hcibook.com/alan/papers/HCI2006-PieTree/*

This paper describes the first full implementation and evaluation of an area-based tree visualization known as the PieTree. The PieTree was first proposed in papers in 1998 and 2000 but has never been fully implemented and evaluated. Informal evaluation was used to enhance the usability of the PieTree and compare it with the more well-known TreeMap. A controlled experiment considered parallel views' effect on task performance time. There were substantial differences between kinds of tasks and in participants' styles of use. Whilst suggesting that further development of PieTrees is worthwhile the experiments underline the importance of careful task fit.

Keywords: PieTree, information visualization, TreeMap, TreeView, hierarchies, hierarchy visualization, individual difference.

1 Introduction

Hierarchical structures are common in computing systems, but in the Internet they are ubiquitous. Some are an intrinsic part of the technical infrastructure of the Internet and Web. Most obvious is the path hierarchy of HTML pages on a website and at a lower level the Domain Name System (DNS), which stores the names of websites and maps them to specific IP addresses, is itself hierarchical. Usenet newsgroups feature a similar hierarchical structure, with groups either existing in isolation, or having related child groups, for example '24hour support. helpdesk' exists by itself, whereas 'alt.activism.death-penalty' is a child newsgroup of 'alt.activism'. Other hierarchies are created within specific websites: directory structures of information sites such as Yahoo! or Open Directory project, category

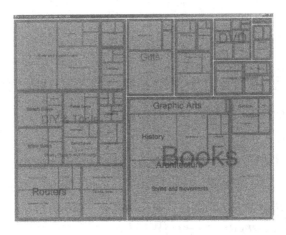

Figure 1: Microsoft Research's TreeMap showing data for a fictional e-commerce site.

structures of content management systems or product categories on eCommerce websites such as Amazon. In browsers and email systems there are yet more hierarchies with bookmark folders and mail folders.

The primary aim of these hierarchies is often to organize textual or graphical information so that it can be accessed easily. For example an e-commerce site may have high-level categories, such as books, DVDs, toys, etc., as well as specific pages for items in that category, such as a certain book. Some visitors may find items by browsing through the categories for the site and others may find a specific page by entering the site through an Internet search engine.

Often also there is some sort of numerical data associated with the hierarchy: number of pages within a folder, number of hits on a webpage, volume or value of sales within a product category. Questions about these numbers are often critical for site owners: 'What are the hot topics on my site?' or 'What areas are being missed by visitors?'

Numerical hierarchical data exists in other areas: for example the size of files on a disk, the stock levels or sales of different kinds of goods in a conventional inventory system, and similar questions can be raised about such data: 'Where has all my hard disk space gone?', 'What is selling well?' Not surprisingly there have been a number of visualizations aimed at this kind of data, perhaps most well known being the TreeMap [Johnson & Shneiderman 1991].

The importance of numerical hierarchical data is perhaps emphasized by the fact that the TreeMaps have been incorporated into several commercial applications. TreeMaps have also been included by Microsoft Research as part of their data visualization components (see Figure 1), and they have been used to visualize data generated from Usenet newsgroups [Fiore & Smith 2001].

In this paper we discuss another novel visualization technique known as a PieTree [Dix & Ellis 1998; Dix et al. 2000] (Figure 2), which like a TreeMap can be used to represent hierarchical numerical data. Like the TreeMap the PieTree maps

Figure 2: A fully exploded PieTree representing a hierarchical data structure.

count/size directly onto area, but instead adopts a circular layout exploiting users' familiarity with Pie diagrams. Earlier work discussed the concept of the PieTree and a partial implementation. In this paper we discuss both informal evaluation of a more fully featured prototype and compare it with Microsoft Research's implementation of the TreeMap. We also report a controlled experiment that investigates the benefits of using the PieTree in conjunction with a TreeView (the outliner style view of trees used in standard file browsers) to generate a parallel view of the hierarchy.

2   Related Work

There are a large number of visualizations focused on simple hierarchies.

Cone Trees [Robertson et al. 1991] are one of the most well known. They present data using a top to bottom hierarchical approach that utilizes 3D techniques to display each level of nodes like a fairground Ferris wheel on its side. They achieve both focus+context by displaying nodes of interest in the foreground (focus) and the rest of the hierarchy (the context) in the background. Distorted nodes can be brought into focus by rotating the tree.

The hyperbolic browser [Lamping 1994] is another well-known technique for visualizing hierarchical trees. In this representation, nodes are positioned in a hyperbolic plane, a distortion technique that allows nodes in focus to be stretched, and nodes in context to be squeezed [Pirolli et al. 2000]. This allows the hierarchy to be drawn in a space efficient manner [Stasko & Zhang 2000].

Information Slices [Andrews & Heidegger 1998], uses concentric semi-circular discs to visualize large trees by using each disk to represent a number (usually 5–10) of levels of the hierarchy. They also include a way of focusing on parts of interest by spawning a fresh disk from a selected node.

Despite research into visualizing hierarchies, visualizations such as the hyperbolic browser and Cone Trees have still failed to make a commercial impact

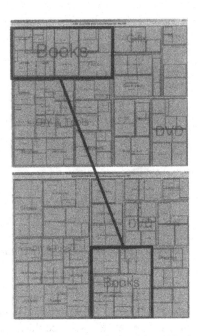

Figure 3: TreeMap item 'Books' changing position when the values change.

outside niche areas in industry and most graphical user interface toolkits only feature the ubiquitous TreeView for visualizing hierarchies. TreeViews, simple outliner-style lists of folders, are found in many applications such as Windows Explorer. Due to their popularity they are familiar to most users, making them a viable option in applications because users already know how to use them [Jacobsson 2002].

A number of visualizations have also been developed that allow you to visualize hierarchies with values attached such as file sizes, Web hits or sales.

The most well known of these is the TreeMap [Johnson & Shneiderman 1991], like the PieTree, it can display hierarchies where both leaf and child nodes contain numerical values. TreeMaps adopt a rectangle space filling approach. They work by slicing and dicing rectangles to create child items. This slicing and dicing is performed recursively (by slicing up child rectangles) until all child items are represented inside each parent rectangle on a TreeMap.

Over the years various improvements have been made to the TreeMap visualization [Wattenberg 1999; van Wijk & van de Wetering 1999; Bruls et al. 2000; Shneiderman & Wattenberg 2001; Bederson et al. 2002] but problems still remain, the biggest two being that the positions of the rectangles in a given hierarchy are not guaranteed to stay in the same position when the items in the hierarchy change value (Figure 3) and the smallest node in the TreeMap may not be represented by the smallest rectangle displayed, due to spacing enhancements suggested by Fiore & Smith [2001] that allowed users to better understand the hierarchy that the TreeMap represents.

Figure 4: Left- PieTree appearing as a pie chart (collapsed). Right- Exploded PieTree showing child nodes and value of category node.

DiskTrees [Chi et al. 1998], like PieTrees, use a circular layout to visualize website evolution. In DiskTrees angular space is allocated proportional to the number of leaf nodes, whilst page access counts are visualized by the thickness and brightness of lines.

Evaluation in visualization has always been problematic and often lags behind new ideas. The CHI'97 browse-off was perhaps one of the most high-profile, if informal, comparisons where expert users of the Hyberbolic Browser were able to out perform the plain Tree View [Mullet et al. 1999]. In more formal evaluation, Cockburn & McKenzie [2000] found that locating items in a Cone Tree was slower than locating items in a TreeView, and Kobsa [2004] found that most hierarchical representations (including TreeMaps and the hyperbolic browser) did not perform as well as the TreeView in Windows Explorer for tasks related to file system management. Cone Trees suffer from considerable occlusion due to overlapping nodes [Spence 2001; Card et al. 1999], and empirical work has shown that Cone Trees become too difficult to comprehend when there are more than 1000 items in them [Carriere & Kazman 1995]. Czerwinski & Larson [1997] found that whilst the hyperbolic browser was better than the TreeView for keeping global/local focus, the TreeView was better for tracking where you had been and was more familiar to users and that they preferred using TreeViews to hyperbolic trees.

3 PieTree External Behaviour

The basic concept of PieTrees was introduced in Dix & Ellis [1998] as an example of the principle of taking a standard visualization (in this case a Pie chart) and adding interactivity. This was developed more fully (and the name PieTree used) together with a partial demonstrator-level implementation in Dix et al. [2000]. PieTrees are seen as normal pie charts when collapsed. However nodes that contain child values can be exploded to reveal the child nodes of that segment. A collapsed PieTree segment represents the sum of the values for a category node + the sum of the values for all its children. An exploded PieTree category segment represents the true value of a category node, and has its child nodes shown outside it (Figure 4). The area of each PieSegment is proportional to the total value of the PieTree. Child values can also be categories and contain child nodes that can also be expanded. This allows the

PieTree to display deep hierarchies. Note that in the case where the top level node has a value it is represented as a small circle of appropriate area at the centre (for example, hits on the home page of a website).

The PieTree allows users to expand and collapse nodes in any order, either the whole tree can be expanded, or just specific nodes. In complex hierarchies users require mechanisms for hiding parts in order to focus on a particular sub hierarchy [Robertson et al. 1991], a requirement met by the PieTree.

Whilst the PieTree can be used in isolation, it was envisaged to be used alongside an outliner-style TreeView so that the two views compliment each other and the structure of the PieTree is made more apparent because of simultaneous folding/unfolding of both – a form of *temporal fusion*. The PieTree is isotropic in nature, so will always have the same width and height regardless of what area it is displayed in on a computer screen. This feature makes the PieTree fit well alongside a standard TreeView control as horizontal screen resolution is usually significantly greater than vertical resolution.

4 Informal Evaluation

To enhance the design of the PieTree visualization, two rounds of informal evaluation were conducted in an iterative process which allowed important usability problems to be discovered. Usability problems discovered in the first round of evaluation were then re-evaluated in the second round. Problems discovered in the second round were then fed back into the PieTree design used for the controlled experiment.

The cooperative evaluation technique was used instead of the standard think-aloud observation technique. This technique, unlike think-aloud, allows participants to ask questions if they become stuck and additionally allows the evaluator to ask questions to the user if it is not immediately obvious what they are thinking [Dix et al. 2004].

4.1 Participants

Eight postgraduate students at Lancaster University volunteered for the informal evaluation. None of the participants were paid for the study. All of the participants had normal or corrected to normal vision. The typical age range was 20–25, with an overall age range of 20–35. None of the participants used in the informal evaluation participated in the controlled experiment.

Participants reported that on average they had a slightly above average knowledge of mathematics and trigonometry. All of the participants reported that they used computers daily. Three quarters of the participants reported using spreadsheets on a monthly or weekly basis, one used them on a daily basis, and one had never used spreadsheets.

4.2 Design

The evaluation followed a 2×2 design with each participant using both PieTrees and TreeMaps for both simple and more complex hierarchies.

The first and third conditions used the PieTree visualization in conjunction with a TreeView to display the hierarchy and the second and fourth used the Microsoft Research TreeMap.

In the first two conditions a simple hierarchy was used containing 3 parent nodes, and 3 child nodes for each parent, each with 12 items. For the third and fourth conditions a more complex hierarchy was used which contained 125 nodes and a non-uniform hierarchical structure with a maximum depth of four child nodes deep. All data was fictional but given realistic names. To make the hierarchies in the third and fourth conditions even harder to understand, a much greater range of values was applied to the items than in tasks one and two.

The conditions were partially counterbalanced to allow for any learning effects. This spread the order in which the visualizations were displayed to the participants and also spread the order in which complex and simple hierarchies were presented.

The participants were not given explicit instruction in the interaction with either visualization as we were interested in the extent to which the interfaces could be picked up by novice or infrequent users. Participants were asked to verbalize their thoughts throughout the experiment. In order to make them comfortable with using this technique they were asked to read the instructions aloud. There was no time limit given for any of the tasks, but the procedure typically took 45 minutes.

4.3 Tasks

For the first two conditions using simple hierarchical data, participants were given the following tasks:

- Find the item with the largest value and specify:

  - What the item is.
  - What the item represents.

- Find the item with the smallest value and specify:

  - What the item is.
  - What the item represents.

- Specify what the data in general represents, and whether or not the items relate to each other.

The tasks deliberately did not define how to find the largest and smallest values; this was left to the participants own intuition. Note that for the first of these tasks both TreeMaps and PieTrees allow the option of efficient heuristic search whilst the second always requires every node to be visited. Both can be accomplished by simply looking at numbers using tool tips, but may, in principle, be aided by visually assessing the size of the targets.

These tasks were deliberately designed not to favour the use of PieTree visualization, but covered a range of sub-tasks one might encounter when interacting in a more exploratory fashion with numerical hierarchical data.

These same three kinds of task were used in the later formal experiment.

For the third and fourth conditions users were also given the task of being allowed to explore the data and verbalize their actions and thoughts as they explored. Users were then given the tasks of finding specific items in the hierarchy that were expected to cause them difficultly (items that were deep down the hierarchy and had very small values). For both conditions users were given items to find which had the numerical value of 1 out of 5282 (less than 1 / 5000 of the visualization). For the PieTree the task given was 'find and highlight the book: What You Wear Can Change Your Life'. In the case of the TreeMap, the task was to 'find and highlight the camera Canon Digital Ixus 40 4 megapixel'.

4.4 Apparatus

The informal evaluation was performed on an IBM Thinkpad R31 laptop computer running Windows XP Professional, with a 14 inch display at a resolution of 1280×1024 pixels. A Microsoft USB wheel mouse was attached to the laptop, as it offered more precision than the inbuilt TrackPoint. Participants' voices were recorded using an Olympus VN-3600 Digital Voice Recorder.

5 Results and Interpretation

Participants did not show any significant preference between the PieTree and the TreeMap. However participants suggested a number of changes to the visualizations, including highlighting the items selected using the TreeView in the PieTree representation.

The major problem with the PieTree was that users believed it was just a normal pie chart:

'OK. Right. A pie chart.'

All participants incorrectly specified the smallest item in the PieTree as being the smallest item that appeared in its collapsed state. Because users thought the PieTree was a pie chart some of them failed to expand the PieTree at all on one of the tasks (they were not specifically instructed to do so):

'OK. DIY and tools, how many page hits? Oh, that includes child items. Oh child items, never thought to do that (expand the items PieTree), that's really cool. Can I go back to other one (task one) and have a look for child items there?'

It quickly became apparent during the first round of evaluation that users expected a greater degree of interactivity between the PieTree and the TreeView, highlighting fine interaction details that lead into re-design. Participants' actions suggested that the TreeView brought benefits to the PieTree, reinforcing the expected pattern of use in the early PieTree papers.

The different aspects ratios of the TreeMap (Figure 5) proved to be a burden when asked to find the smallest item, with participants finding it harder to figure out whether Beans were smaller than Bananas. One of the squarified versions of TreeMaps might have helped this.

Users generally displayed a poor understanding of the hierarchies displayed in the visualizations. This may have been due to the data sets not being familiar to the participants; however some problems seemed more fundamental. In the instructions they struggled on 'techie' terms like parent/child. In the PieTree as noted previously they often failed to realize that there was a hierarchy to expand and in the TreeView they found difficulty distinguishing labels of categories from those of contained sub-categories.

Figure 5: TreeMap items with different aspect ratios (NB partial letters from legends of higher level categories).

---

6 Formal Evaluation

In order to investigate the benefits of using parallel views in the PieTree visualization, an experiment was performed to see whether using a TreeView in conjunction with a PieTree brought any additional benefits over using just a PieTree or TreeView.

6.1 Participants

A total of 16 students undertook the experiment, comprising of 15 postgraduates and 1 undergraduate student all at Lancaster University (6 females and 10 males). The average age for participants was 20–25 years old. All users had normal or corrected to normal vision. None of the participants were paid for the study nor made aware of the study hypotheses.

6.2 Design

A 3×3 within-subjects design was used. The first factor was representation (PieTree and TreeView, PieTree only and TreeView only) and the second factor was task (find the smallest node, find the largest node, find a specific node).

The dependent variables measured in the experiment included task completion time (measured in milliseconds) and the number of correct responses for each condition. There were three trials for each condition in the experiment, creating a total of 27 trials. The trial order was independently randomized for each participant using a pseudo-random number generator.

6.3 Apparatus and Materials

The visualizations were displayed on a Pentium 4 desktop computer running Windows XP Professional with a 17 inch LG L1715S monitor at a display resolution of 1280×1024 pixels. A Microsoft USB optical mouse was used as the input device for the experiment; use of the keyboard was not permitted.

The experimental software was written by the authors to record the task completion time for the stimulus and the item chosen by the participant. The item chosen by the user was also recorded so as to enable analysis of the error totals.

The three visualizations shown to the participants included the PieTree in conjunction with a parallel TreeView (Figure 6), the PieTree in isolation, and the TreeView only.

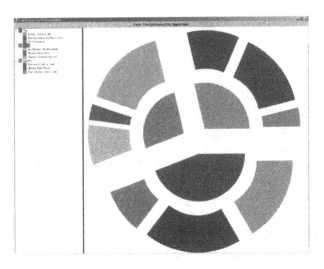

Figure 6: The PieTree in conjunction with a parallel TreeView.

The hierarchy used in the experiment was a hierarchy for a fictional e-commerce store. For each of the 27 trials in the experiment, the value for each tree item was randomly generated between the values of 200 and 800.

6.4   Procedure

The experiment was conducted using one participant at a time in a quiet room. Participants were given instructions on a piece of paper about the tasks they had to perform. After reading the instructions and signing the consent form, they were then asked to watch a five minute instruction video walking through the analysis of the data shown on a sample PieTree for a fictional company called StallMart.

Participants were instructed to complete the tasks as quickly and as accurately as possible. The participants were not told that the area of the segments of the PieTree corresponds to their value, nor were they informed of any strategies that will make the task completion time quicker. They were informed that the values of the data change for each trial.

A post experiment informal interview was conducted with participants in order to establish which visualization they preferred and why, and to discuss and clarify any strategies they appeared to develop over the duration of the experiment. The entire procedure took approximately 20 minutes per participant.

6.5   Results and Interpretation

Over all tasks, the average completion time for the PieTree was nearly 10% faster than the TreeView with the combined visualization between the two. However, this difference is not statistically significant and moreover hides a richer story of individual differences and task interactions.

During the experiment it was observed that different participants adopted different strategies. There were three distinct types of participant:

Task	Representation			
	Both	Pie only	Tree only	*Mean*
Biggest	18.595	16.210	21.590	*18.798*
	(5.62)	(4.63)	(8.92)	
Smallest	16.777	16.236	17.987	*17.000*
	(5.23)	(5.61)	(5.44)	
Specific	9.436	11.444	8.154	*9.678*
	(4.89)	(5.41)	(3.00)	
Mean	*14.936*	*14.630*	*15.910*	

Table 1: Task completion times for task and representation in seconds (standard deviation displayed in parenthesis)

1. those that relied solely on tooltips when finding the largest and smallest values,

2. those that used both visualizations where the stimulus allowed, and

3. those that discovered using the areas on the PieTree aided in finding the largest and smallest items mid experiment.

These three participant types were coded and used in the analysis.

It was noted that the participants who adopted a strategy of using the area of the Pie Segments (Types 2 and 3) appeared to perform better than those relying solely on tooltips (Type 1). Because of the wide variation between individuals we analysed the difference using non-parametric rank statistics as these are more robust to outliers. A Mann-Whitney U test confirmed that there was indeed a significant difference between the rankings of users that utilized the area of the Pie Segments in finding the largest and smallest items, than those that did not ($U = 6$, $N_1 = 9$, $N_2 = 7$, $p = 0.005$, two tailed).

It was observed that making comparisons between segments in the PieTree became difficult when there were several similarly sized segments in the visualization. This was also commented on by participants:

'I found comparing data from different levels to be complex.'

'Pie in the middle is hard to compare- it is like comparing a triangle to a rectangle.'

For angle segments, just as for rectangles with different aspect ratios in Figure 5, it is hard to compare areas. This is a problem for plain Pie charts and arguably these are not a good representation for this reason. However, perhaps just because of familiarity they are an accepted and largely understood visualization and it is on this existing understanding that PieTrees build.

As well as the substantial individual differences there were also significant differences between tasks. Table 1 shows task completion times for the three conditions and three tasks. The interaction effect is significant (ANOVA 3×3×16, $F(4,60) = 4.939$, $p = 0.02$). This is not unexpected. The 'find the biggest' tasks permit rapid visual inspection that can lead to an efficient heuristic search and indeed the PieTree substantially reduces completion times for these tasks (with the presence of the additional TreeView appearing to act as a distraction). The 'find the smallest' tasks require looking at everything, but rapid visual scanning can cut down the possibilities needing to be considered; in these tasks the PieTree still enables faster performance, but more marginally so. However, in the tasks related to finding information about specific values, there is no advantage to size-based scanning and hence, reasonably, the simpler TreeView out performs the PieTree. Again for these last tasks the presence of the PieTree appears to distract from the more efficient use of the TreeView.

We do not have eye tracking or similar data to verify the search strategies used, so the explanations of these results are tentative, however, participants did note the differences between tasks:

'The PieTree was useful for finding the largest and the smallest- it was easy to do based on the area.'

'The more sizes tended to be similar the less useful was the Pie. But typically the Pie was more useful for finding the largest/smallest items.'

'PieTree was useless for finding names.'

'Tree is better for finding a specific item.'

7   Future Developments for PieTree

Like all novel visualization techniques, the PieTree visualization is not without its problems and extra research is necessary to further enhance the visualization. TreeViews become problematic when displaying large hierarchies as users are required to perform a large amount of scrolling. Robertson et al. [2005] suggest using coalesced nodes in TreeViews to overcome this problem, allowing the hierarchy to be visualized in a much smaller space. This in turn allows nodes to be located faster. In future implementations it would be possible to combine the Robertson et al. coalesced TreeView with the PieTree to further enhance its performance when visualizing large hierarchies.

Large hierarchies also cause more fine-grained interaction issues as the nodes towards the leaves become unclickable on larger trees. Perhaps some form of zooming into a part of the tree opening it as a fresh PieTree would be appropriate, similar to that used in Information Slices.

Colouring of segments is also an interesting issue. In principle a planar diagram like the PieTree can be coloured in four colours whilst never having two adjacent areas in the same colour (the famous Four Colour Theorem). In practice the algorithms for doing this are quite expensive, but allowing a slightly larger palette makes this computationally tractable. However, nodes in the PieTree expand and collapse and if node colouring is to be preserved during interaction (it would be very confusing not to!), then it is neither clear how many colours are necessary, nor what an efficient algorithm for colouring would be.

The Gestalt law of connectedness, states connected objects are perceived as a single structure [Nesbitt & Friedrich 2002] and allows for automatic perceptual grouping [Palmer & Rock 1994]. This Gestalt law is exploited in many hierarchy visualizations including TreeViews, directed graphs [Knuth 1968; Gansner et al.

1988], Cone Trees [Robertson et al. 1991] and hyperbolic browsers [Lamping 1994]. This law could be exploited better in the PieTree visualization to help show groupings between nodes, as it has been shown that connectedness is a more powerful grouping principle than proximity, size, colour or shape [Ware 2004]. The Gestalt law of common fate, states that objects moving in the same direction can be perceived as a group [Martinez-Trujillo & Treuse 2004]. The PieTree could again exploit this law when it expands by animating exploding pie segments.

8   Discussion and Broader Issues

As noted the PieTree has previously only had partial implementation and no evaluation. This first implementation as a component within a standard toolkit and evaluation is thus important in assessing the value of the technique.

The informal evaluation compared this first PieTree implementation against the TreeMap, which has had extensive development over many years, and hence the lack of a clear 'winner' between the two suggests that further development and tuning of the PieTree is worthwhile. The specific problems highlighted in the Microsoft implementation of the TreeMap are largely ones that have been addressed in variants of the TreeMap, although problems identifying hierarchy are perhaps more fundamental as this is a bordered version of the TreeMap which should make this easier.

For the PieTree this was more a formative evaluation stage, however, beyond the comments that lead to incremental changes, the fact that users were slow to discover the interactive capabilities of the visualization is interesting. This is probably because it is rare to encounter interactive visualizations even in computer applications or the Web. The familiarity of the PieTree was a two-edged sword whilst making the visualization easier to read, it led to problems where users saw it as 'just' a Pie chart and thus even less likely to explore than perhaps a more unusual visualization might have encouraged.

In the formal evaluation the PieTree did perform better on average than the more familiar TreeView. However, the main lesson we wish to draw (as in so much of interactive systems design) is 'it all depends' – upon user and upon task.

The substantial difference not just in users' 'baseline' speeds but, more critically, in the interaction between visual/cognitive style and visualization strategy is of great importance. It is in many ways 'obvious', but does suggest that effective pre-tests for these styles should perhaps be standard procedure in order to interpret visualization evaluation. This underlines the well known, but often overlooked, importance of providing alternative ways of visualizing and interacting with data. In future experiments in this area it would be good to consider ways of detecting the users' strategies in solving tasks. Eye tracking would certainly help, although analysing the data from this on a dynamic visualization would be very labour intensive or require bespoke analysis software. Also given the level of individual difference it would be good to pre-test participants using standard test of visual/spatial ability, cognitive style etc.

The task interaction is again not surprising, but also so important methodologically. It is not uncommon to see experiments where generalizations are based on a small set of kinds of task ... and in the case of novel visualizations ones where you would expect the new visualization to perform well! We deliberately chose a range of tasks where we would expect good and poor behaviour and this was evident in the outputs. One size does not fit all and visualizations need to fit the tasks for which they are being used.

In any particular task, the hybrid TreeView+PieTree solution was out performed by one of the other methods. It appears that more is not better; users presented with a combined visualization, even with no competition for screen space, were not able to focus on the alternative best for the current task. Possibly this would be different for longitudinal or expert use, but within the timescale of a short controlled experiment participants were not able to learn effective decision strategies. Indeed a simple experiment using any one of the tasks might have led to a rejection of the hybrid approach, whereas in cases where there is a mix of tasks it is clearly the solution to give the most consistent performance.

In summary, the success of PieTrees on appropriate tasks suggests that further work in this area would be fruitful, especially given the relative novelty of the technique. The particular combination of TreeView and PieTree whilst non-optimal in any particular situation appears to be more robust over a range of tasks.

Acknowledgements

This work was supported by an EPSRC MTA studentship on the MRes in Design and Evaluation of Advanced Interactive Systems at Lancaster University.

References

Bederson, B. B., Shneiderman, B. & Wattenberg, M. [2002], Ordered and Quantum Treemaps: Making Effective use of 2D Space to Display Hierarchies, *ACM Transactions on Graphics* **21**(4), 833–54.

Bruls, M., Huizing, K. & van Wijk, J. J. [2000], Squarified TreeMaps, in W. de Leeuw & R. van Liere (eds.), *Proceedings of the Joint Eurographics/IEEE Symposium on Visualization (VisSym'00)*, IEEE Computer Society Press, pp.33–42.

Card, S. K., Mackinlay, J. D. & Shneiderman, B. (eds.) [1999], *Readings in Information Visualization: Using Vision to Think*, Morgan-Kaufmann.

Carriere, J. & Kazman, R. [1995], Interacting with Huge Hierarchies: Beyond Cone Trees, in N. Gershon & S. Eick (eds.), *Proceedings of the IEEE Symposium on Information Visualization (InfoVis'95)*, IEEE Computer Society Press, pp.74–81.

Chi, E. H., Pitkow, J., Mackinlay, J., Pirolli, P., Gossweiler, R. & Card, S. K. [1998], Visualizing the Evolution of Web Ecologies, in C.-M. Karat, A. Lund, J. Coutaz & J. Karat (eds.), *Proceedings of the SIGCHI Conference on Human Factors in Computing Systems (CHI'98)*, ACM Press, pp.400–7.

Cockburn, A. & McKenzie, B. [2000], An Evaluation of Cone Trees, in S. McDonald, Y. Waern & G. Cockton (eds.), *People and Computers XIV (Proceedings of HCI'2000)*, Springer-Verlag, pp.425–36.

Czerwinski, M. & Larson, K. [1997], The New Web Browsers: They're Cool but Are They Useful, Presentation made as part of Industry Day at HCI'97. http://research.microsoft.com/~marycz/bhci97.ppt, last accessed 2006-05-23.

Dix, A., Beale, R. & Wood, A. [2000], Architectures to make Simple Visualisations using Simple Systems, *in* V. Di Gesù, S. Levialdi & L. Tarantino (eds.), *Proceedings of the Conference on Advanced Visual Interface (AVI 2000)*, ACM Press, pp.51–60.

Dix, A., Finlay, J., Abowd, G. D. & Beale, R. [2004], *Human Computer Interaction*, third edition, Prentice–Hall.

Dix, A. & Ellis, G. [1998], Starting Simple: Adding Value to Static Visualisation through Simple Interaction, *in* T. Catarci, M. F. Costabile, G. Santucci & L. Tarantino (eds.), *Proceedings of the Conference on Advanced Visual Interface (AVI'98)*, ACM Press, pp.124–34.

Fiore, A. & Smith, M. A. [2001], TreeMap Visualizations of Newsgroups, Technical Report, Microsoft Research.

Gansner, E. R., North, S. C. & Vo, K. P. [1988], Dag – A Program that Draws Directed Graphs, *Software — Practice and Experience* **18**(11), 1047–62.

Jacobsson, P. [2002], Using a TreeView Metaphor to Visualize Hardware Simulation for Testing, *in* L. Terveen & D. Wixon (eds.), *CHI'02 Extended Abstracts of the Conference on Human Factors in Computing Systems*, ACM Press, pp.850–1.

Johnson, B. & Shneiderman, B. [1991], Tree-Maps: A Space-filling Approach to the Visualization of Hierarchical Information Structures, *in* G. M. Nielson & L. Rosenblum (eds.), *Proceedings of the 2nd IEEE Conference on Visualization (VIS'91)*, IEEE Computer Society Press, pp.284–91.

Knuth, D. E. [1968], *The Art of Computer Programming- Fundamental Algorithms*, Vol. 1, Addison–Wesley.

Kobsa, A. [2004], User Experiments with Tree Visualization Systems, *in Proceedings of the IEEE Symposium on Information Visualization (InfoVis 2004)*, IEEE Computer Society Press, pp.9–16.

Lamping, J. andRao, R. [1994], A Focus+Context Technique Based on Hyperbolic Geometry for Visualizing Large Hierarchies, *in* B. Adelson, S. Dumais & J. Olson (eds.), *Proceedings of the SIGCHI Conference on Human Factors in Computing Systems: Celebrating Interdependence (CHI'94)*, ACM Press, pp.401–8.

Martinez-Trujillo, J. C. & Treuse, S. [2004], Feature-Based Attention Increases the Selectivity of Population Responses in Primate Visual Cortex, *Current Biology* **14**(9), 744–51.

Mullet, K., Fry, C. & Schiano, D. [1999], On Your Marks, Get Set, Browse!, *in* A. Edwards & S. Pemberton (eds.), *CHI'97 Extended Abstracts of the Conference on Human Factors in Computing Systems*, ACM Press, pp.113–4. See http://www.baychi.org/calendar/19970812/ for a brief report.

Nesbitt, K. V. & Friedrich, C. [2002], Applying Gestalt Principles to Animated Visualizations of Network Data, *in* E. Banissi (ed.), *Proceedings of the Sixth International Conference on Information Visualization (IV'02)*, IEEE Computer Society Press, pp.737–43.

Palmer, S. & Rock, I. [1994], Rethinking Perceptual Organization. The Role of Uniform Connectness, *Psychonomic Bulletin and Review* **1**(1), 29–55.

Pirolli, P., Card, S. K. & van der Wege, M. M. [2000], The Effects of Information Scent on Searching Information: Visualizations of Large Tree Structures, *in* V. Di Gesù, S. Levialdi & L. Tarantino (eds.), *Proceedings of the Conference on Advanced Visual Interface (AVI 2000)*, ACM Press, pp.161–72.

Robertson, G. G., Czerwinski, M. P. & Churchill, J. E. [2005], Visualisation of Mappings between Schemas, *in* D. Benyon, J. Gulliksen & T. McEwan (eds.), *People and Computers XIV: The Bigger Picture (Proceedings of HCI'05)*, Springer, pp.431–9.

Robertson, G. G., Mackinlay, J. D. & Card, S. K. [1991], Cone Trees: Animated 3D Visualizations of Hierarchical Information, *in* S. P. Robertson, G. M. Olson & J. S. Olson (eds.), *Proceedings of the SIGCHI Conference on Human Factors in Computing Systems: Reaching through Technology (CHI'91)*, ACM Press, pp.189–94.

Shneiderman, B. & Wattenberg, M. [2001], Ordered TreeMap Layouts, *in Proceedings of the IEEE Symposium on Information Visualization (InfoVis 2001)*, IEEE Computer Society Press, pp.73–8.

Spence, R. [2001], *Information Visualisation*, ACM Press/Addison–Wesley.

Stasko, J. & Zhang, E. [2000], Focus+Context Display and Navigation Techniques for Enhancing Radial, Space-filling Hierarchy Visualizations, *in Proceedings of the IEEE Symposium on Information Visualization (InfoVis 2000)*, IEEE Computer Society Press, pp.57–68.

van Wijk, J. J. & van de Wetering, H. [1999], Cushion Treemaps: Visualization of Hierarchical Information, *in Proceedings of the IEEE Symposium on Information Visualization (InfoVis'99)*, IEEE Computer Society Press, pp.73–8.

Ware, C. [2004], *Information Visualization: Perception for Design*, second edition, Morgan-Kaufmann.

Wattenberg, M. [1999], Visualizing the Stock Market, *in* M. E. Atwood (ed.), *CHI'99 Extended Abstracts of the Conference on Human Factors in Computing Systems*, ACM Press, pp.188–9.

Severity of Usability and Accessibility Problems in eCommerce and eGovernment Websites

Chandra Harrison & Helen Petrie

Department of Computer Science, University of York, Heslington, York YO10 5DD, UK

Email: *{chandra.harrison, helen.petrie}@cs.york.ac.uk*

Guidelines are available to address website usability and accessibility and these often rate the importance of different problems encountered by users. However, users still experience problems when interacting with sites and little research has been conducted to assess which problems are the most severe. Prioritizing problems during website development is needed to ensure efficient and effective use of limited resources. To investigate the issue of the severity of usability and accessibility problems, a study was conducted comparing the severity ratings of problems found in a group of sites by two sets of guidelines (WCAG1.0 for accessibility and the Health and Human Services (HHS) guidelines for usability), by an expert and by users. The research revealed that the majority of the most severe problems are identified in existing guidelines. However, not all of the less severe problems are identified. A significant agreement between expert and users on the relative severity of problems was found, but the expert rated problems more severely than the users. Surprisingly, no relationship was found between the ratings in either the WCAG1.0 or HHS guidelines and the ratings given by the users and the expert. Therefore, we conclude that developers should obtain severity ratings from users or an expert rather than relying on those provided by guidelines.

Keywords: prioritization, usability, accessibility, user testing, visual impairment, dyslexia, WCAG, HHS guidelines.

1   Prioritizing Usability and Accessibility Problems

The literature is filled with information about usability and accessibility problems in
website design and how to avoid them [Chisholm et al. 1999; Koyani et al. 2003].
Fundamental usability issues include identifying the owner of the site, ensuring
consistent navigation, organizing information logically and ensuring links are easy to
use. Accessibility issues include providing alternative text for graphics, not relying
on colour alone to convey information and ensuring compatibility with assistive
technologies. But, although guidelines for both usability and accessibility offer
ratings or levels of the impact of particular problems on users, there is still a lack
of empirical studies to validate these ratings.

1.1   Accessibility and Usability Guidelines

There are readily available guidelines and heuristics to address both web usability
and accessibility. A comprehensive set of guidelines that covers both usability and
accessibility is the Research-based Web Design and Usability Guidelines developed
by the US Department of Health and Human Services (HHS Guidelines) [Koyani
et al. 2003]. These guidelines were developed through an iterative process of
consultation with and validation by web designers and usability specialists to identify
the most important factors in web design, breaking down higher level factors into
specific guidelines and providing research evidence to support the expert claims.
Importance ratings are provided which are based on both the strength of research
evidence available and the experts' importance ratings. Many of the guidelines have
a low strength of evidence rating with a high importance rating, acknowledging the
value of expert opinion but suggesting that more research is needed in many areas of
website design [Koyani et al. 2003].

   To encourage accessibility, the Web Content Accessibility Guidelines
(WCAG1.0) breaks 14 high-level accessibility guidelines into 65 specific checkpoints.
Each checkpoint is assigned a priority level (Priority 1, 2 and 3) [Chisholm et al.
1999]. A Web document or resource must satisfy Priority 1 (P1) checkpoints
otherwise, according to WCAG1.0; 'one or more groups [of disabled people] will
find it *impossible* to access information in the document'. If Priority 2 (P2)
checkpoints are not satisfied, one or more groups of disabled people will find it
difficult to access information in the document. If Priority 3 (P3) checkpoints are not
satisfied, one or more groups of disabled people 'will find it *somewhat difficult* to
access information'. If a website passes all P1 checkpoints, it is Level A conformant;
if it passes all P1 and P2 checkpoints, it is Level AA conformant; and finally if it
passes all P1, P2 and P3 checkpoints, it is Level AAA conformant.

   WCAG2.0 is the next iteration of the guidelines and is currently in its final draft
[Caldwell et al. 2006]. The current draft version is organized into four accessibility
principles: content must be perceivable; interface components in the content must
be operable; content and controls must be understandable; and content should be
robust enough to work with current and future user agents (including assistive
technologies). Each principle includes a list of guidelines addressing the principles.
Success criteria are included to assist in testing conformance to the guidelines.
The success criteria are organized into three levels. Level 1 success criteria must

be reached to achieve a *minimum* level of accessibility. Meeting Level 2 success criteria will result in the website, document or resource achieving an *enhanced* level of accessibility and Level 3 will achieve *additional* accessibility enhancements. Levels 1 and 2 can reasonably be applied to all Web content, whereas Level 3 may not necessarily be applied to all Web content. As with WCAG1.0 conformance statements involve Level A, AA and AAA.

1.2 Priority Levels and Severity of Accessibility Issues

Despite the guidelines available, recent research suggests that accessibility is still a major problem. For example, a Disability Rights Commission formal investigation found that 81% of 1000 websites assessed were not even Level A conformant [DRC 2004]. Possible reasons for non-conformance include developers having limited resources to conduct accessible design and evaluation, and lacking appropriate knowledge. During development prioritizing which issues to address helps maximize use of resources. Therefore, developers need to know what are the most important usability and accessibility problems. Importance ratings for usability issues are available [Koyani et al. 2003] and the priority levels in WCAG1.0 and success criteria levels in WCAG2.0 attempt to indicate which the most relevant accessibility issues are [Chisholm et al. 1999; Caldwell et al. 2006]. However, despite the research evidence cited in the HHS guidelines, there is little empirical evidence to confirm which are the most important accessibility problems for users.

It is also unclear what the relationship is between the severity and frequency of problems. The easiest fixes may take the least time and address the most severe problems. Alternatively, the most severe issues may require more time to address but may be relatively rare. It is also possible that the most frequently occurring issues may not be the most severe but may still have the greatest impact on users. Perhaps it is the cumulative effect of minor problems which has the greatest impact on users. To determine the severity of problems, detailed studies of users interacting with a variety of websites are needed. In addition, if interaction issues classified as accessibility problems also impact on mainstream users (i.e. are also highlighted as usability problems) these should have a higher priority as addressing these issues will improve the user experience for more people. Both usability and accessibility are important, so relative focus and allocation of resources should be on the basis of overall severity. More data are needed to determine the relationship between frequency and severity of problems and overall perception of usability and accessibility.

The objective of eCommerce sites is to make sales and secure repeat business by means of a usable and accessible website. Online selling reduces in-store overheads as consumers who would come into the store can now access the information from anywhere. In addition, eCommerce makes goods and services available at all hours and to people who are perhaps less able to go to a physical location, perhaps due to disability. While the main purpose of eGovernment sites is to convey information and increase social participation, many of the reasons for eCommerce sites also apply in this domain. One of the reasons that eCommerce and eGovernment websites are currently not fully utilized is that users are unable to complete their tasks of purchasing or finding information because sites are unusable or inaccessible to some degree. Therefore, the problems that most hinder task achievement are the most relevant to address in the eCommerce and eGovernment domains. If an issue is severe enough to make a user abandon their task then rectifying it should be a priority for developers.

It is important to explore the impact of the severity of usability and accessibility issues in web design. As well as determining what the most common and most severe problems are to assist in prioritizing, it is necessary to explore what the level of agreement on severity of problems between the guidelines, experts and users is, in order to validate the priorities/importance levels provided in guidelines. To explore these issues a user study of the accessibility and usability of a set of eCommerce and eGovernment websites was conducted as an initial step of an ongoing research programme.

2 Method

2.1 Participants

The participants in the study were three men and three women with a mean age of 32 years, ranging from 21 to 54, including two visually impaired people (VIPs), two dyslexics and two matched aged controls. The VIPs were both registered blind with little useful vision (one blind since birth and one late blind) and used JAWS screen reading software. Both dyslexic participants were diagnosed during high school and had received assistance with reading at school and since. All but one participant were not knowledgeable about human-computer interaction (HCI) with little or no specific knowledge of usability or accessibility or web design. The HCI knowledgeable participant was one of the matched aged controls. All but one participant were regular Internet users, the novice being less aware of technology and workarounds. This was helpful in highlighting problems that more expert users may not have.

The expert in the study was the first author, who has five years experience of working on usability and accessibility issues, in both academic and commercial settings.

2.2 Websites Used in the Study

eGovernment and eCommerce websites were used because they are regularly accessed by the public. Previous research supports using eGovernment sites because they perform reasonably well against accessibility criteria while eCommerce sites are less conformant with WGAG1.0 [DRC 2004]. Three eCommerce websites were chosen on the basis of mainstream popularity and familiarity to the expert (first author), including a bank, a supermarket and a retail catalogue store. Three eGovernment websites were selected on the basis of perceived general need, including a local council, a government employment centre and a licensing authority. Specific details of the sites used in this study have been avoided to maintain anonymity. The consistency of the web content was checked and site history and cache were cleared between tests. The order of evaluation of the sites was counter balanced with alternate participants assessing a website first or second, and each site was assessed by two participants with little or no previous exposure to the site.

		Expert Ratings					Total
		Cosmetic	Minor	Major	Catastrophe		Total
User Ratings	Cosmetic	**4**	3	3	–		10
	Minor	3	**21**	8	–		32
	Major	–	–	**19**	4		23
	Catastrophe	–	–	1	**5**		6
	Total	7	24	31	9		71

Table 1: Comparative severity ratings of accessibility and usability problems by user and expert.

2.3 Procedure

Using task-based scenarios, each user tested two sites with one simple task (which required them to follow one link off the home page) and one more complex task (which required following several links). All tasks required users to leave the homepage and find information on other pages. Users were required to complete the task without using any generic search function that might be available on the site. A task was deemed complete once the participant had the information requested. A task was deemed incomplete if the user decided they were unable or unwilling to continue. If the expert had to assist the user to find the information, the task was also deemed incomplete. The optimal pathway to the goal was compared against the path taken to check absolute success.

Users were asked to 'think aloud' as they went through the tasks. Each time a user encountered a problem (any issue they expressed verbally as a hindrance in pursuit of achieving the task), an assessment was completed in which the user stated the location and nature of the problem, its cause and provided a rating of the severity of the problem as cosmetic, minor, major or catastrophic. The expert, who observed all evaluations and assisted the users when necessary, also made an independent rating of the severity of the problem.

3 Results

Across the six websites tested, 41 individual problems were identified, with 16 of these occurring multiple times, having between two and seven occurrences (making a total of 71 problems). The most common problems were poor or no headings, unclear categories or links and large lists of links or text. On average, 12 problems were identified per website. Based on user group, accessibility problems accounted for 18.3%, usability problems for 81.7%. Table 1 shows the severity ratings of all problems as given by the users and the expert.

3.1 User/Expert Agreement on Severity Ratings

There was a highly significant correlation between the severity ratings given by users and the expert (Wilcoxon Signed Ranks $z = -3.05$, $p < 0.005$). There was agreement on 69% of occasions (numbers in bold in Table 1). However, there was also a significant difference between the users' and the expert's mean severity ratings ($F(1,68) = 9.80$, $p < 0.005$) with most users rating the severity of problems equally

	Users		Expert	
	Mean	S.D.	Mean	S.D.
Control	2.29	0.62	2.46	0.83
Dyslexic	2.08	0.80	2.50	0.86
Visually Impaired	2.76	0.94	2.86	0.79
All users	2.35	0.83	2.59	0.84

Table 2: Mean ratings of severity by users and expert. Scale used was 1 = cosmetic to 4 = catastrophe.

or less harshly than the expert (see Table 2). This effect held for all three user groups. For example, very few of the problems (five in total) were rated as catastrophic by users, whereas the expert classified nine problems as catastrophic (being the total number of tasks not completed by users). On only 5.6% (4/71) of occasions did a user give a more severe rating than the expert (numbers below the bold diagonal in Table 1), by only one rating in each instance. On 25.4% (18/71) of occasions the expert gave a more severe rating, on 21.1% of occasions by one rating and on 4.2% of occasions by 2 ratings (numbers above the bold diagonal in Table 1). This difference between the expert's and the users' severity ratings could perhaps be due to users adjusting their actual severity rating to provide a more positive impression to the expert (an example of the demand characteristic effect, that participants respond in the way that they think the researcher wants them to [see Rosnow & Rosenthal 1997]). Alternately, this expert may be a somewhat 'harsh' rater of problems, or may have been due to the fact that the expert had an overview of all the users performances. The highest level of agreement between users and the expert was for the minor problems, while the lowest level of agreement on the cosmetic problems, but this could be because this category also had the lowest number of problems.

An overall significant difference was found between mean severity ratings given by the three participant groups ($F(2,68) = 3.09$, $p < 0.05$) with VIPs rating their problems the highest, perhaps due to the particular difficulties of accessing the web with a screen reader. The difference between dyslexics, who rated their problems lowest, and the controls was not in fact significant (see Table 2). The VIPs encountered the least problems overall (21), with the dyslexics encountering the most (26).

3.2 Match Between User Problems and Guidelines

The great majority of the 40 major and catastrophic problems encountered (90%), as classified by the expert, are identified in the HHS guidelines. Of those not covered, three were accessibility problems and one was a usability problem. For the minor and cosmetic problems, only 61% are covered in the HHS guidelines. Those not covered in the guidelines tend to relate to aesthetics and trust issues; for example users being unsure whether all products are being displayed, a lack of audio welcoming for screen reader users and the requirement for logging in when searching for information. One of the more frequently mentioned problems was with a duplication of links and categories which confused both a VIP and a control group

	Priority 1 (P1)	Priority 2 (P2)	Priority 3 (P3)	Total
Catastrophe	0/0	6/4	1/2	7/6
Major problem	0/0	4/5	6/4	10/9
Minor problem	1/1	3/4	0/0	4/5
Cosmetic problem	0/0	1/1	0/1	1/2

Table 3: Severity ratings of accessibility problems by expert and users and their WCAG1.0 priority levels. Entries shown Expert rating/user rating.

user. This is in contrast to Chapter 10.7 of the HHS guidelines which advocates repeating important links.

Jonckheere-Tersptra tests showed that there was no relationship between the 'Relative Scores' of the HHS guidelines, computed by multiplying the 'Relative Importance' and 'Strength of Evidence' scores, and either the mean users' ratings (J-T = 61.39, n.s.) or the expert's (J-T = 60.48, n.s.) ratings. Table 3 shows the relationship between the severity ratings given by the users and the expert and the priority levels of the accessibility problems as indicated by WCAG1.0 (for the 22 accessibility problems covered by WCAG1.0). For example, the expert identified 7 accessibility catastrophes, but none of these was a P1 issue according to WCAG1.0, 6 were P2 and 1 was P3. The users identified 6 accessibility catastrophes, 4 were P2 and 2 were P3. The only P1 issue that caused a user a problem was rated by both the expert and the user as a minor problem. No significant relationship between WCAG1.0 priority levels and either the expert ratings (J-T = 65.5, n.s.) or users ratings (J-T = 71.5, n.s.).

4 Conclusions

The significant level of agreement on the severity of problems given by users and the expert shows that an expert can accurately assess the severity of both accessibility and usability problems. This factor is important for the prioritization of resources in the development of a website. However, whether an expert will *identify* all the problems that users may encounter has not been addressed by this research. We would argue that evaluation with users is still vital as they can always behave differently and encounter problems that experts do not fully anticipate [Whiteside et al. 1988]. Indeed, WCAG1.0 and 2.0 both advocate user testing in addition to automated testing as many aspects such as poor categorization cannot be checked using automated tools only.

Many of the problems encountered by users in this experiment are accounted for in guidelines. However, no relationship was found between the severity ratings given by either users or the expert in this study and the HHS Guidelines importance scores or the priorities given in WCAG1.0. This is a concern, as developers may currently be relying on the importance ratings/priority levels to assign effort in the development of their websites. It should be noted that this is only one study, with a small sample of users and only one expert, although the statistical analyses show robust results.

Future research will extend this work, with a wider variety of websites, more users (particularly to allow analysis of the findings from users with specific disabilities) and more than one expert. Future research could also include testing the WCAG2.0 success criteria, when they are finalized to assess the match with user ratings.

References

Caldwell, B., Chisholm, W., Slatin, J. & Vanderheiden, G. [2006], Web Content Accessibility Guidelines 2.0 Draft, http://www.w3.org/TR/WCAG20/, last accessed 2006-04.

Chisholm, W., Vanderheiden, G. & Jacobs, I. [1999], Web Content Accessibility Guidelines 1.0, http://www.w3.org/TR/WCAG10/, last accessed 2006-04.

DRC [2004], *The Web: Access and Inclusion for Disabled People*, The Stationery Office. Disability Rights Commission.

Koyani, S. J., Bailey, R. W. & Nall, J. R. [2003], Research-based Web Usability and Design Guidelines, http://usability.gov/pdfs/guidelines.html, last accessed 2006-04.

Rosnow, R. L. & Rosenthal, R. [1997], *People Studying People: Artefacts and Ethics in Behavioural Research*, Freeman.

Whiteside, J., Bennett, J. & Holtzblatt, K. [1988], Usability Engineering: Our Experience and Evolution, *in* M. Helander (ed.), *Handbook of Human–Computer Interaction*, North-Holland, pp.791–817.

Graph Builder: Constructing Non-visual Visualizations

David K. McGookin & Stephen A. Brewster

Department of Computing Science, University of Glasgow, 17 Lilybank Gardens, Glasgow G12 8QQ, UK

Tel: *+44 141 330 8430*

Fax: *+44 141 330 4913*

Email: *{mcgookdk,stephen}@dcs.gla.ac.uk*

URL: *http://www.multivis.org*

This paper introduces a novel application called Graph Builder, which allows visually impaired people to interactively construct bar graphs using a force feedback device. We discuss the limitations of current technology to allow such interactive construction and explain why, in educational environments, such interactive construction is important. Evaluations of Graph Builder showed that users could construct graphs accurately. However results showed that a large number of 'off-by-one' errors occurred, where the bar was set either one unit too high or too low. Revisions to the mechanism to manipulate bars were made, and further non-speech audio feedback was added. A further evaluation showing that the proportion of 'off-by-one' errors had been reduced.

Keywords: haptics, visual impairment, non-speech audio, graph construction.

1 Introduction

There are currently 11.4 million visually impaired people in the United States [Ross & Blasch 2002] and 2 million in the United Kingdom (http://www.rnib.org). Many of these users interact with computer systems using screen reading software such as JAWS (http://www.freedomscientific.com). This technology, whilst allowing access to textual data, is less good at providing access to graphical data such as the graphs, charts and tables that sighted people use in their everyday lives. Alternative technologies to access such information are available, but these involve creating raised paper diagrams from computer printouts. These diagrams are inflexible as they cannot be altered after production, and the user is unlikely to be able to inspect the diagram until it is produced on raised paper. Lack of easy access to this information is a major obstacle to blind and visually impaired people who are pursuing scientific study and careers [Dimigen et al. 1993]. There are additional problems where graphs and diagrams must be hand-prepared by students, such as in mathematics classes, where automatic generation via a spreadsheet program would not be sufficient for a student to show understanding of the graphs. Currently available technologies make it difficult to initially create graphs as well as change them after creation. Since learning to construct graphs involves making mistakes, understanding those mistakes and revising the graph interactively [Clamp 1997], solutions to allow students to learn effectively are required. There has been little research to provide access to diagrammatic representations such as graphs. Almost no work has been carried out to provide visually impaired users with the ability to interactively construct graphs. Current non-computer based techniques available to construct visualizations have several issues such as the inability to make changes and retain the graphs that are produced. All are unsuitable for communicating data outside an educational environment.

This paper discusses the design and evaluation of a haptic computer based application that allows visually impaired people to interactively construct mathematical graphs; allowing those graphs to be permanently retained, browsed and modified. We start by presenting requirements capture work which highlights the problems of currently available techniques for graph construction, before discussing our novel application called Graph Builder and its evaluation.

2   Background and Motivation

In order to determine the issues involved in graph construction for visually impaired people, a group discussion and interviews were held with visually impaired students at the Royal National College for the Blind (RNCB) in Hereford, and classroom observations were held at the Royal Blind School (RBS) in Edinburgh. At the RNCB, a vocational college in the south of England, a group discussion with six participants and two individual interviews were held. All of the participants were between the ages of 18–24 and were visually impaired when taught graphs at school. Participants studied a range of subjects (such as music technology and English literature), and all used a computer regularly for communication (such as email and Web browsing). Participants were all asked about their experiences of using and constructing graphs. In all cases participants were asked to introduce themselves, before the experimenter posed each of the following questions for discussion.

- In what ways do you use graphs and tables in your everyday lives?

- What sort of tools and technologies do you use to access graphs, and what are your views on them?

- What are your experiences in creating graphs?

- What sort of difficulties do you have when answering questions using graphs?

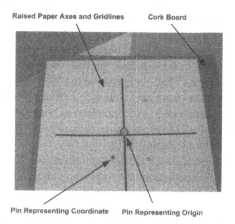

Raised Paper Axes and Gridlines   Cork Board

Pin Representing Coordinate   Pin Representing Origin

Figure 1: An example of the materials used when constructing a graph using the corkboard technique.

Participants were asked to discuss their views on the questions freely. The interviews and group discussion were recorded to allow for later transcription. Each interview lasted approximately 30 minutes with the group discussion taking around an hour. All participants were paid £5 for taking part.

At the RBS two teaching sessions were observed. Each session involved one-on-one teaching between a student and teacher on graph understanding and construction. Both students were between 16 and 18 years old. The experimenter quietly observed as much as possible during the lesson but did on occasion ask the student and teacher questions when relevant. One student was studying Standard Grade mathematics. In this lesson the teacher used a cork board and pins (see Figure 1) to demonstrate simple graph construction to the student, who also demonstrated constructing some graphs for the teacher. The second student was partially sighted and was studying Higher Grade mathematics. She was being taught how to transpose graphs along an axis, with the aid of both raised paper diagrams as well as a page magnifier. No parties at the RBS were paid for involvement in this study.

The most common technique used in schools for visually impaired people to construct graphs is to use a corkboard covered with a raised (swell) paper overlay presenting grid lines. Pins are pushed into the cork, and rubber bands wrapped around the pins to form the components of the graph such as bars, lines, etc. See Figure 1 for an example. This technique, whilst being cheap and simple, has a number of issues. Firstly, the pins used can fall out if not pushed in far enough, causing the student's hard work to become lost. Additionally the rubber bands used can easily fall off the graphs if a pin falls out, or if a pin is removed if the graph needs to be modified (e.g. a bar in a bar graph is set to the wrong value). Since the pins used are sharp so they can be driven into the board, care must be taken to ensure students do not injure themselves. Several participants in the group discussion noted that they had hurt themselves when using such a technique. One final issue is that the graphs created by students are rarely retained after they have been constructed. The graphs must be dismantled so that the equipment can be reused. Several participants in the group discussion found that this was 'a bit disheartening'.

An alternative technique for graph construction is to use a Braille typewriter. Participants in the group discussion noted that this was only useful for bar graphs with a limited number of bars. This technique allows for a permanent record of the graph to be kept, however the entire graph must be redrawn from scratch if a mistake is made. This is problematic since it is the interactive construction, making mistakes, understanding and correcting those mistakes that allow a solid understanding of graph concepts to be built up [Clamp 1997].

An additional problem with all of the techniques mentioned is one of speed. Participants found graph construction to be slow and cumbersome to a detrimental degree on their education. One participant saying:

> 'in my maths exams, if there was ever a question asking me to draw a graph for a set of figures, then I'd just miss it out and go onto the next one. I thought I might as well not even bother trying, it's so time consuming ... I wasn't going to sit there for three-quarters of an hour doing a little graph.'

Clearly any computer based solution must allow graphs to be constructed quickly, with minimum overhead caused by the technology used.

From the observations, group discussion and interviews we can conclude that all current techniques to construct graphs have issues. They are either non-permanent and cannot be retained, or are so permanent that they cannot be modified if a mistake is made. In all cases they are time consuming and 'fiddly'. Our solution overcomes these problems, allowing graphs to be constructed and modified with ease in a timely manner.

3 Computer-based Graph Access

Whilst only one study has investigated interactive construction of graphs, work has been undertaken to provide computer based access for visually impaired people to browse graphs and other mathematical diagrams.

Fritz & Barner [1999] have constructed a haptic-based system, using a PHANTOM haptic device from SensAble Technologies (http://www.sensable.com), that allows a user to explore the plot of a three dimensional function. Unfortunately they do not present an evaluation of their work. Yu & Brewster [2003] have designed and evaluated a PHANTOM based system to allow visually impaired users to browse simple line and bar charts. They have successfully shown that visually impaired users can extract information on the trend of a graph as well as being able to answer more detailed questions about the information contained within it. They also identified that adding non-speech sound to the haptic environment was an effective way to improve performance. They produced a set of guidelines which we have used to construct the novel tool discussed here.

In addition to the studies using haptic systems to allow visually impaired people to browse graphs, there have also been audio based solutions which have provided effective access to mathematical graphs. Mansur's [1985] SoundGraphs pioneered the technique of using pitch to represent the *y*-axis of a line graph and time to represent the *x*-axis. The use of such line graphs has been heavily studied, and have been found to effectively communicate trend information to users [Brown & Brewster 2003]. Unfortunately, only limited work has been undertaken to identify how other forms of diagram such as pie and bar charts can be sonified to be presented to users [Franklin & Roberts 2003].

The work discussed above shows that using haptics and non-speech sound is an effective way to present diagrammatic based mathematical data to users who are visually impaired. It is therefore a logical step to use such technology to build an interactive graph construction tool. Before discussing the design of our tool however, it is necessary to consider the limited work that has been undertaken on haptic and audio based graph construction applications.

There has been little work investigating graph construction for visually impaired people. Yu et al. [2003] have built a simple system using a Logitech Wingman force feedback mouse that allowed users to key in values for a graph and have the graph haptically rendered so that it could be felt with the mouse. The system is similar to the graph plotting system of Microsoft Excel and does not allow interactive manipulation, which as previously discussed is important in an educational environment. An evaluation showed that users could create and browse graphs, and that a combined haptic and audio interface produced lower errors than a solely haptic interface. However due to difficulties in accessing enough visually impaired people, they performed their evaluation on blindfolded sighted people. Yu et al. [2003] also developed an interactive graph building tool for line graphs using the Wingman mouse. Users set consecutive points on a line graph by clicking a haptic grid with the mouse. Their system did not however allow for points to be modified after being set, so users would have the same problems as using a Braille typewriter. If a mistake was made, the user would have to start the graph again from scratch, unlike a sighted user who may just remove the incorrect point on a paper based graph using an eraser and redraw the line. The system discussed in this paper overcomes such issues, allowing graphs to be dynamically altered with ease. Again Yu et al. performed no formal evaluation with visually impaired users, blindfolded participants being used instead. Van Scoy et al. [2001] have constructed a tool that will read and parse a mathematical expression, and produce a virtual haptic representation 'carved' into a virtual surface that can be explored using a PHANTOM haptic device. Unfortunately they do not report an evaluation of their system.

Using an automatic tool to construct a graph, whilst being useful to show the shape of a function, etc., assumes that the student understands the graph type created. This is useful when studying mathematics at say university level, but not when the concept of graphs is being introduced for the first time. As with other subjects simply being told something does not show understanding of it. As already mentioned, it is the interactive construction, making mistakes, understanding and correcting those mistakes that allow a solid understanding of graphs to be built up [Clamp 1997].

Supporting these tasks is a feature that all of the tools discussed above, and the technologies currently used in the classroom fail to do. In the next section we will introduce a novel application which takes account of these issues, as well as

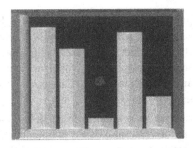

Figure 2: A screenshot of the Graph Builder application showing the recessed 'V' shaped bars. The current position of the PHANTOM in the graph (and thus that of the user) is represented by the cone shaped object. The colours used are of high contrast to aid those with residual sight.

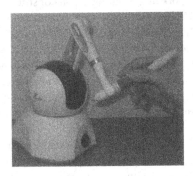

Figure 3: A picture of a SensAble Technologies' PHANTOM Omni haptic device as used in the Graph Builder application. The user interacts with the 'pen' which also contains two buttons for interaction.

overcoming the problems of current graph building techniques as identified at the RNCB and RBS, to allow users to interactively construct simple bar graphs.

4 Application Design

Since, as already stated, there is little research into interactive applications to construct graphs, the approach adopted here was to build an application using guidelines derived from prior work on haptic graph browsing. Our application was based on the guidelines described and evaluated by Yu & Brewster [2003]. A screenshot is shown in Figure 2. The application was constructed using SensAble Technologies' OpenHaptics API. The user could feel the graph by using a PHANTOM Omni force feedback device (see Figure 3) which uses motors to resist user movement providing the impression of a physical object.

The graph is built as a 2.5D object presented on a vertical plane in front of the user, with recessed 'V' shaped grooves to represent each bar. These being easier to follow with a single point of contact haptic device than the raised lines found on swell paper graphs [Yu & Brewster 2003]. The axes were represented as raised cylinders so they provided a contrast to the recessed bars. The background was textured to differentiate it from the rest of the graph, and the entire graph was contained within a box to ensure that a user could not 'lose' the graph. Additionally the colours used for graph features are of high contrast to aid users with residual sight. However since it is difficult to quantify residual sight, participants is all the following evaluations were not allowed to look at the screen. Users could request the names of the *x*- and *y*- axes, the title and the names of individual bars in the graph by touching the appropriate feature and pressing one of the two buttons on the PHANTOM pen. For example, touching the *x*-axis and pressing the button would cause the name of the axis to be spoken using synthetic speech. Our approach allows users to concentrate on the logical units of the graph such as bars, axes, etc., rather than worrying about the smaller details, such as making sure all of the bars are the same width. Additionally, the complexity of the task can be altered. In the evaluations of the application discussed here, users were only asked to set the scale, axes titles and the values of the bars. However, there is no reason why users should not be able to add and remove bars and axes, dependant on the particular feature of the graph a teacher wishes to concentrate upon teaching. Graph Builder makes such scalability possible. Additionally, the application allows the graph to be saved, manipulated and printed at any future date overcoming the limitations of other technologies previously discussed.

With Graph Builder, users can modify the graph by sliding the bars up and down. Users select a bar by touching the top of a bar and holding down the second of the two buttons on the PHANTOM pen. A small gravity effect is then applied to make the bar feel 'weighty', and the user is constrained to moving the PHANTOM pen in a vertical direction only. As the user moves the pen up or down the value of the bar is changed. In order to provide the accurate detail required when constructing a graph, non-speech audio cues have been added to provide specific information about the value of the bar whilst is being moved.

As the user drags the bar being modified over each unit on the *y*-axis a different MIDI note is played, giving the user information about the current value of the bar. As such, one note is played for each unit increase or decrease in bar position. Using different notes should ensure that participants do not become confused over the direction of movement. Counting the number of notes played also provides information about the value of the bar. Using speech to read out the values of the bars was considered but was felt to be unsuitable for an educational environment where the emphasis is on the ability of students to show their understanding of graphs, rather than just get the answer from the application.

5   Initial Evaluation

When evaluating systems for the visually impaired it is commonly difficult to recruit enough participants to perform large scale empirical evaluations. Because of this many researchers choose to initially test and refine their design with blindfolded sighted users, only testing on visually impaired users when a refined system has been developed. This technique works well when there is a developed body of work supporting the underlying application. However, due to the lack of previous work

Food	Calories per Gram
Cheese Curls	12
Mixed Fruits	14
Vegetable Soup	2
Butterscotch Bar	21
Chocolate Chip Cookie	10
Carrot Muffin	17

Table 1: An example table for the graph drawing question: 'Construct a bar graph showing the calories in each of the following foods'.

on graph construction we cannot be sure that underlying assumptions in our design lead to a system which will be usable by visually impaired people. Rather than spending time and effort to create and refine a system only to find out that it was 'wide of the mark' when finally evaluated with visually impaired people, we decided to perform initial evaluations on visually impaired people. If the basic technique is successful, refinements to the design can be evaluated with blindfolded sighted users and ultimately validated with local visually impaired 'expert' users.

5.1 Evaluation Design

The evaluation was a mixed Think Aloud and empirical study, and was performed at the RNCB, Hereford. There were four participants all between the ages of 18–30; all had become blind before they had initially studied graph construction at school. Each participant was paid £5 for participating in the study. Participants who had good domain knowledge of graph construction were chosen since Pinker [1990] notes that such knowledge is one of the key factors in an individual's ability to construct graphs, and we wanted to ensure that a lack of such knowledge did not appear in the results as poor design of the application.

Participants completed a total of 5 graphs each. The first graph was used as a training session where the experimenter helped the participant, ensuring that they had a good understanding of the tool and how it worked. For each graph, participants were given a table and asked to construct a graph from the data in the table (see Table 1 for an example). The table and question were read aloud by the experimenter and could be repeated whenever requested by the participant. All of the questions were based on those found in the General level Standard Grade syllabus [Brown et al. 2004], which is the standard Scottish qualification taken by students in the 14–16 age range. To answer the question participants initially had to decide on the name of the graph, x-axis, y-axis and a scale (how many units of data would be represented by one unit of the y-axis).

This information was requested from the participants, and since the application was not yet integrated with screen reading software, entered into a dialogue box by the experimenter. Participants were then instructed to complete building the graph and notify the experimenter, who could monitor their progress on the computer screen, when they had completed the graph. Participants were encouraged to

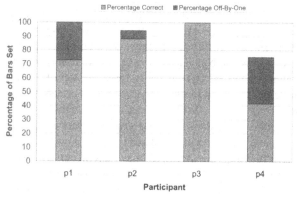

Figure 4: Graph showing the total percentage of bars correctly set by each participant, and the percentage of 'off-by-one' errors, where the bar was set either one unit too high or one unit too low.

talk about what they were thinking and doing during the experiment, and relevant points were noted by the experimenter to be discussed during the interview phase. After completing the graphs, participants were informally interviewed about their experiences in using the application, as well as specific problems that had been noticed during the tasks. Interviews were recorded for later transcription. Overall each participant took around an hour to complete the experiment.

5.2 Graph Building Accuracy

For each graph completed, one mark was awarded for appropriate values for each of the *x*-axis, *y*-axis, graph title and *y*-axis scale. A mark was also awarded for each correctly set bar in the graph. All participants scored full marks for the titles of the graph, the *x*- and *y*-axes titles, as well as the scale for the *y*-axis. Figure 4 shows the percentage of correctly set bars for each participant over the course of the experiment.

The results show that participants can construct bar graphs successfully using Graph Builder, with three participants setting over 70% of bars correctly. However, there are a large proportion of off-by-one errors (68% of all errors) where a bar was set either one unit too high or one unit too low. For example, a bar which should be set at 10 was set at 9 or 11. During the informal interviews with participants, reasons as to the large number of off-by-one errors became clear. These reasons are discussed in the following section.

5.3 Participant Comments on Graph Builder

Overall participant views of the application were positive, and all considered that the concept was superior to existing tools they had used in school. Participants were also positive about the logical construction system, where graph objects are provided and modified rather than users having to ensure that all graph bars are the same width, etc. Participants felt that this allowed them to concentrate on the important features of graph construction. As one participant noted 'it takes a lot of the 'leg work' out of graph drawing'. There were however several common usability problems identified.

Firstly, participants found the method used to select and move the bars problematic and this may have caused some of the off-by-one errors. When selecting the bars, participants found that it was difficult to press the pen in an upwards direction (to keep it against the top of the bar) and then press the button (providing a downward force) without moving the PHANTOM away from the top of the bar and thus not selecting it. Participants tended to use more force than necessary when holding the pen against the top of the bar. When the bar was selected, the upwardly applied force was much greater than the downward gravity effect applied to make the bar feel 'weighty', causing the bar to jump one or two positions before the user stopped the PHANTOM pen moving. Another issue may have occurred when the button was depressed (to set the value of the bar). If the current position was at the borderline of one value and the value above or below it and the PHANTOM pen was moved slightly when depressing the button, an incorrect value may be set and again an off-by-one error occurred. It seems from participant comments that using buttons on the pen of the PHANTOM was not a useful way to modify the graph.

Another issue raised was not being able to determine the actual value of a bar after it had been set. Whilst different MIDI notes were played to provide information about the current value when modifying the bar, it was not possible to precisely determine the bar value at a later point. If the user felt that a mistake had been made, the only option available was to move the bar to zero and then move it back to the correct value. We had considered that using different notes for each y-axis position would allow participants to determine if the value had been correctly placed, but this was not the case. It is likely that these two problems combined to produce the relatively high proportion of 'off-by-one' errors found in the results (68% of total errors were off-by-one errors). See Figure 4. Solving these problems therefore should increase the ability of users to successful produce graphs with the Graph Builder tool.

A final problem was identified when requesting information about features in the graph. As already stated, touching either the axes, or any of the bars, and pressing a button on the PHANTOM pen caused the name of the axis or bar to be read out using synthetic speech. Conversely the background of the graph and the box that constrained the graph provided no information when touched by the PHANTOM. Several participants found this distressing and despite having these features explained to them before the experiment, claimed that the application had broken and 'wasn't working' when it did not respond to requests for information from the background and constraining box. This is an important point since for this user group, as when an application fails to produce sound output it is an indication that the program has crashed. The application should therefore produce sound output for all of the features that a user can touch in the environment.

6 Graph Builder Revisions

The initial evaluation of Graph Builder showed that visually impaired users could effectively manipulate and modify graphs with a high degree of accuracy. However, due to the points raised, several modifications were needed.

The ability of participants to select bars was the major criticism in the initial evaluation. Using the buttons located on the pen as well as the mechanism used to select and lock onto bars proved problematic; as did the inability to review the value of the bar after it had been set. In order to overcome these problems the button used to select bars was changed, with the 'Ins' key (the 0 key) on a standard numeric keypad used instead of the PHANTOM button. The 'Ins' key was chosen since it is a uniquely shaped key on a keyboard and should therefore be easier to find. Using this key means that there is no movement in the pen due to pressing the button to select a bar. Additionally rather than the problematic mechanism of firstly touching the top of the bar with the pen before pressing the button, holding down the 'Ins' key effectively changes the mode from browsing to modifying. With the revised system, as soon as the user touches the top of the bar whilst holding down the 'Ins' key, the bar becomes selected automatically and can be manipulated in the same way as the original version of Graph Builder. Releasing the 'Ins' key changes the mode back to browsing and causes the bar to be set at the current position. Using this method it should be easier to hold the pen steady when setting the bar and avoid the problems that occurred in the original system. In order to make it clear that the user had 'locked onto' a bar, a 'clunk' sound was played when the user successfully selected a bar, the same sound was used when the user set the bar position by releasing the 'Ins' key.

To provide the ability to determine the value of a bar at a later time, the button on the PHANTOM pen which had been used to modify the graph was used to present the value of the bar. Touching the bar and pressing the PHANTOM pen's button caused the value of the bar to be presented. Presenting the value of the bar in speech was considered, however since a potential application of this system is in the classroom, we felt that presenting speech would not be appropriate. Providing speech may be simply providing the answer, rather than requiring the student to work it out for themselves[1]. Instead of speech, the sequence of the notes played when modifying a bar was used. Therefore, if the bar value was ten (and the graph scale set at one), ten notes were consecutively presented at approximately half second intervals. This is analogous to a user with a visual graph counting along the *y*-axis to find the height of a bar. This sequence of notes could be played on demand by the user, and was also played when the user set the value of a bar by releasing the 'Ins' key, allowing immediate review of the bar value.

Concerns by participants of the system having crashed when it did not 'talk to them' were solved by making all of the objects in the graph provide some speech feedback when they were touched and the PHANTOM button was pressed. Navigation feedback was provided, as Challis & Edwards [2001] note that large amounts of dead space (where no useful information is contained) can cause confusion to a visually impaired person. They recommend that no such space exists in tactile diagrams for the visually impaired, but since it is not possible to remove such space from graphs, having that space providing navigational cues is the next best option. For example, the background of the graph provided the information 'move down to get to a bar'. This should reduce the likelihood that participants feel that the application has crashed because it does not provide audio feedback.

---

[1]Later informal discussions with a teacher of visually impaired students indicated that this is partially correct, and it would be better to have both speech and non-speech available as an option.

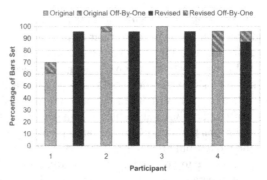

Figure 5: Graph showing the total percentage of bars correctly set for each participant for the original and revised Graph Builder applications, and the percentage of 'off-by-one' errors.

7 Evaluation of the Revised Version

As already stated, a common problem when evaluating applications for visually impaired people is obtaining access to a sufficient number. Whilst the original evaluation used visually impaired people to test Graph Builder, this was due to the novelty of the system, with little prior work indicating its usefulness. Since the first evaluation showed that users could understand and manipulate graphs, the revisions were evaluated with normally sighted, but blindfolded participants.

Four participants between the ages of 18–24 carried out the experiment, which was of a within groups design. All participants were students at the computing science department of Glasgow University, and were familiar with graphs. This is important for the same reasons outlined in the previous study where domain knowledge may have an impact [Pinker 1990]. Participants completed questions similar to the one shown in Table 1 with the initial Graph Builder system (the 'original' system) and the revised Graph Builder system (the 'revised' system). The order in which participants undertook the conditions was counterbalanced. Two sets of questions with similar difficulty were used, with the sets being counterbalanced between the conditions. The graphs produced by participants were scored using the same method as the original evaluation. The results are presented in graphical form in Figure 5 and show that there is little difference between the two conditions. Both conditions produced highly accurate graphs. Notably however, the proportion of 'off-by-one' errors which were prevalent in the original Graph Builder (46% of all errors) were reduced in the revised version (33% of all errors). In comparison to the results of the original evaluation at RNCB, the blindfolded participants had a lower proportion of off-by-one errors with the original system (46% of total errors (7% of total bars set)) than the visually impaired people at RNCB (68% of total errors (16% of total bars set)). This may be down to several reasons. For example, many visually impaired people do not use a pen often which may have contributed to problems when using the pen like interface on the PHANTOM. This indicates that more substantial reductions in off-by-one errors would result if the revised version was tested with the visually impaired participants from the original study.

Whilst there seems to be little quantitative difference between the two conditions in terms of the bars that were correctly set, informal comments by participants expressed preference for several features incorporated in the revised version of Graph Builder. Notably participants liked the ability to review the value of the bar after it had been set, as well as having sounds to indicate that a bar had been selected. Participants said that the addition of such features gave them 'more confidence' that the correct value had been set. However they disliked the value of the bar being replayed immediately after it had been set, finding it annoying, and would like that feature to be optional.

8 Expert Evaluations

The results of the previous experiment are encouraging. In both conditions participants were able to accurately construct graphs, with the number of off-by-one errors being reduced with the revised Graph Builder application. Additionally informal participant comments indicated preference for the revised version. In order to confirm the usefulness of the revised Graph Builder, a further evaluation was carried out using two locally available 'expert users'.

Both participants were between 30–50 years old, were visually impaired and had extensive experience of computer based access technologies for visually impaired people. Both had good domain knowledge of graphs. One participant was an academic researcher at a British university, whilst the other was a transcription officer for the RNIB (Royal National Institute for the Blind). Both had limited experience using the PHANTOM haptic device, and neither had previous experience with Graph Builder.

The evaluation consisted of each user performing two to three questions with each of the Graph Builder systems whilst being asked to talk about what they were doing in a Think Aloud style. After using each system they were asked for their overall comments on it. After both systems had been used, the experimenter discussed participants' comments on both systems and had a general discussion about the previous evaluation studies and what had been discovered. Participants' comments were recorded for later transcription. Overall both participants were able to construct graphs with both systems to a high degree of accuracy.

For the original version of Graph Builder, the main comment that was raised was the inability to review the value of a bar after it had been set. Both participants mentioned that although they felt that the bars had been correctly set, they were not confident in that opinion. One user said that:

> 'if I had been sitting an exam I would have set and reset that bar a dozen times to make sure I had it set correctly.'

These views are consistent with the views expressed in the two previous experiments. For the revised version, both participants suggested that playing the value of a bar immediately after it had been set should be an option and it should be possible to switch off playing the sounds immediately if desired. Again this view is consistent with the results from the blindfolded sighted study.

The first participant also discussed some more problems counting the number of units moved when manipulating a bar. He noted that if the bar was moved quickly, or jerkily, it was easy to lose count of the position of the bar. He noted that this problem was more prevalent in the original Graph Builder where bars were selected by using buttons on the PHANTOM pen rather than by changing modes using a keyboard key, as was done in the revised Graph Builder. This is consistent with the bar selection issues identified in the initial study with the 'original' Graph Builder at RNCB, and provides conformation of the usefulness of the revised mechanism to manipulate the bars.

9 Guidelines

From the work carried out in this paper we can identify the following guidelines to assist future designers of haptic applications for the visually impaired.

All touchable objects should provide audio feedback. Participants using the original version of graph builder complained that the application had 'crashed' when attempting to gain audio feedback about the graph background, even though they were aware that only the axes and bars provided audio feedback. If any feature of the environment provides audio feedback, then all features should provide audio feedback. As was the case with Graph Builder, although participants may be able to feel the object, they may still feel the application is not working if audio feedback is not provided.

Use caution when requiring selection of objects. The major problem with the initial version of Graph Builder was selecting and manipulating bars due to using the buttons on the PHANTOM pen. Changing to keys on the keyboard was preferred by participants. Since it is possible to inadvertently manipulate the object when selecting it (as the users did when selecting the bars in Graph Builder), it may be better to ensure the selection control is physically separate from the manipulation control. Requesting information via the same control (such as bar names and values) however, is possible.

10 Conclusions

For students to be able to understand graphs it is important that they are able to construct them. Understanding of concepts comes from trying to carry out tasks and making, understanding and correcting mistakes [Clamp 1997]. This requires students to be able to construct graphs and easily manipulate them when mistakes are made. Requirements capture with visually impaired student showed that techniques currently used in the classroom are either so permanent (such as using a Braille typewriter) that they could not be easily manipulated or changed, or could only be changed at considerable cost (such as using a cork board). Additionally, the degree of inflexibility of the techniques used makes the process of constructing graphs slow, causing students to avoid constructing graphs in exams and as such scoring a lower mark than if better tools for construction were available. The application introduced in this paper, Graph Builder, overcomes many of these problems, allowing users to interactively manipulate the bars, without the possibility of bars changing by themselves as might occur if a pin were to become dislodged when using the cork board technique. As such Graph Builder provides the permanency of the Braille typewriter technique, allowing graphs to be kept permanently, whilst providing the ability to change and manipulate those graphs as with the corkboard technique. Additionally the 'fiddly' elements of graph construction have been removed. Whilst one participant estimated that it took 45mins to complete a graph in an exam using existing techniques, participants were able to construct 5 graphs in an hour using Graph Builder. Whilst, not all features of graph construction were investigated through this study (participants did not have to draw axes, etc.), the study does indicate that the time taken to construct graphs could be significantly reduced if Graph Builder is expanded to provide effective mechanisms for the currently unsupported features.

Whilst we can consider Graph Builder to be useful for the creation of graphs, we have yet to evaluate its use in a classroom environment. Future studies must consider the impact of Graph Builder in such an environment with students who are learning how to construct graphs, and do not have the good domain knowledge, that the participants in our studies had. Such future development of the Graph Builder application will allow technologies to be deployed which will significantly assist visually impaired peoples' learning and understanding of graphs.

Acknowledgements

We would like to thank all participants and staff at the RNCB Hereford and the RBS Edinburgh. This work is supported by EPSRC grant GR/S86150/01.

References

Brown, D., Howat, R. D., Meikle, G., Mullan, E. C. K., Murray, R. & Nisbet, K. [2004], *New Mathematics in Action S3^2*, Nelson Thornes.

Brown, L. & Brewster, S. A. [2003], Drawing by Ear: Interpreting Sonified Line Graphs, *in* E. Brazil & B. Shinn-Cunningham (eds.), *Proceedings of ICAD 2003*, ICAD, pp.152–6.

Challis, B. P. & Edwards, A. D. N. [2001], Design Principles for Tactile Interaction, *in* S. Brewster & R. Murray-Smith (eds.), *Haptic Human–Computer Interaction*, Vol. 2058 of *Lecture Notes in Computer Science*, Springer, pp.17–24.

Clamp, S. [1997], Mathematics, *in* H. Mason, S. McCall, C. Arter, M. McLinden & J. Stone (eds.), *Visual Impairment: Access to Education for Children and Young People*, David Fulton Publishers, pp.218–35.

Dimigen, G., Scott, F., Thackeray, F., Pimm, M. & Roy, A. W. N. [1993], Career Expectations of British Visually Impaired Students who are of School-leaving Age, *Journal of Visual Impairment and Blindness* **87**, 209–10.

Franklin, K. M. & Roberts, J. C. [2003], Pie Chart Sonification, *in* E. Banissi, K. Borner, C. Chen, G. Clapworthy, C. Maple, A. Lobben, C. Moore, J. Roberts, A. Ursyn & J. Zhang (eds.), *Proceedings of the Seventh International Conference on Information Visualization (IV'03)*, IEEE Computer Society Press, pp.4–9.

Fritz, J. P. & Barner, K. E. [1999], Design of a Haptic Data Visualization System for People with Visual Impairments, *IEEE Transactions on Rehabilitation Engineering* **7**(3), 372–84.

Mansur, D. L. [1985], Graphs in Sound: A Numerical Data Analysis Method for the Blind, Master's thesis, University of California.

Pinker, S. [1990], A Theory of Graph Comprehension, *in* R. Freedle (ed.), *Artificial Intelligence and the Future of Testing*, Lawrence Erlbaum Associates, pp.73–126.

Ross, D. A. & Blasch, B. B. [2002], Development of a Wearable Computer Orientation System, *Personal and Ubiquitous Computing* **6**(1), 49–63.

van Scoy, F. L., Kawai, T., Darrah, M. & Rash, C. [2001], Haptic Display of Mathematical Functions for Teaching Mathematics to Students with Vision Disabilities: Design and Proof of Concept, *in* S. Brewster & R. Murray-Smith (eds.), *Haptic Human–Computer Interaction*, Vol. 2058 of *Lecture Notes in Computer Science*, Springer, pp.31–40.

Yu, W. & Brewster, S. A. [2003], Evaluation of Multimodal Graphs for Blind People, *Journal of Universal Access in the Information Society* **2**(2), 105–24.

Yu, W., Kangas, K. & Brewster, S. A. [2003], Web-based Haptic Applications for Blind People to Create Virtual Graphs, *in* A. Jacobs (ed.), *Proceedings of the 11th Haptic Symposium*, IEEE Computer Society Press, pp.318–25.

Author Index

Keyword Index